The Man Who Cycled the World

The Man Who Cycled the World

Mark Beaumont

Broadway Paperbacks
New York

Copyright © 2009, 2011 by Mark Beaumont

All rights reserved.
Published in the United States by Broadway Books,
an imprint of the Crown Publishing Group,
a division of Random House, Inc., New York.
www.crownpublishing.com

BROADWAY BOOKS and its logo, a letter B bisected on the diagonal, are registered trademarks of Random House, Inc., New York.

Originally published in slightly different form in Great Britain by Bantam Press, an imprint of Transworld Publishers, a division of the Random House Group Limited, London, in 2009.

Grateful acknowledgment is made to the Estate of Raymond Chandler for permission to reprint an excerpt from *Red Wind* by Raymond Chandler © 1938.

Cataloging-in-Publication Data is on file with the Library of Congress.

ISBN 978-0-307-71665-1
eISBN 978-0-307-71666-8

Printed in the United States of America

Cover photograph: © David Peat

1   3   5   7   9   10   8   6   4   2

First American Edition

Contents

Acknowledgments

From a secret ambition, nurtured through university, the world cycle grew arms and legs to launch my career in the adventure world, which I am now able to continue. It is one thing being good at what you plan to do, but it is quite another to find the emotional, financial, and logistical support to fulfill your dreams. For that mountain of help I owe many people a great debt of gratitude. These brave souls said "yes" when most said "no." After achieving my 18,000-mile target, it is easy to say in retrospect that it was a sure bet, but if you looked at my CV and my ambition after leaving university, then I can understand if you would have wished me luck and given your apologies like most did.

I am dedicating this book to Una, my mum, who has been the rock of support for all my ambitions from an early age, and who continues to work with me.

Heather and Hannah, I am very lucky to have two such cool sisters who have always gently ribbed my ways, but who have always been there to support. Heather, a special thanks for all your help with Mum's work while I was on the road, and for the hundreds of text messages encouraging me. Although not family, I would also like to put David Peat right at the top of this list. David has become a great friend and supporter over the last few years, and made the Scottish BAFTA-nominated BBC series *The Man Who Cycled the World* happen.

I had a pretty unique childhood thanks to the rest of my family, including Dad, Granny, Grampa, and Grannie. Dad, thanks also for your help when I was most in debt.

David Fox Pitt (www.eventsandactivities.co.uk) is the man whom I must thank for having the most energy to get this expedition off the ground, through contacts and personal support. Thanks also to Ken Hills for another crucial introduction. I could not have gone anywhere and am most grateful for the capital support from Lindsay Whitelaw at Artemis Investment Management (www.artemisonline.co.uk), Darryl Eales and Rob Pendleton at Lloyds TSB Development Capital (www.ldc.co.uk), and Pia Heidenmark Cook from the Rezidor Hotel Group (pfp.rezidorsas.com).

A huge thank-you to all my sponsors, including Helen Sayles at Liberty Mutual, Helen and Bill at Trident Sensors, Ric Searle at Yellow Brick, Lindsay Manson at Ian Burke Associates, the team at Run4It, Tim and James at The Bike Chain, Sir Chris Bonnington at Berghaus clothing, Graeme Gibson and Ashley Thompson at the Radisson Hotel in Glasgow, Pieter Jan Rijpstra at Koga Miyata, Ruth Casson at Amba Marketing, Lyon Equipment for Ortlieb, Petzl and Exped, Escape Gym at The Scotsman Hotel, Healthlink 360, Footprints Outdoor Shop, the team at Events and Activities, High 5, and Kluge Estates Winery.

For their many skills and giving of time I would like to thank every one of my support team, including Dr. Niall MacFarlane and the technicians at Glasgow University's IBLS faculty, Bruce Murray (www.bcgwebdesign.co.uk), Fiona Lindsay (www.athletesangels.com), Ruth McKean, Craig Ali (www.craigalihealth.com), Bobby Burt, Andrew Robertson, Dave and Judy Denton, Val and John Vannet, Alan Parkinson (www.geobloggingwithmark.blogspot.com), Alan Ferguson and Bill Gold (www.thesportsbusiness.co.uk), Alex Crosby at Wexas Travel, Inge Husselbee, David Lowe, and Heather.

For help while on the road I owe many thanks to Piotr and Jagwega, Albert Payon, the team at ProBike in Poland, Rob Lilwall, Okan Bayramoglu (www.warmshowers.org), Farhad, Farank, Faz and Kirsten, Ali Manoochehri, Mr. Ehsanfar and the Iranian cyclists, Dermot (www.redspokes.co.uk), Nasir Hussain (www.karakorumexplorers.com), the Levvy patrols, Suman Chakraborty, Celia Duncan, Chris and Toi Schofield, Eunice and Phil Cook, Margaret and Mike Whitfield, Sats and Aldo, Stewart Forsyth, Shonnie and Kym Pascoe, Damian Richmond, Guy at the Bike Box, Grant Pedan, Jo Starky, Adam and Catriona Scott, Paul Robertson, Jill, Des and Troy Gilmore, Margaret and Sandy Macfarlane, Tim and Tracy Cooke, Brett Purchase, Joe and Annette Legallet, Hugh and Bill Brown, Simon Levay, Clay Goldberg, Shannon Neil, Greg and Tina

Box, Joshua Rosby, Gary and his family in Baton Rouge, Richard and Chris Reichle, Amy Warpinski, Felipe in Spain, the numerous massage therapists around the world organized by Athletes Angels, Christopher Tiran, the City of Paris transport police, Alberto Ruiz, Tess Mendie, Mike Ridley, and Matthew Dickens at OnEdition. A huge thanks also to the network of British embassies around the world, and in particular to Sir Peter Westmacott for coming to witness the finish.

For the making of a superb BBC documentary and allowing me to share the world cycle with millions around the world, I would like to thank Neil McDonald, Ian Stroud, Jonathan Seal, Peter Capaldi, Steven Jones, Laura Deponio, Jim Preacher, Ian Pugsley, Kaye and Nick the cameramen, Fiona Baird-Crawford, and of course David Peat himself.

Thanks also for the help from Doug Scott, HRH Prince Philip, Sir Muir Russell, Sarah Fisher, Catie Friend, Michael Duncan, Sharon Tonner and the pupils of the High School of Dundee, John Beattie and Katie Still at Sports Weekly, Amarilis Espinoza, Carlos Martinez, Alastair Humphreys, Jenny Kinnear, Andy Barlow, John and Sally Watson, James Bracker, Jamie Corr, Ed Moro, Richard Moore, Irene Johnston, Richard Benner, Rev. Stuart MacQuarrie, Emily Wallace, Kate Richardson, Ray McHugh, Grania, Brigadier John Graham, Gordon Dickinson, Ann and Ally, Peter van der Lans, Stuart McPhee, and Phil White.

Many personal friends are mentioned above, but I still must thank some great friendships that have meant a lot in making my dream a reality. These include Brendan Keller, Phil Bartlett, Grant Fraser, Graeme Brown, Chris Morris, Ally Ford, Emily Frier, Laura Turner, Angus Spiers, Jimmy Clyde, Addict, Dave, Ross, Helen, and Vicx. This list is by no means exhaustive, and to all school, university, and other friends who have listened to, advised, or simply abused me (Spinks!) over the last few years, many thanks. Thanks also to the patience and constant support of Nicci Kitchin while writing this book.

Writing this book has felt like an expedition in itself and was a far tougher challenge than I had imagined. Many thanks to everyone who has encouraged and guided me, including Stan my agent (www.jennybrownassociates.com), Giles my editor (www.booksattransworld.co.uk), Caroline MacKechnie for translating the many hours of audio diaries, Rachel Lin for doing months of first edits and research with me, Mum for all her many reads and edits, Daniel Balado-Lopez for taking me through the copy edit, Madeline Toy for all the publicity, Phil Lord for the design of the picture section, and Matt Johnson for the cover design.

The Tusk Trust, CHICKS, Rainer (now Catch 22), Community Action Nepal, and Cyrenians are five fantastic charities which benefit from the generous support of many people through the world cycle. Many thanks for this fund-raising effort through donating via Just Giving and buying replica world cycle jerseys.

Lastly I would like to say hi and thanks to everyone I met on the world cycle who made the journey so memorable. I hope we meet again and that you get to live your dreams as well.

The Man Who Cycled
the World

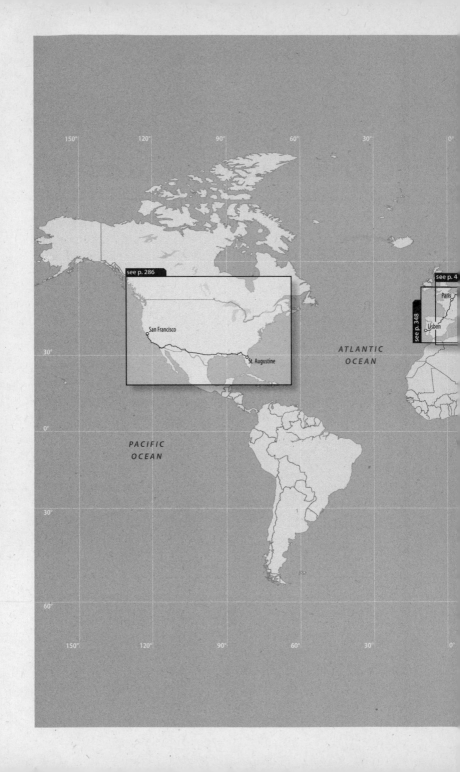

see p. 286

see p. 4

see p. 348

San Francisco

St. Augustine

ATLANTIC
OCEAN

Paris

Lisbon

PACIFIC
OCEAN

150°   120°   90°   60°   30°   0°

30°

0°

30°

60°

150°   120°   90°   60°   30°   0°

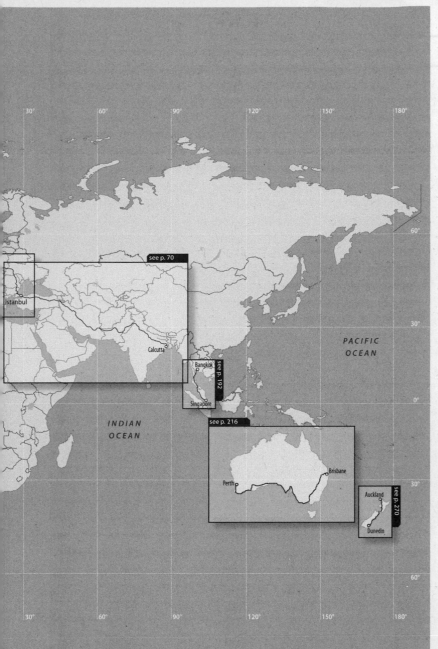

see p. 70

see p. 192

see p. 216

see p. 270

Istanbul

Calcutta

Bangkok

Singapore

PACIFIC
OCEAN

INDIAN
OCEAN

Brisbane

Perth

Auckland

Dunedin

Prelude in Something Major

Eighteen thousand miles. People have cycled much farther than that, but no one has ever truly raced that far.

I would probably never have questioned my desire to cycle around the world if it hadn't been the first question people always asked. It is comforting to think we are in control of our desires. In truth, our choices are the products of influences far too numerous and complicated to grasp fully. "Why would you do this?" There is no good simple answer, and I don't think there needs to be. "Because it is there to be done"—though that doesn't come close to the complex truth.

My motivation for writing this book was to record the adventures of my first major expedition, before time and repetition changed my memories. I have written it as much for my family and friends, and to share the experience publicly, as I have for myself. For everyone involved in the world cycle it was an intense couple of years, and this book is the final chapter, before looking forward to the next adventures.

The four-part BBC1 documentary *The Man Who Cycled the World* was beautifully made and well received, has been seen by millions of people around the world, and was shortlisted for a Scottish BAFTA. However, at two hours, a film could not start to paint a full picture of my six-and-a-half-month race around the world.

A friend recently commented, "I knew what you had done from following your website, but it was not until I saw the documentary that I understood everything you went through and how hard it was." It is always lovely when people associate with my expeditions like that, but I did not have the heart to tell him that it was in no way a true and full reflection of what cycling 100 miles (160km) a day for 195 days was like. This book will also fall short. Because I was alone for the majority of the time, the full value of this journey lies in the frame of mind I was in when experiencing each part of my trip—something that is impossible to re-create. However, such comments were fuel to me to write the fullest account possible.

The most important thing, I feel, is that this story is honest. I have insisted on writing it myself despite having never written more than a few thousand-word essays at university before. So it was an intimidating task.

And the first important truth to set down is this: I have never been a fanatical cyclist. Furthermore, I am a lousy mechanic. When I decided to cycle around the world I had never ridden a race and hardly knew the difference between degreaser (which takes gunk off your gears) and a derailleur (the bit that changes your gears).

I didn't always want to cycle around the world, it just kind of happened.

Leg 1: Paris to Istanbul

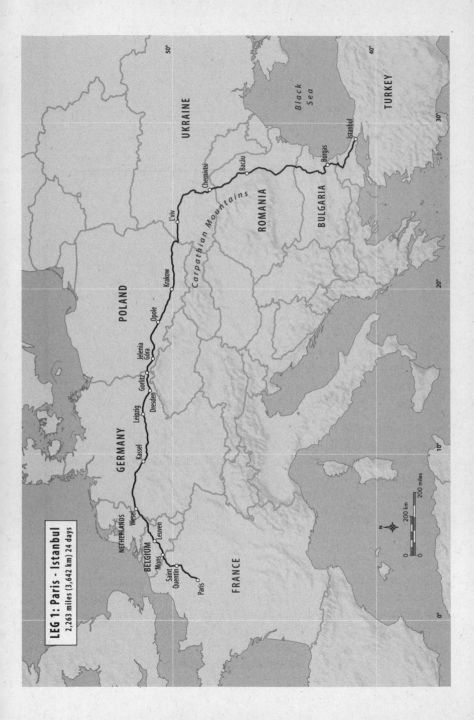

LEG 1: Paris - Istanbul
2,263 miles (3,642 km) 24 days

1

After only 10km, I was exhausted. My legs were fresh but my head dropped and my eyelids started slow-blinking. The surge of adrenaline at the start had passed, and I felt shattered. The last few weeks had been a series of ridiculous and unsustainable routines that had left me completely void of energy at the outset of my 18,000-mile cycle.

By the time our small convoy—Mum, my elder sister Heather, and a friend in a car, plus the motorbike escort to help me navigate the labyrinth that is central Paris—neared Charles de Gaulle airport, I could hardly stay on the bike. This did not feel like normal tiredness but a deep, sleep-deprived exhaustion, the sort that leaves you feeling hollow.

Waving good-bye to the escort at Bourget, a bit farther on, I cycled as far as the next café. I had to stop. I had an espresso and Coke, hoping the life would return to me. But all I wanted to do was sleep. I felt silly as the waiter expressed how impressed he was with what I was doing. It did not feel very impressive. I was pale and felt completely washed out. This was the opportunity of my life and here I was waiting for caffeine and sugar to help me back onto the bike before I had even left Paris.

The start had been a slightly confused affair. For Mum and others it was emotional, but I felt somewhat removed. For so many months all I had wanted was to be on the road. Now, finally at that point, there was no part of me that was sad, or thinking about missing anyone, no part that was concerned about what lay ahead.

The last day before leaving was hot and clear but spent entirely in room 409 of the Radisson Boulogne, Paris. Only in the evening did

Mum, Heather, and I take time out for a send-off meal at Au Vaillant Chez Chemin, a charming wee restaurant near the Porte de Saint Cloud. It was Dad who said a few words and raised a toast. I have not always had the full support of Dad or seen eye to eye with him, but despite our differences I was grateful for his acknowledgment of the task that lay ahead.

We had laid things out, packed, unpacked, repacked, and sorted all day. When laid out on the bed the kit had seemed like a lot. Amazingly, after juggling items between the four main pannier bags to find a balance, it fitted well. It would have been easy to stay up all night faffing and fiddling, but by one in the morning I could do no more. The bike was ready and packed and we were not being particularly productive with the remaining admin jobs. There was too much to do to feel terribly excited.

An integral part of "living your dreams," which I was fast learning, is that the reality is almost always different from what you imagine it will be. In my mind's eye, the day before leaving was a media scrum of international interest, but there were no press calls at all. The media highlight and only pre-departure commitment was a chat on John Beattie's *Sports Weekly* on Radio Scotland, where I had been a studio guest a few months earlier. A number of local papers had covered the story for the last six months, but I felt disappointed. Fame wasn't part of the dream, but I had hoped to share this adventure widely, and to pay back my sponsors for their support.

That afternoon I let my frayed cool show when Heather returned with a late lunch and gave me a ham quiche by mistake. I am normally a vegetarian and this was a meaningless mistake, but it happened to be the tiny event that broke the tension I was bottling. Months later it was amusing to remember this silly overreaction. If I'd only known what I would soon be eating the ham quiche would barely have registered.

Heather spent much of the afternoon finishing a present for me, a lovingly written "advice book" finished with a cover drawing of a stick man cycling around the world. A perfect pocket size, its introduction read, "Here's your little book of useful worldwide info . . . enjoy!" It detailed information and essential phrases for each country, listed all my contact details and emergency information, had an itemized first-aid list, and featured other useful instructions.

My main regret with those last few days was the lack of time for a proper handover with Mum. I was passing over the reins of a year's planning so she could coordinate "Base Camp" from now on. A few months earlier Mum had never even sent an email, so it was not just the "what to do" but "how to do it" that was a very real concern. But we'd run out of time, and I just had to hope that what little we had done was enough, and that what she didn't know she would be able to learn.

At seven a.m. on the morning of Sunday, August 5, 2007, I closed the panniers after the final repack, checked out of the Radisson Boulogne, and pedaled off, fully laden on my new bike for the first time. The early-morning sun sparkled on the Seine as I cycled slowly from Porte de Saint Cloud on Paris's ring road to the start. The bike felt balanced and strong but heavier than I had hoped. I smiled all the way, in no rush, thinking absently about what lay ahead. It was one of the first "moments" of free thought I had grabbed for many weeks. Being a Sunday, the streets were about as quiet as they get in central Paris, and I enjoyed watching the lazy weekend café culture and passing mopeds.

This is the day, I thought, with a new buzz of excitement.

I turned left onto the Champs-Elysées and could see all the way down the deserted avenue to the Place de la Concorde and up to the Arc de Triomphe. This was definitely the time and place to start from. The busiest roundabout in Europe has a calm magnificence in the early-morning light of a summer's weekend.

I am not sure what my expectations of the start were, but again, the reality was definitely something else. When I reached the Arc a few friends and sponsors were waiting for me, and more soon arrived, but by anyone's standards this was a very low-key send-off. I couldn't afford to pay for a Guinness World Records representative to fly out, so I had to make sure we got suitable verification from the start. A friend ran off to buy the morning newspaper to include in a photo and aptly came back with *Le Monde*. With a degree of ceremony, Heather then started the "witness book," which I was to carry throughout. Despite her best efforts, the two gendarmes standing guard refused to sign, but to their credit they did not intervene as we ran about filming, getting photos, and setting up the start.

By eight a.m., the advertised start time, about a dozen family, friends, and sponsors were gathered, looking slightly unsure of what to say or do on such an occasion. My public target was to cycle around the world in under 210 days; my personal target was actually 195. It was an ambitious claim with the current world record standing at 276 days, and given the fact that I'd never cycled for more than a month before. Each person standing there had bought into my dream, however naively. Maybe at that point, having come all the way to Paris, the final outcome was not important to any of them: each person shared in my ambition, and for that moment, this was all that mattered. Whatever was going through their heads, I was truly grateful for their support, and it spurred me on.

David Peat, my BBC director and cameraman, helped bring some humor to the occasion by lying in the middle of the road while my family fended off the traffic for the official start photos. As a man of my parents' generation I was always amazed to see DP's alter ego appear every time he put a camera on his shoulder, which prompted him to run around with the speed and energy of someone half his age. No shot wasn't worth it for DP, and he jumped around to give the impression that many cameras were on the scene. I had only met him for the first time four months earlier, but he was already far more than just "the BBC guy." He was part of the team, a friend to all the family, the only familiar face I would see once out of Europe.

At 8:30 I waved to DP's BBC camera, my friends and family, and pedaled the first rotation, away from the Arc de Triomphe, around the world.

I had always envisioned starting and finishing at the top of the Champs-Elysées, only to get there and realize that the road to Belgium—the first part of my journey across Europe—actually goes in the other direction. In the midst of that last hour of confusion, during snatches of conversations I wheeled over the planned start line on time, simply to stop immediately and spend the next half an hour making sure I was actually ready. During this time it was decided to restart at the pedestrian crossing on the Avenue de Wagram, which runs perpendicular to the Champs-Elysées about 30 meters around the roundabout, and points in the correct direction.

The pedestrian crossing seemed amazingly unimportant as a start line to a circumnavigation. There was no signage or official start line like I had always imagined, it was simply the line pedestrians had to stay within when crossing the street. A bus blocked the road within the first 20 meters, and I glanced back to wave again. As I bumped my way slowly down the cobbled street and out of sight, I smiled and nodded to my motorbike escort. Here goes . . .

Fortified by my espresso and Coke at the café in Bourget, I was on my way again. The sun shone into the early afternoon on the undulating roads north to Belgium, through quaint sleepy villages, thick woodlands, and fields of sunflowers basking in the warm August sun. These scenes did everything to lift my spirits. My thoughts drifted in and out of the present as I started to settle into the bike.

After stopping briefly in Senlis, I cycled on, past a fairytale little château and flat fields of maize with long groves of shady sycamores, then on through Mont L'Avoque and Complegne. Sandy-colored fields broke the maize monopoly, along with areas of lettuce. After the picturesque village of Yvillers the road wound downhill to Verberie, where I met the cars again. It was a Sunday at the start of August, so every café and shop had a VACANCIES ICI sign in its window.

It was important to me that I rode unsupported, carrying all my own kit, but Mum wanted to road-trip the first few days to make sure I was happy with all my kit, and I was glad for the company while I settled in. Considering our limited options, for lunch we sat on the pavement outside a Turkish café to a grand picnic that featured vast amounts of pizza and quiche—the kind of carbs I would need daily for this race. All the urgency of the day's target was put aside for over an hour as we chatted and ate. The tensions and mania of the morning lifted and a brilliant mood set in for the afternoon. I did not care about the delay. This time with family seemed important before I headed off on my own, and moreover, I still felt weak. I needed to ride carefully for the first week to get into a sustainable pattern and not burn out and injure. My greatest fear was a repetitive strain injury like tendonitis in the first weeks.

This break and refuel gave me a refreshed energy for the afternoon and rekindled my competitive spirit. By midafternoon I was suddenly finding the initial joy of company testing. A number of towns we passed through seemed to cause confusion, and rather than figure out my own way through, multiple phone calls were required to make sure everyone got through together. Compiègne, a larger town with Tudor-style houses, proved our greatest challenge.

By 5:20 I had made it to Saint Quentin. Every instinct urged me to go farther—there was daylight, time, and, most importantly, I hadn't yet done 100 miles, my daily target—but I was finished. There was no other town within easy reach and I wasn't going to camp while Mum was still with me. I might as well get a good recovery night and massage.

I have rarely been in such a state. My fatigue manifested itself in frustration and a short temper. As we sat in the town square, which had been turned into a huge artificial beach, eating dinner, I sat quiet and subdued as Mum and Heather tried to stay conversational. Back at the hotel I fell asleep immediately.

After a good eight hours' sleep I rolled out for day 2. This was it, the pattern was set, I was off around the world. It was pouring rain but I didn't care. This was exactly where I wanted to be.

2

I would not go as far as blaming or thanking my unusual start in life for everything out of the ordinary that has happened since. Born a slightly monstrous and hairy 10.9lb on New Year's Day 1983, my only complaint was that it happened in Swindon General Hospital, which is now a block of flats. I have nothing against Swindon, but having lived 99 percent of my life in Scotland I have always considered "Place of Birth" to be somewhat of a scar on my passport. It seems like an unnecessary entry in terms of personal details, and misleading in terms of identity.

You don't tend to question things to which you know no alternative, and thus, while I had a very happy and "normal" childhood, I now know that in the company of a psychologist I could easily blame it for everything which has happened since. Heather, my sister, who is eighteen months my senior, had already started at a traditional primary school in Kilmacolm, near Glasgow, when my parents decided to set up farm on their own after managing others. This move took us to Perthshire, in the foothills of the Highlands, and the fairly remote valley of Glen Ardle, about 70 miles north of Edinburgh. Hannah, my little sister by two years, and I never even started primary school. This decision typifies Mum's outlook as an entrepreneur and freethinker, which undoubtedly helped shape how my sisters and I are.

At the age of five I was entirely oblivious to Mum's reasons for deciding that school was not for us. She had seen how it was changing and dampening Heather's spirit, so without any formal training she decided to home-school us all. It is often hard to separate what you remember from what you have been told in stories countless times, or what you've made up from looking at old photos, but I do have many fond early memories of "school" on the farm. It was great fun. It was not until I went to school at the age of ten that I noticed what little I might have missed out on—perhaps a few social norms. Life in overalls and Wellington boots was a constant adventure: riding as soon as I could walk, skiing shortly after, and helping (or hindering) farm work for as long as I can remember.

Crowhill Farm is a hilly 80-acre smallholding reached by a mile-long dirt track. It sits on a hillside below a large forest that hosts a labyrinth of dirt tracks, which annually used to be turned into a circuit for the Scottish RAC rally. It was therefore a haven for any child to grow up in. I bought my first farm car when I was twelve years old. By the time I left, aged seventeen, I knew every mile of those tracks from horse riding, cycling, walking, and driving my cars and motorbike.

Dad was not from farming stock, so to speak, so his decision to start his own farm was bold. But it was Mum who was always the source of real direction in the family. Their dream was an organic farm. This was a good fifteen years before such things were fashionable, let alone profitable, and certainly not on this scale. They built a goat dairy with sixty animals and bought hundreds of free-range hens. The eight small, hilly fields that stretched out below the house down the valley side to the river held sheep and cattle. Mum's passion was always the horses, and when I was young there were often new foals around and new ponies coming and going. At one point we had thirteen horses and ponies, each with their own story; they became part of the family. A good example of why we ended up with so many is the case of Smokey and Laddie, two scrawny, fleabitten New Forest ponies. These once wild ponies were at the markets being sold for dog meat when Mum stepped in.

I cannot remember a lot of structure to my early schooling, but I can remember sitting around the kitchen table studying, and being visited occasionally by the local education authorities. Apart from the normal curriculum, we were also taught cooking, gardening, and Italian. Every Saturday morning I also went to an art class, and I learned to play the cello from an early age. We were fairly free to do what we wanted. We probably didn't have many friends, but we had each other, and you don't miss what you don't know. Despite this quiet upbringing I was never shy. Mum remembers how I enjoyed being onstage in poetry and music festivals all over Scotland when I was as young as eight.

My very first memory is of skiing in Switzerland, at the age of four—the only family holiday we were ever taken on. All subsequent early memories are of being on the farm. I was once the proud leader of the FAF (Family Army Force), which was how my sisters and I organized our daily adventures for a number of years. These are too varied to mention but included a number of dens and rope swings, fishing trips with onion bags, and many camping expeditions with some very old canvas tents.

Our most ambitious venture was instigated, I think, by Heather, my second in command. The *SAS Survival Guide*, which doubled up as the FAF guidebook, gave us the idea of making our own clothes out of rabbit skins, and this meant setting lots of fence-line snares. This is a cruel way of catching animals and not to be promoted, and I have a feeling this might be publicly frowned on as a childhood pastime now, but while being ultimately fruitless, it was amazing fun and very memorable. (Before the animal activists stop reading, it is worth pointing out that we were not hunting for the sport as I don't think we were old enough for that to appeal to us. We were simply exploring and learning about our world, and our world was the farm.) After the snares were set we then had to check them regularly, which meant walking a couple of miles. Unfortunately the shift pattern for this quickly fell apart, as it was mostly fruitless and therefore boring. It didn't help that Hannah, my younger sister, would not do it on her own. At the time Heather and I frowned on this seeming weakness in the ranks, but in retrospect, she was only seven years old.

Eventually we got ourselves four rabbits. (I can only remember snaring two rabbits, which means that Dad might well have shot the others, though our hunting pride would not have allowed us to admit that at the time.) It wasn't enough to make three sets of clothes, or even one child-size coat, but there was ample for a pair of size 4 shoes.

We soon discovered that curing rabbit skins is not easy. After borrowing a kitchen knife and skinning them, we sat in the driveway and dissected them—a process that took ages as it was also a biology lesson. Then we got an old sheet of plywood to stretch the skins on, fur side down, tacked out with nails. The youngest troop was then sent to find a hand-sized, flat-sided piece of slate to scrape the hide, before being sent back to the kitchen to ask Mum for some table salt, which was rubbed into the hide. This was repeated regularly to stretch the hide and keep it supple. We then sketched the designs of the cuts we needed for when the hide was ready to stitch.

But then for some reason the project was shelved. Quite literally, we shelved the skins, on the sheet of plywood in the false ceiling in the goat parlor. Out of sight and out of mind, they stayed there for the next ten years until the steadings were sold to be converted into a country mansion. I wish I'd been there to see the workmen's faces when they found our rabbit skins.

When I did start going to school, I attended a fantastic place called Edradour which had a system all of its own and retained a lot of the freedoms of home-schooling. It was during the few terms I was there that I first had ambitions on the bike. One day I announced to Mum that I was going to cycle to school, and I did. It was 18 miles over moorlands and a hilly pass—a fair marathon, especially as I had never even cycled off the farm before.

In stark contrast to Edradour I was sent to my local primary school for the last term before secondary school to help ease the transition. I learned almost nothing as I was bullied and found the classes boring. When I then turned up on my first day in a school of 1,300 pupils in the middle of a city I inevitably got gently bullied for a couple more years, until I learned the ropes. But school is a cruel place. Even once you have changed, your reputation goes before you. It is almost impossible to move on from that initial stereotype.

At that time, to be a cool kid at Dundee High School you had to be good at rugby. In all those years of persevering I don't think I ever scored a try. I wasn't any better at playground football. A Chinese kid called Hunter and I were always picked last. Everyone else had played football and rugby by the time they were twelve, and because I was labeled as terrible, I remained so.

But I loved sport, and my passion for skiing and cycling grew as I slowly gave up on school sports. Our next-door neighbor was the head of ski patrol at Glenshee, the ski resort nearest my house, and on good snow days I would get a lift with him and spend my time skiing, often on my own. Skiing was my first sporting love. I went at every opportunity, bought the magazines, watched the races, and talked about it with my friends all the time.

Cycling was different: I wasn't, and never have been, obsessed by cycling. My first proper bike was a white Peugeot mountain bike, which I rode about for years on the farm tracks. I was eleven when I read an article in the local newspaper about a man who had just cycled from Land's End to John O'Groats. This inspired me, so I got the car road atlas out and started planning. Mum, always keen not to dissuade enthusiasm, suggested that I try a shorter cycle first, so we settled on a route across Scotland.

The summer before going to high school I cycled 145 miles from Dundee to Oban with a friend called Lachlann, and our dads. Mum and I spent days going door to door getting sponsorship, and we raised £2,000 for Save the Children and the International League for the Protection of Horses (ILPH). This gave me a chance to meet the Princess Royal and get my adventures in the local papers.

A few years later, during my second year at high school, I went back to Mum and Dad with the ambition still to do the End to End. We went through the same planning and fund-raising, only on a bigger scale, and over thirteen days in my summer holidays I completed my first solo, the 1,038 miles from John O'Groats to Land's End. Mum and Dad drove the family car the whole way as support and the ride raised £3,000 for Calton Athletics (a drug rehabilitation charity in Glasgow) and, again, the ILPH. This expedition afforded me my first chance to speak on local radio and attend a number of events. The whole project was amazing fun; I enjoyed the planning and networking as much as the cycle. Within school the achievement also created small ripples and gave me the buzz to do more.

However, around these cycling trips I didn't cycle that much. I bought a road bike when I was fourteen with the intention of cycling more, but didn't actually do that much. In my last few years at school I followed the Tour de France a bit and saved up for a better bike, but I never actually joined a club or even looked into cycling in a race. In my last year at school I spent all my savings on an incredibly expensive model which I hardly ever rode. I eventually sold it during my second year of university to fund summer traveling around Canada with my girlfriend.

In my last years of school, I decided I would go to Harvard. I haven't a clue where this idea came from. I had never been to Boston and they didn't even offer the course I wanted, but I just liked the idea of it. So I studied for and took my SAT exams for entrance to American universities and had my interview with a Harvard alumnus. It all went very well until it came down to the finances: it was going to cost $27,500 a year in tuition fees alone, before the costs

of flying there and living there. I'd gone to Dundee High School with
the help of the Assisted Places Scheme, so this kind of money just
wasn't possible.

In my excitement I had hardly bothered filling out UCAS forms as
a backup. You are meant to fill in four or five choices, but I had
simply put Edinburgh and Glasgow. I had set my sights on being a
civil engineer, and I was accepted on to the course at both
universities, but then I had a last-minute change of heart. I'd decided
to go to Glasgow University, for no real reason, so I picked up their
prospectus to choose again, wishing I had done more sciences so that
I could study medicine. I then discovered that if I was changing my
subject I would have to go through UCAS again the following year,
which meant taking another year out. This wasn't an option, so
Mum encouraged me to drive to Glasgow and speak in person to
people in the departments I was interested in.

I had no idea what I wanted to do, but I narrowed it down to law
and economics, as I figured you could get a good job with either of
those. I saw the law professor first and he wasn't very friendly or
encouraging. Slightly disheartened, I entered a building that looked
like it had been designed by a toddler, the Adam Smith Building
of Social Sciences, to meet a very excited economics professor who
took one look at my grades and after a five-minute chat accepted me
into the program. That sorted, I went off to Europe and forgot all
about it.

I spent my gap year in France and Italy, and it was the most important year for learning of my life. I left school with the ambition
of being a ski instructor and headed off to the Tignes glacier in
France to improve my skiing. It was a good thing that I went on to
pass the exam as I had already secured a job in the Aosta Valley, in
northwest Italy, as an instructor for the season. It was the perfect
opportunity to shake off the last of school's insecurities, for teaching
is the best way to become a better communicator. I had the most
amazing twenty-two weeks there.

After coming home, within weeks I was bored of the bar job in a
club I'd secured and started looking at another adventure before
university started. Within a week of finding a job on the internet I
was on a farm just north of Toulouse driving tractors, building poly-
tunnels, and planting flowers. There were a number of local workers
there and I was the only British worker, apart from the owner, who

spoke any French, so I found myself in charge of projects and organizing the other laborers. It was a superb summer, and by the time I turned up at Glasgow University I could hardly remember what I was studying.

I quickly shaved off the Mohican I had grown and was dropped at the student halls to be met by a wrestling-mad American and a rugby-mad Scotsman. Brendan, the American, was to become one of my best friends, and a flat mate throughout my university days. Ross, too, remains a good friend.

Around the ski season and farm job I had managed to fit in another big cycle, my longest yet. Mum found a leaflet about a group who were planning to cycle the 1,334 miles from Sicily to Innsbruck, up the spine of Italy in the footsteps of Second World War Allied troops, in aid of Erskine Hospital. It was the perfect summer adventure, and as a group, the perfect introduction to cycling abroad. Or so I thought. The expedition was a success in that between us we raised £50,000, and we did make it in the end, but halfway up Italy some of the group fell out and two groups ended up making their own way north. As the youngest team member I sat quietly through most of the fallout, but at the same time learned a huge amount about logistical planning and teamwork that would come in very useful later.

My four years at university were fantastic, though I did spend most of my time involved in anything but my subject. I wasn't a bad student and went to almost all my lectures, but I found I couldn't focus for an hour. My final degree was economics and politics, simply because I thought that economics should get me a job while politics interested me. For my first years at university I was planning to go into finance afterward. I had no idea what this meant but I was motivated by the money and thought it would buy me the lifestyle I dreamed of.

I was given the opportunity to go to Boston, where I had wanted to study, but this time to do an internship with Liberty Mutual, a Fortune 500 insurance company. For two months I worked in corporate employment, which had absolutely nothing to do with what I wanted to do. It did, however, bring me some amazing opportunities, like flying across the States in the private company jet, and going to see the New England Patriots in the corporate box. The most valuable thing I took from that summer was a single conversation I had with a man called Gene Harris. Gene wasn't my direct boss but worked in the department, and he took me to the football game. He told me about how he had traveled and seen so much after university before starting his current career in his late twenties.

I looked at some of my fellow interns, living the Ivy League dream the way I had wanted to, spending every university holiday working for the company that would then hire them. They were scarily bright and hardworking but dull as dishwater, and with almost no worldly experience. My perspective on what was important in terms of a career changed that summer. I knew then that I wasn't going to race into the City and try to do what our institutionalized world expects of young people. I wanted to make my own path to success.

I can't remember when the idea first occurred to cycle around the world, but it was at some point that autumn, during my third year at university. I had become ski race captain, and then in my third year vice president of the ski club. At the same time I also became involved in the overall Sports Association as treasurer. The planning, financing, and networking were exactly what I enjoyed, and I learned a lot. The top of the pile was the sabbatical role of president, and I set my sights on this. The election for the post is a public student vote, and the 2005 GUSA presidential election between Farmer and Monty (me) produced the largest turnout for years. I lost, and was absolutely gutted. It hadn't even crossed my mind that I wouldn't win, and it ruined all my plans. My presidential year would also have been the year of training and preparation for cycling around the world.

When I graduated in 2006 I realized that I still needed a year of planning, but I was starting from almost nothing. I hadn't cycled seriously in years and had fairly serious student debts and no sponsors. I also needed to make sure I could actually do the cycling. My greatest concern was not the physical side of things but the time I would have to spend alone. Therefore, to prove something to myself and to have something to take to sponsors, I set myself a training cycle.

I got a cheap flight to Oslo in early August and headed north. I had no set route, no flight home; I was simply planning to try to cycle as far and as fast as I could for a month. By the time I reached

Trondheim after four days my back wheel was broken and I had to buy panniers for the front of the bike for the first time. I was on the old mountain bike I had ridden around university for years, and I suddenly realized that I actually knew very little about touring. I hadn't even used a camp stove before.

Not only was the bike breaking, but I also had tendonitis in the left ankle. I can remember phoning home after a couple of days and having a long conversation about the realities of my plans. I explained that I was going to send half of my kit home because the bike was too heavy, and that I had to start thinking about the cycle differently. I couldn't try to race all the time because it was breaking me physically and wasn't enjoyable. I had to enjoy the journey and just try to stay on the bike for long hours to get the big miles.

Bike fixed, I headed north, up the fjords to Bodo and then over to the Lofoten Isles and up to Narvik, 300 miles north of the Arctic Circle. I purposefully wanted to find the emptiest place possible so that I could see if I enjoyed being alone for long periods. From there I cut through the most northerly road in Sweden and then south through the thousand lakes in Finland. By this time the tendonitis in the left ankle was very bad, and I also had it behind the right knee, which squeaked like blocks of polystyrene when I walked and was incredibly painful—but I could cycle.

In Helsinki I set my sights on Warsaw, and Mum booked my flight home from there. Through Estonia, Latvia, and Lithuania my body got worse and worse. I don't think I could have kept going another week, but I loved it. The sense of freedom, the daily adventures, and the things I saw dispelled any doubt. I would have to put in a lot of training, but I could race around the world. In thirty-one days I had cycled 2,700 miles.

I returned home on a high—and came straight back down to earth. Phil, a flat mate from university, had decided to do a master's at Edinburgh and I decided to get a flat with him again (it would have been difficult to stay in Glasgow and give up the student lifestyle). Our first night there we went to our new local in Broughton, and after Phil bought the first round I went to buy him a pint back and was left with two pence in my wallet. I was on my overdraft limit at £2,000 under and had two credit cards in debt. I hated asking, but Mum and Dad had to help me out until I found work. I was completely broke.

Then, that same week, I went back to Glasgow to see my girlfriend of four years and discovered that the relationship was over. To start with I assumed it was a short break, but as the weeks went on I never heard from her. It was a tough period of insecurity and doubt. I felt I couldn't show doubt in my plan to others in case they started doubting me, but I couldn't shake the feeling that if I had just got a job like everyone else and stayed in Glasgow, then my life would have been very different.

The dream was still on, though. While still at university I'd realized that if I only had one chance to have this adventure then it should be as big as possible, so right from the first brainstorms I was set on cycling around the world. I researched what had been done before and got in touch to find out what the world record was. I was amazed to discover how many people had cycled around the world by different routes and distances. But only a few had ever gone for the Fastest True Circumnavigation of the Globe by Bicycle. An Englishman called Steve Strange held the record, at 276 days. His website showed an incredible world tour and told of how he had cycled 65 miles a day on average for over nine months.

From my experience, admittedly only on the good roads of Europe, I thought that this was very beatable. I speculated that with the right training I would be able to cycle 100 miles a day sustainably. This was hugely naive—I had no idea of the roads, weather, political situations, or other possible delays—nevertheless it was how I set my target. To get the Guinness World Record I would have to cycle 18,000 miles, start and finish in the same place, go in one direction, and pass through two points on opposite sides of the world, among other criteria. Eighteen thousand divided by a hundred gave a figure of 180 days, and I then added a day off every fortnight to allow for delays with transfers, rest periods, illness, and anything else unexpected. Therefore, long before I had researched how or proved that I could actually do this, my target was to cycle around the world in 195 days.

To give myself an extra margin of error my sponsorship proposal, a two-page introductory document, had as its title "Around the World in 210 Days." When you have never ridden a race in your life, have never cycled more than 2,700 miles, and have never cycled 100 miles a day for a week, let alone half a year, claiming I could break a world record by two months was a hard sell. It took eight months to get my first capital sponsor, and that was only £500 of the £25,000 initial capital I needed. It was just enough to allow me to give up the day job I had for one month. For three months I had opened the mail, photocopied and filed papers for an engineering firm. The only good part of this was that it was 7 miles from my flat, so a good distance to run to and from as part of my training, which I was struggling to fit around the day job and the night job: planning a major expedition.

To go from punter to pro in one year was the goal, and along with securing sponsors and media interest in the absence of a strong track record on my part, to do that I needed to put some science behind the ambition. I got in touch with the sports science faculty at my university. Dr. Niall MacFarlane and his team of technicians were more than happy to put me through my paces and I completed a range of lab tests to find out my critical power output, the most efficient cycling position, cadence (pedal strokes per minute), heart-rate range, and aspects of diet.

I had sold my good race bike during university when I had no money for half of what it was worth and now had only an old mountain bike, which had been worth a couple of hundred pounds when new. Scouting the local pages, I found an old Fausto Coppi for sale in Greenock, just outside Glasgow, for £250. It was at least five years old and not nearly as good as what I had sold, but it had a strong aluminum frame and, while being slightly small, was good enough to get going. This was the bike I would ride every mile of my training for the next year and a half.

Once back from Warsaw in September 2006, I had to work until March 2007, when I found my first sponsor. Time was therefore pretty short to train and I ended up doing far more running than cycling as it was always dark when I could get out. From February until July, when the training increased substantially, I would get up and train all morning, and then every afternoon and evening would be spent in the living room-cum-office of my small flat in Edinburgh, planning. In my year of training I never cycled 100 miles once, partly owing to a lack of time but also because I tried to do all my training at a much higher intensity so that when I got on the trip it would be easier, but just for much longer each day. The training was tough and pretty lonely. There was little joy in cycling the same 60- or 80-mile loop alone, day after day, just to come back and sit in the flat, alone, to email people who never emailed back.

I spent months sending out letters and emails to any companies I thought might have an interest in my ambition. One out of ten would respond, and that would be a no. It was demoralizing, and I got nowhere for months. I talked it over with a friend, and he suggested I use my networks to get an introduction; someone might then actually open the door and sit me down with the decision-makers in these companies. My answer was that I didn't have a network of contacts, and his response remains the best bit of advice I have ever had: rather than ask people for money, he said, ask them who they know. People are proud of their relationships. It worked. I changed tactics, and within three and a half weeks I had the minimum money I needed to go.

Artemis, my title sponsor, was found through a fourth stem of the network and is the best example of how this works. I asked my cousin Catie if she could help with any contacts. She introduced me to her old boss Neil Laughton, a man who had been integral to the start of Bear Grylls's career. Neil couldn't help personally but he introduced me to one of his best friends, a man called David Fox-Pitt, who runs adventure challenges in the Scottish Highlands for charities. David asked if I could drive up and see him, and I soon found myself at a dinner party on the banks of Loch Tay telling a group of strangers how I was going to cycle around the world. The next day David called and asked if I could get a proposal to him to take to HBOS. They said no, as did some others. Then David gave me an introduction to Lindsay Whitelaw at Artemis Investment Management. After meeting Lindsay and having a brief informal chat, he called a few days later with a yes. I had a title sponsor.

A second example was how Ken Hills, an investor I met one evening when supporting Mum at a work function, introduced me to Lloyds Development Capital. The LCD managing director also seemed to barely study the proposal, and just bought into the expedition on the basis of the introduction and the strength of our discussion. It was then up to Rob, his marketing director, to ask me all the more specific questions about how an expedition like mine planned to give back to sponsors. It was a good question. At that point I could promise little more than a few newspaper articles.

My last of three major sponsors was Radisson Hotels, my old

employers while at university. They were actually the first to agree to support—a real surprise as I was just a barman—and gave generous capital and sponsorship in kind throughout.

I knew that what excited me about the cycle wasn't necessarily the main hooks that would make it a commercial success. But, without telling any lies about my background, I needed to be as professional as possible; there was little value in trying to sell this as a post-university adventure and charity cycle. I wanted to ride for charity again, but learned from early press releases that the newspapers were less likely to run the story if the main point of the expedition was the charities. I needed to package it differently. That's why I made it a world-record attempt with a charitable aspect. I would be riding for five charities: Community Action Nepal, the Tusk Trust (conservation in Africa), the Rainer Foundation (support for young people), CHICKS (Country Holidays for Inner City Kids), and Cyrenians (support for homeless people).

From the very start I realized that a documentary would be a major key to the profile of the expedition, and therefore the return on investment for sponsors. It so happened that Andrew Robertson, a friend from the cycle trip in Italy, had been flat mates with a BBC director and cameraman. And so it was, over a cup of tea in his house in the West End of Glasgow, that without warning I was handed his phone to speak to Mr. David Peat. I launched into my usual sales patter. David sounded interested, but cautious. Over the next month I heard nothing as he took the idea to people within the BBC to see if there was interest. There wasn't.

Then I met David face-to-face for the first time in the canteen at the old BBC Scotland headquarters in Queen Margaret Drive, Glasgow. After some time chatting over a coffee, he spotted someone across the canteen, jumped up, and came back with one of the main producers. For the next twenty minutes I repeated my plan to take a camera, self-film, and make some unique low-budget TV. This must have sounded so naive—the budget for the documentary would eventually be many times that of the expedition—but that meeting did spark some real interest, and a few months later, at the start of June 2007, we got the green light to start filming. From then on David Peat was with me regularly, filming any important meetings and training sessions. I had no relevant experience but thought that he seemed to be filming a lot. It was only much later that he told me why. With a laugh, he explained that if I got to Belgium and had a puncture and came home, they still needed a film, hence the tens of hours of footage for what was initially meant to be a half-hour documentary.

I had to begin the cycle in early August, not to mention stick to my daily target, if I wanted to hit the best climatic windows in all regions. Paris had been decided on as the starting point, as it was the closest high-profile point to the UK, in order to tie the story in with the UK media. The antipodal points I had to pass through were Madrid and Wellington, and there was no way I could cycle in an easterly direction from Madrid and get back to the UK, so France was chosen. A Sunday was selected as the start day as it was the quietest day of the week in Paris.

In those final weeks in March before the major capital support came in I had been seriously worried about having to put back the whole plan by a year. It felt like I had been pushing a rock up a mountain since leaving university. But now, with all the sponsors and the BBC support in place, there was absolutely nothing stopping me from going. I had pushed the rock to the summit, and now it felt like I was madly trying to keep ahead of the ensuing landslide. The project suddenly had momentum, and there was still an incredible amount to be done.

The team of support included Fiona, a physiotherapist; Ruth, a nutritionist; Niall, the sports doctor; Bruce, the website designer; Phil, the treasurer; and a number of advisers and helpers, including a good friend, Bobby, who worked with me over those final months to arrange all the visas and routes. However, while each of them played a valuable part, there was no one to hold the reins when I was on the road. I considered employing someone for this role, but knew it wouldn't be easy. I had spent a year doing all the research and logistical planning—for example, putting together a global network of contacts who could help, if or when needed, along the route—but in truth I'd completely underestimated just how key this job would be and how I would soon need someone on call 24/7 to keep the race on target. I did interview one guy for the job but he was entirely un-suitable; another one who applied never turned up. So I turned to the person who had helped me with every one of my previous expeditions. Mum.

I had kept my plan to cycle the world to myself for a long time. It was midway through my last year at university when I eventually took my mum and sisters out for a meal in Dundee. I will always remember their reactions. I had already partly told Heather, and she and Hannah were very excited. Mum was sitting opposite, and she stayed quiet and just sat back and looked at me for a long moment. She knew I was serious and I had her support from the first, but her concern was the fact that I wanted to *race* this time.

The cycle just would not have been possible on that scale had it not been for the work done at home, soon to be called "Base Camp." I may never know the full story of the incredible parallel adventures Mum had trying to keep me on the road. It is easy to imagine a team of support back in the UK behind such a major expedition, but in truth it was mainly all the work of Mum, calling on Fi, Ruth, Niall, Bruce, Bobby, and others when their specific help was needed.

Mum and Dad divorced when I was seventeen, and Mum became a very successful equine sports massage therapist, so taking on the job of key coordinator for the world cycle was a big commitment. For my part, I knew she was brilliant at networking and perseverance, but was concerned that she did not have the computer skills to take on the job. In fact, she could barely switch one on. In a couple of very brief meetings with her I handed over my laptop and a pile of folders and explained the "simple" role I expected her to fulfill. I then explained how to get onto the internet and send an email—and that was about all there was time for. The rest she learned on her own, with the help of Heather and friends. She single-handedly wrote a daily blog, communicated with all the embassies and global contacts, coordinated the kit being sent to and from me at certain points around the world, worked with the charities, and much, much more. I was entirely oblivious of most of this as she would only ever share with me things that affected me or needed my ultimate decision. Any other stresses or issues she absorbed on her own. I only ever heard about the few times she wasn't coping very well via messages, usually from Heather, to say that Mum was upset, and telling me how many hours she was working.

Like any project manager, Mum's greatest challenge was managing people, balancing those who were being overly helpful with those whose help we really needed but who sometimes weren't doing what they had said they would. I was sorry to hear that some of the people I had made contact with and had trusted to help were not cooperating, and Mum often found it more efficient to do their jobs for them. After hardly involving her at all in the year's planning, she suddenly became my rock of support for the actual race. And to do that she put her own career on hold. As the race progressed I felt bad that it was such a big job for her, but there was nothing I could do from the bike.

A potted account of her time at Base Camp features as a postscript in this book, but I hope Mum gets a chance one day to write her full story as it would undoubtedly be a fascinating read.

Those final couple of months were truly manic. Training went well until mid-June, when I broke my trusted training bike. The new Koga Miyata then arrived in time to do a ten-day training ride in Croatia with Ally Ford, an old school mate, before a final month of preparation. I hardly trained at all in July, just working from dawn till dusk to make the start line in time.

On August 1 I moved the last of my stuff out of the flat in Edinburgh back to Mum's house, packed the car, put the bike on the back, and we left for France. Driving out was Mum's idea, partly to have the chance to do a proper handover. We didn't get very far with it as I spent most of the next three days on the phone, lost in my own world of last-minute preparations. It was, however, lovely to stand on the top deck of the ferry chatting to her as the white cliffs of Dover disappeared behind us. We were off on another adventure, just like ten years before on the John O'Groats to Land's End trip. Except this time Mum would remain at Base Camp and I would be out in the world alone and unsupported.

3

My priority after leaving Paris exhausted was recovery. The routine of sleep, food, hydration, and miles cycled needed to become my new habit. It was no more difficult or simple than the target I had set myself: 100 miles a day.

Mum and Heather were going to stay with me until Brussels. This seemed to make sense, as they are both masseuses. A huge part of me was impatient to get out on the open road alone so I could get into the right mind-set, but I understood that having the car there for the first few days was actually as much to help Mum deal with what I was doing as it was to help me get started. Mum has always had amazing strength and selflessness in her support for what my sisters and I do, and I could see that it was important to her to share the first days with me. She would then drive back to Scotland, alone, to run Base Camp for the next six, seven, or eight months. However long it took for me to get back to Paris.

It was easy riding, flat and warm, as I pedaled into Belgium on day 2. There was little to challenge me; it was simply the scale of the big picture that was getting me down. I was now a few hundred miles into an 18,000-mile race and had expected to be able to hit the ground running, but I was actually struggling to adjust to my new reality. I was impatient to get a few thousand miles down the road, to prove to myself, as much as anyone else, that my dream was realistic.

Belgium looked much the same as France, though steady rain had now set in which dulled the world I was passing through and contributed to my change of mood. Annoyingly, I had to stop mid-afternoon with a puncture—not something I'd anticipated so early on. After clicking the panniers back on after a quick fix and a quicker espresso from a quiet café, I pushed on. Nearing the small town of Mons in the continuing rain along flat roads I hit puncture number two. No big issue, but frustrating niggles so near the start.

Though there was a whole world of camping ahead of me, I was also impatient to get in the tent, not just to save money but to get used to my new routine. But this would be the last night with my family so I aimed for the military town of Casteau late in the evening. Over dinner, it felt like I had not yet started. We shared the same calm that was present at the last meal back in Paris. The Europe I was cycling through was so familiar, and having my family near made Paris feel like a false start. I was still to head into the great unknown.

Day 3 started after five hours' sleep. I knew there was no way I could sustain this routine of bed after midnight. Food and sleep were the main inputs I could control and I would have to make them a far better habit once alone. Mum left at eight a.m. to take Heather to Brussels to fly back to Scotland, before driving home over three days herself. I smiled as the car disappeared. For all that I would miss them, I was finally on the road alone, left to my own devices with nothing to distract. It was my choice to test my stamina and endurance. There's no slant on the Guinness record that says you have to do it solo and unsupported.

Wheeling the bike out felt wrong, and I looked down to find another puncture. Three in twenty-four hours—ridiculous. Punctures are not newsworthy events, but this was getting annoying. Bike fixed, I felt exhausted and decided to catnap for twenty minutes before a fresh start. Three hours later I woke with a start when the cleaner rapped on the door. I jumped up, my contact lenses feeling like bits of dry paper on my eyes. There was no point in worrying, so I smiled to myself at the ridiculous nature of week 1 and wondered at what point the ride would start to resemble my plans.

Luckily, Belgium is very flat, and the day was sunny without wind—perfect for a fast spin. As the day went on, and I hopped from perfectly flat, wide roads to cycle paths and back, I moved from French- into Flemish-speaking areas. My battery felt better charged after my accidental sleep, but I was concerned by a continuing niggle behind my right knee. "Just settling in," I tried to reassure myself. The ligament felt strained and was hurting when I walked. I stopped midmorning to drop the seat and slide it forward in its rails. It was a completely different position from the one I had designed and when

I got back on it felt horribly low. Amazingly, the twinges eased after a few hours and all concerns about a knee injury disappeared.

Stopping at the first town in time to notice a fourth slow puncture, I wasted time in a labyrinth of cobbled streets trying to find a bike shop. It was embarrassing to tell the owner that I had just set out to cycle around the world as he fixed my puncture. To my relief it took him a full twenty minutes to find the problem. After pulling the tiniest of slivers of metal from the tire, he announced that he was confident the problem was fixed.

After a puncture-free afternoon, I finished the day at 147km, which meant a three-day average of 86 miles—far from perfect, but it was too early to start worrying, though in the long run such an average would add a month and a half to the target of 195 days.

It was a relief to be in my tent for the first time; the sense of an expedition was complete now. However, camp one was not ideal. Having tried to stop for 10km, I'd found myself in an army training ground. Skull-and-crossbone signs at regular intervals warned of tanks and firing ranges. At one point I had stopped to pee in perfect time for an army jeep to pull up and ask what I was doing. They clearly did not believe I was planning to keep going past the military zone, and proceeded to drive around me until I was clear. Now in thicker woods, it was getting late so I simply ducked off the road and hid my tent under some trees.

When I turned on my phone, I learned that Mum had not set off for home but was in Au Prince Royale Hotel, just 8km back, where I could have stayed if I'd wanted to. But it was ten p.m. and I couldn't go back. David Peat had called her to say he was back in Scotland and was concerned about my initial aches and challenges. His text afterward, which Mum forwarded, simply read, "Tell Mark, take it at his own pace." Mum mentioned that she might or might not come and meet me in the morning at some point. I fell asleep thinking that it was unlikely she would leave without finding me.

It was easy to feel good now. I was on my own at last, the terrain was fast and flat, the rain had stopped, and the countryside was changing so fast that I started to feel I was making real progress. Tomorrow I would race across Holland into Germany—three countries in a day, an easy illusion of speed.

I love waking up in a tent—which is just as well. I was on the road by 8:30 a.m., which boded well for what I needed to start doing. My only concern was some tightness in the legs, which were obviously taking time to get used to the new daily demands. The final weeks' preparations had been far from ideal in terms of training and some teething pains were expected, which is why I had arranged for a masseur and physiotherapist to shadow me for the first week.

Piotr is Polish but lived in Edinburgh and worked for Athletes Angels, a company that provides masseurs and medical support to a lot of adventure sports and endurance events in Scotland. I was slightly nervous about how this support would work out but was glad for it when I felt how tight my back and upper legs were when I clambered out of my tent. Piotr texted as I set out to say he was en route, driving from western Poland after visiting his family home, and would meet me when I got to Germany that evening. He was twenty-six years old, an ex-competitive swimmer, and very friendly from what I had seen, but I had only met him twice, briefly, so I hardly knew him.

All I wanted to do in that first week was get into a solid routine. The reality was that every day so far there had been distractions preventing this from happening, hence my concerns and doubts about meeting Piotr. His support had seemed a good idea during the planning stage, but now that I was on the road the prospect of continuing company bothered me. Each day I would be doing my own thing, cycling all day and expecting him to amuse himself until we met in the evening. I would then be exhausted, in need of treatment and food before immediately falling asleep. Given that he was a volunteer whom I did not know, I was struggling to see how much fun this would be.

Day 4 turned out to be a great day, the first 100-miler. Cycle paths took me all the way from Belgium through Holland and into Germany. I was enjoying the freedom of these easy miles and was surprised when I saw Mum parked by the roadside. I had forgotten she'd said she might come and find me. At the next town, Bree, we shared a coffee and pastry for an hour and took some photos before she headed off for the Calais ferry. She looked sad to see me go, but after an hour I could delay no more.

Holland would undoubtedly be my quickest country crossing, achieved in a matter of hours, with only a slight delay when I got lost in the town of Venlo near the eastern border. I have never been anywhere with so many bikes. Outside the train station was a sea of racks the size of a five-a-side football pitch which housed thousands of town bikes. Bikes ruled the roads here, outnumbering the cars, but never in conflict as the cycle paths meandered safely alongside the roads. It was cycling heaven, though no one seemed to be in the same rush as me.

Across the Dutch border with Germany, on Route 58, I decided to stay in a hotel in Wulfen. It had rained on and off all afternoon, which I did not mind camping in, but it made no sense to meet Piotr late in the evening in the dark in some wet field at the roadside. Piotr found me hungrily demolishing a bizarre mountain of cauliflower, cheese, and vegetables. Without a common language or translated menu I had been hoping for something more than a pile of vegetables when I'd gestured "vegetarian."

Afterward, on the massage table, Piotr's check-over confirmed the way I felt—absolutely fine. There were some tight muscles but nothing more than small teething issues. The knee pain from the day before had completely dissipated. The main issue was general fatigue, and it was only week 1. I had started exhausted and sleep-deprived and was now piling physical tiredness on top. It was again past eleven p.m. when I crashed out. Lots to improve on.

My route through Germany and Poland took me north of the Alps and was a fairly safe climatic bet in August. The main Guinness World Record criterion was to cycle more than 18,000 miles in the same direction. Therefore, it made sense to do more miles in "fast" countries than in "slow" ones. There are many factors that make a country slow. Hills are not the biggest concern but worth avoiding if possible. The main factors that make a country fast are road quality and prevailing winds, hence my global route took in this big loop north in Europe, following the coast in Australia, and doing a dogleg in America. This was intended to make up for shorter distances covered by taking the most direct route through potentially slow countries such as Turkey, Iran, and Pakistan.

By day 5 on the road it was getting easier to get up and go. However, my motivation was soon dampened by the heavy rain that had rolled in overnight. The German countryside seemed very drab in this wet world.

The hard part in any expedition is not the start, but a few days in, when the body and mind are struggling to get used to their new routine. The big picture was still too much to think about. In half a year's time I would still be doing the same thing every day: getting up, riding 100 miles, trying to find and eat 6,000 calories, drinking six to ten liters of water, and finding somewhere safe to sleep. You cannot just leave Paris and race back to Paris. The world is simply too vast to grasp at the speed of 13 miles an hour. Instead, every bit of energy needed to be focused on making the most of each day, and every moment. The theory was simple; finding this mental zone was the challenge. In reality, each day was different, with unique challenges to stop me drifting into a timeless place where I could just focus on getting the miles done.

By midafternoon I had made good ground, but as I climbed over rolling roads toward the small town of Lichteneu the ominous gray blanket above started to break again with light drizzle. By the high ground I was completely in the clouds, in an eerie stillness, where cars appeared from a fluffy horizon less than 20 meters away then disappeared as fast into a wall of cloud behind me. Off to each side lay fields with rows of crops and tractor marks which painted a strange symmetry in the bubble of murky gray. Pedaling became strangely hypnotic, with no other visual distractions. There was no way of knowing what the road was doing as the undulations sneaked up and road signs jumped out at the last minute to assure me I was on course.

After an hour riding through the fog I started to hear a dull drone off to each side. It was a slow, strange whirling noise that came and went as I glided past, but the curtain of cloud veiled its origin. After some time peering off into the fields I heard a louder noise ahead and a slowly spinning blade appeared, then cut back into the gray, followed by another, before it too clouded out. I was cycling through a wind farm, but the fog made it look like something out of a science fiction movie. It was unusually beautiful. It reminded me specifically of a scene from the 1960s version of *War of the Worlds*, which was a storybook I had listened to on cassette over and over when I was a kid. Ironically, in that rain and fog I felt as bright and happy as I had at any point on the trip. I was finding the zone.

When I stumbled across Lichteneu in this short-sighted world the light rain turned torrential and I pulled up under the cover of a petrol station to consider my options. It was getting dark fast, hours before it should, and the rain was settling in for the evening. The small town seemed deserted and there was no sign of anywhere to stay. If I had not felt so good about the day it would have been miserable. After calling Piotr, who was up ahead, and agreeing to meet at the station, I went inside and bought some food, hoping to find warmth again in my wet clothes. While standing back outside by the pumps, thunder sounded close overhead, followed by a flash that lit up the clouds spectacularly.

Piotr pulled up. Apparently there was a hotel just a couple of kilometers off the road which was showing on his GPS. I had no bearings or sense of what was around me, but from what I had seen on the main street I was pleasantly surprised that there was somewhere I could dry off so close. The bad news was that it was down a side road and the turnoff was behind me. There is nothing more demoralizing than going back.

As soon as we turned off, the narrow road swept downhill and Piotr raced ahead. Over 3km later I was still flying around sweeping corners to the zing of wet roads, not a dwelling in sight as we disappeared into a rural valley. As the road forked with an option to cut sharp left I called ahead to Piotr, who had also found nothing and was being sent in circles by his GPS. The road going left was at least in the correct direction, and far more appealing than going back up the climb in the cold rainy darkness. The car appeared out of the fog ahead and Piotr agreed with my plan, annoyed at his GPS but convinced that the hotel had to be somewhere close. "Please don't go too far ahead," I asked. "Any turnoffs, please stop."

I was soon resigned to the fact that there would be no chance to dry out that night: this would be a bizarre place to put a hotel. Sure enough, after 2km another road cut left, back up the hill to Lichteneu. Piotr looked dejected with this wild goose chase and his false promises. Opposite the turnoff was a thick wood with a small path leading a short way in where farm vehicles could be parked. Apart from the thick nettles and torrential rain it was a perfect camping spot as it was slightly raised and obscured from the road. I couldn't face the climb back to the main road now; it could wait for the morning.

An hour later, having cooked a pot of quick rice in the porch of the tent, I sat scribbling my stats for the day in the logbook, listening to the rain battering off the tiny tent. The heavy splodges coming off the trees made it sound heavier than it was. Piotr had parked the car just off the road, blocking the path and any view of my tent, and I dashed across. He had put the backseats down and arranged his luggage down one side to create a makeshift bed. We must have looked hilarious for the next half an hour as we attempted to perform a massage in the back of the car while trying to keep dry. The boot lid gave some cover, but Piotr was soon soaked. It was only nine p.m. when I crawled back into my tent and tried to remove my jacket and shoes in a space little bigger than myself so that everything else didn't get damp.

There is an incredible snug peaceful feeling to falling asleep to the sound of rain pattering off canvas just inches from your face. It had been a successful 174km. I would settle for another half year of that—just without the rain and the 6km detour at the end.

The next day took me quickly into eastern Germany. For the first time since France, having enjoyed the company of so many cyclists on the maze of cycle paths through Belgium, Holland, and western Germany, I felt alone on the roads. Day 6 included an 11km climb to the town of Mulhausen, eclipsing the Low Countries' total climb of 1,370 meters. They were the first hills I had encountered, and they came at the right time to help the legs settle in. These first weeks were so crucial for the long-term sustainability of the small muscle balances around the joints. I had learned a lot from the 2,700-mile training run the year before, when tendonitis in the ankles and one knee meant I could not have carried on. This was the reason Piotr was here, and this was what a year of training had been focused on avoiding. Happily, I felt like I was getting stronger without any of the niggles that had caused concern for consecutive days.

The hills were also a welcome change of scenery and helped the feeling of progress. Momentum had been achieved. The bike was running well and I felt fit. I was heading east as planned, at 100 miles (160km) a day.

4

The start of week 2 was celebrated with more heavy rain. I love waking in the night to heavy rain on the tent, then falling asleep and finding it has stopped by dawn. But as I sat cross-legged in the tiny Terra Nova tent, peering out while eating the leftover quick rice from the previous night, it was raining even harder than before, and the wind had picked up. As I packed the bike the low gray skies gave no sign of change. Piotr was still asleep in the back of his car and I refrained from waking him as I pushed the bike out of the field.

In eastern Germany the countryside changed quickly. Leipzig was an obvious target today, a perfect 100 miles away and a big town where I could get shelter to dry out my soaked camp. With a clear target, week 1 in the bag, and bike and body feeling good, I soon forgot the misery of the rain. Just after lunch it eased slightly, then after a while it stopped and I was left pedaling along to the delightful zing of standing water. After half an hour in the dry, the trick is to wear your jacket inside out to dry the inside as well before packing away. Gore-Tex or not, you get drenched within a few hours in heavy rain, especially when you're sweating.

Flying down a fairly big downhill, through some hardwoods and past a farm steading, I braked hard to take a sweeping right and left. As soon as I banked the bike slightly left I released the back brake entirely and eased the front to let the bike ride out the corner. Immediately I heard a sharp cracking sound from the back of the bike. My heart sank. I did not even have to look; I knew the sound well. A broken spoke.

Spokes should not break through lateral strain like this if the wheel is built properly, but everything about the bike was a trade-off in terms of strength, speed, comfort, and weight, and the wheels were no exception. To get techie for a moment, the two biggest decisions were if I should ride mountain bike wheels or road wheels (26-inch and 28-inch circumference respectively), and if I should ride a traditional gearing system with a cassette of cogs where the chain is moved by derailleurs to different ratios, or an internal gearing system where all the gears are held within the back hub (center of the wheel). The massive advantage of this is that the chain has no lateral movement, like a track bike, and lasts much longer, helped by the fact that you get less grit and grime as there are fewer external parts. The cons are that it is expensive, if it breaks you cannot fix it yourself, and lastly—and at this point most importantly—it only supports a thirty-two-spoke back wheel. Most back wheels on road bikes have a minimum of thirty-six spokes, but if you are being very safe you could build a back wheel with as many as forty-eight spokes, which could happily seat an elephant. At 6 feet 3 inches and 14 stone I was in the margin of concern in terms of wheel strength, especially once the bike was fully laden with five pannier bags. The smaller the wheel, the shorter the spokes, and therefore the stronger it will be. Riding a road wheel with only thirty-two spokes on the back had been a concern from the start, which is why I had taken the manufacturer's bike and got the wheels rebuilt specifically with strong double-rimmed wheels (twice the strength, to stop the spokes pulling through) and used tandem bike spokes which thickened out near the rim for extra strength.

A broken spoke is not in itself difficult to fix on the road, but after one week out of a possible seven or eight months this break reawakened all the debates about kit choice. Did I have the right setup for the job? It might be simple enough to fix now, but a serious wheel breakage outside Europe with no help for thousands of miles and I could wave good-bye to the record.

A few hundred meters from the corner, still downhill, was a small town. Like others I had passed that morning it was gray, shuttered, and sleepy-looking. As I slowed to find somewhere, anywhere, flat and sheltered to fix the wheel, it started raining. I pushed the bike into an old brick bus shelter set back from the road and quickly found the break. A broken wheel so early on was one of my worst fears, and it had happened just as I was starting to hit a good routine on the bike. I was struck with a sense of utter dread.

Focus. I would fix the spoke, get back on the road, and worry about the long-term reliability later.

The light in the shelter was very bad, but after taking the pannier bags off, turning the bike upside down, taking the wheel off, and removing the tire and rim tape, I could thread in a new spoke. To true the wheel (make it rotate straight) you must tension all the spokes evenly, which is easier said than done while sitting in the dirt in a bus shelter. Unless you build a wheel on a proper rig and tension all the spokes together it is almost impossible to get them perfectly true, especially when you have never built a wheel before, like me. But after ten minutes' spinning and tweaking I was reasonably happy. It was fixed, but not perfect, absolutely nothing stopping it from happening again. I had four spare spokes for the back and two for the front for the rest of the world.

I was pleasantly surprised and pleased with my wheel build as I pedaled out into the rain again, keen to make up lost time. Leipzig was still a sensible target and I really needed shelter to dry everything out.

Leipzig's sprawling suburbs are very run-down. Walls of graffiti accompanied me for miles to the center. It is a city of over half a million people and located just past the border of Germany's easternmost federal state, Saxony. For a city with a millennium's worth of history and famous for its university and trade, it didn't look that spectacular when I arrived.

I decided it made more sense for Piotr to find me at a hotel rather than the other way around. Right in the city center there was a big hotel across from the train station, and I made my way through the bucketing rain to find it was a pricey four stars and evidently the nicest in town. Back on the bike, I weaved through slow rush-hour traffic to get to the right-hand side of the road. The traffic was two lanes deep and in the central area two sets of tramlines ran parallel to each other. As I turned left to feed into my lane I went to cross the second set of tracks, but as soon as my front wheel mounted the first rail it slipped, as if on black ice. Without a moment to react, and with my feet still clipped into the pedals, I hit the ground hard, looking into the oncoming traffic to see a bus hit the brakes and a car on its outside stopping as well.

Luckily the bike landed on a pannier bag and seemed undamaged as I jumped to my feet and dragged it back upright. I pushed my bike to the side of the road and then ran back to pick up a pannier bag which had come off. A few people got out of their cars but no one approached, maybe because it was raining. I was so annoyed with myself. I hadn't been concentrating properly. The bike was fine and the bag clipped back on easily, but unfortunately it now had a small hole. My injuries looked superficial—just a grazed knee—but after a few minutes in the cold rain I could feel it starting to seize up. It had obviously taken a knock.

It was getting late, and as I left the city center there seemed less and less chance of finding a hotel as I passed yet more run-down retail shops and boarded-up windows. I was close to turning back, as I simply could not face camping after the rain, the broken spoke, and the crash, when I picked up signs to another hotel. I had followed one of these breadcrumb trails on the way into town and just got lost, so wasn't hopeful.

The dot-to-dot led me to a large out-of-town shopping center and a very plush-looking hotel. It looked expensive but I was out of options and I called Piotr with directions. Standing under its huge canopied reception and looking around at the pouring rain and glistening car park, I smiled. It had been a shite day. I was a drowned rat with blood running down my knee. The thought crossed my mind that they might not even let me stay looking like this.

Fifty-four euros was a surprise result for a luxurious suite for two. After food, shopping for the next day's food, emails, drying everything, a massage, and truing the back wheel once more, it was one a.m. once again by the time I got to bed. Piotr's cheery banter was very welcome after such a tough day, but on the bright side I had made 162km despite it all.

I slept in till 6:30 and my first thought when I woke was a continuation of a bad dream I had been having about broken wheels. I hated that nagging concern about reliability. So much research had gone into getting the best kit yet here I was, week 2 on the road, questioning it all over again.

I waved off Piotr, who was driving on to Poland to see his father and then coming to meet me in the evening. I felt very tired so I decided to use the internet to write a web blog to wake me up. But Leipzig seemed determined to be unkind to me from first to last. As I rushed to pack the bike I noticed Piotr's big laptop sitting on the table. Despite trying many bungee cord and repack options there was no way I could carry it so I left it at reception for him to retrieve. I knew he wouldn't be amused when he found out and I felt bad for being unable to carry it.

Kicking myself for a slightly late start, I cycled out of Leipzig on day 8 after a big bowl of pasta. It looked like a perfect cycling day with some cool cloud cover and a gentle tailwind. It was truly a beautiful day, and the road, which gently rose and fell with wind farms on every horizon, was amazingly quiet. As the day went on I tried to rationalize and suppress my fears about the wheels.

I didn't get off the bike for the first 80km, only stopping at the small town of Greuban after three hours and seventeen minutes for some food. Coming into Dresden, I dug out the bullet cam (a small camera which could go on my helmet or handlebars) for the first time—and then promptly got lost. It was a beautiful place, especially when doused in sunshine after a fast morning, and in contrast to the soaked horror of Leipzig. Dresden is still associated with one of the most controversial acts of the Second World War, when Allied bombers obliterated much of the inner city, killing thousands of innocent civilians. Forty years spent in the Soviet bloc changed the city further, but it looked a splendid and friendly place as I cycled in.

Meeting Piotr on the road out the other side was trickier than I'd hoped and we lost some time, but then found ourselves on a long, straight, forested road just 30km from Poland. Miles of roadworks and houses made it difficult to find anywhere good to camp. After hours of looking, Piotr came back having found a beautiful spot up a small lane into a field. It was shielded from the road by some corn on one side and a few low young trees. After a massage and a big dinner I was determined to get an early night as Piotr set off for the drive back to Leipzig for the laptop. Things seemed to be on track after all the teething challenges of week 1.

I am not superstitious, but the 13th was not good to me. It started well, cycling over beautiful rolling terrain with clear blue skies for the first time since France, into the first miles of western Poland. Piotr arrived as I sat in the morning sun having breakfast. He had been too tired to drive back during the night.

The back wheel seemed to have held up well since my rebuild and today's plan was to pile in some big miles and hopefully find a good bike shop to get the wheel set up properly. A few hours in, a loud twang brought that plan crashing down. I actually laughed at this rotten luck, pulling on my brakes and into a lay-by. I hung my head for a moment before kicking out the bike stand and looking at my second broken wheel.

Having a Polish friend now seemed incredibly useful, and Piotr was on the scene within half an hour to make a series of urgent calls. It turned out that the nearest bike shop, Pro Bike, was 30km ahead. They were very busy and said they couldn't help, but Piotr explained what I was doing again and they finally agreed to see me. Limping the hilly miles with a wobbly wheel into Jelenia Goro, I found a small workshop with mainly town and kids' bikes. On the far wall I did, however, spot a few race bikes, which gave me some hope that these guys were experienced.

After taking off and piling the panniers to one side, I handed the wheel to a shy-looking mechanic. I spoke no Polish and Piotr knew nothing about bikes, but we managed to explain my situation. After some time spent making calls and trying to figure out my options, Piotr told me that the mechanic thought my spokes were over-tensioned for such a heavy setup and also that they had been cut too short and were pulling out from the nipples (the bolt part which the spoke screws into at the rim). My best option was to let him rebuild my wheel with new spokes, Piotr explained.

I felt completely unqualified to make this decision. The workshop hardly looked like cutting-edge technology, and I could not even discuss my options as all my questions seemed to be getting lost in translation. "OK," I agreed eventually, out of choices. I couldn't believe I was getting a new wheel built in a tiny shed in Poland just over a week from the start.

Decision made, I assumed that the rest of the day would be a write-off. "When will it be ready?" Piotr asked for me, earnest as always. The mechanic pointed at the number two on the clock on the wall. It was nearly half past twelve, so this did not fill me with any more confidence; in fact, it dashed any hopes I had of a professional job. My original wheel build, by a professional wheel builder, had taken the best part of half a day. I looked desperately around the sparse workshop and conceded. It was hopeless.

We walked away, and I felt a knot of dread tighten in my stomach.

My bike was broken to the point where I could not carry on. Did I get a complete overhaul with traditional gears so that I could have a rear wheel with a normal number of spokes? I reasoned that the system I had was built for this kind of riding so it must work, but I failed to convince myself. While this was only a nuisance and delay in Europe, it would almost certainly end my race if it happened anywhere between Istanbul and Calcutta. I had a little over a thousand miles to find a permanent solution. And as we walked up a hill into the old town center to find some lunch, I was not convinced that this one-hour rebuild was it.

Jelenia Goro was stunning, with a surprisingly bustling main street. We sat outside a small pizzeria watching the world go by. It was hard to stay stressed for long here. Piotr babbled away enthusiastically about Poland and caught me noticing a group of beautiful girls walk past, which sent him into an excited monologue about how Polish girls are the best in the world. Moments like that were important in terms of putting the expedition into context: it was a race for the world record, but I had to continue appreciating the chance to see the world.

Sitting there, it felt like a spell had been broken. Since Paris I had been head down, ignoring the world I was passing through. Now, having been forced to stop, I could properly see this world for the first time. If my wheel had not broken I wouldn't have had this chance to draw breath and make sure I was actually enjoying my journey. I could only make the most of each moment and not distract myself with what I could not affect. It seemed very clear, so for now, with my bike in bits, I enjoyed a good lunch in a beautiful town in Poland with my new friend Piotr, who seemed to be bursting with pride for this opportunity.

Back at the shop, word had spread about my ambition and the owner, a smiling man with a trim beard, introduced himself in broken English. The wheel was ready and was presented to me amid a huddle of shop workers who looked expectantly at me. I flexed a couple of spokes toward each other to feel the tension and the knot of dread immediately came back. I smiled at the retiring mechanic and said thank you but I was actually very disappointed. I had never felt looser spokes. They had an incredible amount of flex on them and were much thinner than the ones that were now scattered on the workshop floor.

Trying not to sound rude, I turned to Piotr. "Can you ask him the reason for making the spokes so loose?" I have no idea what Piotr said, but from his gestures and tone I realized there was no reason to be worried. "They can move to take any bumps and pull from the side," Piotr explained simply to me. "If they are tight like before they are good for a race bike but will break when you have too much weight on the bike." This theory made sense, but my wheel still seemed extremely loosely made.

After fitting the bags back on the bike I ended up leaving some Polish zloty on the counter after both the mechanic and owner refused any payment. For the second time, in the second bike shop since the start, I felt silly as the team waved me off—I certainly didn't feel like I deserved any hero's send-off. But for these amazing people it didn't seem to matter. For them, the dream was enough. It was the ambition and not any past achievement that they loved.

The friendly owner insisted on joining me for the first 10km out of town, saying it was a complicated route. After two well-signed turns we cruised up a long hill. His big motorbike idled lazily by my side as I puffed and panted to set a reasonable pace, feeling the effects of our big lunch. His limited English was almost impossible to converse with over the engine noise, but we managed to talk about his racing background and how he was now the sole importer for a brand I had never heard of but which he assured me was the very best. I was beginning to feel less awkward about saying the right things in situations like these. A comfortable silence is far better communication than misunderstood small talk.

By the time he left me I realized that I had not thought of my wheel once because of his company. I now looked down as I pedaled deeper into the Polish countryside to see it running perfectly straight and true. If it broke again at all before Istanbul I would change to normal gearing system on a forty-spoke wheel—decision made. For now, it was time to stop worrying about it.

Sitting in my slightly sloping tent that evening in a hay field set high above the road (Piotr had left to spend the night with a friend nearby), I looked out at an incredible sunset over a wide valley below me. The road through the afternoon had continued through lush countryside and under blue skies, promising a hot week ahead. Considering I had written the day off at midday it was a result to have finished on 140km. Assuming no more breakages, my confidence was growing with every day I maintained my target of 100 miles. I ate a big meal of couscous sitting on a round bale of hay. Afterward I lay in my tent, crying with laughter as I listened to some Billy Connolly sketches on my laptop.

Waking on day 10, I stumbled out of the tent early. It was another great morning and looked to be much hotter, after a soggy week 1. The bike rolled perfectly over the next 181km. It was a cozy 40 degrees at lunch as I headed into the arable central belt of Poland, having passed the big hills of the borderlands.

The following day was even hotter, over rolling hills with a headwind. At 176km I could sense my confidence soaring. My fears were quickly dissipating about the back wheel, which was as loose as ever but riding true. I was now more distracted by my sunburn. I was famous for a strong nose, which was now bleeding, the week of rain having made me complacent about the need for sun-cream. Other than that, physically, apart from the inevitable leg fatigue, I felt great and fresh each day with the support of Piotr's evening massages. Piotr made it so easy to call on him when needed but leaving me to do my own thing. Any initial frustration about not being able to just get on alone had gone. The only drawback was the lack of sleep, as every evening ended late, after an hour's treatment on top of everything else that had to be done.

Poland is a forgotten gem. The Poles are some of the most welcoming of all Europeans and the country has some of the most scenic riding I have done. It was always interesting to see a country changing at the speed of a bike. After a fast morning, lunching in the midday sun on heavy Polish cuisine—the abundance of fried eggs, potatoes, and pasta was very welcome, but I struggled to find a love for the national delicacy of sauerkraut—left me lethargic as I pedaled for Krakow. Early afternoon I passed Auschwitz, which almost went unnoticed as the signs I passed bore the Polish name, Oświęcim, which Piotr translated for me. 1.1 million people died in concentration camps in the area around this small town. In the basking midsummer sunshine it was impossible to get a sense of the history but it left me thinking about the places I was flying past.

As I approached Krakow I had a number of road options. Krakow, the former capital of Poland, is one of the largest and oldest cities. Sensing the inevitable delays of getting through a big town, and looking at the contours, I struck off onto a smaller road which would take me directly east. This was the wrong decision. The road deteriorated to one of the worst tarmac surfaces I have ever cycled on and for the final 40km all my fears about the back wheel came back. Broken tar is many times worse than dirt and rubble, its sharp edges threatening to break wheels turning at any speed worth traveling at. The panniers sat evenly on the bike, with as much weight at the front as possible to offset the imbalance of my weight being over the back, but the total weight on such broken roads was a worry.

The edge of the road was worse still. I snaked the best line until passing cars pushed me back near the edge. I stopped twice and with a sense of the inevitable gave the back wheel a spin, looking at how it cleared the brakes. Amazingly, it was still spinning perfectly. This was truly a horrific road but these jelly wheels were bumping and bashing happily without fault. Riding through the outskirts of Krakow, I was on an absolute high. I had struck gold in that sleepy town with its worn workshop. The bike had just passed its greatest test yet with flying colors.

That evening, after enjoying my first shower since Leipzig, I looked at a map of Europe for the first time. I was doing it. That was my first 1,000 miles done; only seventeen more of those to go.

I had to start getting to bed before midnight. Correct sleep patterns were one of the biggest factors that determined my energy and mood. For the first week or so it had been a low priority, but in the last stretches of Europe I was starting to consistently hit my 100-mile-a-day target. However, I knew that this was the easy part. Food, roads, culture, climate, and much more were soon going to make this tougher.

Eastern Poland was hilly and hot after the fast miles of the North European Plain. Turkey and Iran were going to be scorching so I was actually grateful for the gradual acclimatization. It's easy to wish for anything but what you have, though. I realized that a week ago I would have given all my rations for the rain to stop and a bit of this sun to come through, and the thought amused me. Now, a light shower would be heaven sent.

As was becoming the routine, lunch was a welcome break at about 100km, during which I looked ahead to set a reasonable target for the afternoon. It was a good thing I did this because almost every early afternoon I would feel lethargic after a big lunch. I would have struggled to roll on without this focus.

Just past seven o'clock I was climbing out of another big dip in the road and spotted Piotr's Audi waiting at the top. We were a bit short of the town of Rzeszów. I glanced down at the cycle computer, which read 165km. I knew I could go on, but this was to be one of the last nights with Piotr. I felt I should stop and take the time to have a proper treatment before the months alone. I had been fighting this argument backward and forward in my mind all afternoon.

"There are some hotels here or we can go into the center." Piotr pointed to a side road. "I have been into both, looked at rooms, and got prices," he continued. I smiled at the obvious joy he was getting from his self-appointed role as Polish fixer. He described the first as a normal hotel, quite cheap and clean, then said, "The other is, um, blue, looks a bit *different*, but is cheaper. It is very smart, just . . . different." Not much to go on, but intriguing.

"Which would you choose?" I ventured.

"Both are fine," he replied unhelpfully.

I respected his impartiality in giving me the facts and letting me decide, but his tone told me something. "Let's just go for the cheapest," I said. "I will follow you."

Piotr smiled and jumped in the car. "I hope you like!" he shouted out the window as he pulled out.

I followed the car up a single tarmac path between fields and houses, which looked more like a farm entrance than any hotel. The road turned right then left around some building works and after a short distance opened up on the left into a wide car park. The building facing me was a large L shape, baby blue with gold gilding. The entrance porch was protruding from the corner and had a huge coat of arms above the door. However, I did not immediately notice any of this. Pushing the bike across to where Piotr had parked, I found myself standing close to an elaborate marble fountain spouting jets out of stone mermaids into a wide basin. On the far side, nearest the door, were four ladies, two sitting, two standing, dressed in tiny dresses and skimpy tops, each with a cigarette hanging from red-lipsticked mouths. They were stunning. We were too close to pass comment as Piotr got out of the car, but his look answered mine: "I have no idea." As if to put me at ease, he did say, "The rooms are fine and it is good food."

The foyer was very dark, with deep red velvet sofas around the edge of a long room and heavy gold-framed mirrors on three walls.

The wallpaper, also deep red, absorbed any ambient light. I felt like we had walked into a 1950s Soviet palace. It felt strange to be standing in Lycra in what could have been a plush nightclub. Behind the thick black marble desk sat a young man with slicked hair. He had very good English and spoke over Piotr's initial translation. After we'd handed over passports and paid for a room he responded to my glances around the room. "It is owned by a family from Ukraine," he said, pointing at a coat of arms on the wall behind him. "We have a show six days a week, in the restaurant," he added helpfully, pointing past me into a hallway. We thanked him and I asked if I could bring the bike into the room.

"Why did you give me a choice?" I laughed with Piotr as we went back outside. "This place is amazing!"

The heavy old Russian style continued through the hallways to our room. It was sickeningly rich and looked like a fancy dress set. I would like to call it tacky but it was so ornate and elaborate that I had nothing to compare it to. After a quick shower and stretching off Piotr and I ventured through the deserted hallways in search of food. The restaurant was through a thick velvet curtain and didn't look like any restaurant I have ever been to. The room was about 30 meters across, with booths of circular sofas around the edge of a slightly raised central area, which took up most of the room. On the back wall was an entrance through another heavy curtain, straight onto the stage. A couple of disco balls hung overhead. A bar was tucked off stage right.

The whole place was dimly lit and a young waiter showed us to a dark leather booth. He handed us both menus but immediately ignored me when he realized Piotr was Polish. He was attentive to the point of being awkward and Piotr looked startled by his pampering. As soon as he had gone, Piotr leaned over, stammering, "What is this place?" I laughed out loud.

The other strange part was that it was almost entirely empty. Off to our left was a group of three men in suits, but otherwise there was no one there. It didn't quite make sense. We were in the middle of the countryside, yet here was a hotel and dancing club with shows six days a week without an audience. Maybe we were too early. It was evidently an expensive business.

Of the showgirls we could see no sign. After two massive plates of omelettes, potatoes, and salad in our coolly lit booth, listening to eighties pop, our ever-attentive waiter told us that the show started at ten p.m. Perfect. Time for a massage and to write the logbook.

We were about to get up and leave when a man I had not seen before walked over. He was very short but built like a tank—his arms were abnormal. Tucked into his snug black trousers was a tight silky red shirt, the short sleeves stretched and bunched up above these most ridiculous of arms. The neck was open to the second button, revealing a heavy gold chain necklace. His Marine-cut hair framed a bony face, which was looking somewhat aggressive. There were a number of loose stools on the stage side of our table, directly across from me, and he threw his leg over one and sat down without a word of introduction. I glanced at Piotr, who looked as blank as I felt. Our newcomer placed a bottle of energy drink on the table with some ceremony and then gravely extended a handshake to each of us.

I would love to know what was said next. He spoke to me in Polish, and Piotr answered. I had no idea what Piotr was saying but I had to admire his natural charm, which was immediately disarming. The man cut into Piotr's conversation with a few seemingly curt comments and I sat back, finishing my drink and conscious not to look worried. The guy had incredible presence, and I noticed our waiter hovering just out of view of him by the bar, always looking over. I have little experience of such things, but if I was to cast a Russian-style mafia boss then this would be what he looked like, except perhaps he was a little young and too short. He was a triangle of a man, his squat frame and insanely large shoulders and arms making him the Ukrainian Johnny Bravo.

Minutes of Piotr's chat passed before JB broke the tension with a swig of his bottle, which appeared to require his whole flexed arm. An open hand shot back across the table and he nodded as he wrung my hand, acknowledging me for the first time since Piotr had butted in. I held the iron clasp for a second time and looked him in the eye. My mind flashed back to Tete and Arnaa, a couple of Estonians I had worked with on a flower farm in France when I was eighteen. They had always given and expected the most intense look and shake of respect. After an age, though probably no more than five seconds, my new friend seemed satisfied and sat back, looking around for the first time. The camp waiter was there in a second. I had no idea what had just happened but we now seemed on good terms.

JB spoke to Piotr, gesturing at me. "He wants to know how you'll break the world record for cycling around the world and why other cyclists have not been here."

I tried to bullet-point my answer for Piotr to translate. "Guinness World Records are based in London. Anyone can try to break a record. I must cycle 18,000 miles, I mean 29,000 kilometers, going in the same direction, passing through two points on opposite sides of the world and starting and finishing in the same place. Others have not been here because there have not been many. The last was in 2004 and he took a very different route. He did not come to Poland." JB looked blankly at me so I added, "I have enjoyed cycling here. I enter Ukraine tomorrow."

He nodded, seemingly happy, and took another swig of his energy drink. He spoke to Piotr again then got up, like a bulldog. Piotr was visibly relieved and laughed nervously. I had missed most of what had been said but the message was universally understandable: *you are on my turf and it is my rules.* I was glad Piotr had been there to explain.

The camp waiter returned with the bill and a DVD from the owner featuring a film of the dancing girls. This was too good to miss, so after a massage in the rather cramped room we returned to the restaurant/club. The first act had six girls wearing what looked like huge frilly doll gowns, although when they turned it was revealed that they were only frontal dresses and their backs were completely naked, apart from a thong. They moved about the stage with tiny steps, in synchronized dance to a polka. Six suits were now watching the show, but the place was otherwise still empty.

The stage was cleared for a few minutes while the smoke machines went into overdrive, flooding onto the floor, wafting cool mist toward us. It had a strange smell. The lights were so low now that I could barely make out what the girl who then appeared was wearing. She shuffled forward, swaying and twirling her arms in time to a slower beat. She wore a string thong and—it took a minute to figure out—nothing else. She looked like she was wearing a tiny top in the low lights and smoke, but that was probably just my expectation. She was only a couple of meters away, looking at me, solemnly dancing. It was not particularly sexy, although she undoubtedly was. It was very professional, but in the context it felt seedy as she ran her hands over her small breasts for the benefit of the eight men lurking around dark tables on deep velvet sofas. Piotr looked similarly intrigued but slightly uncomfortable. I declined a second Coke and went to bed, amused and confused.

I woke with a start at eight a.m. I had slept in. It was hard to stay annoyed as I surveyed the scene around me: my deep red silken bed-sheets were gold-trimmed and framed by a heavy engraved wooden headboard, the red wallpaper was so elaborate it looked more like a carpet, and the mirror on the far wall looked like it weighed a couple of tons. I woke Piotr, who followed my lead by swearing when he realized daylight was already streaming in the window, then pausing to laugh out loud at our crib.

Breakfast was served back in the club, where the weirdness con-tinued. An amazing buffet seemed to be just for us. The place looked cold in the light of day. Very loud rock music, presumably Ukrainian, was playing. Two suits were drinking vodka shots in the opposite corner, their ties and jackets now abandoned. Two younger women were wrapped around them and drank with them. They were definitely not wearing suits, just knee-high boots and little more than underwear. Halfway through my first bowl of cornflakes one of the girls dragged her guy past us, through the velvet curtains and off to the rooms. I sat there in my Lycra, comforted by Piotr's similar bemusement. We agreed over breakfast that this place, this *faux palais*, was undoubtedly a money-laundering venture by a Ukrainian family. JB had mentioned that he was the younger brother in a family business in Ukraine.

The night before, somewhere between the mafia dinner and the dancing girls, I had spent some time studying the map. To my surprise and annoyance I realized I had cycled 200 miles farther to this point than I had expected to. I kept waking during the night worrying about this. The implications were that I would be in Istanbul a few days late, but on a grander scale, if you multiplied this error by what I had left I would be nearly 2,000 miles out. I had no idea how, after so much planning, I had got the distances of Europe so wrong. Mum was immediately on the case and I could do little more at my end but keep pedaling.

During the day I got a text from David Peat reassuring me that meeting him in Istanbul a few days later was not an issue. A second message from Bobby (the friend who had helped with the maps) told me that I would inevitably do more miles on the road than planned.

Even so, 10 percent seemed too much. Mum then called Guinness World Records who also agreed that differences between maps and reality were not a problem and to be expected. Despite all this reassurance, as the day went on I became obsessed by the discrepancy and eventually got Piotr to mark out 10km on the road according to the car. Easier said than done when his car measured miles. Still, when he scratched a mark on the ground after 6.25 miles my bike computers agreed. It was some relief that at least my recorded statistics were correct. Not being able to provide verification for my world record was another of my greatest fears.

I came across the Ukrainian border before I had expected to. It was 3:30 p.m. and I had already done 117km—not bad on these constantly rolling roads.

I had not given this border enough consideration after flying across other European borders with just a glance at the EU sign of a circle of yellow stars on blue. But this was different. It is a major border into the European Union, and the EU is somewhere a lot of people want to get into. It therefore stood as the gateway to a different standard of living and lifestyle. Security was tight, big gates by robust-looking toll buildings with large central offices and heavily armed guards.

Borders often involve queues, but nothing I saw subsequently compared to that Polish/Ukrainian border. The long line of cars, vans, and trucks waiting on the Polish side included many stuffed full and piled high. I wondered if it was a luxury of the rich to shop in Europe or if there was such need in Ukraine that anyone who could just popped into Poland for supplies. The vehicles included many old Ladas, the likes of which disappeared from the UK at the end of the 1990s, whose owners completed the stereotype by being dressed in dark heavy clothes despite the heat, many of them smoking.

After pushing my way to an area where the road opened out into a park before the border, I surveyed the scene and called Piotr, who caught up after a few minutes having managed somehow to bypass the queue. Plan A had been to drive across with me and have one last, longer, and thorough massage before leaving me for good tomorrow morning. However, this queue looked prohibitive, so Piotr called over a young Polish guard who was directing the traffic and chatted earnestly, as was his way. These guards had a real presence and I was again impressed with Piotr's confidence in any situation. His openness was quite disarming, and not for the first time over the past week I made a mental note to learn from his approach in potentially tricky situations.

It turned out that on the Ukrainian side there was over ten hours' worth of traffic trying to enter the European Union. Even if it had been half this length it would have been crazy for Piotr to go across for one treatment. He would have to spend ten hours trying to get back, which was pointless, especially when he planned to drive non-stop to Paris the next day, in time to propose to Jagwega, his girlfriend.

Being Piotr, this new challenge was merely a nuisance. He ran back over to the guard.

"Right, he is a nice guy, he has family from my town. I can leave my car here and get a lift across with any car here, then get a bus back tomorrow morning, go through security as a pedestrian, pick up my car, and go . . . no problem."

"OK, that could work. But how would you know where to get a lift to once in Ukraine?" He couldn't contact me as he was out of credit and his phone battery kept dying.

"I can find a call box and ask where you are."

"Do you have any Ukrainian money?" It occurred to me that I didn't even know what the currency was.

"No," he confirmed.

The conversation continued, exploring the pros and cons. Ultimately, though I did not wish to sound negative, it felt like a huge effort for one last treatment. The previous few days through Poland had been so rushed, always running late into the evening for different reasons, so the massages had been rushed. This was to be an important session to iron out any niggles in the legs before I carried on alone, but in light of the queues, the communication difficulties, and the money situation, it was more hassle than it was worth.

As we chatted, it struck me how important Piotr felt it was to come with me and do his job as planned. I had never before experienced this level of support from someone who had been a stranger a week earlier. Despite my initial concerns, Piotr had enjoyed our road trip across Europe. I had hardly seen him yet he had shared my adventure in a way that had obviously meant a lot.

A decision needed to be made. It was now past four p.m. and I had no idea what I would find in Ukraine. "It doesn't make sense, Piotr," I said finally. "Get a head start on your drive back to Paris."

He looked pained and even suggested he do a massage there and then, in the queue at the border, but at last he agreed. I waved until his black Audi disappeared back into Poland then turned to push my bike toward the border. I had never made such a close friend in such a short space of time. It is amazing what circumstances can do. Our leaving hug was one shared between great friends.

5

The guards on both sides were dressed in stiff uniforms with dashes of polished leather, and brandishing excessive hardware. The first soldier on the Polish side waved me through without delay. I dismounted and pushed my bike forward, entering the canopied Ukrainian border control. I felt intimidated by the mood of the place but I wasn't worried: I knew Mum had been in touch that morning with the Ukrainian embassy, who said they'd be informing the border guards I was coming.

There were two lanes of vehicles whose drivers were doing paperwork through open windows. A guard who was wandering down the line looking at the cars stopped when I approached then walked briskly over. I immediately felt judged for not being in line, but there was no point in waiting with the cars. He scanned my passport briskly and pointed to a third booth off to the left of the others, which seemed empty.

As I drew level I saw through the window that there were three guards inside chatting. Two younger soldiers flanked a heavyset man who sat by the window. He looked down and made a beckoning gesture with his whole hand, which I took to mean "give me your passport." I have seen armed police before and heavily armed military, but never at such close quarters had I seen guards with semi-automatics. I felt completely helpless and wished I had thrown a pair of trousers on; among these guys I felt silly and naked in my Lycra. The lack of any common language didn't help. The whole situation was most nerve-racking.

The man in the booth looked at my passport and pushed a form through a narrow slot in the window. I filled in the boxes and handed it back. He seemed to read without understanding and eventually came out and stood closer than was comfortable in order to ask the same questions that were on the form. After a while he got stuck on one question: "Why?" "Tourist," I repeated. The point of contention seemed to be all the visas in my passport. "I am going to cycle through these countries," I added helpfully, but he talked over me to his colleague, who laughed and openly gestured toward me, making me squirm a bit more. Without another word he turned and walked toward the main building, still with my passport. After ten minutes he returned and started speaking Ukrainian to me. I had no idea what he was saying, but I could tell he was repeating certain names. I gestured that I did not understand. His manners seemed friendlier, but despite my best efforts I could not answer his questions.

Then he said something that caught me off guard: "Blah blah blah Champions League blah blah blah!"

Was he talking about football? I tried not to look startled or relieved, both of which I felt. "Glasgow Celtic," I said, trying to sound upbeat. He beamed, and agreed enthusiastically.

Shit, the international language of football, and I did not speak a word of it.

I pointed at myself and said, "Glasgow, Rangers, Celtic, yes, good."

This seemed to work. "Yes," he said, and broke into another monologue.

The second, younger guard who had remained inside now wandered out, lifted his baton, and lightly tapped first the back right then the top pannier bag on my bike. "Guns? Narcotics?" He looked at me intently.

"No," I answered.

He walked off without another word or acknowledgment, seemingly content with that answer.

I gratefully took my passport as it dropped through the glass and waved weakly at the guards who were already deep in conversation. They hadn't smiled at all and it had taken over forty-five minutes to get through.

I had no Ukrainian currency, so when I stopped at a fuel station to buy some food and water I was hugely relieved that my credit card still worked. With no idea what the exchange rate was, I guessed and took out 200 UAH (Ukrainian hryvnia) at the first ATM, knowing that a drink, pastry, and ice cream had cost 7 UAH. As soon as I stopped a couple of workmen immediately came over and started to talk at me while touching and fiddling with the bike. I was worried by all the attention and I felt unsafe with the military presence that kept passing on the road.

The contrast with Poland in terms of wealth was massive—the roads, houses, cars (mostly Ladas), and the way people dressed. The roads were not terrible but also not great, and I knew it would be slow going if it continued like this. The roadsides crumbled into the dirt but I didn't dare cycle out from the edge as the driving seemed pretty reckless.

All afternoon I battled an upset stomach so I decided to stop again for some Fanta and Coke to see if acidity and sugar would counter it. At 7:30ish I was very relieved to see the "Hotel Mirage" at the roadside. Along the way I had not seen any signs for hotels or rest-houses so my hopes had been low, and I was very concerned about camping. For 80 hryvnia (about £7) I was given a nice simple room, but was not surprised to find an old shower with no hot water.

Unfortunately, my introduction to Ukrainian cuisine was not impressive. The mushroom soup turned out to be stock water with soggy noodles and chewy mushrooms, and the omelette—the only other vegetarian option on a twelve-page menu—was truly disgusting. Some very grating bar music helped make my decision to have an early night an easy one.

The next day, my first full one in Ukraine, would take me eastward toward Lviv and then south to the small town of Ternopil. When I woke at 6:30 a.m. the rain was battering off the windows. I went downstairs, first going outside to check that the bike was safe. Over breakfast I checked the map and was disappointed to learn that Lviv was farther away than I had thought. I guessed that the waitress the night before must've meant 50km, not 15km. This meant at least one more night in the Ukraine than I had planned. And at that point it was not something I was looking forward to.

As I set out, the legs felt fine—this was now two weeks on the road. I smiled grimly. It felt like I had come a long way to get here, but in the grand scale of things it was only a fortnight out of seven months. I buried the thought quickly so it wouldn't put me in the wrong mood for the day.

The road to Lviv deteriorated and was often dogged with road-works. Rain fell throughout the day so I bobbed away to my iPod under my helmet, starring at the mirrored road in front of my wheel, but little else. Little gray villages came and went, but seemed empty.

For the first time ever I was in a place where I could not read the road signs. Naively, I had assumed they would all have English translations on them, like I knew they did in the Middle East and Asia, but during that first full day cycling outside Europe I realized that I had overlooked researching Ukraine properly in my preoccupation with the greater concerns of Iran and Pakistan. Leg 1 was meant to be smooth running through familiar territory to get the bike and body warmed up. The cultural evolution was supposed to wait until leg 2, so Ukraine was a bit of a shock. The roads, food, weather, and people all seemed cut out of a tougher cloth than the Europe I had just left. I wondered if this was just a first impression or whether it would be how I reflected on Ukraine.

By midmorning the roads were busier. There was no room for bikes—not that I had seen any others. I turned off my music: the thunder of the rain was too loud and I'd grown nervous of the trucks that flew past. At one point a police car drove past, lights flashing. Rolling down the window, the driver shouted something and jerked his thumb over his shoulder, pointing back. Unsure of what he meant, I looked over my shoulder to see an oversize load whose concrete tunnel section overlapped the curb by meters. Throwing the bike onto the soft soil by the roadside, I ducked as two of these lorries hammered past.

The plan was to avoid Lviv at any cost. Cities and towns are slow going by bike. The problem was, I couldn't read the street signs. Soggy in the rain, I stood trying to match symbols on the map to symbols on the signs. The bypass around Lviv was being dug up so was sporadically excellent and then horrendous. On the sections they were still working on the road was now a single lane with no traffic lights. Cars from each direction had to make a dash for it. Each of these sections was too long to make it at bike speed so I had to jump off every time the opposing traffic bore down on me.

Lviv is regarded as one of the main cultural hubs of Ukraine. Designated as a world heritage site, it begged a closer look, but all I saw was a gray cityscape as I cut to the south.

There was nowhere to stop for a proper lunch and not much food other than bread and cheese at a few small places, so I nursed hunger pains all day. I was focused on cycling until late regardless of distance, but as the afternoon wore on there were fewer and fewer houses and I started to get concerned about where I would end up. I passed a few garages but they only sold fuel, Coke, and water. After 6:30 I decided to stop at the first place I found. I really didn't want to camp after such a tough day, not just because the weather was miserable. I also didn't feel completely safe.

The first petrol station I found only sold fizzy water but I bought a few bottles anyway, to cook with in case I was camping. The man there spoke no English but I understood that it was 20km to a hotel. It was 7:30 and I had been on the road for eleven hours but there was no choice. Thankfully it was mainly downhill, and because the clocks had gone back in Ukraine there was a bit of extra daylight.

The day got a shade grayer as evening drew in and I suddenly came across Hotel Monaco, set off to the left. It looked entirely out of place after the empty expanse I had just come through. Entirely self-conscious of my drowned appearance, I parked the bike and walked into a dark corridor which opened into a large bar and restaurant. A large middle-aged lady wearing a long skirt and frilly blouse with a huge silky scarf draped around her neck and over her shoulders quickly came from behind the bar and hustled me back into the corridor. I glanced into the restaurant in an effort to figure out why.

"Do you speak English?" I ventured.

"No." The answer was curt.

"Français?"

"No. Lei parle Italiano?" she demanded impatiently.

I had studied Italian for a year at university and when I was very young at home. I might not be able to string many sentences together, but I did know some words. "Una camera per una notte per favore?" I scrambled together.

She beamed, the icy demeanor evaporating. "Si, certo."

"Quanto costa?"

Her reaction gave me confidence. We conversed very basically for a few minutes as I explained where I had cycled from and she explained that she was either Italian or married to an Italian, I was unsure. My Italian dried up just as she asked for money, and I sensed her suspicion. The room was 200 UAH (¤30) and they didn't accept cards, which seemed bizarre. I had no way to pay. "Non è problema," I said slowly, wondering how to explain that I'd have to cycle into town to get money. Then I remembered the US dollars stashed in the bottom of my bag for emergencies. Matron immediately agreed on $40. I didn't bother doing the conversion, I just wanted to get to my room, and I could tell there was no point attempting to haggle.

The room was surprisingly posh with a large en suite and I ran about happily, hanging things everywhere to dry out. It was a great haven at the end of such a tough day.

After a shower I threw on shorts and a T-shirt and ran downstairs. The restaurant was now half full but gloomy, its heavy wood beams and dark walls reflecting little of the dull bulbs that glowed overhead. In one corner there was a mini stage where a few people were setting up a keyboard and microphone. Matron immediately bustled from around the bar and took me back into the corridor. I followed, confused by her manners for the second time. I explained I wanted dinner and she led me back inside, but this time upstairs to a small empty balcony area over the restaurant below. It was deserted and she offered me one option, a small table in the corner.

I had my room so felt more confident to question her now. "Si possibile mangare in restarante principale?" I tried in appalling Italian. I was being hidden away, but didn't understand why. It was a very average, old-fashioned-looking hotel but I felt she was ashamed of my presence, as if I had turned up at the Ivy.

Matron looked awkward and gestured from her head to toe. I was dressed wrong. I excused myself, chuckling, ran upstairs, zipped the bottom half onto my shorts, making them into trousers, and checked in the mirror. I only had one T-shirt so there was nothing I could do there. It seemed rather ridiculous to insist on such standards for a small, half-empty, out-of-town place. When I presented myself for a second time I was deemed acceptable. I earned myself a small table at the edge of a very small dance floor in the main restaurant.

There was no menu, but Matron chatted away in Italian about options. I didn't understand a word. "Non carne si posso?" I asked, still struggling for the words. I was so hungry I would eat almost anything, just not meat. "Certo," she smiled, and left.

In complete contrast to my day, the next few hours were an utter joy. I was alone for the first time in foreign lands, experiencing the unexpected. A plate of fish arrived; it was the first time I'd eaten fish in about four years. There were about twenty people in the restaurant as I began eating, just as the music started. A middle-aged man in a flowery shirt played the keyboard and a young lady with dyed fiery-red hair sang over a heavy backing track. They played a range of Ukrainian cheesy pop in this strange karaoke style—it was brilliant, and perfectly fitting. As terrible as they were, each tune was catchy and I felt swept up in the mood. As my plate was taken and replaced with chocolate cake, a murmur went up as another tune started, obviously a national favorite. A few people clapped lightly in time with the beat and a group of six girls took to the stage and started dancing. They were customers but I had not noticed them dining. They danced with complete abandon and each seemed more beautiful than the last. My logbook simply commented, "I wish I could video this scene—I can't go to bed while this is going on. The music is all Ukrainian catchy pop and the girls are amazing."

I woke after a few hours' sleep to the sound of loud drunken chatter and laughter outside my window, and felt terrible. After a few minutes trying to get back to sleep I got up and was very sick. Eventually I fell back asleep. When I awoke, my stomach finally felt better. I had breakfast in my room and then got a late start out into the pouring rain. Luckily, it soon dried up and the better roads allowed me to cover 135km that day.

I camped 5km past the Dniester, a spectacular deep-flowing river. I had crossed this on a narrow stone bridge which led up a steep climb to long tree-lined roads framing fields of crops. The road rose and fell as far as the eye could see in a straight line in each direction. I stopped and cooked on the roadside, before ducking into the fields once it was dark.

That night was a disaster. After twenty minutes in the tent someone came past on the track a few meters away. There were no lights, but I could hear them walking, pause for a minute, then carry on. Ten minutes later they returned but didn't stop. I lay there feeling trapped in my small tent, unable to see or confront them. I scrambled out of the tent and searched the area nervously by head torch, but could find no one. It was nearly midnight before I dozed off. At 12:30 a massive storm started overhead; torrential rain bucketed on the tent. Eventually I fell back asleep, only to wake suddenly at 2:30 feeling really ill, similar to the night before—a horrid bloated feeling. I clambered out in the pouring rain to be sick. I instantly felt better and was able to get back to sleep after resetting the alarm from 6:30 to seven.

As if on cue, the rain stopped at 7:15 as I stepped out and quickly packed camp. Everything was wet. To round off an interesting night, a large hairy cream-colored spider crawled out of my tent as I rolled it up, which slightly alarmed me—I had never seen a cream spider. I simply could not face the leftover couscous, which just reminded me of being sick, so skipped breakfast until the first shop, where I devoured a tub of Nutella with some bread.

I still thought it was the fish that had made me ill—perhaps my body wasn't used to it—but after being sick again I wasn't so sure. Ruth, my nutritionist, was worried that it might be something to do with my sodium levels, not being able to replace all the salts I was sweating out. Needless to say I felt dire for the first few hours on the bike. It was only 35km to the first main town but I was so weak. The sun started to break through as I got there and I stopped at a garage for some salted peanuts.

By midday I had only done 40km, having pushed two of them through a town where the cobbled streets were so rough I was worried they would break the wheels. Looking ahead, I saw it was hilly all the way to the Romanian border, but the shining sun made me feel better. Despite the terrain, the roads around the national parks in the south were the best I experienced in Ukraine and it was beautiful riding.

The border area was well signposted for a couple of kilometers with many places to change money. All afternoon, my thoughts were preoccupied by one thing. By the border I had made up my mind. I had not eaten properly for days due to the foreign choices and lack of vegetarian options. I was living on a lot of bread and had to eat more or I'd continue to grow weaker. Being a vegetarian was just not an option here and I was certain it was only going to get harder. My indignant comments about never eating meat regardless of my situation back in Scotland now seemed very naive.

Sitting in the sun, outside an empty café, a kilometer from the Romanian border, I tucked into a big chicken leg and chips for the first time in many years. It felt strange, even wrong, to be eating it, but it was the best meal I'd had in weeks. It tasted fantastic. My vegetarianism has never been about the taste of meat. Having grown up on a farm I had always eaten and enjoyed meat. It was simply through a dislike of many industrial farming standards and the cruelty in commercial abattoirs that I preferred not to eat meat when given the choice. In Scotland you almost always get this choice.

Exiting Ukraine was much easier than the entry had been. The Ukrainian guard took his time but the Romanian joked as I left, "There you go, two minutes!" His colleague idly patted my pannier bags without comment and moved on.

What a contrast. I was back in Europe, and everything was suddenly far less foreign. Maybe it helped that the sun was shining, but from first impressions Romania looked amazing: great roads, beautiful villages, and scenic rolling hills.

I paused after border control to look at the map. A man sitting alone at the roadside put out his hand as he read his paper and said, "Welcome to Romania!" I smiled and thanked him; it was a charming gesture. The first garage was incredibly well stocked compared to the sparse supplies I had found in Ukraine, and despite some big climbs I felt so much stronger after that big meal at the border.

After 42km I arrived at the first town. It was seven p.m., but I felt so good I decided to push on to Fălticeni, another 22km away. It got dark by 8:30. I pedaled hard through my new wonderland, enjoying every detail. I shared the road with many horses and carts, and at the sides I passed shepherds in the fields. As it grew dark I stopped to film a stunning sunset as two old shepherds took their flock across the roads ahead of me. One of the men paused on the road, lifted his crook to me in a high salute, and smiled. The day finished with a long sweeping descent through orchards, past a dam, and into town just as night fell.

I soon found myself in a busy town center but no hotels in sight. After the previous night being sick in the maize fields I wanted nothing more than to dry everything out and have a good night's sleep. I stopped a passing police car, and the officer simply called out "Follow" and gave me an escort for the last 2km. Despite a very grumpy hotelier, who only amused me further, I was so impressed with Romania. Dividing the UK pound by five made my very basic hotel room about £15.

Back in the UK, Mum was very concerned about my night sickness and general weakness. Over dinner I spoke to Dr. Niall MacFarlane from Glasgow University, Ruth, and Mum, who had also been speaking to Healthlink 360 (a specialist medical helpline for travelers) for advice. It was reassuring: basically I had to eat more, get some more electrolytes (sports drinks that hydrate and replenish salt and sugar levels), and take it easy for a few days, although I obviously couldn't do the last bit. In truth I was already feeling much better and just craving a good night's sleep.

The next few days in Romania passed easily. Day 17 was through the north of the country where every village was selling local woven wares on the roadside. I passed an old lady and young girl sitting together weaving brooms, and others making baskets out of straw. After a perfect 80km morning to Roman, I got a bit lost in Bacău, a city situated at the foothills of the Carpathian Mountains, but had a good afternoon ride and camped 20km north of Adjud in a maize field.

Istanbul on Sunday was our new plan after the mileage miscalculations as far as Ukraine had put me back by two days. I examined the maps by the light of my head torch in the tent and realized it was a tough target with no room for any more delays or miscalculations. While concerned by this, I also heard from Mum that the British embassy were saying it was not possible to get through southern Pakistan and that I would have to take a train. I buried this potentially major issue for later, along with the fact that I also had to quickly figure out and let Mum know what things I needed sent out to Istanbul with the BBC, and got some sleep.

Day 18 took me through larger, more industrial towns in the south where vineyards now filled the countryside. It was my first 200km day. After a really fast morning I had covered the 140km to Buzău by 3:30 p.m. After the sense of chasing a tough target to get 160km a day until Romania, this newfound momentum brought a new level of energy.

Midafternoon I reached the small town of Râmnicu Sărat and stopped to get some water and food. A man beside me at the garage counter simply took these items from my arms and bought them, saying something that included the word "bicicletta." It was a lovely random act of kindness. I was covering the ground well and feeling better because I was eating more. The difference in my mood between now and a few days ago was huge, and I kept on, finally pushing my bike over a railway line and camping in a field near Urziceni after 205km.

Though it was flatter, it was also getting hotter each day. Little did

I know, but I had seen my last rain for two months. I knew by the time I got to Turkey in September it would be very hot, and the hotter it is the more you sweat, hence the concerns about my salt levels. It also poses other challenges. When you can't clean your clothes regularly the salt buildups are a catalyst for skin sores, in particular saddle sores. Saddle sores are an inevitable inconvenience when spending hundreds of hours sitting on a bike seat. Unlike the soles of your feet, your bum is not designed for such constant wear. Saddle sores are a unique kind of pain, and the first weeks of a trip are always uncomfortable as you build up conditioning to it. Spinning through Romania, these sores made more of a song and dance than they had before, partly because of the heat but maybe also because I was less preoccupied by the bike breaking down or being ill anymore, and it was something else for the mind to concentrate on.

Day 19 was an average of 36 degrees. Even at night it was starting to get uncomfortably hot. I slept with the tent completely open and without a sleeping bag or liner all night, and still lay there sweating. It was an unnerving thought that Turkey lay ahead, hotter and hillier.

I should have stopped for more food in the morning but was out of Romanian money so pushed on, hungry. The south of Romania was far more familiar, with large industrial farms and tractors instead of horses and carts. The north had been how I imagine Italy was a generation ago.

The last section of road to the border was empty and I paused before crossing and went on to the checkpoint, which seemed deserted. After a minute a border guard came out of the large white building beside the roadstop and explained in very good English that this border control was not open yet and that I must take a ferry across the Danube. He directed me back up the road to a side route. I had seen no signs, but when I turned up I found a small queue of cars and trucks. It was meant to be just 5 RON, or Romanian leu (£1.20), for bikes to cross but I had not expected a ferry and had just spent my last money. After explaining this to the ticket office the young guard waved me through for free. The thought of backtracking to the last town was awful and I was grateful once again for Romanian generosity.

The unexpected break while waiting for the ferry was welcome, and I watched the passing trade float up and down. The river was busy with boats. It stretched out far wider than I had expected and I assumed the far bank was Bulgaria. After ten minutes a tug turned up, pushing a large floating platform approximately 20 meters square, which had on it a few lorries, half a dozen cars, and a few dozen people. The raft was open-topped with a shallow ramp at each end and a thin railing on both sides to keep everything penned in. Although I had not even expected a river crossing, it ended up being a fairly major maneuver, taking nearly half an hour.

As I pedaled off the ramp into a small port on the far bank and up a steep road for about a kilometer, the signs indicated I was still in Romania. The customs house was after a turnoff to the right, but easily missed if you were not looking for it. It took less than a minute to get through. The guy offered me water with a beaming smile and said, "We have been waiting for you for three days!" Not a great morale-boosting comment but thank you, British Embassy, for your help.

I headed into Bulgaria. The contrast was huge again. I found myself in big wooded hills instead of open flatlands and confronted with another very foreign Russian-looking alphabet. After being used to regular service stations in Romania I was caught out when trying to find somewhere to get supplies. There was nothing. Not a single house on the horizon for the next 25km. When I eventually found a village it was five p.m. and I had to settle for a croissant and a bottle of Coke to keep going.

It was almost dark by the time I camped behind a long line of trees off to the left of the road in an open field. There was no need to put the tent up as it was so hot so I just lay there, the whole valley below me illuminated by a bright moon, thinking about the day's ride and what lay ahead. David Peat was now en route to Istanbul with new tires and bits of kit, and I could sense the end of leg 1. Bike and body had been tested and were coping well. The bad news was that the British embassy continued to have real concerns about my plans to cycle through Baluchistan. They were insisting that I not do it, but this 1,000km stretch through southern Iran and Pakistan was my only option through the Middle East to Asia with the visas I had.

I buried these concerns again as there was nothing I could do about them now, and fell asleep.

*

Take my word that 171km including a 1,500-meter ascent in an average temperature of 37 degrees Celsius is a tough day at the office. It was my second day in Bulgaria, and for the first time I found myself lying at the side of the road on a big hill, too tired and hot to go on. It took twenty minutes and dunking my head in a trough of water I found at the side of a field to get going again. By the hilltop I reached woodland, which gave some shade, and the trees painted stark shadowy patterns as I enjoyed a fast descent, cooled by the breeze my speed created. I had been sick again during the night but woke feeling fine, albeit very hungry, at 5:30, lying in the open to the sound of chanting coming from loudspeakers in the town a kilometer away. The early-morning Muslim prayer call would take getting used to; I was more startled than charmed. I deduced from the pattern so far that I seemed to get sick when I went to bed too full.

The day was a struggle. The cycling was tougher, but it was more than that. I couldn't stay focused.

The following day I woke fresher. The next night I would, or should, be in Istanbul, and that got me up, eager to finish leg 1 and have a day off.

When you're getting up at 6:30 a.m. and are on the road until late in the evening, a lot can happen. I found myself thinking about each day more and more in isolation. The general pattern each day was the same, it was the same tough routine, but the context and stories seemed to change. The big picture, in this sense, was too big, too much to consider, let alone focus on. So there I was, in my world, focusing on what I could control—the here and now. I was starting to love it, each and every moment, even the toughest parts.

It was just as well my mind was starting to deal with this pace of life as today I would cycle into Turkey, into a whole new world again. The Turkish/Bulgarian border is on top of a mountain. The last town in Bulgaria was in the valley bottom before the big climb and seemed almost deserted except for a large cycle group who were also riding from Paris to Istanbul, having taken six weeks. I had lunch with them, chatting mainly to a young girl around my age from New Zealand. They were the ultimate mixed bunch and I enjoyed comparing Europe in six weeks to Europe in half that time. Everywhere in the town seemed shut but I sat outside a closed café, eating a sandwich made from my own supplies.

The long winding climb to the border meant that this diverse group was soon strung along the length of the road. I set off after them, overtaking some and meeting the rest at the top. It then took ten minutes to persuade the border guard that I was not with them so I could go through alone, without waiting a further hour or more for the slowest to climb the hill. Fifty US dollars buys you access to Turkey, and the immediate reward was the best downhill section yet: mile upon mile of gradual descent from wooded mountaintops to a more arid open land where the towns started.

In the first of these I stopped, wary of leaving my bike but keen to explore and find some food. A plump middle-aged man walked up as I scouted the various vendors for food. "Come, you want food?" I tried to decline, assuming he was trying to sell me something. He rushed off and came back a minute later. "This is my brother, perfect English." His brother was taller, thinner, and smartly dressed, and did indeed speak perfect English. He was also more reserved than his brother and gave the impression that he was not altogether sure why they were bothering speaking to me. The first brother persevered. "Every time drive Bulgaria, eat town, kebab . . . you like?" I smiled at his enthusiasm and the image of him eating a town. He seemed very genuine. Though I had recently weaned myself onto chicken, the thought of a bloody red kebab was almost too much. Then again, what choice did I have?

Leaving my bike on the busy street, I followed the brothers into a rustic café with bare walls and plastic tables. Quickly forgetting that it was very bloody meat, the real issue was that the kebab I was presented with was also made of pure fire. After four bottles of Coke I felt like I was being very rude, but I didn't care. The sweat dripped off my brow. I faced each mouthful like a set of heavy weights, psyching myself to keep going. It was, however, very filling, and I listened as the brothers told me their life stories.

They were the academic and the entrepreneur, it seemed, and you can guess which was which from their appearance. The short, fatter Del Boy had hotels and other businesses in Istanbul, but he explained that it was too populated, the markets saturated, so he was looking to invest in Bulgaria, which had a foot in the EU. It was for this reason that his son was at university in Sofia, where they were driving now. He slapped the silent one sat next to him on the back. He then proudly showed me pictures of his properties and new hotel on his mobile. The taller brother had a diploma in economics and English and was a lecturer.

I thanked them profusely for their kindness after a while and explained that I had to race on.

Before leaving town I went next door to a small shop to pick up supplies. The owner proudly boasted that he would accept any money in the world and that my little Bulgarian or US dollars were no problem, although I am fairly sure he charged me a good commission for the transaction.

As I passed through towns, villages, and a number of factories in the countryside, I noted that the Turkish flag, a red banner with crescent moon and star, always flew high. The Turks were obviously a proud nation.

It was to be a long afternoon, but I was determined to get within striking distance of Istanbul. It was nearly dark when I stopped after 163km, having climbed nearly 2km during the day. When I passed a big military base outside Kirklareli, the only sizable town that day and the capital of the European part of Turkey, the soldiers on duty gave me an enthusiastic wave and one, alone on a corner watchtower, pulled a solemn salute. The buzz of adventure hit me again as I waved back before cycling on into this new world.

This last day to finish leg 1 had been the biggest yet, by a good length: 210km, over 1,775 meters ascent in an average temperature of 34 degrees Celsius. I double-checked the stats, smiling and weary.

The last 30km had been the scariest riding I'd ever experienced. Istanbul is one of the largest cities in the world, with well over eleven million people in the city itself, before you start counting the greater Istanbul outlying area. With people at a density of over 2,500 per square mile it is fair to expect traffic jams, even on a Sunday evening. This is not cycling for the fainthearted, or for those with a short concentration span—you will not survive. The traffic often spans three lanes in each direction and each slip road was a leap of faith, the traffic merging and approaching much faster than I could get across the gap in the road. The last miles were over huge rolling hills, each hiding the true distance to the center of town. I had never entered a city with such sprawling suburbs. "I must be nearly there," I repeated for the final few hours, always thinking it could be no more than ten minutes away.

At times the traffic was going so slowly that I was able to go faster and weave my way through to keep going. At one point a bus that was passing slowly started drifting to the right, getting closer and closer. I hit the brakes and fell back to its back wheel, but not in time to clear the back end: its wheel arch caught the front left pannier bag and pushed the front wheel right and into the high curb. The front right pannier bag bounced off the edge of the road and I dropped behind the bus as it drifted wide again, oblivious to the mayhem it was causing. It felt like driving the dodgems. There was no room for me on these roads. It was truly dangerous cycling.

I could hardly speak when I did finally pull up. I felt frazzled and exhausted after an incredible 210km day, undoubtedly the toughest day's riding of my life.

Leg 1 had thrown up a diversity of challenges, some of them most unexpected. At the end of it, however, I felt physically great and mentally focused on carrying on. It was a great learning curve, and I felt glad to have had those experiences so early. The breakages, ill-nesses, and saddle sores made me realize how little I actually knew about long-distance cycling. I was being fueled mainly by ambition, as opposed to experience. I laughed to think of how amateur my other cycles had been compared with this.

The leg 1 race had started at 8:30 a.m. on Sunday August 5 and ended in Istanbul on Sunday August 26 at about 8:30 p.m.

Leg 2: Istanbul to Calcutta

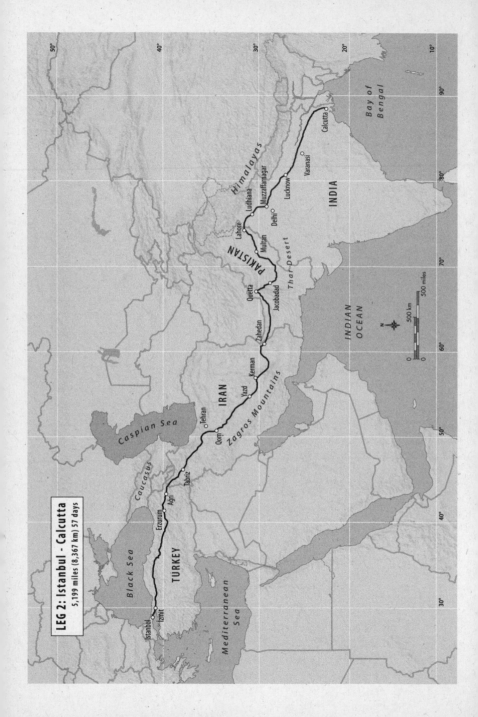

LEG 2: Istanbul - Calcutta
5,199 miles (8,367 km) 57 days

6

I had traveled 2,277 miles in twenty-two days—exactly on target, and in spite of many challenges. Paris seemed a long time ago, yet this was one of the shortest legs of my tour of the world. It was too much to consider, and for the moment I simply enjoyed having made it this far on time.

I had meant to arrive in Istanbul fully conditioned to take on leg 2, where bike and body would have to be far more self-sufficient. There would be little medical and mechanical support at hand, the roads would get worse, food become scarce, water unclean, and cultures so very foreign. However, the reality had been that the wheel had broken, I had been sick, my route setting had been over 200 miles off target, and I had been forced to eat meat for the first time in years. But now the bike was running perfectly and I was feeling better. I just hoped the mileage error was a one-off. What's more, getting through these challenges gave me confidence.

It was annoying to have to take two days off at this point, but I wasn't underestimating what lay ahead and I needed a good recovery. My plan before leaving had been a day off every fortnight, but I soon knew that this was not realistic. There was no way I was going to take a day off in the middle of a section if I felt fine and could easily carry on. By the same token, now that I had made it three weeks without a day off, while it was tempting to carry on after a day and put a day in the bag, I really needed two. It didn't take much persuading by Mum to convince me. Niall and Ruth were also very keen I take the extra day to recharge the batteries.

The rest days were anything but restful, but I did enjoy every moment. Like my time with Piotr, sharing this part of the adventure with David made me realize what I was missing by doing the rest alone. He stayed with me until the second lunchtime, before flying home. I would love to say that we also got to explore Istanbul, but we hardly left the hotel, except for numerous short trips into the old town behind the hotel for our regular meals—I had an intensive eating schedule.

The old narrow streets were absolutely charming and led up the steep hill to the Sultan Ahmed Mosque, more commonly known as the Blue Mosque because of the color of the tiles on the inside. At night it was indeed blue thanks to some clever lighting. Behind this and to the left was Istanbul's oldest and most famous mosque, turned museum, the Hagia Sophia. It was unmistakable because of its massive dome and is considered to be one of the original and best examples of Byzantine architecture. For over a thousand years it was the largest cathedral built on earth.

Even this tiny quarter of Istanbul in which we were staying deserved a long explore, but we had no time, except to walk through and admire. I was just glad David was with me, as there was something around every corner that I wanted to discuss. True to his thrill-seeking nature, one of David's favorite discoveries was where the train tracks went over the narrow street just above head height. The sleepers had been laid onto a simple cast-iron structure so when a train went overhead you could look straight up at its undercarriage less than a meter above you. The effect was thrilling as a din of heavy carriages clattered overhead.

The rooftop of the hotel was a flat tiled area David had already discovered during the day he spent waiting for me in Istanbul. The view from there was spectacular. Istanbul is situated on a natural harbor called the Golden Horn, and the old town formed the protective lips of this harbor around Seraglio Point, which I had cycled in the last mile to the hotel. I looked east across the Bosphorus at its wide part, in awe at the size and volume of shipping. To the north I could just see the massive silhouetted Bosphorus Bridge, the Golden Gate–style structure connecting Europe to Asia. Closer to the hotel, but out of sight from the rooftop, was the more famous but less stunning Galata Bridge, the original link between the two continents.

I had asked Mum to send out a few things. She had, and a few more. Of the massive suitcase DP brought out, his own things were confined to about a quarter. The rest was mine, and far more than I could carry on the bike. It was like an early Christmas stocking going through it all. One of the items was a small black box. This was a dog repeller, which lets out a supersonic sound that only dogs can hear. This was our response to concerns about stray dogs in Turkey and Iran, which I had read about on many cycling blogs. Istanbul is full of them, so on our next wander uptown I was intrigued to test this out, to disappointing results. Most didn't seem to hear it, and those that did just looked at me. It looked like I would have to rely on a simpler self-defense.

The most important bits of kit that had been flown out were spares for the bike and some more ration packs of food. The tires had lasted quite well but were not strong enough for the rougher roads to come so I upgraded to a thicker and heavier set. The rooftop was the perfect workshop. I rolled out an old Persian rug that was in the stairwell and set about servicing.

The truth was, I couldn't wait to get going. It was a massive unknown, cycling and traveling alone outside the Western world for the first time. I was also enjoying the race, and excited about being on target. I wanted to build on this. I had proved to the team and myself that this routine was possible by completing leg 1 in time, but we all knew that leg 2 was where the real test of bike and body would lie—over 5,500 miles from Istanbul to Calcutta through Turkey, Iran, Pakistan, and India.

One evening something happened that left both DP and me a bit shaken. It was an event I vowed to learn from. A physiotherapist had been arranged to come and treat me, but instead two men turned up. They were brisk from the start but I didn't suspect anything was wrong until at the end they demanded much more money than had been agreed. It was an insane amount by UK standards, let alone Turkish prices, but DP and I felt the situation was threatening and decided it was best to pay and just get rid of them. It was a valuable lesson: you have to know how to set your price and stand your ground.

Once DP had left on the second afternoon, I took a taxi across town. The cash machines, to my amazement, gave out US dollars, and I withdrew $500 to be stashed in small amounts around the bike for use in Iran and Pakistan, where I couldn't withdraw money. Next I bought a Turkish SIM card. Turkey was the first of the big countries so I would save a lot by using a local phone number. I also found a bike shop, the last I would see for months, to pick up some final bits of kit.

The British embassy in Istanbul had been a great source of advice, like those in many other countries, and they were keen to meet up. I still had a lot to do but arranged a chat over a quick coffee in the old town behind my hotel. Four of their staff arrived with a surprise guest. Rob Lilwall was another cyclist who had been helped by them and he was on his way home from Siberia after an amazing three-year cycle. What I'd thought would be a short break and sociable coffee was therefore a really useful conversation about what lay ahead. Rob had just come through Turkey and Iran, albeit much slower than I planned to, and his comments quietened a few of my concerns. These were replaced by even more excitement about what lay ahead.

It had been a difficult section to research. I'd had to be careful when assessing the risks as there were so many misconceptions and unknowns about the places I was heading to. I couldn't cycle around the world without entering these countries, and bogging myself down in unfounded fears bred by "what ifs" seemed futile and counter-productive. I had to focus on the everyday concerns, and food and water in some parts were going to be a real concern. I had left Paris overweight on purpose so that I would have reserves, but the sickness meant I had already lost more than I should have. I met Rob at the right moment to give me up-to-date information about the everyday challenges on the road ahead.

Mum had been busy balancing some conflicting advice on the best way out of Istanbul. The British embassy had told her I would not be allowed across the Bosphorus Bridge. It seemed that the Asian side was potentially even more dangerous than what I had already done. The Bosphorus opens on to the Sea of Marmara and there was a strong argument for getting a ferry from outside the hotel across the strait to the town of Yalova, which wasn't much to the east and would take me immediately onto quieter and faster roads. However, if it was possible to cycle the whole way, I reaffirmed that that is what I would do.

On Wednesday, August 29, I set out, alone again, for the Bosphorus Bridge. Unfortunately, the British embassy were right: due to the high number of suicides, walkers and cyclists are no longer allowed across and I was turned back to take a short commuter ferry for the princely sum of 1.30YSL, or Turkish lira (55p), across the river to the Asian side.

Unbelievably, it took over four hours to clear Istanbul. I pedaled through endless suburbia and industrial plants, but it wasn't nearly as scary as the European side, despite the three-lane traffic, and I was able to enjoy being back on the bike. For the next 1,200 miles I would remain on this road, route D100 through Turkey to the Iranian border.

My first observation heading east was the astonishing number of petrol stations. You can tell a lot about a country from the number and style of its petrol stations. At the first of these I discovered Ulker Biskrem, a Turkish biscuit which comes in apple, fig, and chocolate varieties; it would become a staple for the next weeks.

The area was very industrial and not great for cycling. At the end of the day I met a friendly nineteen-year-old guy on a scooter who wanted to know what I was doing (but didn't speak any English that I could understand). He followed me as I cycled through his village looking for somewhere to stop, which made me a bit uncomfortable, but I had no option but to camp. I finally camped in a fig grove 20km from Sakarya, where lots of little frogs surrounded my tent.

I woke to the sound of three old men working on the fig trees near the tent. They carried on as if I wasn't there, pushing ladders against the trunks and climbing up. They weren't harvesting them, and I couldn't figure out what they were doing. I quickly stowed the tent and packed my panniers, then pushed the bike down the rutted field track. I looked back to see that they had all stopped working and were staring after me. I waved, but they just blankly looked back, so I walked on.

As I pushed on I passed beautiful valleys and views, broken up by frequent suburbs with lots of garages. The roads got gradually worse, and long climbs alternated with long downhills. I stopped briefly in Bolu for supplies, then pedaled on until 7:45, when I set up camp near the road in a well-hidden quarry area. The next morning, I had a breakfast of pasta, chocolate cake, and biscuits, then set off into more big, long hills.

I lost a bit of time going the wrong way out of Gerede as the road I was on, the D100, turns into the D750 toward the capital, Ankara. To carry on down the D100 you actually had to take a turnoff. It was a big downhill and I flew past the turnoff without realizing. Luckily I saw a sign and figured out what had happened, but it was annoying to do a few extra kilometers back.

I really struggled to do the 100-mile targets in Turkey. The roads themselves were actually OK, but my speed very much depended on the quality of the hard shoulder, which I was forced onto most of the time along with tractors and slow lorries. It was just so hot and I was starting at about eight every morning and cycling each evening into the dark.

I was really concerned for the last 40km of day 3 since Istanbul, as it was such slow going through this deep gorge of a valley with hills and a headwind. Plus I was not passing anywhere for water, which is the minimum I needed for camping. Finally, after seven p.m., I found a small garage with three old men and a very chatty lady who, despite not speaking English, acted like a granny figure, wanting me to stay and chat. One of the old men was drinking some apple-juice-colored drink out of a Coke bottle (unlikely to be alcohol) and had an old pistol tucked in his belt! It looked like something out of the Wild West in a leather holster, but he did not look like someone who would use it. I made my excuses and quickly left this wonderfully eccentric group as it was sunset.

I tried to camp before town but there was nowhere, and by the time I had made it through it was very dark. My first try to find somewhere off to the right was hopeless and I got shouted at by a farmer. I cycled on and pushed the bike into a young pine forest on the left.

I was by this stage almost exactly halfway through Turkey, in the Amasya Province.

There was no wind, so it felt very hot. I was following the river for most of the day but gradually ascending all the time. The real climb started when I left the river 7km from Susehri and found myself on a long gravel section. It looked like they had been redoing the road and had forgotten to come back. For much of the day there was so much tar on the road that it had melted in the sun and was sticky, and then the loose gravel stuck to the wet tar on my tires and got caught in the mudguards, so it was quite slow going. At the end of the day there were kilometers of loose gravel with sand on top of it. Every time a bus or a lorry went past it was just unbelievable, like a sandstorm, and I had to stop as the sand got in my eyes. I even had to push the bike for a couple of short sections where the gravel was very loose.

And so Turkey continued. The heat and hills made for hard miles, and each day was not hugely different from the next. After getting used to border-hopping every few days in Europe, this sameness took some getting used to. I would always keep several levels of targets in my mind: the big picture, the section, and the very short term. The big picture of the world was always there and thoughts of the finish would flit through my mind from time to time. Within that I would consciously be thinking of the next country or area I was targeting. However, even this was too big to affect directly, so most of my thoughts were focused on the very short term: getting through each hour, and keeping the food and hydration right. The challenge in Turkey was that there were far fewer milestones in the medium run to punctuate the short-term achievements, and this change in perspective in terms of mental focus was difficult to adapt to. It was tough cycling.

As keeping well fueled was now the main concern every day, I would stop when I passed any place that looked like it made the sort of food I needed, whether I was hungry or not. Turkey is not an ideal reintroduction to an omnivore's diet as the meat is some of the heaviest and darkest I have ever eaten. Burgers and kebabs were the standard fare, served with a glass of black tea. After a few situations where I felt I was being charged "special prices" I quickly got into the habit of securing the price of a meal by getting them to write it down before agreeing. As long as you stood your ground and acted confidently like they did, I found the Turks to be very respectful. Often when I stopped I would be approached by locals, and I found them very friendly. However, it was only ever men who spoke to me. In fact I saw very few women.

Turkey is a fascinating blend of Eastern and Western cultures, wrapped in a strong national identity. Apart from America, I have never been to a country that flies its national flag as much. After over 600 years of the Ottoman Empire, the Republic of Turkey was founded and first presided over in 1923 by Mustafa Kemal Pasha. A decade later he was gifted the name Atatürk (meaning "Father of the Turks") by the new parliament, and his image is everywhere in Turkey. Like any new country it clings especially tightly to its identity.

As I traveled east, Turkey became noticeably less developed with worse roads, less industry, and fewer towns. People spoke less English too. I started having to carry food and water for longer stretches.

The Eastern Anatolia region has the highest average altitude, is the largest area, and has the lowest population density in Turkey. Though the changes each day were subtle, by the time I reached Kurdistan, which makes up the eastern part of Eastern Anatolia, the contrast with the Bulgarian border area of Marmara was vast.

Over half the world's Kurds live in Turkey and, along with Kurds in neighboring countries, they have long been fighting for their own independent state. Between 1984 and 1999 this escalated to open war between the separatist party Partiya Karkerên Kurdistan and the government. Like many such movements the PKK is considered a terrorist organization, and the outcome of this conflict was widespread unrest and depopulation in southeast Turkey. The scars of the struggle and the sentiments of the Kurds were still very evident.

Erzincan and Erzurum were the two big towns I had been aiming for in eastern Turkey, and after a week they were now in my sights. The routine through Turkey was going well, but after over 700 miles I felt the need for a one-night break from the tent, somewhere I could handwash my shorts and have a shower at least. The saddle sores were not getting any better with the salty shorts and dirty skin. My plan was to stop in either town, whichever fitted best at the end of a day's riding. By the end of day 31 I was a perfect 100 miles from Erzurum.

I'd had a record slow start to the morning on day 30—24km in two hours, with a 600-meter ascent—and it was pretty hot for climbing like that. I needed something to bring that average speed up or it would take a long time to get to Iran.

I stopped at this quaint little truck stop on a bleak hilltop with an amazing view. It was set back off the road in a dusty car park. The shed itself had rustic wooden walls and a corrugated roof that stretched out over the front to form a canopy that covered a couple of tables—welcome shade from the relentless heat. A bath with soft drinks and a constantly running cold tap made for another very welcoming feature beside a stall of fresh fruit. Inside, two men served tea and food from a kitchen comprising a tall brass tea boiler and a small ring hob. The younger one threw together a mixed dish of fried meat and eggs, soaked in oil, served with a pile of stale bread. It was much-needed fuel after a big morning.

It was just really nice and quiet. Two truckers turned up and I shared some tea with them. I suppose I was there for about an hour—a normal lunch break.

Then, I don't know where they came from, but at least fifteen guys turned up and the truckers I was having tea with immediately got up. I thought the timing was just coincidence until one came back and tapped me on the shoulder. Once he had my attention he bent down and said really quietly in my ear (he didn't speak much English), "Bad Turkish man."

I was alone at the table as the group of men approached. I picked up my stuff quickly and started packing it away into the bike—my camera, wallet, phone, and logbook. The two guys who ran the place went from being really friendly and laid back to being really flustered and running around. The new arrivals didn't look armed and didn't look particularly nasty but they certainly weren't a smiley bunch. As I was packing up, one of them walked into the young waiter who was carrying a couple of Turkish teas and the glasses went smashing to the ground. Rather than apologize, the guy who had walked into him stood and glared at him. The waiter ran off.

It took about five minutes to pay because the owners were stressing out about the fifteen guys, who were just sitting around waiting on teas. This stop was not on the tourist trail, and these guys weren't truckers. I wondered if they were a mafia-type gang, or maybe part of a separatist movement like the PKK. In any case they were obviously infamous and acting above the law. The tension was high and I was close to leaving without paying. Eventually the older guy said, "Six lira." Anywhere else, that meal would have cost over twice that, but he seemed to just want me out of there.

The two truckers I'd had tea with had waited for me. They drove with me for the first kilometer. I didn't know whether to be more worried about the truckers following me or the unknown men back at the truck stop.

The next 30km from the lunch stop to Erzincan were very fast, and after demolishing a ration pack and some fresh fruit a man gave me for free from a roadside stall, I made a huge push in the afternoon to compensate for the slow morning. I camped in soft sand on the riverbank and slept well. By afternoon of the next day I'd finally made it to Erzurum.

Erzurum—its name means literally "Land of the Romans" in Persian, showing its importance in history—is a beautiful town and home to one of Turkey's largest universities, Atatürk University, named after the republic's founder. Maybe it was freshers week when I arrived: I wasn't the only one lost, and the first three people I stopped for directions had no idea where they were. To this day Erzurum is known as "The Rock" as it is the most southeasterly NATO air force base. It must be a tough place to call home at nearly 2,000 meters in altitude. The day I visited was well over 30 degrees Celsius, and it often drops below minus 30 in winter.

The ride into town had been fine except for two separate stone-throwing incidents. This phenomenon had occurred a couple of times before in the villages and countryside, but this was worse. The first time, two days earlier, a shepherd's boy had thrown a pebble from a long way off in a field and then waved madly at me. I waved back as the stone fell a safe distance short. On the long gradual descent into Erzurum a group of older boys, in their late teens, saw me coming from a long way off and turned to face me. I saw all six of them stoop and pick up stones. As I drew level, from short range, across the width of the two-lane road, they pelted me. Luckily none hit my head, as I would definitely have been badly hurt from that range, but two of their stones bounced off the bike. It was a malicious gesture, and they shouted after me as I pedaled on as fast as I could.

Almost everyone I had met since Istanbul, normally over a glass of tea in a petrol station, had warned me about the eastern province and Iran. Everyone I spoke to seemed to distrust and dislike Iran. Such sentiments did not ease my apprehensions about the next stage. It seemed to me that the Kurdish people's dislike of the government and their oppression manifested itself as a dislike for anything that they saw as representing the West. I continued to meet charming people, but I also saw, on a daily basis, petty acts of defiance and encountered some initial coldness.

My last full day in Turkey was a kind 645-meter ascent—the smallest day's climbing since Romania. I woke inspired by the people I had met late yesterday and eager to see as much as possible before the unknown world beyond the border, 175km ahead. The roads steadily fell apart as the day wore on, so there was little time to daydream and reflect while on the bike.

About eleven a.m. I found myself in a wide valley with a winding creek below me, about 50 meters off to the right. There had been no fences for most of the journey through Turkey. Beyond the creek, a large flock of sheep was being herded in my direction by two young boys, next to a bank of moraine. Drawing level, I spotted their three dogs as they clocked me. The taller of the boys called something, and the dogs leaped forward, forgetting their job, and turned toward me. Had the boy set them on me or tried to stop them? The first dog was huge with a shaggy brown coat, the others were darker and a good bit smaller.

A surge of adrenaline hit me and I hammered the crank, shifting up. Looking right again I could feel the panic in my stomach as my mind raced. I suddenly realized that the creek was between us and the dogs would stop there. But with my next glance I saw the first dog leap effortlessly across and I felt myself panic a bit more. The beast bounded across the rough ground and onto the road about 30 meters behind me. It was soon catching up. My head spun around helplessly looking for an out, for any defense. It was futile. I was climbing a hill so I wasn't going fast despite my best efforts, and within seconds he was just a few meters behind.

I reacted instinctively, throwing on my brakes. The bike skidded and I clipped out, jumping simultaneously to the right-hand side, putting the frame between the dog and myself. His momentum took him into the back pannier, which he bounced off. Barking, snarling, and jumping as though on a chain, he snapped at the bike, eyeing me. I looked desperately over to the shepherds, who were watching passively. Feigning calm, I looked back at my tormentor. As quickly as he had attacked, he spun around and ran off. I threw my leg over the saddle and struggled to pedal with shaking limbs. At the brow of the hill, lungs screaming and legs feeling like jelly, I looked back to see the dog paused at the roadside, watching me.

By lunch I was laughing about it, still shaken but relieved. Adrenalin is an amazing high, making the mundane seem vivid, helping you see the world differently. That morning I noticed far more of the world I was passing through, my senses sharpened.

My rule for lunch was always to choose the busiest place, as good food was more likely. The more people, the less chance they were all wrong. That day's choice was on the right by a sweeping left in the road. Behind a number of big trucks were a small but busy car park, a central water fountain, and then an open terrace with small plastic tables. In the bare interior, three rows of plastic trestle tables led to a canteen-style serving counter. A number of young Turks ran about taking orders and shoveling food. I spent a few minutes trying but failing to get served, confused as to why I was being very obviously ignored. Lingering near the counter trying to get someone's attention, I watched one waiter as he brushed past me to the open door and noticed a man, who had just sat down, beckoning me over. After introductions to his friends in very broken English, he asked me to sit, and continued by buying half a chicken and a pile of rice for me.

These men were businessmen from Ankara, and they talked enthusiastically, though not completely intelligibly, about the development of Turkey and the beauty of Kurdistan. In their eyes it was an age of opportunity, and I enjoyed their open charm and exuberance. What I liked most is that they didn't ask anything about my cycle after establishing that I was on my way to India. None of the men looked even vaguely fit but to them my aim seemed reasonable. They gave the impression that, like each of their enterprises, every man's venture was sacred and not to be questioned.

After an hour I had to excuse myself, but before leaving I needed to pay and get water. My new friends would have none of it. "My pleasure," the large man said as he stood and wrung my hand. I finally conceded, adding, "But I need to buy water."

"This is not problem. Water outside."

I looked through the open door to where he was pointing. I felt rude to say that I needed bottled water instead and knew that they would not let me pay for this either. I thanked them again and left, filling my bottles at the fountain. Everyone else was drinking it so it should be fine, but I hated taking the risk, so I popped in a couple of chlorine tablets. As I pedaled off, this chain of events made me realize that while eating my very dry meal I had been drinking the glasses of water they had poured me without thinking. Cursing myself for this stupidity, I tried not to worry about it as I headed for the border town of Doğubeyazit.

The road to Doğubeyazit, like so many others in Turkey, alternated between silken tar and unrideable terrain without warning. At one point I had to push the bike at full arms' length, struggling to get enough purchase through the shifting gravel and up a long hill as thundering trucks created sandstorms and pelted me with flying gravel. I stopped briefly in the town to pick up as many supplies as I could with my last Turkish lire. As one last taste of the opportunist Turks, I was given a bill almost twice what I'd expected. Unable to argue the man down, I ended up spending the first of my US dollars to cover the bill.

By nightfall I was riding down the straight, flat road to Iran. It would have been easily possible to ride on for another 20km before dark, but there was no point. I could not cross the border tonight and it was unwise to camp too close: I knew there would be a few checkpoints and a section of no-man's land.

Mount Ararat, Turkey's largest mountain and an extinct volcano, is famous for its theoretical link with the biblical story of Noah's Ark. As I cycled east it soared up on my left, looking bizarre in the evening heat with its snowy peak rearing out of arid, sandy brown hills.

There was nowhere obvious to hide away a camp as the ground was so open and featureless, but eventually I had to stop as I could go no closer to Iran. It was hard to distinguish between the slow rise of the valley bottom and the hills to my right, but there was a break in what looked like a bank of earth which ran as far as the eye could see, parallel to the road. Had it not been for some loose stones and a shadow at the break, this bank would have been invisible from where I stood, blending into the rest of the hill. After waiting for the road to clear in each direction, I sprinted the 100 meters or so off the road, over stony grassland. Perfect. I pushed the bike through the gap I had seen and hid behind the bank of earth. It was the old road, and this small break was where it had fallen down, allowing herders to take their animals across. I could see the sheep prints and droppings at the bottleneck.

Pleased with my find, I quickly erected the tent and sat behind the bank, just shielded from the road, eating by the light of the setting sun, contemplating what lay ahead. I had never felt such a sense of anticipation. This really was the point of no return. If anything serious happened to bike or body between now and Calcutta, which was over a month away, I didn't know how it would be fixed. Mount Ararat was the perfect backdrop for this moment of deep thought. I felt happy with what lay ahead but also incredibly alone. It was the first time I had truly felt a long way from home.

After enjoying the last rays of sun and watching the odd truck thundering toward the border, I retreated to the tent and called Brendan, one of my best mates from university days, who lives in New York State. I needed to share this moment of trepidation. He is a good guy for this: no drama, just a welcome break from my own thoughts. For the first time since Paris I also sent a text to a group of friends. It felt like the end of a chapter.

7

The Iranian border area was completely barren, with a number of field guns standing solemnly surrounded by sandbag walls. I had decided it was wise to wear baggy shorts over the cycle shorts for the border, but apparently this was not enough. We were alone, just me, a handful of guards, and a solitary hut in the middle of a featureless plain. On hearing the advice I kicked the bike onto its stand and started to change into my trousers. "No," the soldier protested. He looked around at his colleagues nervously. "Please be quick, Kurdish women watch." I followed his searching gaze to the empty horizon. Throwing my trousers on as fast as possible, I took back my passport and waved them good-bye. "You might find Liverpool a shock after this," I thought as I pushed into no-man's land.

It was getting hot, climbing to over 35 degrees Celsius, like yesterday. Cycling in trousers was immediately uncomfortable. I soon reached queues of lorries that weren't going anywhere, their drivers standing in small groups, chatting. Each of them stopped and looked at me. It was evidently as slow to leave Iran as it was to enter, though there was very little traffic coming the other way.

Before I could get near the gates a number of men approached me, offering to change money. The first few did not persist and I had room to push on. Maybe I should've said no to them all but I wanted to cross the border with some currency as I had no idea what to expect on the other side. The patter of an older man was that the black market was better than the banks at 6,000 rial to $1, as opposed to 4,500 rial. He reassured me that he had done it for twenty-five years and always gave a good rate. I figured it was worth changing just $40 to be safe. Even at whatever inflated rate he was selling to me, he then tried another swindle by giving me 205,000 rial instead of 240,000 and saying that the 5,000 was "extra" and "free." I showed him the calculation on a scrap of paper and he apologized for the "mistake." I was eager to move on. More people were gathering and I felt very vulnerable, having shown all my money by mistake. I took the notes he counted out in front of me only to find that by some slip of the hand I was still short. I laughed. I had just watched him count it out. Shouting out, I expected him to walk on, but was surprised when he turned, walked back without comment or expression, handed me five more notes, and walked away. I had been ripped off, but at least it was at the rate we had agreed.

The last Turkish guard was half asleep, and opened the big electric rolling gates without checking my documents. On the Iranian side a tiny policeman checked my passport and asked me where I was from, sending me to a building with a slap on the back. There was only one passport window in a small room with one guy doing data entry on tens of passports, handed over by bus drivers. After I'd waited ten minutes he realized I was on my own and took my passport. Without looking at me he glanced over the visa details and stamped it, then took me through and introduced me to a colleague.

This second man, dressed in a smart suit, didn't look much like a policeman. He took me into his glass-walled office and explained that he had to register all tourists entering Iran. After giving me a map—which was kind but unhelpful, as only in Farsi—he asked me where I was going. Leaving my bike with a guard, he then personally walked me through to the bank, a tiny room next door, and waited while I changed $100 at a rate of 9,600 rial for $1. I fought the urge to laugh, and to pass comment on the ridiculous number of notes I got in return. My single $100 note was worth a 5-centimeter-thick wad of Iranian currency. With a shake of the hand and wishes for a safe journey, I made my way into Iran. It had been far easier to enter than Ukraine.

The road from the border raced down through dramatic red rock outcrops and cliffs. The contrast with the flat, featureless Turkish side was absolute. The roads were perfect. I had heard this would be the case but hoped it was not simply a borderland novelty. There was further good news when I saw the first sign, which read 250km to Tabriz—a reasonable target for the following evening. It was also a relief that the signs were in English as well as Farsi. I had forgotten to research these details.

As I passed through the first town, where the road deteriorated, my eyes were everywhere. There were almost no points of reference with the world I had just come from. I stopped briefly in the outskirts as I didn't feel brave enough to face the busy central street yet and had a meal of some nondescript meat with flaky flatbread, washed down with Zam Zam, the Iranian version of Coke (and Fanta and Sprite). This was arranged through gestures.

In the afternoon I didn't pass many other towns and the riding got harder. It felt hotter with a noticeable headwind, and the scenery was back to wide arid hills, stripped of features save the odd boulder outcrop, and with no place to hide a tent. This was a concern and meant I had to reach a town. But then I had no idea how to find somewhere to stay.

Ev Oghli was my only option and I hardly stopped all afternoon to reach it, sweating uncomfortably in my trousers (I needed to get some light tracksuit bottoms instead of these hiking trousers). The road reared up to a long, slow climb with 30km still to go. I had to fight a hot headwind and lost any chance of making my target. Over the top I raced into the dusk. An immense sweeping road opened into another wide valley and I could see the lights of Ev Oghli twinkling on the horizon. But I had to stop. Until I knew Iran better, I couldn't risk riding into the dark. I was less than an hour away from the town but it was too far.

I had read on a cycling blog about someone sleeping in tunnels under the road in Iran. I could see the viaducts of these every few kilometers and they seemed my only option. The possibility was exciting. I braked over a few tunnel sections before judging the third to be big enough. I paused, pretending to sort my panniers while a few trucks cleared, before jumping over the crash barrier, lifting the bike over, and clambering down a steep bank. It was perfect. The tunnel was about 3 meters across, and the right side of the road, where I was, was very low but possible to climb into, gradually opening up to about 4 feet on the far side of the road. Its brick walls and concrete floor seemed clean, as it was too low for a toilet stop or animal walkway. Despite being in the middle of nowhere the viaduct had its own streetlight. I unpacked the food, stove, and film gear and made a few crawls and clambers through to take it to the far side, where I could cook at the entrance, under the street lamp.

Hidden by elevation but under the lee of the road, this felt like a real adventure in a new world. I had suffered for the lack of food during the day's ride and threw a huge pan of pasta on. I have never liked tuna, even before becoming a vegetarian, but it was my only option now. It was impossible to replace what I had burned into a shrunk stomach and I felt uncomfortably full half an hour later.

Through the tunnel I could see my bike's silhouette at the far end, and I did more shuttle crawls back with the kit. After blowing up my rest and laying it along one of the walls, I locked a long cable around the front wheel and then along the dirt onto my back pannier bag, which would be my pillow. If the bike was touched I would wake up immediately.

After crawling into my sleeping bag I lay there for ages, uncomfortably full, taking pictures of my unusual camp. It was strangely quiet, even when traffic passed, despite the road being only a couple of meters above my face. There seemed to be small fires burning at a number of points on the wide plain below and I tried to figure out what they could be.

I woke suddenly, with no idea of the time and forgetting momentarily where I was. My stomach was cramped in pain. I could have cried out. I crawled out of the hole, past the bike and, checking that there were no cars coming, clambered on all fours up the bank of stones. Some car lights appeared and I moved to a shallow gorge a short way up the hill where I leaned on a large boulder and was violently sick. A few minutes later I was still there. The cramp had passed but I felt weak, my eyes streaming. Under the light of the clear starry sky I glanced at my watch. I had been asleep for less than an hour.

The tunnel felt uncomfortable and bare now and it took me ages to get back to sleep, only to wake within a few hours to crawl out to be sick again. It was utterly barren out there. You couldn't pick a lonelier place to be ill.

I hardly slept for the rest of the night. My sleeping roll kept deflating. Normally this wouldn't have mattered—I didn't notice once asleep; I'd simply wake up in the morning on the ground—but now, sick and sleepless, I tossed around on the concrete bed feeling bruised.

Sunrise was just before six a.m. and I was already awake. It was 180km to Tabriz; looking at the map I could see there was little before it. The plan had always been to take a rest day in Tabriz before the long stretch through the rest of Iran and Pakistan to Lahore, during which there would be almost no opportunity to break. I needed one more than ever now. My stomach was feeling better but I was incredibly weak, and 180km seemed like such a distance in that state. I pushed the bike up the steep bank and hit the road. It was 6:55.

Thankfully, I had read the map wrong. After 150km I met Farad, as planned, by the airport, an unmistakable landmark on the outskirts of Tabriz (Farad's brother is a family friend from Scotland). He greeted me with the customary kiss on each cheek. "Lovely to meet you," I said, standing back. "I hope you have not been waiting long?"

"Yes," replied Farad blankly, turning and signaling for me to follow as he got into his car.

This could be interesting, I thought. I hadn't imagined Farad would have only a little English.

Farad drove a car that was identical to a Peugeot 405, but it had a different name on the trunk, and I struggled to keep track of it in the busy streets. I hadn't been sick again but was so weak, my stomach churning. Off the main roads, I followed the car down a network of narrow dusty streets with high windowless walls on each side. The last thing I needed at that moment was a puncture just a few miles from the end of the day. Laughing at this last stroke of bad luck, I eventually made it into central Tabriz.

When we got to Farad's house there was no way I could describe how ill I was, so I called home and explained what was going on to get the ball rolling to find a solution. After a shower I joined the family around a mat on the floor. We each sat cross-legged eating an amazing picnic of exotic foods. I could only communicate a simple thank-you, and out of politeness the family refrained from chatting to each other, so we sat in silence until Farad's two young nephews arrived to translate. My appetite had not returned but I forced some down. One hour at a time, I thought to myself, but I could not face the prospect of getting back on the bike. That evening I was still hoping that the worst had passed, having not been sick all day.

I did not until much later understand the challenge of finding a sports massage in Iran. On the short walk from the house to the clinic where one had been arranged, I took in Iran. Every woman wore a headscarf, some of them covering the entire face, most in black. Considering this conformity, I was surprised to see most men wearing shirts and jeans.

Inside an old building we met Dr. Radin, a small man with a trim goatee and delicate square glasses. He greeted me warmly and I told him about my sickness, stressing that I hoped it had passed. Seemingly satisfied after a few questions, he introduced me to a junior doctor who showed us through to what looked like a hospital ward, trolley beds lining each wall with various machines set up between them. It was going well until I told him that the only underwear I had was a pair of Speedos. Apparently this was an unacceptable amount of leg to show, so I was carefully tucked in with towels.

Only once this was done was a young nurse allowed to come in, dressed in black with an open face scarf. She was undoubtedly very beautiful, but in the context of Iranian culture I felt like a pervert glancing down at her slim figure. She avoided any eye contact and the young doctor stood by the next bed, doing nothing, apart from maybe checking that nothing untoward happened.

She wheeled over a fabric blind and pulled it over the bed, across my waist, then thwacked on a pair of hospital gloves. I felt incredibly uncomfortable and not the least bit relaxed as she massaged my calves and thighs. The context made me feel like I was doing something deeply wrong. It was not entirely awful, just different, and she went through a system of moves rather than stopping and working out any specific tightness.

That done, she disappeared, and the screen was dropped. It had all been very brief but I assumed it was over, until the young doctor wheeled over a large box. He explained he would now relax the muscles with electricity. Trying not to look concerned, I just nodded.

A large fabric pad was put on my left calf as I lay on my front. It was damp and heavy, and hugged the skin. The machine was turned on and I felt a mild shock that made my leg twitch and jump. He then left for five minutes, to let the current gradually grow stronger. By the time he returned my left calf was cramped, the shocks having caused the muscle to seize. I was clutching the bed linen and trying to focus through the pain. He did the same with the other leg. I didn't want to protest, it all seemed very scientific, but this was the most pain I had ever experienced during therapy. After twenty minutes my thighs had received the same treatment.

Without any explanation this time, the attractive nurse reappeared with a trolley piled with thick red towels. She proceeded to take one and place it on me from the knee down, and another from the knee to the waist. They were damp and very warm, about as hot as I could bear. She then piled a few more on top and left again.

While all my clothes were being washed, Farad had lent me a very fetching pink short-sleeved shirt. For a few minutes I was fine, enjoying the warm relaxing towels. Then the heat started to become uncomfortable, like being in a slow cooker. After five minutes I was dripping and my pink shirt now clung to me, saturated. I felt like I had gone twelve rounds, sweating and weak. It might well have been the best treatment available—it was certainly the strangest—but I will never know.

Back at the house it triggered my illness, and I was very sick again, this time with diarrhea too. Hoping desperately it would disappear in the night I tried not to tell my kind hosts, but after a fourth trip across the courtyard to the long drop Farad looked concerned, and I pointed to my stomach and signaled that I would try to sleep.

Before bed I called home again. It looked like water poisoning. It had to be that table water in Turkey.

When I woke I could barely walk, let alone cycle, having spent most of the night being ill. After numerous calls to Scotland I took the hard but only possible decision to rest up another day. Every instinct wanted to fight on, but I was heading into the hardest part of the journey. Perspective on the big picture is always hard when on the road, but it would have been rash to carry on in this state.

Dr. Radin had invited me for dinner. I wanted to sleep all evening and night to recover but thought it would be rude to refuse, as my illness seemed to have passed. His flat was on the top floor of a simple-looking building, but behind plain wooden doors was another world. The entrance area opened into a vast living room with elaborate sofas and seats in a wide circle around the edge. Tabriz is the Persian carpet capital of the world and the floor was decorated with some amazing designs. The decor was in marble, and a number of expensive-looking paintings hung on the walls.

A table was set out along the right-hand wall where a huge buffet awaited us. It seemed my arrival was a good excuse for a party, and soon there were about twenty friends there. Everyone sat around the edges and I sat quietly, not quite knowing what to do, taking it all in.

Dr. Radin was a natural host, bounding about, making introductions. I asked him about the music when Enrique Iglesias came on, and he proudly pointed to a massive flat-screen television that looked out of place on the far wall.

I hardly ate anything, which was just as well, as the etiquette was confusing. It seemed that whether you wanted something or not, you must initially say "No, thank you." This went on for a few minutes until it was unclear if the person actually wanted it or just didn't want to offend the host. I watched one man refuse a plate of chicken nibbles over ten times, the offers and refusals getting more and more animated until he accepted. Before I observed this, I'd happily accepted the first offerings with a smile and thanks. I have no idea if this caused offense.

If you took away the decor and manners, it could easily have been a party back in Scotland. The buffet went on for hours, a lavish mix of courses and delicacies. Toward the end, one of Dr. Radin's friends sat next to me. "You see," he gestured openly, "we have democracy behind closed doors." He laughed and then looked at me seriously. "Remember this when you go home. Write it in your book." I could not think of anything appropriate to say, so simply agreed.

After the meal, another man came over and said to me, "I will play some Azerbaijan music with my wife for you." He sat at a baby grand piano in the corner and his wife produced a guitarlike instrument. After that, each couple got up in turn and played some music or did a dance. Dr. Radin spent half the time on the floor dancing. A younger couple got up and danced around each other, close and suggestively but avoiding any contact, and clapping loudly in time with the music. It was mesmerizing. The rest clapped and cheered in time.

Then Dr. Radin took to the floor and turned to me. "OK, Mr. Beaumont, you will now show us your Scottish dance."

He was serious, and I paused, unsure of what to say, a roomful of eyes on me. The only Scottish dances I knew were country dancing ones, not Highland dancing. At least if I had known Highland dancing I could have embarrassed myself with a short solo and then passed the buck to the next act. There was no way I could take a partner for country dancing: I didn't fully understand their customs of contact and didn't feel comfortable about breaking them. "Thank you, doctor," I replied with a smile, "I cannot dance, I am sorry."

There was a general murmur of encouragement, and I remembered the game of over-modesty that was being played out again. How do I say no and mean it? Eventually, Dr. Radin moved on, but not without great awkwardness on my part, and he took to the floor to show some more of his exuberant moves.

I was privileged to be allowed behind closed doors into a private world of freedom. It was a world they had obviously wanted me to see, and we finished the evening with many photos to remember it by.

The next day I was feeling better, just washed out. Having slept for the best part of a day and a night I just needed to prepare for heading off. This was tough. After two days off I could feel my focus slipping, momentum halted.

A young relative of Dr. Radin called Farad and insisted on meeting me. He claimed to have helped a lot of cyclists who passed through Tabriz, so despite my best intentions to rest up I went out to meet him. Hamed turned out to be the most intensely annoying character. Early twenties and extremely goofy, he was excessively excited to meet me and positively bounced as we walked to a café. I tried to be patient with him, just wanting to go back, sleep, and recover. I tried to listen through his patronizing monologue to glean any gems of wisdom as he took charge of my Iranian section. The one great tip seemed to be "avoid Tehran." Tehran is the capital and the largest city in Iran with over seven million people, and I could see the sense: it would be another Istanbul and could be entirely avoided by cutting south a bit earlier. My planned route was an easterly tack toward Tehran and then cutting southeast to avoid Afghanistan in the east, toward Pakistan. To my dismay Hamed ended up inviting himself back to Farad's to look over maps. At the first opportunity I excused myself and got some more rest.

The road out of Tabriz is a long climb, and I still felt weak, not helped by five hours' sleep. A short distance out of town a friend of Farad's who insisted on being my escort passed me. His business was car batteries and he was driving a blue pickup with large drums somewhere to get acid. He drove ahead a bit, got out, leaned on his hood, and waited for me to pass, then repeated the routine. Eventually, at the top of the hill, he flagged me down, having bought a watermelon from a roadside stall and cut it into fat slices for me. What a sweet luxury. We could not communicate at all, so I simply thanked him.

As we went on, it was obvious that he was annoyed with my speed, especially when I stopped to introduce myself to a group of motor-bikers who turned out to be from Croatia and Austria. The truth was, there was no need for an escort, and having just been sick I wasn't prepared to push myself to go faster than was comfortable; but there was just no way to say this without offending. The motor-bikers were heading through Baluchistan, and were extremely concerned. When I told them I was doing the same, they laughed. "You are mad, this is impossible, on a bicycle?" Their camaraderie was charming and made me acutely aware of being alone on my journey. They were facing the same concerns with the humor and banter of good friends, and for a moment I envied them.

I had been told of a new highway that was being built to Tehran, which I soon found, just after my voluntary escort left me. The pros were that it should mean perfect roads and less traffic, but I was con-cerned looking at the map that it would avoid a lot of the towns the old road went through, and therefore supplies.

Just as I turned onto this highway, two road cyclists passed me, the first I had seen on leg 2, clad in full cycling kit. Since entering Iran I had sweltered under my trousers, worried about offending in my shorts, and they were now sticking to me after the long climb since Tabriz. I stopped and stuffed them into my pannier bag, laughing at the unnecessary discomfort I had put up with.

By midafternoon my concern about the new highway was confirmed. I had not passed a single shop, and eventually I had to detour a kilometer in the wrong direction to find a small store. A dozen boys of all ages crowded around; four men sat inside. A number of rope mattresses along the walls gave the appearance of a community center. This was a decision point. The old and new roads now diverged. I sat outside, eating biscuits, staring at the map, trying to figure it out. The new highway looked more direct and would undoubtedly be faster, so I took the risk and cycled back along the road I had just turned off.

It was almost definitely the wrong decision. For the next few days, though I enjoyed the best roads since Germany, I was punished in the searing heat, with no shelter when I stopped. I quickly ran out of food and had to ration water. The days seemed to drag with the constant worry of no stops or supplies. The plan had been to take it easy for a few days and recharge my batteries, but that was not possible here. This was relentlessly tough riding.

On night one out of Tabriz I stopped by a big hill of a stubble field and waited for the road to clear so I could make a dash for the brow and camp on the far side. A couple from Tehran took my idling as a sign of a problem and stopped to help. I avoided telling them why I had stopped, which led to a long lesson on reading Farsi numbers to help me understand road signs, then a more general lesson on the history of northern Iran. They were charming. The man left me his contact details and offered to do anything he could to help while I was in northern Iran.

The second day on "the lonely highway" started well, at 5:30 a.m., with a breakfast of Iranian flatbread with soft cheese, the end of the honey, and a packet of biscuits. Eight hours' sleep is a great cure and I felt stronger, only with a slightly sore throat, probably as a result of the heavy traffic fumes when leaving Tabriz. After 50km I had passed nothing, not a single house, and stopped to look at the map again. It was midday and I realized I had 120km to do by dark or I would be on biscuits for dinner. The recovery ride was over. I had 900ml of water at midday and it was the high side of 35 degrees Celsius. I hardly got off the bike all afternoon, counting down the hours. I knew I had about six hours' riding to do and there was no point in getting upset about it. I averaged 19km/h for the rest of the day, which is not fast, the undulating roads adding up to a 1,500-meter ascent.

As it got dark I made it to the first inhabited place I had seen all day, a small rest area just short of Zanjin. I was hungry and parched; one bottle had 100ml of water left which I had been saving in case of emergency. I was badly dehydrated and would have eaten anything. I ate hamburgers and sandwiches until I was full again. It was all they had and I couldn't have cared less in that state. It had been scary out there without enough food and water.

There is a tough thrill you get from setting such a target. Under normal circumstances—unladen, flat, cool, and in full health—120km would not have been a big target, a five-hour pedal. But that day had proved one of my hardest-ever rides. I'd fought waves of weakness and broken down the distance into two lots of 60km, then into smaller units in my mind to make them go faster.

As I sat at the roadside eating, a guy approached. He spoke very little English but seemed very keen to talk. He wore black overalls and signaled that he worked in the petrol station, a few hundred meters farther on. He seemed to be a big Ultimate Fighting Championship fan, and despite knowing a bit myself he soon ran away with the conversation, illustrating chokes and locks as if we were playing charades. He seemed a perfect new friend.

"Is there anywhere near here where I can sleep?" I asked, pointing in the direction of the garage.

"Yes, no problem," he repeated a number of times, slapping me on the back happily.

The town was off the main road. It was dark but I had to trust him. We walked down the road together and he asked me to wait away from the lights by the pumps. I did so, increasingly uneasy. After twenty minutes I was about to go and find him when he appeared. He would not look at me as he spoke. "I asked my boss if you could sleep in the garage and he said yes, if the police were told . . ." He stumbled for the right words. "So I called the police who said that all tourists must stay in hotels and so you must go to the town center." He never actually said so but he looked incredibly sorry. "Thank you," I tried to reassure him.

I pushed the bike toward the road as if to cycle into town, but was really looking about for anywhere to hide. I noticed a bank of dirt about five meters high running parallel to the road. Checking that no one could see me, I switched off my head torch and scrambled over it. I was less than 100 meters from the garage but hidden in the wasteland of a building site. After clearing an area of thorns I threw the tent up quickly and locked the bike outside, with the other end of the cable attached to my pillow bag inside again. I was utterly exhausted.

Having congratulated myself for a tough ride into Zanjan, I now paid for it. Despite the kinder terrain I managed only 131km at a painful average of 18km/h. Those two days of hills and lack of proper food had left me exhausted. My right calf was tight and cramped all day. However, it was a much better day. The wind now blew steadily from the south and I was off "the lonely highway." I had rarely felt as bad as those first few miles, barely able to raise my eyes above the front wheel. It was only going to get tougher and I needed to recover fast, so I made a decision within the first 5km to have a recovery ride, not to take my heart rate above 110 beats per minute all day. I tried not to worry about the lack of miles. The annoying thing was that it could have been a really big day because for the first time since Romania it was very flat. The long-term average will take care of itself if you take care of yourself, I kept telling myself.

Late in the day, after eating, my energy came back and I found myself in a vast plain with flat horizons, worried where I would camp. It was almost dark when I spotted a few small banks about 100 meters off to the right and decided it was my only option. Making a dash when no cars were near, I cycled onto the dirt. Incredibly, the ground simply fell away at the banks, down a steep path into a dry riverbed that had been completely hidden from the road. The bed ran parallel to the road and as far as the eye could see but was sunk, about 20 meters lower than the plain, so was invisible until you were on it. I pushed the bike down the precarious path and set up the tent, using stones to peg it as the old riverbed was as hard as concrete.

The following day, I woke stronger, ready for the big miles again. I cut south, my easterly tack since Istanbul over. This was a milestone, and I was now heading into southern Iran and Pakistan, the areas people seemed most nervous about.

After hitting the sacred 160km (100 miles), I skirted west of Tehran, climbing gradually all afternoon and then coming onto a huge plain with two massive factories in the middle of nowhere. These had skyscraper turrets and cranes, were mainly white, and were of a scale that made the vehicles in the car park look like toys. I stared at them as they got bigger—there was nothing else on the horizon—then slowly pedaled past, not daring to take photos.

Finally, I freewheeled in the dusk for the last 15km into the town of Saveh. My only contact in Iran, other than Farad, was a man called Ali who lived in Yazd, a few days farther to the south, but he had other networks and a young dentist called Hadi met me as I cycled into Saveh and kindly showed me to a small hotel—a good thing, as it had no sign. It was wonderfully simple but clean and cost $17. A bed and a shower! It had only been three days but I felt in greater need of these luxuries now than after the whole of Turkey.

Afterward, I enjoyed a long walk into town, feeling like a new man in a pair of tracksuit trousers Farad had given me. Stopping in one of the many small restaurants, I ate a huge kebab and rice. "So much for being a vegetarian," I'd mused when I scanned the menu for options. The streets were clean, and though not busy, people of all ages were out. It felt safe, and I wandered back slowly, window-shopping.

It had been a huge improvement of a day. It would have been hard to keep up the style of the previous week. My cold was moving from my throat to my head, which gave me a really stiff neck and headache, but in general the batteries felt fuller. The fire was back in my belly, and I had a bed for the night.

With every mile I now moved toward Baluchistan. The change in direction, now southeast, took me straight into what had been a side wind. Therefore progress was slow as I cut back onto more major roads. Apart from the wind it was a fairly uneventful day, until later on.

Qom is known as one of the major religious centers of the Middle East, and the epicenter of Muslim faith in Iran. After Tabriz I had given up on cycling in trousers, but now I put them back on, not wishing to stand out more than necessary. For the first time in Iran, the English translations on the signs disappeared altogether as I cycled into a maze of suburbs and market streets. Toward the center I was forced to ask directions from half a dozen people. Most did not speak enough English, or I did not understand their instructions. Eventually, I cycled past a young man with an English book under his arm. A student—perfect—and I found he was delighted to practice. Despite the help, it was late by the time I found the correct road out. On the south side, the suburbs seemed to stretch even farther, and as darkness fell I was still passing rows of buildings and the odd streetlight.

In this situation I needed to act fast. Maybe I should have stopped in Qom, but I had not seen anywhere and it would have been a short day. As it was I had still only covered 140km. There was nowhere obvious to hide away and camp. Eventually I passed a couple of fields on the right, with a boulevard driveway and a large brick farm building. It looked deserted, so I ducked off the road and hid until the road was clear. The building was around 20 meters by 10, set 30 meters back from the road. On both sides were open fields and I decided to hide by the far wall so traffic in my direction could not see me. Ideally I would have hidden behind the building, but it was open to the farm track and was very exposed. A bunch of trees next to the road meant that when it was dark the headlights of oncoming cars wouldn't stray this far.

The trees stretched out in a long parallel line, marking the far side of the field, and behind this were a number of bright lights. Some were like streetlights but others seemed like white stadium floodlights, and I peered closer, trying to figure out what they were. I concluded it must be a factory or something industrial, which was far from ideal but at night should not be a problem.

Crouching with my back to the building, I boiled some water and threw on some couscous and ate a large cake. I kept low and covered the flames, trying desperately to go unnoticed. After an hour I still felt uncomfortable. There was a lot of traffic on the road and even on the farm track. It was certainly too open to put the tent up, so I cleared some scrubby weeds on the narrow path at the field's edge and set up my sleeping bag.

As I dozed off, uneasily, a loud call went up, startling me. It was a call to prayer coming over loudspeakers from the floodlit area on the other side of the field, but so loud it seemed to be all around me. Sitting up, I surveyed my surroundings in time to see a single light coming along the road. It turned off and continued along the track straight for me. I guessed it was a motorbike from the engine noise and lay low to miss the dancing headlight, hoping it would turn onto the main farm track. Twenty meters away now. I jumped up: it was going to drive right into me. The rider stopped immediately, and I threw on my glasses quickly and walked slowly toward him. My head torch did nothing to penetrate his headlight and I could not see him until I had walked right up to his side.

He was a middle-aged man, dressed in trousers and an old scruffy jacket. He spoke to me in Farsi. I stepped back slightly, swiveled my head torch so it wasn't blinding him, and opened my hands to show I didn't understand. Then, pointing back up the track where I had been hiding, I gestured "hands on head" to show I was sleeping. He just looked at me. I guessed he was the farmer, or a worker at least.

A minute passed. He said something else in Farsi and I replied this time in English to make it clear that we did not understand each other. I sensed his indecision and realized that this was my chance to make the decision for him. I stepped forward, gestured "sleep" again, waved as conclusively as I could, and smiled. Without waiting for a response I walked away, and as I got back to my sleeping bag he restarted his motorbike, turned, and drove back to the road.

It suddenly hit me: I had been spotted rather than been stumbled upon. He had purposefully driven over to question me. This made me nervous, and I racked my brains, trying to think where he could have seen me from. I lay in my sleeping bag for over an hour, worried that people would return now that they knew where I was, before falling asleep.

Uncomfortable on a broken mattress on top of a solid path, I struggled to stay asleep. I couldn't move at night but felt unsafe staying. As a last resort to help me sleep I got up at two a.m. and had to put the tent up, but only half up as the path was too hard to peg and I was half asleep. Since people knew I was there, I saw no point in hiding now.

At 5:30 I woke and quickly packed. Dawn was just creeping over the hills to the east. I was soon joined in the field by two workmen who started pulling huge bundles of whatever was growing in the field over their shoulder and along the ground, using a rope.

It proved a better day, the wind subsiding slightly and the road continuing to stay flat. It was frustrating to make only 161km.

Each day south grew more arid. The desert was meant to start at Yazd but in my ignorance I would have suggested I was already in one. After a fast morning on day 45 I hit a long three-hour climb, which combined with the headwind in the early afternoon. I didn't care. I felt stronger and back in the zone, where I could deal with anything.

On the outskirts of the town of Na'in I paused to look at the map. The main road was a ring road but after that was a big gap, with nowhere obvious to camp. There was no way I could camp again without more supplies, so I decided to cut off the road into the town. The map suggested I could rejoin on the other side.

Within a few hundred meters a small white hatchback pulled up in front of me and a guy jumped out, waving for me to stop. His English wasn't very good but he seemed to be offering to show me into town, that I could stay with him, and something about a friend. He was tall, well dressed in a shirt and trousers, and about my age. I didn't trust him. He seemed very friendly but I felt as though he wouldn't offer his help without the hope of something in return.

"No, thank you, I am just stopping for water," I said, and began to cycle on.

"Follow me!" he called after me, jumping back into his car without another word.

Sure enough, he drove ahead, and there was no way to lose him. I tried to think through my next move.

As the town got busier he stopped and flagged me down again. There was no sense in cycling on as he would catch me in a second. I pulled up to find him talking to another man, of a similar age but shorter. This did nothing to ease my growing concern.

"Hello, my name is Hanif." The shorter man spoke well. "I would like to offer you my house to stay tonight. I want to practice my English." He looked at me expectantly, as if this was a very normal proposition.

"Thank you very much, my name is Mark," I answered. "I am just picking up supplies and carrying on tonight." I didn't want to draw attention to my plan to camp.

"This is impossible." He pointed at my bike. "There is desert for two hundred kilometers until Yazd." I knew that Yazd was 180km at most. "We are friends. I own a computer shop. You can stay with my family. This is my town. You cannot go on tonight. Where are you from?"

I explained my story, and Hanif translated, wide-eyed, for the taller man. This bought me enough time to think. They might be right. There certainly hadn't been anywhere in the open country where I could have camped in the last 20km.

"OK. Thank you very much for the offer but I cannot accept. But can you please show me a hotel?"

I followed them to a guesthouse, which from the street was a narrow unmarked staircase I would never have found alone. They helped carry my bags and bike up to a small room where they then stood, expectantly. I just wanted to be left alone: I had to plan closely the next few days in the desert and was tired. Initially I had found their friendliness suspicious, but now I saw that they were very genuine and simply wanted to spend time with me, and I had no wish to be rude.

We ended up in a small restaurant eating pizza for dinner. They spoke endlessly and with pride about their town and Iran but also about its limitations and their idealization of the West. I tried to balance some of their rather naive impressions with the realities—the excess, the waste, the crime—but there was no way to persuade them that the grass was not greener on the other side. They were charming, true gentlemen. We walked the streets of Na'in after, stopping at Hanif's computer shop, where he burned me a CD of some of his favorite photos of Iran.

It had been a shorter day than I had planned at only 147km, and it was frustrating not to hit my target, but I went to sleep reenergized by the evening's company, a distraction from my own world.

8

On day 46 I had no choice but to get to Yazd, a city surrounded by sands. It was a 180km ride in an average of 35 degrees and I was there by midafternoon. I had flown the first few hours at 30km/h—an unprecedented average in the gentle descent to the sands. The early finish the evening before had left me feeling the strongest yet in Iran.

Ali, my only personal contact in southern Iran, was a friendly man who worked with a friend of the family. I called him and waited by a number of big roundabouts, each with elaborate modern art statues in the middle. As I sat on the grass, a group of five youths walked up, pointing and chatting. One wore a Manchester United top and I called out "Manchester United," smiled, and gave him the thumbs-up. I have no football allegiance but was happy to see something that reminded me of my world. He was maybe sixteen, soft-looking, with black scraggly stubble and curly hair. The guy next to him seemed to be his brother. They shyly came and sat with me when I beckoned and the Man U guy spoke enough English to explain that they were all from Iraq, but had been living in Iran for four years to escape the war. "I will go back in a few years when it is safe and become a doctor," he said in earnest. I admired his conviction. At that moment Ali pulled up and I followed him into town.

The Silk Road Hotel, in which Ali had booked me, was a spot of multiculturalism amid this closed world. In terms of people it felt like every hostel I have ever been to; in terms of setting, it was a haven of Iranian culture set in a tunneled and arched building next to a bustling street market and a huge mosaic-fronted mosque. Ali left me for a while, and I sat in the large open courtyard listening to native English as something novel. Strangely, I felt no need to join in.

Social stereotypes can be found in every hostel in the world, and they are amusing to observe. There was the young couple doing their own thing over in the corner with a *Lonely Planet*, a young hairy man with a guitar proudly telling anyone who cared to listen how he had spent the last years traveling the world, an older man who was reading a book quietly, looking like the nomadic traveler, and four other guys, each going through the initial meeting FAQs.

Lastly, and to my surprise, were a group of ladies. They didn't fit in, especially in Iran, and I eventually introduced myself. It turned out that one was from Edinburgh, though originally from England, another was Norwegian, and the others were from around Europe. They were studying Farsi in Tehran and were on a tour of the country. Sharing a bag of fresh pistachios that Ali had given me, I enjoyed a conversation with women for the first time in over a month. Some things you don't value until they are no longer there!

I was used to eating at ground level in Iran, but never fine dining. Ali and I pulled up in a very dark alley after a driving tour of Yazd past the university and night markets, and walked through an arched wooden door. The entrance looked like a wine cellar but once inside it opened into a large domed room with sandy mosaic tiles and smaller domed rooms in open plan around the edge. The centerpiece was a large stone fountain. We sat on a raised platform to the side on a Persian rug, ate, and chatted the evening away.

It was a pivotal point, a fitting moment of calm before heading into the dangers and solitude of Baluchistan. From here I was cycling against the official advice of the British embassy. I would be uninsured and would soon be under armed guard. In the morning I would be giving Ali my BBC video gear to send home: it was too much of a risk to carry it and be misunderstood as a spy. But for the moment I was eating like a king in the company of a gentleman in a country I now loved.

I went to bed late that night and didn't get going the next day until 10:30 a.m. I'd felt weak due to lack of food, so I ate two breakfasts then stopped after 30km for rice and kebabs. I just couldn't stay on the bike. I felt weak and incredibly saddle sore. I can't describe this constant pain in any way that does it justice, and I was not in the right mental state to override it. When I could stay on the bike, I hunched over my front wheel feeling powerless, my stomach in my throat with relentless grief. The five hours' sleep hadn't helped, but I realized that this lack of focus was in part because of the mental break I had taken the night before. I had fallen out of the zone.

By late afternoon I had covered a pitiful 70km, which would normally have taken just over three hours. The sands had started as soon as I left Yazd and it had been a barren day staring at gray tar. I was too sore to feel lonely but I was very alone, my momentum broken.

At 5:30 p.m., as the sun set, I saw lights on the horizon and knew it must be Kermanshan. There was no sense in camping from now on because of security concerns. I saw a fuel sign on the map so pushed to reach the town, not caring that it was only a short distance ahead— or so I thought. The horizon in a desert is much farther than you think. After nearly an hour I was still pedaling hard toward the lights in the growing dusk. The road slowly rose and fell, so occasionally I lost sight of them, and the closer I got the more they seemed to fade. My concerns and confusion grew, my legs screamed, and the pain in my backside was indescribable. After another fifteen minutes, to my relief, the lights started to move off the horizon and I finally turned into a large truck stop.

I found the place bustling with hundreds of men and a few women. The front car park was directly off the road that came in the opposite direction; I had cycled in through a rear truck park. The row of buildings included a couple of shops, a restaurant, and then a mosque at the far end. I pushed the bike along the crowded pavement, unsure what to do. There was no town in sight and nowhere obvious to sleep. For a long time I just stood and watched, wondering when it would get quieter so that I could curl up in a corner.

At the end of the shops and restaurant a small crowd huddled together. I pushed forward to see what was going on and found an old man in a small stall handing out cups of tea. Leaving my bike, I joined the gathering and took a few cups gratefully, unsure what to do about payment, just following those around me. After a while the metal boiler he was pouring from evidently emptied and the crowd slowly dispersed. The old man was left to clear up.

"Hello, do you speak English?"

He looked up and peered at me, expressionless. Throwing my hands out to symbolize confusion, I then signaled "sleep." He continued to look blankly so I repeated the gestures, more enthusiastically. He

````

got it, or at least seemed to, and pointed toward the mosque. I stood back for another ten minutes, sipping my tea, sure that he'd misunderstood.

"Excuse me." I stopped a man in a suit, the first I had seen, hoping he would be more likely to speak English. He didn't, but walked off and came back with his son, who was in his teens, who answered directly, as if it were a very silly inquiry, "You sleep there."

"In the mosque?" I questioned.

"Yes."

His definitive tone made me slightly more confident and I wheeled the bike inside. Huge rugs covered the floor and strip bulbs dully lighted it. Around the edge, curtains were used to partition sections. I went into one of these, parked the bike, set up my sleeping bag, and went off to find food. It felt strangely safe there, away from the bustle.

Just 94km in five hours' riding—it was a day I needed to forget about. After two burgers and a kebab and rice at the restaurant next door I spoke to Mum in a hushed voice from the mosque, then slept from 8:30 p.m., curled up on a huge rug in the corner.

The next day I felt much more energetic and made good time, covering 161km before stopping at a hotel in Rafsanjan. I cycled through a lot of pistachio nut fields that day, which made a nice change to the desert. At one point a white van pulled up ahead and waved for me to stop. Two men stepped out and asked me for some of my water. I felt slightly awkward as I was in the middle of a desert, rationing my water to the next town, and these guys were in a van; but considering where I was, and feeling slightly defenseless, I didn't want to refuse.

It was also interesting to note the change in people over the past two days, increasingly wearing long smocks and slacks instead of shirts and trousers, with some wearing long desert headgear. In terms of ethnic groups I was moving out of the Persian area and into that of the Balooch. I would pass Kerman the next day and I had to call ahead to the police to discuss the next section. Ali called from Yazd to check that everything was OK and said he might have a contact in Bam, two days away.

Each day grew hotter, which seemed apt, symbolic of the apparent danger. Day 49 took me through Kerman and over a perfect 100 miles to a small truck stop called Mahan. It was an exceptional morning, 102km in just over four hours. I passed many more pistachio fields
````

and later on a number of huge cement and other nondescript factories. The spaces in between were always sand now, whereas they had often been gravel and scrub farther north. After a very flat day there was an unexpected climb to finish. At the top of the climb I stopped and could see all the way to the small truck stop, marked on the map, 10km ahead. The sun was setting behind the mountains, and it looked like a perfect oasis in the midst of an arid emptiness.

To the British embassy's credit, despite our decision to go against their official advice on Baluchistan they kept in touch every day to make sure I got through safely. A few days earlier they had given Mum the contact number for a Mr. Ehsanfar, who could help me get through southeastern Iran. The only details we were given about this man were his name and phone number; we had no idea who he was. They had also given us the contact number of a proactive cycling character in Tehran called, funnily enough, Ali. Ali had some connection with an organization called Cycling for Peace, but details were again sparse. There was nothing I could do from the bike, but I could sense Mum's considerable task to pave the way.

That day was spent, for the most part, trying to juggle phone calls and thinking through the characters involved in the next section. There was the embassy, Ali in Tehran, the elusive Mr. Ehsanfar, and then eventually Ali in Yazd, who was called in to make sense of the translations. Tehran Ali spoke very good English, but as the negotiations wore on it became clear he was not the most rational player, taking on few of the facts and trying to dictate the situation.

Midmorning I'd called him, and he'd said something about calling back and hung up. Ten minutes later I got two texts from him saying he had spoken to Mr. Ehsanfar, who said he would meet me and arrange safe travel from Zahedan, but that I must catch a bus from Bam to Zahedan "especially because you are an Englishman." I was annoyed he had made this decision without actually speaking to me and talking the situation through. He had only just been contacted, was up in Tehran, and had little idea what I was doing.

I don't believe I was underestimating the risks of the area I was heading into. I knew that other cyclists had cycled this way and I was reluctant to go along with the bus plan, as long as I only traveled during daylight hours and stayed on main roads. After a few hours thinking the plans through I texted Ali back and told him as much.

The truck stop was on the right of the road: a line of stalls, a mosque, an elaborate tile fountain, and a trough for washing and drinking. I could not see any fuel. As in Kermanshan, I had no idea where to start.

As I stood there considering my options, a middle-aged man with a trim mustache and slight stoop came over. "Do you speak Spanish?" he asked in English.

"No, but you speak English?"

"Of course, but I used to live in Barcelona, I prefer Spanish." He laughed. I found him immediately likable. "My name is Ali," he said as he shook my hand. No surprises there.

Ali insisted on organizing food for me at a grotty stall with a very dirty, fat, and dour owner. Thirty thousand rial, or £2, got me half a chicken with some green salad and a carton of orange juice. Ali explained that he was opening a shop here and to come and get him after I'd eaten, and wandered off.

As I sat in the dirt on my plastic chair, a young boy of about ten came and sat opposite me. After a short silence during which I'd smiled and waved a hello, he started talking to me, without pause, and at length. He must have chatted for nearly ten minutes and I sat there, simply watching. At first I was uncomfortable at my inability to converse, but then realized it didn't matter to him that I blatantly didn't understand. He was bold and inquisitive, gesturing occasionally to illustrate a point. After a short pause he got up, shook my hand, and left without a backward glance.

My next visitors were less amusing. A group of five young guys, all of whom looked to be in their midteens, took it in turn to come forward and shout at me. I understood that I was a novelty to them and that they were excited, but after half an hour of them running up, boisterously shouting in my face, and running off I was getting slightly irritated. One eventually redeemed himself by bringing over a packet of biscuits for me, seemingly embarrassed about his friends' behavior.

As it grew dark I pushed the bike toward the shop fronts—about a dozen in total, mostly food stalls, but a couple were car workshops. I found Ali in the last of these, behind a closed garage door, painting the ceiling. He was in his fifties and had been to London and through Europe. He'd worked in textiles in Barcelona for a few years and had a degree from India, where he had lived for five years. Now living in Kerman, he taught English and Spanish. He had a well-traveled and educated air about him and I thought he seemed out of place trying to open what he hoped would be another roadside food house.

He placed the roller brushes in a tub of turpentine and casually asked, "Do you smoke?" I said no. "Because I would like to make you a joint. Maybe you like opium? We are near Afghanistan here." I declined but tried to show my gratitude for his strange offer. "Ah, you don't do drugs." He was now using a small brush to fill in the corners. "I was the same before I lived in Barcelona, but I did everything there, it was crazy." It was a small room and needed a lot of work, but he seemed to be alone. "I realize that in Europe most people get drunk, but when you go to someone's house here some people drink, some smoke, and some take opium. It is all the same, people like different things. All the drugs come over from Afghanistan with the lorry drivers, who are all on opium when they drive as well. You should be careful on the road." The conversation and his situation seemed at odds with my first impression of this man. Regardless, he was very friendly, seemed harmless, and it was nice to speak to someone.

After locking the workshop, he asked whether I'd like to come back to his house for fruit. I declined, as politely as possible, and explained that once it was quieter I would sleep in the mosque. "No, there are rooms you can have, come."

I followed him back along the shops. Around the back, next to the toilet block, he knocked on a door. He seemed to argue with the guy who answered for a few minutes but assured me everything was OK. The room turned out to be a small old office or something similar with no bed, but a desk, a single hob, a bookshelf, and a pile of rugs and blankets. Apparently the argument had been about the price: the guy had been asking for 30,000 but Ali had insisted on 25,000 as I was a friend—a saving of 35p. With a lock on the door it was perfectly fine, and I thanked Ali, who then left.

It was 155km to Bam tomorrow, so I went back to shop for a few supplies. I was sure the guy was overcharging me and he dropped the price when I questioned him.

The next morning I got a text from Mum, which read as follows: "Ali (in Yazd) spoke to Mr. E. He is head of cycling federation in Iran. He has now got Bam to border sorted. He had wanted you on a bus between Kerman and Bam . . . says be careful off the road until hour after sunrise and hour before sunset. Ali speaking to him again in the morning (now), then will call me. Spoken to J and S Watson [who had recently cycled through Baluchistan] for over an hour . . . lots to tell. Stay at Akbar's guesthouse in Bam. They speak good English and have latest news for all travelers . . . retired teacher who helps everyone. White Light. x." It sounded positive. "White Light" was Mum's way of saying good luck.

I was already past Kerman, where Mr. E now wanted me to get a bus from, and there was no way I was going to go back. Looking around, I could not see why everyone was so against me riding. There seemed no imminent threats, though I realized I was not fit to judge.

It was a fast and beautiful day in the desert. Anything over 20km/h average was above target, and that day I managed nearly 24km/h. However, the concerns and confusions about what lay ahead remained, and it became clear that the authorities really did not want me on the road.

Bam became a known name around the world on December 26, 2003, when an earthquake flattened the city and claimed around 25,000 lives. Five years later the center still looked like a building site with piles of debris everywhere. The first place I was directed to was a strange extravagance amid the rubble with a sweeping driveway and marble lobby. It was so posh and seemed completely out of place. Because I had no idea what Akbar's was, it could easily have been it.

"Is this Akbar's guesthouse?"

"No, this is a four-star hotel." The receptionist looked slightly offended and gave me a map with directions to a couple of Portakabins with beds in them a few kilometers farther on.

A big Lonely Planet sign hung outside but it was a very unlikely-looking street, with tumbledown buildings and a couple of shops operating out of the back of metal shipping containers. I went to one of these but there was little other than biscuits for sale. To my joy, however, I did find some eggs.

There was no answer on the doorbell, so I rang the number on the sign. No answer again. Ten minutes later a guy turned up on a motorbike waving a mobile. He spoke hardly any English, which is why he had not answered my call.

I was the only guest. It was a lovely little place and I made full use of the kitchen. Akbar's guestbook was full of warm comments from just after the earthquake onward when he had set up again in this temporary location. Akbar himself was in Tehran. I would have loved to learn more about his work, and about Bam.

That evening was my last chance to sort the next stage of the cycle. Tehran Ali had sent me a rather blunt message informing me that I'd have to pay between £150 and £170 for car rental or get a bus. Yazd Ali had begun negotiations with Mr. E and arranged for a couple of cyclists to meet up and ride the 300km from Bam to Zahedan with me, where I'd then meet a police escort to take me to the border. There would be a car that would help carry the supplies, which I'd have to pay for, which was around £75. Yazd Ali was being proactive and sensible, presenting me with the facts so I could make an informed decision rather than just trying to tell me what to do. I felt as though I could go on by myself provided I was careful, traveling only by day and staying out of the busy places, but that it would be irresponsible to go against the advice I'd been given. Mum was amazing, as usual, through these negotiations. It was a frustrating end to a 166km day, but Mum was in good form and happy for the first time in days, and it seemed like we had reached a reasonable solution, so I went to bed relieved.

I was up and ready at 6:30 a.m., as arranged. I feasted on a huge dish of scrambled eggs, leftover pasta, and very stale bread while waiting for the Iranian cyclists. Three hours later, when they still hadn't arrived, I could wait no longer. After half a dozen phone calls home since getting up to go over my options, and knowing that ahead lay some big hills and tough riding, I set out alone. I was nervous, all the risks I'd been told about floating around in my head. I set myself lots of small targets for the day in an attempt to stop my mind from wandering from the task at hand.

Halfway through the morning the call came through that my escort was still coming but had not left yet. They had found a vehicle and I did not need to pay for anything anymore, I just had to sit tight in Bam for the day. By this time I was already halfway to the town of Faraj, where I eventually stopped for lunch. Faraj is a small desert town with widely scattered low buildings. I ordered a pile of chicken and rice from a roadside stall at the far edge of the town, feeling very vulnerable. Men lay out on rope-mesh bed structures, hiding from the blistering sun.

At one point a man approached me and gestured for some water and I gave him about half a plastic bottle. In return—not that I expected anything—he reached his hand into his pocket and into my open palms poured a handful of seeds. With a slow nod he walked off. I examined them and tried a few but decided they were far too much hassle to take out of the kernels for what you got. A week later I was still finding some in my pocket linings.

The shop owners and men were giving me nothing but respect and the only reason I was worried was because of all the concerns that had been voiced about this area. Looking ahead on the map I was troubled to see the desert stretches getting vast. For the first time I bought a lot of water, stashing six 1,500ml bottles on top of the back and front panniers. The added weight felt massive, and I put some more air in the tires, concerned about pinch punctures.

The afternoon was a slow climb from Faraj with a headwind. The sand picked up and whistled through the tires and over my feet, but thankfully didn't rise farther. Midafternoon Mum called to say that the escort had left and should meet me soon but if I got to an army checkpoint before that to wait there.

The army base was the biggest I had seen yet, a fort-style building surrounded by a barbed-wire fence, with corner turrets and a walk-way on the wall top patroled by soldiers. A couple of scraggly trees stood on the roadside next to it. I sat under one of these trees for hours. The guards kept wandering over and pointing at me from across the road. To pass the time I did a phone interview with BBC Online and tried again to suppress the inevitable frustration at being held up.

At one point a huge Mack truck, the likes of which had been tormenting me throughout Iran, thundered to a stop next to me. The driver had a huge mustache and wore a baseball cap. Apparently, to change gear often takes two hands, which explains the way these beasts often seemed to drift in the road. With nothing to do I wandered around, admiring it up close. The driver seemed equally intrigued. I shared some grapes he offered, then clambered in after taking a photo of him in his cab. The pride he took in his vehicle was charming, and even with the few words he understood and spoke we managed to exchange some stories about the open road.

As it grew dark, the soldiers came out of the base again and called me in off the road. I sat in the sand by the entrance guard post for half an hour, unsure what to do or say, aware of how tricky my situation would become if my escort didn't turn up soon. The soldiers seemed friendly though and I felt no threat, just annoyed at having wasted most of the afternoon when I could have pushed on in the daylight.

Night fell, and a blue pickup truck pulled up, driven by a small, tubby, middle-aged man with a big beard. Out of the kingcab stepped three teenage boys. By this time I was waiting by some military vehicles inside the base. One of the young soldiers tapped me on the shoulder. "Don't trust them," he said. Looking into the dusk, I could see the driver talking to some of the soldiers. Don't trust them? This was the escort that had come from a British embassy contact. I had no choice.

I pushed the bike out and a couple of soldiers dropped the chain barrier, with a nod of mutual respect. The teenage boys and driver silently shook my hand and we loaded the bike into the back of the truck, although I had no idea where we were going.

Once I was sitting in the front, with the three boys cramped in the back, I tried to ask where we were going and who they were. They did not speak a word of English between them, absolutely nothing. Almost everyone I had met in Iran spoke a few words of English, especially teenagers. Worried about where they were taking me, I called home. Mum was on her way to the gym, taking her first time off after an intensive week, having assumed all was fine now I had met up. She immediately called Ali in Yazd, who called me back to help translate what was being said.

I stared out of the window as the desert night whizzed past. After 50km of silence we stopped at a large house and unloaded the bikes. Two of them were mountain bikes with large knobby tires, entirely unsuitable for long-distance road riding.

To my surprise, the youngest boy, who looked no more than fifteen, now spoke to me. He had obviously been asked to give me a message from the driver, who was standing nearby. He looked uncomfortable, stammering for the right words. "Tomorrow, cycle from here." I tried to remain composed but turned to the driver, evidently the real source of the statement. "No, we cycle from there," I said, pointing in the direction we had come from, and turned, leaving no room for discussion.

Without any language it was impossible to tell if I was being offensive, but in my mind I had been advised to have and had now been provided with an escort to get through this part safely. And what was the point of an escort if it did the same job as the bus I was trying to avoid? Not being able to communicate made it twice as frustrating. I tried to monitor my body language to look strong but not rude. After a meal of chicken and rice, eaten in a silent circle on the floor in the hallway of this unknown house, I set up my rest and slept on the floor.

Sure enough, the next day started at 5:30 a.m. with a beautiful drive through the desert at dawn, back to the army checkpoint. I would have loved to know who these guys were, and their understanding of their role with me. There were misunderstandings and tensions which could not be explained away but there was no point in feeling awkward about the silence, since there was nothing to be said.

I knew what lay ahead that day as much of it was what we had already driven. The start was flat desert riding toward a wall of mountains. Then things just got hillier. The main climb was long, hot, and stunning. To start with the road rose gently up the foothills, following a deep boulder valley. It then rose sharply over 15km to a col, cutting through a number of tunnels and sweeping around rock outcrops.

The escorts were a great challenge. The youngest was on a road racer but the two in their late teens were on mountain bikes. My initial concern was that they would be really slow on their fat tires, but the opposite was the case. They were fresh, riding completely unladen bikes, and had obviously been told that I was racing. I couldn't explain the hare-and-tortoise theory of ultra endurance racing. If I'd gone as fast as they wanted to I would have been injured or tired out in a week and would have had to take time off to recover before making another sprint. Going at a stately 20km/h all day every day was obviously not their idea of a buzz, and from the start they set off like the clappers.

The van sat on my back wheel all day, the boys talking openly among themselves about me, then dropping back, holding the window and chatting to the driver. They all had good kit with full Lycras and seemed fit. However, at one point I managed to ask them how far they had cycled before, and the farthest was 100km. These guys were kids, used to races that lasted a couple of hours. I had no idea who the escort driver was but I did know that he was getting increasingly irritated as the day went on. The thing I didn't understand was how this group sufficed as a safety escort. If a situation of real danger cropped up, what would some teenagers and a middle-aged, unfit, unarmed civilian do about it? Admittedly they knew the area, and there is always strength in numbers, but I hardly felt that they were on my side.

By the afternoon, and despite my best efforts to communicate and ask them to ride in a group, there was an obvious tension. After an hour's climbing, plodding at a sustainable pace, the middle kid dropped back from the others, who were riding together a good distance up the road. "Fast," he said as he shot ahead, gesturing for me to follow. I didn't respond. Ten minutes later the oldest one dropped back, past me to the vehicle, which was laboring slowly behind. After a minute he too was on my shoulder, this time gesturing urgently, with an angry expression. "I am not going faster," I shouted at him. "I have to do this for half a year, every day, do you understand?" He obviously didn't understand a word, but my anger had trumped his and he disappeared up the road to report the bad news to the others. I sat there, spinning up the longest hill I had seen in weeks, cursing my guides as they cursed me.

At the top, we stopped. It was an incredible view and there was obvious relief among the guys, even some friendly gestures, joking about completing the long climb.

"Stop here." The driver was pointing at his watch.

The youngest was pushed forward to translate. He pointed at the driver. "Zahedan, work."

We had to stop because the driver needed to be back in Zahedan by 4:30, I deciphered. It was early afternoon, and we were about to freewheel some fast miles on the long descent. There was nothing I had seen all day that concerned me, so I took a quick decision. There was no way I was stopping at just over 100km, and I communicated as much to the boy.

"No . . . stop," he said. It was obvious he wanted to say more but hadn't the words.

It felt like a standoff, but I didn't feel I was being rash. They hadn't met me yesterday when planned and now wanted to stop after half a day; at that moment I didn't care if I was offending their sentiments. If they respected my mission and their role in it then they would not be asking to stop here.

I pushed off. There was no point in trying to explain, but I did gesture for them to go on once more.

A fast descent does everything for morale, and the guys raced about me, smiling and gesturing happily, their arguments forgotten. After a few hours the van passed us and pulled into a lay-by and the driver got out, waited for us to pull up, and started loading the bikes into the back. I took the map out of my pannier, quickly identified where we were, and checked the cycle computer: 150km. I wasn't stopping yet. At this speed I could do 10km in twenty minutes, and I signaled this to the driver using my fingers. There was no angry gesturing this time, and he did a "go now" motion with both hands. It was nearly 4:30.

I finally stopped at a military checkpoint, and two of the boys stopped behind; the other had stayed in the van because his bike had been loaded. We were still descending but it had flattened out. It was an epic day's ride. It would have been a dream day if I had been alone.

There was a lot of interest from the soldiers as we loaded the bikes and I felt truly intimidated for the first time. A number of them had shin-length black boots, dark trousers, jackets, and a black scarf wrapped around their heads and over their faces. Semiautomatic rifles hung around their necks and they held these loosely, with pistols on their hips. They all looked hard as nails, unsmiling and unmoving. The ones with the desert face masks looked the most terrifying of all. One of them stood close by as we tied the bikes down. You could just see his eyes looking out from the scarf. I tried to unglue my gaze from him, worried it would provoke him, but I couldn't stop myself. He was magnificent, every part the desert warrior.

Zahedan was only a short drive away and we were all dropped off at what turned out to be a recreation center and shown to a couple of bunkrooms. This time I was given a room to myself, with beds for twenty-four, and the boys were shown to another room. The center manager spoke reasonable English and insisted on taking me swimming—"good for your muscles." I was starving and not hugely enthusiastic but agreed. It was the strangest swim I have ever had. The pool was your average 25-meter setup but packed with men only. There was no room actually to swim, with guys bobbing about in every possible space. Many seemed to be learning, so there were a number of grown men with armbands on. There should be nothing odd about paddling with just men, but it was. Still, it was a nice change, and after a session in the steam room and an ice bath I felt refreshed.

I then met Mr. Mehdi Nazemi, an accountant for Mr. Ehsanfar. "I am at your service," he told me, with a half bow. He looked to be mid-thirties. He was letting himself go but there was still evidence of a more active youth. He was here to translate for Mr. Ehsanfar, who joined us at a restaurant with his son for dinner. After all the aggro of the arrangements, Mr. E turned out to be a lovely guy. Despite the lack of English his mannerisms were international and I could see the respect he earned from everyone around him. He was small, probably in his fifties, with a smoker's gray complexion.

After the meal Mr. Nazemi bought a takeaway of more rice and chicken from the restaurant, I assumed to take home with him. When I was dropped back at the dormitory it was 10:30 p.m., and I was horrified to find that the boys were still there, pale and tired. I had learned over dinner that they were members of the youth team that competed in the area. Mr. E was employed by the Iranian government and was director of the Iranian Cycling Federation. The guys were undoubtedly fit and talented, but I could not believe that they had been left for five hours after riding a century without food.

There were no arguments or questions the next morning. The driver knew I would insist on cycling every mile, and we drove back to the military camp. The other guys looked terrible, goofing off and delaying us until nine a.m. While tempted to say "I told you so," I felt truly sorry for them. They looked wrecked. The bounce and energy were gone. None of them had ever ridden 100 miles, let alone on con-secutive days. They had hardly drunk all day yesterday, each with only one small bottle on his bike, then had sat around after a long moun-tainous day's riding without food. Obviously they were now stiff and hurting.

I wasn't much better. I had a headache which felt like it was cracking my skull. It was no dull ache but a sharp splitting pain that made bright lights and moving my head almost unbearable. For the first few hours I stared at the road in front of my wheel with slit eyes, drinking all my water and hoping the painkillers would kick in. I hate painkillers. You can't monitor the problem if you cover the pain up, but when it gets that bad you have to take them.

Fortunately it was a fast day, the road gradually descending, and the wind was behind us. It took just five and a half hours to cover the 150km to the Pakistan border. This time the driver had split as soon as we started and we'd made it back to Zahedan riding in a bunch; there was no racing ahead today. It was unclear where we were meant to stop. The driver was evidently meant to have returned after a few hours as the boys kept trying to call him. It was another two hours before he appeared. By then I was very worried: none of the guys had any food with them, we were all out of water, and we'd passed nothing all day, having skirted Zahedan. By the time the van arrived the boys looked very weak. The youngest fell off his bike badly at one point, cutting his leg and arm, when his front wheel hit my back pannier. They were quiet all day.

He found us as we passed an outdoor prayer structure, a 10-meter-square platform with a roof held up by corner pillars. A dozen or so men had stopped and were going through their Muslim prayers as we sat on the edge and devoured the rice and chicken the driver had brought. But there was no water. We all had to fill our bottles with Zam Zam.

After eating, we rolled out and finished the day by a long line of trucks near the Pakistan border, almost friends. It seemed sensible to stop a good distance back from the border and I gladly loaded my bike into the van, having accepted Mr. E's offer of one last night's comfort in Zahedan. I was glad I had. Looking around this barren desert, there were no options to camp out or take shelter.

Back in my dormitory, I was left for ages, repacking for Pakistan, unsure what the evening's plan was. The manager appeared after a couple of hours. "Are you able to do an interview for the media?" He looked unsure of himself.

"Of course," I said. I had no reason not to, and was not surprised after seeing the businessman that Mr. E was. "Is it for the newspaper?"

"No, it is for the television. Are you able to do it now?" He looked at me expectantly.

I wanted to eat, but realized this wasn't really an option and followed him down the short corridor and outside. It was now dark but two large lamps floodlit the center of the courtyard and the camera was already set up on a tripod. About ten men stood around waiting and I stopped short, unsure what to do.

I met a man in a smart suit, evidently the interviewer. Mr. E was standing at the back by his car, out of the floodlights. I looked around at the crew. They were all staring at me expectantly and I shook their hands in turn. "They want you to put on a long top," the manager translated. I had on my cycle strip with short sleeves and a pair of tracksuit trousers, but they were insisting on full cover for TV.

As we made our way back to the dorm I decided to question the manager more closely about the interview. "They might ask you about why you are doing the cycle," he warned, "if you are cycling against war or for another reason."

"I have no political message," I told him, "please tell them that. I am cycling for sport only, for charity, and for a personal journey."

Thankfully, I was never asked this. "What do the people in Scotland think of Zahedan?" was as political and awkward as the questions got. "I have had a wonderful welcome here and am looking forward to telling the Scottish people what a great place Zahedan is," I replied.

The manager did his best to translate but I could see he was nervous and struggling with the job. An Iranian friend later found a transcription of this interview on the internet; it was not complete or entirely correct. On the whole it was the strangest press conference I have ever given; but I did enjoy it.

Mr E would not let me leave without accepting a gift, and there was a choice. The first was a large wooden statue of a cyclist, and the second was a small round plaque with an Arabic inscription in gold. Neither was practical to carry on the bike, so I accepted the plaque as it was smaller.

"You will invite us to your wedding!" Mr. Nazemi bellowed, and translated loudly for his wife and Mr. E and his family.

"Of course. Please thank Mr. Ehsanfar again for the kind present."

"We are at your service," he said, repeating his catchphrase.

I would have enjoyed more time with them, but was keen to crash out, and I couldn't stop thinking about what lay ahead. Pakistan.

9

I woke in the bunkroom early as arranged by Mr. Nazemi, but he was late. When he did arrive he brought some dates, dry bread, and a bag of milk, which I ate on the floor. At seven a.m. an old yellow taxi turned up and we managed to cram the bike in the boot, its lid pulled over the protruding front tire with some string. My new friend gave me a kiss on each cheek and held my hand. "You will invite me to your wedding," he repeated, then gestured to the driver. "He will take you safely to the border."

I smiled and nodded. "Thank you so much again for all your help, my friend."

"At your service," he replied, with his half bow.

The drive to the border took over an hour. Absentmindedly, I watched the passing world while eating dates. At the edge of town, without warning, we stopped at a roundabout. The driver left the car and returned quickly with a young man who got into the back. His clothes were rags and hung off his skinny frame, his hair and beard were unkempt. "OK?" the driver gestured. I guessed I was paying for his ride but had no complaints. All I cared about was getting to the border with no further delays.

As we neared it I could see the long line of trucks we had stopped by the previous day. Pointing and gesturing, I told the driver that I wanted to be let out.

"No . . . border."

"No," I replied firmly, pointing again and turning to him to stress the point. I was not prepared to miss the distance between here and the border.

Seemingly put out at not being able to carry out his orders to the letter, he dropped me at the side of the road without another word.

The Iran/Pakistan border is like no other I have seen. It is simply a barrier across the road with a small single-room building off to the right. Many men milled around, but no women, and I nervously left the bike and followed a young guard who directed me to the waiting area. Men sat on seats on the dirt on each side, and as I walked through there was a stirring of mumbles and gestures at my presence. Everything set me apart from these men, from my skin and clothes to my height. I tried to act calm but every eye followed me to my seat. A number of men immediately approached offering money exchange. I refused as firmly as possible but they lingered, waiting for me to change my mind.

The desert stretched out as far as the eye could see into Pakistan. Except for this small office, there was nothing to see. I needed more food and water, and I had very little money. My mind raced through what I did have in terms of rations, adding up how far I could go without restaurants or shops. Mum had warned about how hard it would be to find food in the next stretch, after conversations with people who had done it, but there had been little opportunity to stock up. Besides, I couldn't carry enough for a week. I would just have to eat whatever I could find.

The man studied my passport, then my face. "You will get a bus to Quetta." It was a statement rather than a question.

"No, I will cycle," I replied. "I have asked for an escort to Quetta." Mum had reassured me that the Pakistan Transport Police, or Levvy, would be there to meet me.

A short pause hung in the air before the man continued. "OK." He held up my passport. "Wait outside." He turned to the next man, and I walked out to my bike to wait for the police escort.

Catching the registrar's attention, I asked if there was anywhere I could change money. Pointing back outside, he simply said, "Yes." The voice of authority was directing me to the black market. Maybe it wasn't considered the black market when it was the only market. My US dollars were running low, but Pakistan has links with Western banks and I hoped I could get money out when I got to Quetta, 600km ahead, through the Baluchi desert.

I pulled some dollar notes out of the bike and looked up to see three sellers walking over. There was still the one guard by the door, about 5 meters to my right, but I felt very uneasy as each of them hassled for my trade. I kicked myself for not having learned from the last few border crossings to find out the exchange rate before arriving. I had no idea what their money was worth and certainly did not believe the quotes. The main trader, the first man who had approached me, had an aggressive manner as he earnestly repeated his offers. It was not a welcoming negotiation using charm, like at the Turkish/Iranian border; but I could not go on without some local currency. Putting my hands up to signal for a break in the torment, I reached for my phone, which simply intensified the mutterings of the group around me.

"Mum, I need to know the Pakistan/dollar exchange rate."

Over the past three months Mum had become incredibly proficient on the computer. A currency search was, however, a new task, so I quickly helped her through a Google search for an online exchange rate converter. Before I could get an answer a man dressed in gray appeared and beckoned me. "Mum, don't worry, I have to go, the escort has arrived. I will call back later on." It was nearly a week before I got phone reception again.

Accepting the trader's offer, I changed $100 and left. I couldn't tell from his reaction if he had ripped me off.

I pushed my bike through the deep sand and back onto the road. The policeman who had come to get me was small and old, and carried a rifle which looked just as ancient. A blue Toyota pickup was waiting on the road, which was empty as far as the horizon.

A guard came around from the passenger side. His big beard and deeply wrinkled face gave him a nomadic, unkempt look. The driver, who remained behind the wheel, was younger, early thirties perhaps, with a big mustache that overshadowed a small jaw. He looked haggard and wild.

The policeman and older guard chatted briefly before turning toward me. It was clear that neither spoke any English, so without explanation the bearded one gestured that he wanted my bike. I let him wheel it forward. At the back of the truck he went to pick it up. "No," I protested, "I will cycle." I pointed to the road. Beardy shook his head and motioned for the policeman to help him. Frustration filled me and I found myself walking over, taking the handlebars, and pulling the bike away from him. "I cycle," I repeated firmly, and threw my leg over. Beardy and the old policeman spoke angrily to each other for a moment then gestured for me to go. Without looking back I wheeled around the pickup and headed into the desert.

After 10 meters I heard them shouting at me and I looked back to see them pointing angrily across the road. Ah, of course, I was back on the left-hand side of the road. It was not a great start to Pakistan.

Day one was tough riding, with the police on my back wheel all day. Sand whipped up by a big side wind from the right stung my face and eyes despite the sunglasses and took the already sunburned skin off my nose, making it bleed. We passed a couple of checkpoints, isolated posts in a sea of sand, but nothing else. Lunch was a tin of baked beans, eaten while sitting on the stone floor of a simple square police room, its doorway open to the road, waiting for the new police escorts to arrive from the next area. Apart from the shell of an old car, half buried in drifting sand, there was nothing around. The sun baked down relentlessly, making the sands scorching to the touch. A lorry passed, full of camels, and I hid to the side of the hut, taking photos secretly so the police wouldn't see. As hard as it might be, I wanted to act as little like a tourist as possible so that the police would treat me with respect.

That morning the reality of crossing Baluchistan hit home. However surreal and challenging my escort in Iran had been, this was something else. It was far emptier, and the presence of a pickup with armed policemen driving slowly on my back wheel all day was hard to get used to. It made me realize how subconscious my ride patterns were. I rarely sat on the bike pushing the same speed for set periods. Ideally, a day would be broken up into four sets of two hours at 20km/h, a total of 160km. The reality, however, was that I stopped whenever I felt like it and for periods of ten or twenty minutes would often slow slightly, dropping the cadence to give my legs a break. Now when I did this the escort would pull alongside, assuming I had had enough and was signaling to throw my bike on the back. I had to keep going strong whether I felt it or not, or these police were going to make it difficult.

The desert is a beautiful place with a real magic to it. It is a great place to think. In normal solo riding you have a slide-show world to occupy your thoughts. But in the desert, with nothing for the eyes to focus on, your mind just drifts off into an almost trancelike state.

I heard a rattling noise up ahead which pulled me out of this dream world. The heat haze on the road distorted everything more than 50 meters ahead, so I stared in disbelief as a lorry approached. In the desert heat, this could easily have been a mirage. What I saw looked entirely out of place (not that I had much authority on the subject). It was an old truck elaborately painted with swirling, dancing shapes and mosaic-style paintings. Some of the wood panels were carved intricately. The loud rattling and clanging came from the front, where the bumper was lined with chains in a row with metal weights at the bottom of each. It looked like something out of *Austin Powers* and I wondered whether they or I was more startled by the sight that greeted each of us. Must be hippies, I thought as I cycled on, living in a time warp out here.

Half an hour later a similar vehicle passed, psychedelically painted but completely different from the first. These trucks are remarkable-looking things, and they remained a feature of the Pakistan roads.

That evening I reached a small settlement, though I had no idea when we were going to stop or how far we would go. It was not my choice, and I had no way to ask. The Baluchi people are traditionally nomadic, and this first small settlement—made from mud and sand, simple squares with flat roofs—blended into the desert. I pulled off the main road onto a dirt road when the pickup signaled, then pushed my bike into an open courtyard as instructed by the Levvy, who drove on without explanation. It was a large, bare, sandy space framed with three walls. I pushed my bike over to the left and sat by two huge urns, each 4 feet tall, under a 2-meter strip of shelter which ran along the left and back walls. On this wall stood a lone guard, between two barred doors, which I assumed were stores.

While trying to avoid the guard's idle stare, I rummaged in my pannier for some biscuits; I hadn't eaten well all day and felt exhausted after being shadowed all day. A pillar initially blocked my view of the barred doors, but after a few moments I leaned forward, having heard a noise that broke the desert silence. Standing there, dressed in dirty rags, hands on the bars, were two men. They were hairy and gaunt, and they stared blankly at me. Another appeared from the shadows behind them and he too wrapped his fingers around the bars. I sat there, gazing back, expressionless. I had never seen prisoners before. Regardless of their crime, seeing men locked together in a tiny room in the open desert, my natural reaction was absolute shock. The guard turned and idly waved his rifle at the prisoners, who continued to stare back, unmoving.

After some time I got up and waved an empty bottle at the guard to try to signal that I needed water. Propping his rifle against the pillar, he lifted a slab on top of one of the urns and used a metal cup to fill each bottle. I slipped a chlorine tablet into each, hoping that five liters would be enough rations for a night and day. I had two 750ml bottles on the frame and a couple of big bottles strapped under the bungee cords on the back of the bike.

I had only been in the jail courtyard for about twenty minutes, though it felt like much longer, when one of the pickup's guards reappeared. Across the road I was shown into a bare concrete room. It was a good size with a long-drop toilet in one corner and a basic metal bed in the other. A new guard walked in and shook my hand. He had on a heavy jacket and sported a big beard that framed a broad smile. It was the first smile I saw in Pakistan.

He'd brought with him a tray with a pot of tea. What a joy. As I sat on the bare concrete floor I marveled at this strange luxury, and even more at the fine porcelain cup and saucer that accompanied it. The old Commonwealth had influence even here. Just a day ago in Iran, tea was served, as always, in a glass; it would now be a cup and saucer until Calcutta, I guessed. The tea was also white for the first time, and tasted really strong, and a bit strange. I guessed it was the milk. There was no way to keep milk without refrigeration around here, it was too hot. Maybe it was camel's milk, I speculated. I was brought up on goat's milk and guessed camel's would be equally strong.

This new guard seemed immensely house proud and pleased to welcome such a strange guest, and when I used hand gestures to indicate that I needed boiling water he quickly returned with a big gas burner. The heavy wooden door was then closed and bolted shut.

As I cooked up a tin of eggplant bake with some pasta, a latch on the door kept opening and I could hear other men talking and see eyes looking in at me. I felt like a zoo animal, though was thankful at least to be locked in their better jail, and on my own. The only small window would've given a great view of the desert if it hadn't been covered with tarpaulin to stop the sand blowing in.

For the first time since the start I was not my own boss. My guards now dictated my timings and distances. On my second day in Pakistan I swapped onto the second patrol midmorning with five unlikely-looking policemen and repeated my wish to cycle. The police uniforms in these parts were loose-fitting gray jackets, with large badges pinned to the shoulders. The men were all wild looking, mainly bearded with weather-beaten faces. Whenever I glanced back as I cycled, they looked bored and impassively back at me. Why were five armed guards needed, I wondered? Their rifles looked so old they might have made better spears, and few of the men looked physically fit. Was there a real and imminent danger which I was underestimating?

I was missing the video camera, which had been sent back home. My audio transcriptions, logbook, and photos were my only records through this amazing part of the world, and this was a shame. I'd enjoyed sharing the tough days with the camera when there was no one else to talk to. It would also be four days until I got mobile reception back and could call Scotland.

I found going to the toilet in the middle of the desert, at the road-side with no cover in front of a group of armed policemen, a challenge too. Ever since I was young I have got stage fright when peeing. I can't help it. If I am at a public urinal and a man stands next to me the flow will immediately stop; it doesn't matter how much I need to pee. On top of that challenge I was wearing bib-style cycle shorts that had shoulder straps, so I had to remove my top before I could pull them down. This process meant I was pretty much naked as I squatted on the roasting sand, eyes closed in an effort to force myself to go while those five police officers stood at the road-side watching me.

I rode for eight hours and thirteen minutes on my second day in Pakistan. The wheels were turning for six hours and fifty minutes of that, and I finished after 175km. My escort gave me all the benefits of a support vehicle, in that they forced me to keep going beyond pain and fatigue, without any of the moral support, in that they herded me at a 25km/h average on the flat desert road. The wind had picked up as the day went on and drifting sand raced across from the left. To start with it flew at hub height, so I would often lose sight of the road completely. Amid this veil of sand I felt as though I were floating. As the wind increased the sands rose higher, forcing me to wear a buff over my face to act as a shield. I kept looking back as the pickup's engine got lost in the sound of the wind. Twice they pulled level to stop and give me a lift. I simply shook my head and con-tinued. I was conscious that without language I might come across as rude, but my only weapon was to look determined.

The only main stop of the day came before the Levvy changed. At one of a number of barriers across the road we went into a small hut to the side for shelter from the sandstorm. It was completely bare except for an old rug on the floor. In one corner one of the guards rekindled an open fire on the ground, and I sat down as instructed, wondering where they got the wood from. He then hung an old-fashioned metal teapot over the flame, using a rudimentary tripod. The others sat around ignoring me, and talked. The wind howled in, as there was no door, so we all took refuge next to the walls. Once the tea was made we sat closer in a circle, eating dates that were handed around and drinking sweet, milky, strong tea. The men took a few dates, chewed, and talked, pausing to spit the pits on the floor behind them. This had to be one of the most bizarre tea parties I had been to. Spitting on their own floor that doubled as their bed seemed quite primal. I shared a packet of Digestive biscuits with them, although rather hesitantly, as they were among my last supplies.

Midafternoon I reached the first proper settlement in Pakistan and was escorted to a small shop. For 350 rupees (about £3) I bought some biscuits, a cake that had mold on it, two tins of baked beans, a tin of tuna, and a bottle of Coke. When we left, the wind suddenly dropped and the sand returned to ground level. This also brought a slight change of scenery, some gravel and scrub appearing in the endless sands. I was literally chased by the afternoon's patrol and fought to suppress my growing frustration at their taunting when I again refused their lifts.

For the last 5km into the town of Dalbandin a motorbike escort came to join the pickup. This was the first proper town I had seen in Pakistan and it differed hugely from what I had left in Iran. The main street was dirty, and it bustled with traders and stalls on the rutted dirt road where the tarmac ran out. No one spoke to me, so there was no choice about where I would stay, I was simply led to the police station.

The Pakistan police colors are red and blue, drawn as blocks with a diagonal divide. The outside of this much larger station looked like a fort, and its large blue and red gates opened without warning as our convoy turned into a courtyard with a number of half-scrapped pickups. My patrol disappeared into the buildings, leaving me alone, their job done. As I stood there wondering what to do, a number of policemen wandered around, watching me closely but avoiding any contact.

Reassuring myself that they must be as nervous of me as I was of them, I kicked the bike onto its stand and had a look around. The upper floor stood wider on the left, with a number of columns forming a walkway. I noted that these were the first painted buildings I had seen in Pakistan: apart from the gates, it was whitewashed. Farther down the walkway were two barred doors, and I walked outside one and looked in. I tried not to stare; the dark concrete room held a number of prisoners, most sitting on the concrete floor, some standing leaning on the walls.

"Don't go near there," came a voice from behind me, in perfect English. I turned and saw a man unlike any I had so far encountered in Pakistan. He was freshly shaven, except for a thick mustache, which was neatly trimmed, and dressed in a clean, unworn robe. He had a distinct air of importance about him. I extended my hand. He took it and introduced himself as the chief of police, while gesturing flippantly around. "You are American." It was not a question.

"No, I am Scottish."

He didn't reply, just looked mildly puzzled, maybe annoyed at his wrong intelligence. "OK, you will not leave until the morning." Then he turned to walk away.

It took me a moment to process this. "Excuse me," I called after him, "where should I sleep?"

"Here," he answered quickly, as though it was a stupid question. He then paused before adding, "Maybe you can sleep there," pointing to the back of one of the broken-down pickups a few meters away. "Just don't go near there," and again he pointed toward the jail. I saw that a couple of the inmates had come forward to the bars. I thanked him despite my continued confusion, and he walked off.

I was not about to sleep in the middle of a busy police courtyard on the corrugated floor of a pickup. It was obviously up to me to look after myself and I decided not to ask any more questions. I opted to sleep under the stairs as it was the quietest corner and went to ask for some rugs or blankets to sleep on. The police chief was sitting on the floor of a small staff room drinking tea; another man handed me a thick bed of matting. I felt a buzz at this small victory and strangely house proud of my new nest. After a while I ventured back to ask for some gas to cook on, which resulted in an invitation to cook in the mess, which then turned into a source of entertainment for the Levvy. The chief of police watched me throughout, a fat cat among his workers, eating dates and passing orders. Casually, in an attempt to break the awkwardness, I asked him whether he ate pasta. "No, I am not rich," he answered curtly.

Later on he asked whether I wanted to go to the market with him. As we passed through the heavy gates, I asked him if it was safe to go without other police. "You are safe when you are with me," he replied. "This is my town."

The busy streets did seem to part as we walked through, and he walked unarmed and without a care. He seemed proud to promenade me at his side, as though I were a prize, a symbol of his position. Refusing the multitude of fly-infested fruits and fresh foods he pointed out, I eventually bought some honey, tinned mango and pineapple, chickpeas, three bottles of mineral water, bread, and a tin of condensed milk for 550 rupees. There were no staple foods to take with me but I was happy that I could at least eat well that night.

On the way back the chief bought some flatbread, cooked as we waited in the street by some boys. One kneaded the dough on a mat on the pavement, a second baked it in a stove below street level, lifting it out with his thick mitts, and the third wrapped it in newspaper and sold it. The market was bustling with men, bikes, and the odd stray dog, and I kept looking around nervously as a tail of inquisitive teenagers and young men followed me. My guide didn't seem to notice or care and walked through the crowds as if they weren't there. I stood out for being white and wearing Western clothes, but he also stood out for being so well dressed and well groomed.

It was too hot to use a sleeping bag, so I felt very exposed. But I was tired so eventually I slept, only waking when a policeman walked on the stairs or someone called across the courtyard.

The next day started slowly. Being controlled by men I couldn't communicate with continued to prove frustrating. After being told to be ready at seven a.m. I sat on my mat until after nine waiting for the patrol to get ready. They, in turn, were equally frustrated when I refused their lift, insisting on cycling again. The chief of police was nowhere to be seen, so there was no way to communicate this properly, though in all honesty I don't believe he would've represented me.

This escort had four guards, two sat in the front and two in the back on some bench seats which ran over the wheel arches. The vehicle was open but had a frame which canvas could be put over, giving them something to hold on to on the rough roads. As soon as we left Dalbandin, they overtook and shot off. It was a hot morning (the day would be scorching), but at least the wind had died completely. Despite my growing love/hate relationship with the Levvy, I immediately felt vulnerable without them. Nothing I had seen since entering Pakistan made me feel threatened, but I was now alone for the first time in this country.

I passed three checkpoints that morning, and at each my escort was waiting, drinking tea. At the first they made me stop and hang around for twenty minutes before they were ready. They then stayed with me for fifteen minutes before passing and disappearing again. My feelings of vulnerability soon passed, and I loved the freedom of going at my pace again and letting my mind wander without their presence on my tail. At the second stop they were waiting but simply waved me through, catching up half an hour later, accompanying me for ten minutes before racing on.

In the afternoon the sands gave way to thicker scrub and I saw mountains for the first time appearing on the horizon, off to the right. But as the afternoon drew on, my concerns grew. I had barely stopped all day, it had hit 46 degrees, I was exhausted, and my left knee was becoming increasingly sore with twinges from the tendons. I had been told that the roads were about to deteriorate; currently it was passable but I knew they could change quickly. Every instinct said stop at Padag, the next village, but when I arrived my elusive patrol was there and waved me on. I stopped, tried to reason with them that I should overnight in Padag, but they signaled that there was nowhere I could stay and I must go on. I was hurting, and the conditions meant I would probably not make the next town, but I had no choice.

At the next checkpoint the police waved me on, and this time simply didn't follow. I didn't know whether to be relieved or concerned. After an hour I concluded that they were probably not coming back and got the map out to consider my options. It was 50km to Amad Wall and I was in the midst of barren scrub. The police were meant to be protecting me, after twenty kidnappings in the region in previous months, but they had left me alone. A more practical challenge was that without a police station to stay in I had no idea what to do at night. There was nowhere to camp safely because it was too open and desolate, and the towns had no obvious traveler's shelter. I was right in the middle of the region, on my own, heading for nightfall, and all I could do was just keep going. I decided it was better to reach a town and approach the locals on my own terms rather than try to hide out and be found at night.

The last few hours' riding were grim. My body ached all over and my knee was a particular concern. It was hard to focus on anything else and I quickly became aware of just how tired and dirty I was.

Still a distance from Amad Wall, I came across a few houses scattered among small scrubby fields. They looked out of place in the desert. Three separate groups of children threw stones at me. They missed, but the incident did not help my mental state.

And then the road did worsen. It suddenly halved in width to a single track of broken tar with banks of sand which often covered the road, forcing me to dismount and push the bike through. At one point, in the middle of a long straight, I passed a burned-out bus; the road now went around it. It was a ghostly sight and I wondered about the story behind it.

Eventually I reached the outskirts of Amad Wall and came across a stall, a small wooden frame with a table. I stopped to consider my options. I didn't feel scared, more hesitant in the situation I found myself in. The man at the stall asked me to stay longer and I was half tempted to ask if I could go home with him, but decided to cycle into town and try to find a police station. Amad Wall looked tiny, though, and I wasn't hopeful. Low mud-colored walls lined each side of the road. These were the homes of the Baluchi, and I had no idea how to make an approach. Amad Wall was not like the settlements I was used to, with commercial centers and places to stay.

Up ahead I spotted some lights, and as I got closer I saw that they were strip lights, hanging at the roadside. There was a small stall set on a wooden platform, and out front were a number of large plastic drums with big funnels on top. A group of men sat under the strip lights. Taking a deep breath, I got off and wheeled toward them.

"Hello," I said.

They had been watching me silently, and one got up and walked over. "Hello, my name is Aman Ullah Assani." He shook my hand and I asked whether there was a police station in Amad Wall. "Yes, Amad Wall," he repeated, smiling back.

I thought about how I could simplify my question. "Police, Levvy, here?" I asked.

"No, no police—come."

I sat on what turned out to be an old bench seat from a pickup and tried to introduce myself to the remaining men. None looked more than thirty, and none spoke any English. Aman returned from the back of the stall with a pot of tea and poured us all a cup. He seemed to be the owner and could speak a little English. I learned about his ant problem, which was evident as there where thousands crawling everywhere. Laughing about this broke any initial awkwardness. They started laughing again when I put a sugar lump in my tea. They then taught me to put the lump in my mouth and to drink the tea through it as a better way. Four sugar lumps and one cup of tea later, I tended to disagree.

Within half an hour it was completely dark. I made one last effort to ask for the police, but Aman repeated that there were none here and that I must stay with them for the night. I could see nowhere else. I was in their hands now, and thought them trustworthy.

Aman sent one of the teenagers into the town on his motorbike. The boy returned half an hour later with a metal bowl of meat and rice. The meat was a rough stew and I could see parts of cartilage, arteries, and lungs. Without spare water to boil for ration packs, this was it. I didn't want to be rude and refuse it, so I dug in without a second thought. I was almost glad it was fairly dark, and my hunger stopped my imagination lingering, but this was as animal as it got. I reflected on how I had reacted back in Paris a few months ago when a bit of ham made it into my quiche. What I would have done for some quiche right then! It was very spicy and texturally questionable, but I finished the lot, aside from a few mouthfuls, which were subtly spat back into the bowl.

Aman, in the meantime, had found a map of Pakistan and I showed the group my planned route. My story was answered with a long and nearly completely understandable explanation of the history of the Baluchi people. Aman described the Baluchi as strong and honorable, unlike their neighboring tribes, whom he described as inferior and untrustworthy. He pointed in turn to the main towns I would pass through and waved a finger over much of the rest of Pakistan, describing the people in the regions around Quetta and Jacobabad as being a range of things including thieves, corrupt, and bad to their families. "I friends, here good, not good man here . . ." He seemed to have the strongest sentiments about closest neighbors, giving those in Punjab and the far north the benefit of his partial trust. Each time he stated a strong feeling he would repeat this in Baluchi to his friends, who would rally in support, pointing at the map, nodding. Occasionally while we spoke a car would stop and a couple of the men would run out and fill it up from the fuel containers with the funnels.

After a few hours I gestured that I must sleep. Amar seemed flustered, as if he had mistreated his guest, and I tried my best to calm his apologies, thanking him for looking after me. Next to the stall was a small shed with a flat metal roof that opened onto the road. In the middle was a single rope-woven bunk on a metal frame, which Amar pointed at. "This is your bed?" I asked. "I can sleep on the floor." He would have none of it and explained that he'd sleep on the bench we had just been sitting on.

Two of the men came and stood watching quietly while I dug out my logbook and wrote up the daily stats. Aman reappeared when I was nearly finished and called them away, apologizing for their manners.

I took my top pannier bag, which was a roll-top dry bag, and emptied it. After blowing up the therma-rest and unrolling my sleeping bag I repacked the tent in another pannier, filling the empty bag with all my valuables, and padded it out with clothes to make a pillow. Again, I ran a long cable between it and the bike so that if anything moved I'd be woken. Lastly I put my knife in my right pocket and tried to sleep. I was exhausted and knew I couldn't face a day of riding on no rest, but every instinct told me not to sleep, so it took a while to doze off.

At one point I woke to the sound of a loud engine and men's voices. My glasses had fallen off, but I found them quickly. By the petrol containers, not more than 10 meters away, was a bus, one of the old-fashioned ones in the movies with diagonal window frames. A couple of men were by the door, arguing, but this is not what caught my attention. The bus was full of cows. I propped myself up on an elbow to get a better look. There was no mistake: the back end of the bus was filled with cows. How do you get a cow onto a bus? I laughed to myself as I drifted off again.

I woke suddenly to men shouting and a bright light on me. Before I had time to get up a man was above me. I recognized his jacket: it was the police, and it was clear from his shouting that I had to move, now.

I fumbled about, unlocking and reattaching my makeshift pillow. It was two a.m., and I felt wrecked. The blinding headlights of the pickup stayed on me as I tried to think clearly.

"How far are we going?" I asked.

"Not far." He spoke good English, but that answer was incredibly unhelpful.

Within five minutes I was ready. I saw Amar standing next to his stall, looking exactly how I felt. I felt sorry for him and walked over to thank him. He didn't respond, just looked at me blankly. My last thought before bed had been to give him my spare head torch as a present, as during the evening the generator had died a couple of times and there had been minutes of fumbling around in the dark to get it working again. As I set off I realized I had forgotten to leave it with him, but it was too late to go back.

The pickup let me go ahead and I rode in its headlights. I was surprised how cold it was but I doubted the temperature was actually that low: it was just my body failing to deal with the shock of the situation. I had no idea how far I had to cycle so I pedaled slowly, my left knee painful and very stiff.

Thankfully, after just a couple of kilometers we pulled up. My legs screamed in pain for ten minutes. I was too tired to complain as they led me through the now familiar red and blue gates and into an empty cell, locking the door behind me. A single bed lay in one corner. I was asleep in seconds.

At seven a.m. I woke to someone opening the door. A young policeman walked in. He stammered in broken English that I was to be ready to leave in half an hour, then left. My contact lenses felt like a pile of grit as I looked blearily around at my cell. There was a police uniform hanging on a hook and I was amused by the thought of trying it on. By the door was a metal ring with a lead and plug. I didn't recognize it but plugged it in to find it was some sort of electric stove. What a find. I threw some water into a pan, which quickly boiled, and made up a ration pack. There were only a few left, and apart from that I only had some dry biscuits for the morning.

It was day 57 on the road and I was aiming for Quetta, except according to the map I didn't want to go as far as the city, I needed to cut right toward the Indus Valley. Part 1 was nine hours on the road to a checkpoint in the middle of nowhere, where I wanted to turn east; part 2 was the remaining 20km into the city of Quetta, which took another hour and a bit, when the police wouldn't let me take this turnoff. It had been the toughest four days' riding of my life but I was through the Baluchi desert.

That last day in the desert can most aptly be described as long and hot. After the relative flatlands since Iran, it was back into the hills, with a 1,400-meter ascent over arid switchback roads. The day was full of checkpoints, and at three of these my patrol also changed. The pain in my left knee had eased a bit but the tightness in my leg was a worry, and the hill climbs weren't helping. The reason for this pain was that I was not riding at my own pace. I wasn't covering any more distance, I had just been pushed to ride faster and for longer than was comfortable and then forced to break for far too long, my legs cooling off before going again. The thought of riding alone after Quetta kept me going. Though I doubt I could have got through without them, the Levvy certainly made my days harder.

I was now on the southeast tip of Afghanistan, only a few miles from Helmand province, and the scenery changed quickly. Before reaching the mountains, which had been getting bigger around me, I cycled through the first of a number of vast refugee camps. The Levvy patrols grew nervous passing near these camps. One stopped, refusing to move on until an additional motorbike guard joined us. I wasn't aware of any threats or aggression but their nervousness was infectious. I passed a number of white UN Land Cruisers and bill-boards in English and Hindi advertising the work of Mercy Corps in the area against meningitis. I felt strangely removed from the realities of this war-torn world as I cycled past craggy hills with large rock mosaic signs for different military scout groups, and seas of tents in the open plains between.

The grade of the road into the mountains was not gradual. When it got steep it reared incredibly, and the psychedelic trucks labored. I passed one bus on a steep slope with its engine seemingly spread over the road, and a couple of men working away at it. I marveled at such incredible ingenuity and perseverance; it would never be expected in the West. A while later a small white car that looked like a Fiesta passed us, which was nothing out of the ordinary, except for its load: a goat in a cage on the roof. My lowest gear was barely enough to deal with the gradient on the rough tarmac and I strained in the

35-degree heat, until I met a kinder incline. Looking back over my shoulder gave a breathtaking vista over the desert floor. In the foreground the pickup crawled in second gear behind me.

Ten miles before cutting east, off the high ground and down into the Indus Valley for the turnoff for the town of Sibi, the road deteriorated further. Then it stopped altogether. The tarmac ended and a rubble and dirt road continued. I had been following a meandering river off the high ground and could see another climb ahead, from where I hoped to be able to see Quetta. The lorries that now constantly passed threw up clouds of dust which hung around me, impossible not to breathe in, stinging my eyes. The steep climb looked like a quarry pit, as trucks scrabbled for grip. It was a bike breaker, and the patrol stopped twice on the 3km climb to take my bike. Each time I refused.

I made it to the turnoff by Sibi, but the police wouldn't let me camp behind their huts, claiming it was too dangerous and I was a kidnapping risk. They called an escort from Quetta, and I had a horrid cycle in the dark into Quetta with multiple motorbike escorts.

At that point I thought I would have to cycle back up the broken road to that turnoff in the morning, so a wasted 40km loop. I was completely disoriented as I passed miles of colorful street stalls and packed streets the likes of which I had never seen. My front light was not working for some reason, so I was reliant on the headlight of the motorbike escort behind me, or the sporadic streetlights. Thankfully, within the city we were back on tarmac and I could look far enough ahead of my front wheel to keep going in the darkness.

I was taken to a big police station with a hotel beside it, and left at the gates. "Tomorrow at here, eight," the policeman said, tapping his watch.

I protested. "No, thank you, no escort from here." I had had enough and was past the danger zone. Those few who had recently been escorted through Baluchistan stated that from Quetta it was safe enough to continue alone.

"Not possible," he replied simply. "Eight time."

There was no point in arguing with him: he was simply carrying out an order. He waited at the gates until I disappeared into the hotel.

It was a very basic foyer but could have been the Ritz for all the luxury I was used to after the police cells. The man behind the desk continued his phone call for ten minutes as I waited, looking at me occasionally as if he hoped I'd disappear. He eventually hung up and gave me a room. While he was photocopying my passport, a small old man appeared and spoke urgently to the young hotelier, who translated for me.

"You are cycling from Europe?"

I said yes, confused.

"You are a day late," he stated as a matter of fact. "You were in the newspaper yesterday," he continued in perfect English, nodding to the old man, who was peering at me closely.

I left them and found my room, off a large courtyard. I was completely baffled as to why the police had told the papers about me while trying to keep my profile low in order to protect me.

I closed the door and was truly alone for what felt like the first time in over a week. The simple room had a single bed, small table, and a large fan overhead. The toilet had a long drop, a shower head but no basin, a small sink, and a broken mirror. I peered at myself in the moldy mirror and laughed aloud at the face that appeared. I looked haggard. Dirt in my hair and beard, my eyes sunk into my red, leathery face. I had not changed out of my shorts or top for over 400 miles and had done no washing of any description. A light sprinkle of cold water was all that was on offer but it felt heaven sent.

That evening I sat in the grassy courtyard outside my room and ate a huge bowl of egg fried rice. For the first time since Iran I could call home. It was great to hear a familiar voice, and despite the relief I felt I couldn't hide my annoyance at being in Quetta, which I thought I could have avoided, and being in the papers. At least for the first time in many days I was able to switch off completely when I went to sleep, without fear of being watched or woken.

The hardest thing about my routine was keeping the mental focus; after reaching one target I had to go straight on to the next. Since Zahedan my target had been getting to Quetta, no matter how tough. I had made it, but now I had to get to Lahore.

I woke at seven a.m. and quickly packed. My first thought on waking was that I wanted to avoid the police escort. By ten past eight I reasoned that they were late, so I got my bike, which was locked in the car park outside, and left quickly. My rupees were almost gone, so I went in search of a cash machine. Despite the promise that Iran would be the only country where I could not withdraw, none of my three cards worked. The bank opened around half past ten and I waited for the exchange man, though he didn't turn up. I finally persuaded another worker to change my final dollars.

Back on the saddle, I recognized a Shell garage but soon came to the realization that I had no idea where I was going. The previous night I had blindly followed the police motorbikes and had taken no notice of the route. The streets were insane. Rickshaws, bikes, and motorbikes shared a laneless space with everything from oxen pulling carts to trucks. I passed a large golden globe sculpture in the middle of the road, just past the garage, and was determined to keep going in the same direction until I hit the outskirts, where I would ask. There was no point asking directions here, I thought; my every instinct had to be focused on staying safe. Also, once I was in the flow of the traffic it was hard to stop.

As I peeled onto some smaller streets and back onto main roads, my sense of direction told me I was still heading out of town in a fairly straight line. On one of these wider roads the traffic was in two lanes each way, although so many things using that space were of different sizes and went at such different speeds that each simply fended for its own space.

I was cycling slowly, held up with a car to my left which was only just moving. A tractor pulled up on my right. Its trailer was a flat platform at handlebar height and wider than the tractor, and the boy driver was concentrating on going forward. I was pushed left, but the large trailer tires were wider still and I had nowhere to go. A wheel hit my right back pannier, which sent me left into the wing of the car, and the bike went down hard. Luckily I went between the car and a cart, and a cyclist behind me was able to swerve. Half the street stopped as people suddenly crowded around.

The car driver was a well-spoken older man who insisted on taking me to the hospital. I wasn't hurt, or at least not badly; I just lay there shaken up for a minute before getting up. My right leg, side, and arm were grazed and bleeding, and I'd cut my right shoulder. I picked the bike up, spun the wheels, and checked the frame, almost oblivious of the shouting and traffic jam around me. It was fine. The bike had fallen on its bags again and, thankfully, there was no real damage. The adrenaline hit and I realized I was shaking. Quickly thanking the driver for stopping, and reassuring the petrified tractor boy that I was OK with a thumbs-up, I pushed off, wanting nothing more than to get out of there.

After twenty minutes I was still in thick traffic when I saw a big golden globe in the middle of the road. My heart sank. Pulling to the side I had a second look and then back down a side street, where I could see a Shell garage. I will never know how, but I had spent the last forty minutes cycling in a perfect circle. In such a situation you have to laugh. I then did what I should have done long before and asked the way.

A young man in a rather fetching tweed jacket agreed to cycle with me and we set off, having a traffic-dodging conversation about his studies and my travels. After passing where I had crashed we took a sharp right over a bridge. I could not remember crossing this the night before but followed anyway. Left off the bridge he pointed straight, bid me safe travels, and pedaled off. Over the next 10km I recognized enough in the daylight of what I had seen by night to believe I was on track.

On the outskirts a large sign spanned the tarmac road: straight on to Sibi. I could have leaped for joy. The road was good and wide, with more refugee camps and many brick factories to each side. The tall red chimneys smoked lightly as I watched donkeys and men carrying massive loads of bricks from wet molds to huge stacks of fired produce. Ahead lay more big mountains, and my heart sank again. I felt liberated with no escort, but there was not much left in the legs, and I was bruised from the morning's tumble. The batteries were low after the last four days.

10

A day of downhill riding took me all the way to Sibi. I could not believe I'd managed 174km after such a poor start and the way I felt. It was truly one of the most spectacular day's riding I have ever done, definitely the most breathtaking since Paris. I had expected that first climb to go on for ages, but it simply cut through the first hill and then down, down, down. When it flattened out and then inclined I once again settled in for the long climb, only to summit within minutes and then descend for another half an hour. I hadn't realized how high Quetta was. The road chopped through the arid mountains in amazing shapes, shadowed by the railway which cut a daredevil path through tunnels and over bridges at impossible angles.

The road was filled with many psychedelic trucks, each uniquely painted and carved. Those without the rigid backs had huge canvas loads which bulged incredibly on either side, dangerously heavy. These descended at a painfully slow pace to prevent their brakes from overheating. We leapfrogged each other every time we went from steeps onto flats and back again. One, which I passed a number of times, had a family perched on top who posed excitedly for photos as we zipped downhill. I had been keeping my camera in my back pocket since Iran so I could take photos without stopping when under guard.

Once the valley flattened out, it followed a wide fast-flowing river past a huge collapsed bridge. One end had fallen down but was attached, and I stopped to watch in disbelief as a man on a motorbike somehow still managed to cross. Farther down, the valley got greener, and then for a while it closed in to form towering cliffs, which the road hugged, then I crossed the river on a stone bridge, and on the left bank started to cut through deep tunnels and over-hangs. It was spectacular. I freewheeled, taking photo after photo.

Each time I passed a police checkpoint without stopping I got a rush of adrenaline—like the excitement of a fleeing prisoner. When I was finally stopped the guard went off to radio someone and I knew my escape was over. After a half-hour wait a motorbike turned up, and without any mention of having given them the slip in Quetta we set off together. I had been recaptured!

I was taken to the police station despite asking to be taken to a hotel. Another passport check in a room full of policemen drinking tea. They were all chatting, ignoring me, as I stood by the wall, completely unsure of what was happening.

"Will you sleep here or in hotel?" asked the chief of police, addressing me for the first time.

"Hotel," I answered with utter relief.

After a short night escort we arrived in the main street and pulled up at a dilapidated building. There was no sign outside and I followed the policeman inside, leaving the bike in the corridor as we continued upstairs. The policeman spoke briefly to the hotelier and then to me, saying they would be back in the morning to get me. I tried to take my bike up to my room but the policeman insisted it was locked away until their return. I tried to object but he was adamant, and wheeled it into a cupboard. Once he'd gone, a couple of boys helped me up with my bags.

I walked out to find a place to get food but didn't trust anywhere, so back in the resthouse—you could not call it a hotel—I asked, three times, for some boiling water. A boy finally arrived with a two-liter 7UP bottle full of murky, tepid water, which I threw into the long drop. I got out my stove to cook the last food I had on the floor—some noodles and my last ration pack.

There had been voices outside and doors slamming for much of the night, but at seven a.m. the place was deserted. After knocking on a few doors, a bleary member of staff came to the reception. I already had my bags downstairs and saw my opportunity. "I need to get my bike out so I can go to the police station," I said, pointing to the road outside. The young man hesitated, unsure if he could make this decision. I tapped my watch, pointed at the road again, and repeated, "Levvy, police."

Ten minutes later I had slipped out of Sibi, and was on the road to Jacacobad, 170km ahead. There were two police stops in the first 130km, both small huts at the roadside with a chain across the road, which now lay on the road surface so cars could drive through without stopping. The first guards saw me too late and didn't react, but the second lot waved me down, calling out. They were just two men sitting on a bench, and I could see no motorbike or vehicle that could follow me, so pretending that they were waving greetings I simply waved back, shouted a cheery "good morning," and carried on. I glanced back to see them standing at the roadside staring after me and laughed, feeling a buzz of excitement at having run the gauntlet.

I had more strength today, or maybe it was the tailwind and flatlands helping. As the day wore on I entered the thick marshes at the edge of the Indus Valley. The humidity gradually increased, making for uncomfortable riding.

Strike three, and my luck ran out. I guessed the last lot had radioed forward as there was no way to cycle around the next police, who quickly pulled the chain up as I approached. There were only 30km left to Jacobabad, so I followed the bumper of the pickup, trying to chat to the two policemen sitting in the back. One was twenty-four and married with two children, the other twenty-five and engaged. Time always passed quickly during these mutually intriguing, cross-cultural, simple conversations.

Jacobabad was a very dirty bustling town. Off the tarmac artery, the dirt roads were a now familiar mayhem consisting of everything that needed to move. The police again seemed abnormally nervous, but I could not see why. This made me slightly nervous. I was not given the option to stay in the police station and was shown to a hotel by the central crossroads. The owner had obviously been forewarned and rushed out when we arrived. The town center was a mass of moving people, half of whom seemed to crowd around the bike and police as soon as we stopped, peering in, a din of voices. The four police stood around me in close security as I wheeled my bike inside. I was convinced that if I had been on my own I would have avoided some of this drama. I closed that world out with relief when I was left in my room.

After a "shower" using a mug and a cold tap, I opened the bedroom door to find a policeman on guard. He was just a teenager and started to panic as I went to walk past him. I explained that I was going to eat, using my best charades. He accompanied me, looking uncomfortable, and stood outside the restaurant downstairs. The small room was full of men. One, about midtwenties, started a conversation, explaining that he wished to improve his English, which was already excellent. He was about to start studying medicine and was the first highly educated Pakistani I had met. He spoke openly and seemed to be the only fluent English speaker in his group. It was fascinating to hear his views on Pakistan and the rest of the world, his education, and his love for his country. In response, as I finished the best meal I'd eaten in weeks, I answered as best I could about the journey I was on. He shed some light on the tough time I'd experienced with the police, explaining the traditional view on someone my age, unmarried, and traveling alone: I was seen as strange. He laughed.

I needed to get some supplies. The young policeman refused again, indicating that I needed to go back to my room. It was absurd: I could see no danger that would stop me going 50 meters across the road to the shop. I walked past him, making for the door. He ordered me to stop, standing in my way, waving his rifle in one hand. I saw an insecure boy dressed as a policeman. I asked reception for the manager. After explaining my need for food and a lengthy debate I was allowed out, under the condition that the hotelier and two policemen accompanied me. I had never before shopped while under armed guard. The policemen shooed away any potential crowds with their rifles and the shop owner looked wary and nervous.

After half an hour, finally alone again, back in my room, there was a knock at the door. I opened to find a man dressed in a smart suit who looked out of place—a city slicker in the rough part of town. He introduced himself as a member of the Intelligence Police and told me he needed to ask me some questions. I looked out to see if my door guard was still there and down the otherwise empty corridor. I smiled and shook his hand. "Come in."

For twenty minutes he examined and copied my passport, asking questions and filling out forms. I perched on the bed, trying to look relaxed. I had no idea if I was in trouble for having given the police the slip that morning or if this was simply a local bit of standard bureaucracy. He was younger than I had initially thought in the dull light of the corridor, and his tone became more conversational and less accusing. By the end he seemed genuinely intrigued. Regardless, I was still hugely relieved when I was able to bolt my door shut again.

During the night the room phone rang four times, but every time I answered there was a short pause and then the person hung up. When I left, I confronted the manager. "You cannot call my room many times in the middle of the night," I almost shouted, surprised at my own anger.

"I am very sorry, Mr. Beaumont, we had to check you were there."

There was nothing more to be said. Evidently whole conversations about my situation had taken place that I was not involved in. Regaining my composure, I thanked him and left.

That day I experienced, for the first time, absolute poverty, and it made me feel ill. Even the desperate situations of the refugee camps a few days earlier did not seem to compare to this forgotten land where there were no aid organizations, no prospect of change. In the morning, until the Indus river, the road and buildings were raised just out of the swamps. The towns and villages seemed piled high with litter and waste which filled the air with the putrid smell of rot. Children were as dirty as the animals and I passed a number of people simply lying at the side of the road, alive but helpless. The wasted legs of one man sitting on the roadside had obviously never been used, and he stared at me with a ghostly calm.

I felt trapped by my police guard and ridiculous for my egotistical focus. What was the point in my journey when there were people like this, without any choice? You can read about poverty but you can never understand the reality. Poverty is not really about the line between needs and wants, the dollar, or any Western standards of living; it is the reality of seeing, hearing, and smelling a standard of life that is indescribable. I had hit a few psychological lows since leaving Paris, but nothing compared to this. It took days for me to reason through that, for right or wrong, there was a greater good than myself coming out of my journey, and that it was not folly.

In the midst of all this, a convoy of three passed me. The front and back vehicles were vans with gun turrets, and the middle one was a blacked-out car. The car began to track my speed, then the back tinted window rolled down and a bearded middle-aged man looked out. He told me to stop, that he was a politician and he'd give me a lift to Sukkur. I thanked him but refused, and he pulled away without another word. It seemed he would stop for a white man but was happy to drive along with tinted windows, ignoring the poverty of the people. He probably had nothing to do with what I was experiencing, but he became an outlet for my emotions. Perhaps blaming him helped appease my feelings of guilt. I can imagine from inside a car at four times my speed it is easy to miss the horrid details of the world I was passing through.

Once on the Indus Highway I was stopped after 40km, this time by a highway policeman. He was dressed in a tan-colored uniform instead of the Levvy's gray and was absolutely charming. He had heard on the radio that I was passing and welcomed me warmly, saying that he had met some Scottish cyclists before. I wondered if they were John and Sally Watson. Mum had been in regular contact with them to find out how to get through Baluchistan safely, and without their help I probably would have taken alternative transport to Quetta. They had also experienced great frustration with their escorts, but had spoken of meeting one incredibly nice policeman around here. After buying me some biscuits he gave me his number, asked me to visit him any time, and waved me on. I was touched by his generosity as he'd apologized for not being able to do more for me, saying that he was not paid very much.

In contrast, I finished the day with a very grumpy and sarcastic set of guards at the town of Daharki, where I was given no choice but to stay in the police station. Before passing through the blue and red gates a good crowd of mainly children and men had gathered. My room was the gatehouse, next to the road. It was whitewashed, about 4 by 3 meters, and was bare except for a number of small lizards. One of these creamy-colored creatures had died in one corner and become a feast for hundreds of ants. At the back was a long-drop toilet and tap. Sliding windows with bars faced the street and the police courtyard.

I was left alone and, using a bowl, washed from the tap and changed. Those who had been locked out now peered through the outside window, which was high for most children but eye level for the men. I assumed they would soon leave, but an hour later I was starting to feel like a caged animal. Eventually one bold kid realized that he could slide the window open from the outside, and I then had a windowful of faces shouting questions at me, chattering to one another.

A guard had been put on my door and initially he tried to shoo my tormentors away, but soon gave up. After another hour the door was unlocked and I was told to follow the guard. In the main courtyard sat a ring of policemen chatting around a table. A young and very goofy-looking teenager introduced himself as the son of the captain, who was away. It was clear that he was there to translate.

"What is your name?" one asked. "Are you American?" another asked, and was immediately corrected by the men in the escort who had seen my passport. "Are you married?" the first man asked again. They didn't ask anything more interesting and instead laughed and talked. It could have been about anything, but their manner made it seem as though it was directed at me.

"Can I sleep somewhere else?" I asked the captain's son. "The children will not leave the window." My excitement at having someone to communicate with soon evaporated. It was clear that he was in awe of his police friends and wasn't going to speak to me to undermine that. I asked him twice more before an answer came back, straight enough: "No."

More laughter.

"Can I please get some food? I must go to the shop."

"There is no shop open," he mumbled, to more laughter.

I was merely their entertainment for the evening. After sitting for a further five minutes, forgotten in the background, I decided I needed to get food. I'd seen a number of shops on my way in, so I got up and walked off. This got their attention. The boy called after me to stop.

"I have no food," I repeated.

Three police were sent with me. The tallest, in his twenties, seemed embarrassed by his colleagues' behavior and tried to say so, speaking in broken English. Like the pied piper, our small group grew, and in the few hundred meters to the shop the street literally filled with a following crowd. This time there was no door control and as soon I walked in the shop was rammed with people. At the counter I quickly bought a box of rice and a number of unknown savory bakeries. Pausing at the counter, I took my camera, stretched my arm above my head, and took a photo backward. A snapshot of the mayhem.

Back in my room I was left alone, but not on the outside. The kids' confidence grew as the police's enthusiasm to deter them waned. A constant slideshow of small faces accompanied my dinner of fiery rice, which, incredibly, had been served on a cardboard Tesco quiche box. As I sat there writing up daily stats and notes in my logbook, some kids started to throw small stones in. There seemed to be less of them now but the same few kept coming back. "Hello, how are you?" they shouted, over and over again. "What is your name?" My attempts at engaging them in conversation to satisfy their curiosity succeeded only in doubling their number and noise.

It was easy to understand that a child in this closed world would be fascinated when a white man cycled into town. What I could not understand or forgive as easily was the policemen, who also kept opening the window and gawking at me.

I needed sleep, so finally I determined to ignore them. A faint light filtered in and I could only see the kids' faces by the light from my head torch. I was sure that when they couldn't see me, they would soon leave. I had just crawled into my sleeping bag when the court-yard window opened again; it was a red-haired older guard who'd been the main jester earlier. He had decided to show me off to a new face. I jumped up and slammed the window shut. They didn't open it again.

A few hours passed. I lay on the concrete on top of my broken therma-rest, awake, the odd stone hitting my sleeping bag. My head was covered and I was sweating, trying to ration the little water I had. I had flashed my head torch up a few times to see the same faces staring in. I felt wretched, and frustration was taking over.

I got up, without much thought for my actions. The faces shrank back onto the street but I put a hand up, beckoning them to come closer. The oldest boy looked about twenty and I had noticed him encouraging the others earlier. He moved boldly toward me. I struck forward with an open hand, catching him around the side of the head, cuffing his ear hard. He jumped back with a yelp and fell to the ground. I blew up my rest again and lay back down, ashamed of having lost it. They didn't come back again.

For all its challenges, day one of five to Lahore was over, and I was on target.

The Indus is described as the lifeblood of Pakistan. From its source in the glaciers of Tibet to its delta on the Arabian Sea, the river covers a distance of 2,000 miles and supports most of Pakistan's agriculture and industry. I was now following it north.

There was a delay before setting off when the Levvy pickup wouldn't start. It was 7:30 but already a large group of kids were standing at the open gates, staring. The policemen again tried to put my bike in the back and drive me, but the time for diplomacy had passed. They backed off and, after a few angry words, drove out. As I followed them out of town, I once again took some blind photos over my head of the kids running and cycling after me.

Within a few kilometers the pickup started tooting its horn and the men gestured for me to go faster. I plugged in my music and ignored them. Five minutes later the pickup appeared beside me. The red-haired man was in the passenger seat, pulling a face and signaling to cycle faster. The pent-up frustration exploded inside me and I threw on both brakes as hard as I could. The bike skidded to a halt and I threw it onto its stand. The vehicle pulled up and the three men got out.

"No escort!" I bellowed at them, pointing back toward their town. "Go, go! No police!"

They looked stunned.

"You should be ashamed!" I continued, not really thinking about what I was saying. "You are an embarrassment to Pakistan and so are many others in your force."

They had no idea what I was saying but I'm sure the message was clear. I had cycled into Pakistan over a week ago in awe of these rugged armed men. I now had no respect for them.

Without another word I mounted and cycled past them. They followed, but at a distance, and I never saw them again. The message was evidently passed on as after the patrol changed I was left to my own devices and only saw the police when I stopped. Only at the end of the day did the last patrol come up and sit on my wheel for a while before stopping me. "We must go now, it is late." He was a large officer with a fantastic mustache and a name badge saying Mohammed. He stepped forward and gestured that he wanted to put my bike in the back.

There had been ample time since my blow-out that morning to regain my cool and I went through the old routine, pointing at the globe on my shirt, then at the bike. "I must cycle, thank you."

Mohammed and his men stayed behind me for another minute, then drove off ahead. I cycled on, wondering what had happened. After ten minutes I saw the pickup pulled up on the left by a large shed and car park, and a number of other police vehicles were parked nearby. I suddenly realized it was six o'clock and they were here to break their fast for Ramadan, the ceremony that takes place during the ninth month of the Islamic calendar. That is why they had suddenly insisted on giving me a lift, and been annoyed when I'd refused.

My patrol men seemed surprised that I had got there so fast and gestured for me to sit down with them. A long mat had been spread with dates, nuts, and sections of banana. After saying a few words they all started eating hungrily and encouraged me to join them. One had a huge black beard, and I noticed him watching me closer than the rest. I caught his eye, and he slowly lifted his hand to his beard and nodded his head. There was no doubt, and I felt a burst of pride: he had just complimented my beard. That made up for any previous insult.

That night I stayed in a police station in Tarind Muhammad Panah. I was shown into an office on arrival where a gray-haired, clean-shaven man was talking sternly to a couple of men. I prepared myself for another testing evening.

"Sit down, please," the officer said, turning to me with a smile. "You must be hungry," he added in perfect English. He took a few notes out of his pocket, called a man in, and sent him for chicken fried rice and some tea.

It turned out that he had traveled to London and Canada, and he asked about my travels and told me about his family. "They would not give me a visa to travel to Canada to begin with," he explained, shaking his head. "I have worked for the police force here for thirty-two years." He sat back proudly. "I have a family here—why would I want to leave and run away?" He was great company after the trials and scorn of the last days, although I couldn't help but feel slightly uncomfortable as I sat in his office eating dinner in my Lycras while he sat there half doing paperwork and chatting while picking at a bowl of dates on his desk.

After my meal he told me about the regions of Pakistan and their cultural differences. I was most intrigued by how each had its own headdress—something I had noticed. He pointed out the picture on his wall of the founder of Pakistan, Muhammad Ali Jinnah, and explained that his picture was only ever on the walls of the boss's room. The man in the picture had on a woolly-looking hat that was only worn by the ruling classes. This and a shalwar kameez, the baggy trousers and long shirt which I often saw, was the national dress of Pakistan. I learned that the common man most often wore a sindhi, which looks like an embroidered cotton skull cap, except each region had a different shape of cut at the front.

"How have you been treated by the police?" he asked.

It was a loaded question and I decided on an honest answer. "I could not have got here without them but they have made it very difficult as well. I realize that they do not understand what I am doing and they have treated me badly at times."

He sat back, looking despondent. A man walked past the half-open door and he gestured toward him. "Most of them are idiots and animals—it is a problem," he said, then changed the subject.

I admired this man; he seemed to be a born leader in a troubled world. From his resigned tone I detected a lifetime of patience, an educated and rational man who had given himself to lead selfish thugs.

I was shown to a room next door and given a string bed. A large fan kept me cool overhead and I slept well. I remained on target for Lahore: day two down, three to go.

I'd woken at two a.m., my stomach in a knot of pain. I'd bolted out into the courtyard and along to the toilet just in time. This was the first of half a dozen runs to the long drop before 6:30, when I got up. At 6:50 the pickup was ready outside and the guards wanted to go. The head officer wasn't there to explain, but I could not leave without food. I sat on my bed, with ten minutes to wolf down the rice, take some Loperamide—a general-purpose antibiotic—and one Imodium for my upset stomach and push the bike out. I felt weak after a night of diarrhea and my stomach still ached, but just three more days and I could stop in Lahore.

The next day was terrible riding, 100km of rutted roads and lots of roadwork. I turned off the main road to Multan to avoid the city and having to cycle two sides of the triangle.

By the end of the day I made it back onto the main road, now on the section between Multan and Lahore. Right on the junction where the roads met was a hotel and the Levvy gave me no choice but to stop there. After shouting abuse at me for the last five hours they now wanted to stop for photos and to have my address to keep in touch!

I was expecting the police guard to remain, but they just left me.

The rush of excitement that I felt surprised me. I felt like jumping around and celebrating my freedom but instead stood there staring and smiling insanely, long after they had disappeared. I hadn't realized how much I had been bottling up the pressures; the sense of freedom was immense. I was still sick though. The Imodium had done its job but I was suffering from having pushed it through food poisoning. I didn't feel like it but I knew I needed to eat.

The hotel looked as basic as the ones I had stayed at in Quetta and Jacobabad and I quickly washed before going for food in the restaurant. There I was met by Mahmud, the sixty-eight-year-old caretaker, who ended up joining me for tea after I had eaten some rice. Mahmud was looking after the hotel for his younger brother. He had a full head of gray hair, was tall for a Pakistani, thin and well dressed but casual. When he spoke, he looked straight at me and pronounced his words slowly, in perfect English—the presence and confidence of a lifetime. My immediate impression was of a man who thought far more than he said, and meant exactly what he did say.

After I answered him briefly about where I had traveled from, he started telling me about his travels when he was my age. He had driven to Europe three times and once all the way to Britain, where he toured Scotland and visited Glasgow. It was bizarre to be sitting in the middle of the Punjab talking about his memories of walking down Sauchiehall Street and seeing the shipbuilding on the River Clyde. "I used to be able to drive through Afghanistan and Iran without any problem too," he added, "but that is all changed."

His company and conversation were wonderful and I wished I could have spoken longer, but my stomach was sore and eventually I needed to excuse myself to go and be ill. On the way out Mahmud reduced my bill by 125 rupees.

I woke the next day with mixed feelings about my new freedoms. As I packed up and had breakfast I half expected the police escort to turn up. To my surprise I almost wished they would, only so DP who would meet me that day could film part of this important chapter.

It was flattish, easy riding all day and I covered 102 miles in a speedy seven hours, no doubt helped by the huge morale boost of meeting David Peat, who was filming the last couple of days into Lahore. My dysentery had now passed and I could sense the end of Pakistan. By the end of the day we'd made it past the big town of Montgomery, where I was sorely tempted to stop, but continued to the village of Otara. I only had 130km left to Lahore. I had nearly done it. My five-day target was about to be achieved.

When I pulled up at the Hotel Avari, the most luxurious in the country, on Sunday, October 7, the first thing I did after getting off the bike, before even checking in, was call home. I had left the real Pakistan. Lahore is almost exactly 6,000 miles from Paris, so I was a third of the way around the world. Over the last miles into the city I completely lost motivation as I mentally unwound after weeks of absolute focus. All the suppressed pains, like the saddle sores and the legs and neck, suddenly seemed much worse than they had been before. Having worn the same top since Iran, I was absolutely filthy too.

The place was a palace, the nicest hotel I have ever seen. This would have been a strange luxury in a normal situation; after a few weeks of police stations it was insane, and I marveled at every pristine detail.

I'd made a good start on the minibar by the time DP knocked. We had two days to get a lot done, and my first priority, which was maybe an unnecessary luxury, was to get rid of the beard. It was a great beard, and made me look as local as I ever will, but shaving it off was almost a symbolic gesture: I'd come through the wilderness. DP was very up for hitting the streets of Lahore to find a barber with a wee street stall to give me an open-razor shave, but I was somewhat relieved when the concierge organized a car to take us to a professional barber shop instead.

I hardly recognized myself. I had lost a stone and a quarter (8kg, or 18lb) in just a few weeks. A checkup and blood test the next day showed that I was fighting fit apart from a few low reserves, but I needed to put some weight back on. I spoke to Ruth the nutritionist and Niall the sports doctor back in Scotland, who both expressed concern at this rate of weight loss and encouraged regular energy and fat foods. I could not have eaten more in those two days to make up. DP did a great job of trying to keep up with me as we sampled every one of the hotel's numerous restaurants.

On the first day off we didn't leave the hotel once. On the second day I ventured out to service and fix up the bike with the new tires DP had brought out from Scotland. Later I got a taxi into Lahore for an hour to see a bazaar and get a sense of the city. It was mayhem. I have never been in a street with so many people.

I'd always known Baluchistan was going to be a tricky area. It was difficult, but the dangers were different from what I'd expected. Rather than the things the police were protecting me from, the difficulties were in fact the police themselves for most of the time. The contrast between Iran and Pakistan was huge. Geographically and physically the cycling was very similar: it's a big flat desert and you've got the same challenges finding your food and water. But the people changed, and the culture changed hugely, and with that the reception I got. On top of desert riding, with the heat, the sand, and everything else, sat the emotional burden of the feeling of resentment I got and, I suppose, the isolation. Many of the police I'd been in the hands of in southern Pakistan had acted like I was a waste of time and a freak.

It had been a shock to the system, and I was glad to be through. I took five minutes to call and thank Nasir, whom I had never spoken to but who had arranged everything between Mum and the Pakistan police. I couldn't have got through without him.

11

The Avari was not the real Pakistan, it was a ridiculous world of luxury with poverty on its doorsteps. This reality hit me hard when I left Lahore. I was wearing fresh Lycra for the first time in weeks, had lost the beard, was well fed, and felt as though I had recovered. I no longer felt part of the landscape and culture, but like a Western tourist for the first time. It took nearly an hour and a half to leave the city and get to the Wagah border crossing.

The elaborate border-closing ceremony on both the Pakistan and the Indian side is world famous. I could see where this happened— there was a tiered seating area for spectators—but when I arrived it was business as usual. I was taking photos of no-man's land when I noticed a guard was watching. I cycled past the small border hut on the Pakistan side and heard him calling. Guiltily hiding my camera, I wheeled back and walked into a small, dim room. A hundred meters later I did the same for the Indian authorities. Both were some of the least official border controls possible.

The simple wooden desk in the Indian office looked like a heavy old kitchen table, and a single naked bulb hung low overhead. Apart from a few pictures the walls were bare and dirty. The guard here was as welcoming as could be. Sitting on a border post all day every day must get very mundane, but he seemed genuinely intrigued with what I was doing, asking questions even after stamping my passport until I made my excuses and left. I found it strange that there weren't more people waiting to go through but didn't want to ask why.

The short ride into Amritsar was a joy, taking in all the new sights. India immediately seemed different from the Pakistani Punjab, though the changes were hard to define. Perhaps it was just more organized. It seemed busier, people everywhere, regardless of town or country limits. Small differences were the most amusing, like the vast number of hugely overstacked rickshaws. The traffic was definitely denser but the roads were the best since Iran.

Everyone who goes to Amritsar visits the Golden Temple. It is the heart of the Sikh community and one of the most extravagant symbols of identity ever built. But I spent my time in Amritsar trying to buy an Indian SIM card and then trying to change $200 in a bank, whose security guard carried a twelve-bore shotgun. Useful for shooting rabbits, but I hoped he knew what would happen if he tried using it in a bank.

I had slept for only four and a half hours the night before in Lahore, and I was soon suffering. My left Achilles was also giving me twinges as I settled back into the bike. By the end of the day I realized that in India the words "restaurant," "hotel," "resort," "palace," and "pub" are interchangeable. This caused much confusion. Many roadside cafés were called hotels but had nowhere to stay. I ended up pulling up at a simple white "resort," set back from the road. Its banner would have looked more at home in Florida. Inside was a large hallway with a huge stone spiral staircase but there was no one at reception. The place looked deserted. I called, then shouted, and was about to give up when a young man appeared. The prices seemed expensive, at least by Pakistan standards.

After wheeling my bike up the stairs, I was happy to find a simple, decently sized room. Mum had again sent out a huge selection of food and I was reluctant not to take it all, so I decided to make use of the stone floors and well-ventilated en suite by setting up the camp stove and making couscous. Halfway through boiling the young man reappeared with a solid knock at the door. After closing the bathroom door, and making as much noise as possible to cover the sound of the jet burner, I answered. "Thank you, I will not need dinner." He looked puzzled. "But I might come for tea after." Then I closed the door quickly.

Over the next few days I raced southeast toward New Delhi. India continued to surprise. I realized that this was as much the result of a comparison with what I had come from as a reaction to the place in isolation. It was certainly far more developed than I'd expected. I passed Sikh men in smart suits and turbans driving SUVs and luxury cars. Each town had the sort of shops that suggested an entrepreneurial market with more than simple needs catered for. I hardly felt like I left towns all day: each blurred into the next, and the volume of people as well as the general standard of living in the Punjab were impressive. I passed what looked like very organized, productive farms, utilizing the high labor supply. I could also feel a much stronger Western influence. It was so refreshing to see women riding motorbikes and people walking down the street hand in hand and everything not seeming so censored.

My favorite discovery in India was the abundance of awesome vegetarian food. I had not consistently eaten vegetarian since Europe. Back in Scotland before I left, Ruth, my nutritionist, had taken me to a number of restaurants offering cuisines of the countries I would visit and set up meetings with the chefs so I could be taken through the types of food I would encounter. Ruth then explained their nutritional value to me, and this now proved very useful.

The good food showed, too. I was flying. Day two in India I rode 205km in just under nine hours on the bike. This was the perfect start and showed how fast my body could recover when pushed.

Cycling along one more open stretch, I was amazed to see the golden arches a few hundred meters up ahead and decided I needed a pit stop. McDonald's is my hell, but it does provide an international, free, clean toilet network. Before I got there I spotted an elephant walking up the road. I had never seen an elephant before. It was amazing—just an elephant walking along the road. It was much smaller than I'd imagined. This one had paint on parts of its face and ear, and decorations around its neck. It moved very slowly, in a steady lollop, and I stood off to the side of the road as it was led toward me by a young man and boy.

I assumed it would walk right by, but the man raised a large stick as he drew near and led the elephant off the road and to a stop right in front of me. I didn't know what to do, so raised my hand to say hello. The man smiled back and pointed at the elephant, then at me. He then walked around to the right shoulder of the animal and pointed up onto its shoulder, then at me again. He was asking if I wanted to get on. I didn't know what to say, but it seemed too good an opportunity to miss.

The young man took the initiative and raised his staff, resting it on the elephant's forehead, and pointed at the ground with his free arm. To my amazement, the beast slowly bent its front legs, got onto its knees, then lowered its hindquarters as well, until it was lying on the ground like a dog. It was now too rude to refuse, so when the boy beckoned me toward the tail, I went over. A rope snaked down the animal's back and looped under its tail, and the boy gestured for me to hold it and pull myself up. Most people are smaller than me, but this boy and the older friend were especially small, and not just because they were standing next to an elephant. I felt ungainly and huge as the boy pushed my legs then feet up and I clambered onto the beast's back.

I grew up riding horses, but an elephant with a simple cloth saddle is somewhat different. Straddling this vast back certainly opened up the hips and it felt like a very strained yoga move even before we rose, shudderingly and unevenly. Once up, I laughed nervously, like a big excited kid, and looked down at the beaming man with the staff. From my passenger's seat (I was under no illusion that I was in control of this thing), I looked forward to a very bony and surprisingly hairy head. I never knew elephants were hairy, but this one had tufts of wiry black hair shooting straight up.

It got up, then it started walking. Firstly the left shoulder disappeared under me and I rocked forward and to the left alarmingly. It was too far to fall without injury and I grabbed the back of the saddle, my knuckles scraping Dumbo's tough leathery hide. Then the left shoulder appeared again, just in time for the right one to go, and I shot front right suddenly. It was like the slowest bucking bronco imaginable. But at least on a bucking bronco you can catch your balance when it comes up quickly before going the other way. On an elephant, there is no such recovery.

We were off, to the amusement of everyone who passed at the roadside. After a minute, once I got used to compensating for the elephant's leisurely stride, it was actually going well. But it was painfully slow, and I had no idea where we were going. I decided it was time to thank them and get back on what I had previously thought to be the most uncomfortable mode of transport.

We had gone all of 100 meters or so but it felt like an epic journey. As Dumbo bent both knees and fell forward I slid down his left shoulder and back onto terra firma with a bump. I had managed to snap a few wonky photos from on high, and I now took some of the elephant men with Dumbo. There was no point in acting all cool and not the excited tourist, like I usually would. It was an elephant! They seemed to want nothing, just a handshake and my thanks, but I felt a bit awkward about this so gave them some money—not much, but it was gratefully received and I sensed it had been the right thing to do.

The adventure left me starving—I'd only had some leftover couscous and a packet of fig rolls for breakfast—so I cut back by a few hundred meters to a roadside stall where I thought I might find lunch. At the entrance to the McDonald's car park was a big menu on a placard and I was astonished to see that it was mostly all vegetarian. Of course, I had almost forgotten: most Hindus and many Sikhs are vegetarian. At last, a McDonald's where the veggie burger rules! I marched in and feasted.

After this I sat on the bike for a solid three hours, energized and far less sleepy, then stopped at the next McDonald's for four more veggie burgers and chips and some ice cream. This is the only time you will ever hear me endorsing them, because they were the last I saw. McDonald's will remain the dumps for me, except in the Punjab, where they are damn good.

That afternoon I focused on getting to the town of Ambala. It was incredibly fast, on perfect roads, and despite the astonishing volume of traffic I again passed the magic 200km mark. That came rarely, only when all the factors converged: good roads, flat terrain, a tail-wind, no niggling muscles, good food, rest, and nothing to delay me en route. But you normally suffered for them the next day, so it was important not to get carried away with the momentum of a good day. A 200km day had little value if it was followed by a 140km recovery ride.

A small boost that day was that there was some harvesting happening in the area and lots of old combines were on the road. On a flat stretch I could happily spin at 22 to 24km/h. These harvesters all seemed to travel at about 28 to 30km/h, so for a few short sections of about 10km I managed to speed up as they overtook and sit on their tail. In their draft I could happily go at their speed. It probably only happened for a total of 25km but they were fast miles, which provided a psychological high point.

At 180 rupees, Neel Kanth was a very cheap hotel, and with good reason. I lifted my bike up two flights of stairs then ran back for the bags before being shown into a tiny bare room overlooking a busy junction. The noise of incessant horns and people trading flooded in through the window, so I closed the shutters to try to find some peace. Having not washed for long sections in Pakistan and Iran you would think by now I was used to this feeling, but I felt really grotty. It was not good old dust and dirt; this was a day of breathing in truck exhaust fumes, and now I was stuck in a small pollution box. I needed space and peace and I usually only got that when asleep, but the constant din was enough to send a man insane. Only a few days in and I already craved silence, if only for a few moments.

I slept terribly and struggled to focus on the road the next day through the eye strain and skull-splitting headache. However, when it gets tough, the most important thing is to keep going even more than usual. "At least if I stay on the bike I am covering ground," I kept saying to myself over and over. It was an obvious statement but it needed saying when every impulse urged me to curl up on the road-side or check into the next hotel I saw. After a rubbish first few hours, I'd fought through and started flying. In the end it was another great day, pushing 190km. And there was no reason for it not to be, despite the traffic: it was very, very flat and the quality of the roads continued to amaze me.

I had long dreamed about my 18,000-mile odometer. Along with the bike, it would be one of the great artifacts from the expedition. That morning, this dream was crushed. I had not actually chosen my master cycle computer, which was a corded unit attached to the right side of my forks, and my mechanic in Edinburgh had picked up a unit with a 10,000km limit, instead of 100,000km. The mix-up took a minute to work out when I went to complete my log at the end of the day and the odometer read only 146.7km. This meant I had to add 10,035.93km to every day's total in the written logbook from now on.

After four hours' riding southeast, like the previous days, I turned left, off the main road, to cut north and around New Delhi. I knew the big city would delay me massively, and from there I was cutting due east anyway, so I might as well skirt the city and then pick up the main road east. The change was immense and it was immediately much slower going, with narrow potted roads, especially through the many villages.

From the turnoff, for about 10 miles I had the company of two young brothers on their motorbike. Most bikes slowed as they passed me to have a closer look, and a few tried to chat, but this was the first time one had stayed with me for so long. Their escort helped the time pass. Meeting them was my first insight into this generation of highly skills-educated Indians with very little life experience. They were engaging, well mannered, and interesting, but had never had the opportunity to travel beyond their area.

If all went well I knew I would be finished with this section of small country roads in a couple of days. It was like cycling into a Rudyard Kipling novel, through sections of jungle with monkeys everywhere. I stopped at one point to film men using oxen to dredge silt out of the river, whipping the laboring animals up the steep banks as they pulled heavy trailers of sand to be used in construction proj-ects. The silt is a mixed blessing, providing regular enrichment of the soils but also building up and blocking channels and filling up the river courses, making flooding more likely; but then the floods spread the silt and fertilize the land.

It was hot, averaging 32 degrees but hitting 40 at one point. But it wasn't nearly as muggy as I had feared India might be, and the light and shadows were magical as I moved through tree-lined avenues and twisty forested parts, then into open farmland, with small fields being worked by hand or cattle.

This detour allowed me to see the real India, rather than just the highways, but the downside was there were very few roadside places to stop. I didn't pass any shops for hours and by late afternoon was very hungry, and feeling weak for it. By nightfall I made it to the town of Muzaffarnagar and was again determined to find the correct road out of town so I would be facing in the right direction in the morning, to avoid a frustrating small-town traverse.

I was now out of the Punjab region, and therefore out of the main Sikh area. Most of the rest of India is Hindu and I had seen evidence of this all day, having passed many small colorful shrines. It was only on reaching Muzaffarnagar that this seemed unusual. There was some sort of big Hindu festival on and I had to literally walk across town, pushing my bike in the stationary traffic. It felt like a particularly wide load in such close quarters. The traffic was barely moving at all, but this didn't stop men from sitting on their horns. The sound was incredible.

Through asking people, I finally found myself, slightly irritated, on the east side of town. The last man I asked for directions was a rickshaw driver who, instead of replying, beckoned me to follow. I had not asked for accommodation but he took me directly to Raj Mahal, a tiny guesthouse almost invisible from street level, hidden on the top floor above a restaurant. I dared not take my eyes off the road, so I would never have looked up to see its faded sign on the second floor. The cyclist asked me for nothing, so I assume he got paid for bringing in business.

Despite having not asked, this was exactly what I wanted, and a good step up from the pollution box in Ambala the night before. After washing with a small plastic bucket from the cold tap, I descended one floor to a hearty vegetarian meal of my new favorite, shahi kofta with vegetable fried rice.

I could hear the festival sounds outside and went out for a quick explore before an early night. I desperately needed another big sleep as I was finding these Indian roads exhausting. Maybe it was the level of concentration required. The streets were poorly lit and still insanely busy, despite it being late evening now. No one hassled me, but it didn't feel totally safe, and I was intimidated by the incessant volume. Local music blared from tin speakers attached high on lampposts, and the crowds were like fast-flowing rivers that had to be navigated carefully; you had to spot the far bank a good distance before exiting so you could forge your way across. Before long I came across a small central area decorated and ready for ceremonies, the only such space around, but it was at that point empty. It was all amazing, another world I had underestimated that would take serious time to explore. But I was exhausted and needed my room, above the maddening crowds.

The following day was the second of my cross-country traverse around New Delhi and was very warm. At the end of the day I was surprised that my watch told me it had been an average of 30 degrees, although it had hit a toasty 43 degrees at one point. I realized that the main reason for the uncomfortable riding was that it was now getting increasingly humid. I knew that a lot of muggy wetlands lay ahead, not to mention the jungles and expected monsoons in Thailand and Malaysia, but after the dry heat of the desert of Baluchistan this new type of heat was going to take some getting used to.

It was another very exciting day in terms of the world I was passing through. It was wild, vibrant, untouched India, the bits tourists don't get to see. However, in terms of the roads it was suddenly like being back in Kurdistan, constantly slow going and wheel-jarringly broken. Through a number of towns it was unclear if the road had been dug up or never properly built as it went from broken tar to rutted mud with banks of loose dirt which caught the front wheel, and was like cycling in porridge. On one country section I passed a team of twenty men digging up the tar by hand with pick-axes. They stopped, stared, then shouted and waved at me, with the same workmen cheer you find the world over, happy at their tough job, perhaps because they had one another. All day I passed donkeys, cattle, and horses pulling carts of local produce, mainly high piles of a green, stalky crop which the driver would sit on top of, holding the reins and a long whip. But by the afternoon, despite this most beautiful of worlds I found myself in, I had resolved to get back to a highway as soon as possible and stick to it. These minor roads were simply too unreliable, and though I might have to do extra miles, it didn't matter. What did matter was the speed with which I covered those miles.

Late in the afternoon I got back onto the highway, and turned left toward Calcutta. It was already more developed but was slow riding. Though less potholed, the traffic levels were immediately tenfold, and I was still some distance away from the nearest town when dusk started to fall. I felt dirty, sore, and tired after a day of navigating ter-rible roads. Then, in the midst of an industrial sprawl, I saw ahead some high floodlights so bright that they made the surroundings look dark. Until I drew close, I assumed it was a big factory. What appeared were the pearly white gates of a five-star hotel. Its entrance had high pillars above symmetrical curved driveways that enclosed a huge fountain. It looked incredibly out of place. I struggled to see what purpose it served, considering the standard of living I had been traveling through.

My next decision was instinctive and slightly out of character: I turned in, drawn to the light. Out of the wilds I now felt twice as dirty and disheveled. "Let's just find out what it costs," I told myself as I left my bike with a slightly wary-looking parking attendant. It looked magnificent next to a deep-blue Range Rover.

I jumped two steps at a time up to the entrance area, a canopied courtyard where the driveways met the front door. The doorman, who wore a funny hat with a feather and a jacket with tails, tried and failed to hide his shock as he scanned me from head to toe in my grubby Lycra. I was obviously not their usual clientele.

I clattered in my cycling shoes across the polished marble floor. The pretty receptionist had a far better poker face. "Good evening, sir," she said, smiling.

I smiled back, aware of the dirt on my face. "One room please?"

"Certainly, sir, our standard rooms are $150. Will that be OK?" This question was soaked in genuine doubt, as if I might not have realized I wasn't in a motel.

"Yes, thank you," I replied, and handed over a Visa card. "Thank you, sponsors," I thought to myself.

Rarely in my life have I shown such extravagance. It had cost all of $500 in cash to get through the whole of Iran and Pakistan, ridiculously below budget, so this did seem like insanity. I felt like a mischievous kid. My last few motels had looked fit to be kennels, which made this place seem even more lavish. It didn't make sense to make the trip as tough as possible, but this was opulent; there was no avoiding the fact. Still, the same place in Europe would easily cost five times as much (as I tried to justify it to myself), and it was bang on 160km—perfect. I caught myself laughing aloud as the bellboy scurried after me to the lifts, pushing a trolley full of dusty and battered pannier bags.

The room was vast, and gilded in gold paint. I looked back at the line of dirt my shoes had left across the cream carpet. The room had a chandelier and one of the biggest beds I have ever seen, dangerously high with silky ivory-colored covers. And of course there was a minibar, most of which I devoured in the bath, the nuts, chocolates, crisps, and soft drinks lined up along the edge. I had no idea what I was celebrating, but it was amazing fun. Dinner was bizarre because the hotel seemed so empty—not surprising considering where it was. I was the only one in the restaurant, which meant that the five waiters were embarrassingly attentive.

It was the perfect opportunity to get online for the first time since Tabriz, a month ago at the start of Iran, and I sat in the lobby after dinner tapping away happily while tucking into chocolate gateaux on sale from a small coffee bar by reception.

On day 71 I woke feeling like a new man. It was a hard place to leave though, and once gone, having wheeled out after a vast buffet breakfast at nearly nine a.m., I kicked myself for not being stricter. I met a Swedish couple during breakfast, the first white people I had seen since entering India, and the first blonds I had seen since Europe. I found myself watching them with fascination, which gave me a small insight into what it must be like for these Indians to see me. I wasn't going to miss the chance actually to speak to people and they seemed as keen to chat. The husband explained that this town was one of the big industrial centers in northern India and that he came over a few times a year for metalwork business. His wife then piped in that this was a new hotel; the rest in town were terrible and she had refused to come before this one was built. At this the long-suffering husband nodded. I left them to it, and tucked into my smoked salmon and omelette.

Highways were now the way forward, despite lacking the amazing scenery I passed on the minor roads. I averaged 23km/h that day and covered 181km, despite the late start and often broken roads. The roadsides were almost all flooded, so there now seemed to be even more bodies crammed onto the roads, with a constant path of walkers down each side. Many of these were women with large bundles of crops or twigs balanced on their heads. When the road got too broken it was often easier to leave it and bump along the walkers' path as it didn't have the same broken edges as the tar, despite being uneven. Just a few hours into this heavy traffic and once again I felt clammy with matted hair, the hotel a distant world. By evening it was like it had never happened, and I was forced to ride into the night, unable to find anywhere to stop.

Riding at dusk in India is not just dangerous with the many bikes and vehicles without lights. Swarms of bugs came out of the flooded fields at the roadside. In the growing darkness they looked like dense clouds and caught in my hair and beard. I clamped my mouth shut and snorted out a couple that threatened to be inhaled. It was a great relief to find a motel in the middle of nowhere and get inside.

It remained incredibly flat, which was helping the mileages. A 75-meter ascent that day made it the flattest since leaving Paris. The following day was the same, pipping this tiny total by 5 meters. I managed another 180km, but it was tough as the legs were feeling it from pushing such big miles the previous day. There was no cruising, and it was exhausting riding on these constantly changing and manically busy roads.

The previous day I had made it to the town of Bareilly for a late lunch; on day 72 I pushed a similar morning mileage to Sitapur. The main difference was the increasing humidity, and just before Sitapur the heavens opened. I should have seen it coming, but as it hadn't rained since Bulgaria I had almost forgotten what it was like. Here it was very warm and almost pleasant, except for how it turned the fine silt on the road into very slimy mud, which slid the wheels about and splattered into the mudguards until they were blocked up and the turning tire rubbed as if I was riding with the brakes lightly on.

From Sitapur I set my target for the day to the town of Lucknow, the capital of Uttar Pradesh, the most populous state in India. Later on, and still miles from the town, I hit its suburbs, which told me it was going to be an even bigger place than expected. This made me nervous again, for I'd have no choice but to cycle in at night. The traffic soon got very dangerous and I was pushed off the road completely a couple of times.

Looking at the map and imagining I was coming into the town at nine o'clock, I could see the road I wanted actually cut out at about one o'clock. So when I passed what looked like the turnoff for a ring road, I stopped and asked. It wasn't shown on my map, but the thought of missing the town center on a ring road at dusk was perfect. The first man didn't understand me, the second wanted to sell me some plants he was holding, and the third confirmed that this was a ring road. I wasn't convinced, so I asked a fourth, a truck driver, who agreed emphatically as I pointed north and repeated, "Gorakhpur?"

Getting back onto the slip road proved tricky given the flow of traffic. Once I was on it I saw that it took the form of a narrow walled flyover—a scary gauntlet to run—before opening up on the far side into a two-lane highway. The only challenge was that it looked far less likely to find somewhere to stay in these outskirts. Then again, there was no chance of camping where it was so populated.

After a few miles a teenage boy on a bicycle, whom I had just over-taken, pulled alongside again. This had been a recurring game over the last few days: boys on bikes would race and overtake me, then pedal away until they tired, whereupon I would steadily catch up and overtake again. Sometimes this happened two or three times before they gave up and stopped hopscotching me. However, this boy caught up and stayed with me. This had also happened a few times, and they mainly just stared at me for a while before drifting back. But this boy started talking. His English was broken but I did manage to ask him if there were any hotels ahead, to which he responded in the affirmative, by the road off to Gorakhpur. Perfect. After a few kilometers I signaled that he should go on: it was far too dark and busy to ride two abreast. He didn't seem to understand this and simply pedaled on, barely looking where he was going, chatting happily as I strained to understand.

Like most people I had seen in India he was riding a Hero bicycle, with its single speed, steel frame, sit-up-and-beg style, and pulled-back handlebars. Hero seemed to have monopolized the market with these traditional steeds, mainly because they would go on and on, maintenance-free, for ever. Huge billboards for HERO CYCLES were painted on farm buildings in the most rural spots, miles from any other advertising in the towns. These bikes were everywhere, and ridden by everyone. They seemed classless, which is saying something in a country like India where the caste system seems to manage the whole society.

The ring road was a lot quieter than the road I had left but was still used at every speed possible by laden rickshaws, pushed by their owners because they were too heavy to cycle, trucks, and cars. As it was a bigger town, there also seemed to be fewer animals on the road. There was still the odd "holy cow," a wandering beast that seemed oblivious to its locality and was free to roam wherever, often across roads, because of its revered status in the Hindu faith. Throughout my time in India this never ceased to amuse me. It seemed utterly bizarre to come across a big cow lying in the road, lazily chewing its cud, as the traffic drove around it. It was such an odd juxtaposition of tradition and faith with modern technological life and education. Still, I have no doubt an Indian would find "normality" odd on a visit to Scotland.

My new friend tried to ask me another question as we continued to cycle along, but I could not understand. I had just managed to find out that it was only a few kilometers to the turnoff that I wanted. I turned to ask him to repeat his query. As soon as I saw his face I knew something was wrong. I'd taken my eyes off the road for only a second or two but it was too much. My front left pannier crashed into the back of a moped and my front wheel was thrown right, and before I could even hit the brakes I hit the boy on his bike. My bike crashed down on its left side and I sprawled forward into the road. I hardly hit the ground before jumping back up, still running forward with the momentum. I stopped and turned to see that the moped had fallen off the road and the driver had been thrown off. The boy on the bike also lay on the road but right in the middle, our bikes next to each other. My mind raced. I hadn't even seen the moped, and I remembered looking up the road just before turning to the boy on the bike and it being clear.

The bag that had hit the moped was lying on the road. I picked up my bike quickly, immediately checking the wheels. They were fine, running straight. The other riders were also now on their feet and I walked over to the boy, who was limping badly. I hoped it was just a dead leg, but even in the late dusk I could see blood on his knees.

It took a moment to click: the moped's lights were off. Then I noticed the dirt track that joined the ring road. All of a sudden it made sense. Without his lights on I hadn't noticed him at the roadside. He must have pulled out without looking. I began shouting angrily at the moped driver, who was picking his vehicle up. Amazingly, the engine was still running.

The boy was definitely in a worse state than me, walking around with a limp and holding his right arm at the elbow. Both limbs were moving, though, and I took that to mean they weren't broken at least. He and the moped driver were now talking to each other in Hindi, so I walked over and picked up the boy's bike. He immediately came over and took it off me. "Thank you, sorry, no, thank you." He seemed embarrassed. I had knocked him off but he was acting like it was his fault. He wheeled the bike forward but the back wheel was completely locked and skidded along the ground, as if the brakes were stuck on. But it was more serious than that: the crank, the metal rod attached to the pedal, was completely buckled into the back wheel.

I struggled not to stay angry with the moped driver. Of course it had been an accident but it was now almost completely dark on a busy road and I just wanted to move on, leave this behind. The boy and I tried to pull the crank back by hand, then turned the bike over and tried to hit it straight with a rock. Nothing worked; it was thick steel. He was at least limping less now and kept uttering apologies and saying he was OK. The moped driver had in the meantime disappeared back down the side road without a word of apology.

In the end there was nothing I could do—his bike needed to be fixed properly—and after about ten minutes I went over to my own bike, which I had left on the curb, and tried to fix the pannier back on, only to find that the bracket along the top had snapped on impact. Trying to suppress the unreasonable anger I was feeling, I strapped it onto the back of the bike, under some bungees, as best I could.

The boy was going to have to walk home. I had no idea where he lived; it could have been miles. I couldn't help anymore, but it would cost him to get his bike fixed, and maybe go to the doctor, so I went and got some rupees out of my wallet and gave them to him. He was still acting embarrassed, despite being by far the worse off both in bike and body, and protested. I had no idea of the cultural etiquette, but the economic practicality was that I could better afford for his bike to be fixed and the accident certainly hadn't been his fault, so I refused to take the money back and said good-bye, shaking his hand and wishing him luck. As I cycled away I found myself shaking, furious that the incident had happened and feeling pain in my arm and knee for the first time.

I soon found the turnoff and went left. Within a couple of kilometers I hadn't passed anywhere except roadside shops and was getting worried, assuming the suburbs would thin soon. This was not ideal motel territory. And then I spotted it, off to the left, the perfect wee establishment. I was glad to stop. My leg hurt and under the car park lights I could see blood from where my shorts ended to my knee. I would have to ask them for ice.

The car park was half empty, and I left the bike in a bay by the door. The reception was deserted except for an old lady behind the counter who looked very bored.

"We have no more rooms tonight, sir," she said, barely looking up.

Surely not. "I need any room, please, I am on a bicycle."

"Sorry, sir, we are full this night."

There was no way of telling if they were actually full or she just didn't want to give me a room. I looked around and caught sight of myself in a mirror. I did look pretty rough, but surely that wouldn't make a difference. Apart from the blood on my leg, I just looked like a dirty traveler. And around here I probably looked like a rich traveler.

"OK, can you please tell me where the next nearest motel is?"

She looked up properly now. "No motel, but hotel back in Lucknow, on a bike maybe an hour."

My heart sank.

It was a horrid wee cycle. Not only was I hurting but I was going back and it was late and dangerous on these roads. I felt incredibly vulnerable as traffic thundered past as if I wasn't there. I pulled off and stopped a couple of times with the sound of an engine approaching from behind.

I was mentally resigned for a big ride back into town, so I was relieved to see, within fifteen minutes, a big hotel off to the left. There was a long pause as the receptionist checked room availability, then I was in, finished for the day. It was far more than I wanted to pay, but I didn't care. After locking my bike outside, I carried the bags to the room and peeled off my Lycras.

Road rash is what you get from the grater effect of tarmac on skin, and though mine wasn't deep, my right thigh was very tender. My right hand was also cut, despite the glove being intact. After a very stingy shower, I threw on some antiseptic cream and went for dinner. After an awesome buffet I felt much better and managed to take a phone call from BBC Online about the last week, as well as telling Base Camp what had happened.

The important point was that I was fine and the bike was fine; the only damage from what could have been a serious crash was a broken pannier fitting. The tops of the bags have two clips which secure around the top bar of the pannier rack. One of these clips had broken off along a 10-by-5-centimeter section of solid plastic, part of a bar which makes up part of the skeleton of the bag, which showed the force of the impact. I'd had to stop a few times because the bag fell off the back, so before bed I got out some superglue and tried to reattach the seared plastic.

At 184km it hadn't been a bad day, despite the crash, and I went to bed thinking of the young Indian whose bike and body had saved me from a much harder fall. I hoped he was OK and wasn't offended by my giving him money. It had felt like the right thing to do.

12

October 16 was a poor mileage day, mainly due to a swollen right knee but not helped by the roads. Lunch was brilliant. I stopped at a roadside restaurant, though the word is far too grand to describe these food stops. Like most of the others, this one had a wooden canopy and dirt floor. The eating was done on wooden benches, each a few meters long, and the cooking was done in huge metal pots on an open brick fire. It took a line of these pots, which were a couple of feet deep, to make enough tea and stews for the fifty or so people who were there. In the middle of this space was a man on a raised floor toasting pakora and unknown lumps of food in what looked like a meter-wide wok pan. Boys in their early teens ran the floor, back and forth with teapots and plates of rice-based dishes. All the customers looked like workers. This was no-frills roadside food Indian style, and it was superb.

I'd asked for a plate of whatever the wok man was cooking and he pushed four balls of food into the pool of sizzling oil before him, squashed them flat with his spatula, and sporadically moved them and turned them. After a few minutes he took a small bowl, scooped them in, then from a number of other bowls around him sprinkled on some chopped onions, mixed spices, and yogurt. Lastly he called for a spoon, sat it on the top like a spade in a sandcastle, and proudly handed it to me, reveling in the plying of his trade.

Late in the day a motorbike with two men on it pulled up. This too was a regular occurrence, but this time they stayed with me for longer than a good stare and a snap on their mobile phone. After a few kilometers nothing had been said; they just stared blankly at me, so I broke the silence. They were both middle-aged men, and the amusing part was that the passenger blatantly had no interest in speaking to me and was soon bored. However, for the driver, Christmas (or the Hindu equivalent) had come early and he beamed happily at me for over an hour. He was a local businessman, spoke good English, and despite the dangers and challenges of holding a conversation on these treacherous roads, I enjoyed having someone to speak to. At the next town he insisted that I stop and have tea with them. It was hard to say no, despite the slow afternoon.

After the crash and mayhem of the past few days I'd just wanted to hide away. I actually craved to be in my tent, a small space hidden from the real world, a familiar cocoon where I could recoup. All afternoon I'd watched out for any opportunity to camp out, but in four hours from lunch there was nowhere. There were people everywhere, and where there weren't people, it was flooded. So at nightfall I found myself cycling into the town of Ayodhya. I rode to the far side without finding a single sign for accommodation, so had to stop.

There was a police post at the roadside and I asked the officer where to go. I was by a busy crossroads and I suspected any instructions would be both unclear and complex. They were both. Option one was to go back into town and option two was a long way farther on. Lastly, almost as an afterthought, he pointed to a building a few hundred meters away, across the intersection, saying, "Or you could stay there." I thanked him and wheeled on, baffled by his monologue.

The road was packed with buses and people in festive mood. The building I had been directed to didn't look like a motel, more like a block of flats, with people milling in and out. There was no way to wheel my bike through the narrow gates, so I risked it and dashed in.

A man sat behind a desk in the busy but very bare hallway. "No, you can't stay here—not for tourists," he said. He pointed back outside and farther down the road, giving directions to a place nearby. People were sitting in groups around the buses and others were dancing to a radio blaring Indian music, while a number of stray dogs ran about. The streetlighting was poor, and in this busy, dark scene I felt very out of touch. It seemed as though everyone here was together.

The house I had been directed to looked deserted and I walked around in the dark, watching monkeys in the trees and finding three locked doors before giving up. It was completely dark at this far end of the street, except for the moonlight and my head torch. As I reached the gates again someone called from behind me in Hindi and I looked up to see an old man standing on a balcony on the first floor. He scurried down some outside stairs to the driveway.

"Hello, is this a motel? Can I stay here?"

He looked at me, very closely, obviously not understanding. He wasn't scary but the whole scene was spooky and I felt uncomfortable, so I simply smiled, waved, and cycled off, glad to be back by the junction, out of that strange street.

Not quite knowing what to do, I went over to a boy sitting on his rickshaw. He hardly spoke English but seemed to be saying that a motel was close. "OK, I will follow," I gestured, unwilling to submit to any more lost wanderings. We went back past the bemused-looking policeman, and I resigned myself to the fact that we were now heading back the way I had come. But we soon took a left fork, onto very quiet back streets. In the dark, under the odd dull street lamp, over broken roads, I followed the rickshaw for what seemed like ages, but was probably only 3 or 4 kilometers.

I had completely lost track of where I was, when he finally turned right toward a grand but dilapidated house which I would never have found alone, and which bore no sign. I thanked him with a tip and wheeled inside to find wide, empty corridors running the length of the building and a huge stairway. It looked more like a haunted school than a hotel, but for the bargain price of 600 rupees I was given a simple room with air-conditioning. AC always costs a few rupees more, but it was well worth it not to wake up in the middle of night sweating profusely.

From India I couldn't cross overland into Myanmar, Bangladesh, or China because of border issues; my only option was to fly for the first time. Flying is necessary and allowed by Guinness World Records rules, and this would be the only time the clock stopped on the circumnavigation. I had booked my flights between continents back in Edinburgh, months before leaving, but with full flexibility so that if I needed to I could jump on the next available flight whenever I arrived at the end of each leg. At my current speed, and despite all the bad roads in India, I was on target to get the exact flight I had booked all those months ago, on Tuesday, October 23, for I had a week and about 700 miles to go.

The thought was exciting, and it recharged my energy. Iran to

India had been an incredible adventure, but in terms of the race I couldn't wait to move on; I felt I had been in the wilderness for long enough now. Above all else I craved space. I spent every day surrounded by people, constantly jostled and on edge but rarely actually interacting. It was a strange feeling: I either wanted to stop and engross myself in the Indian way, or get out.

The next day, Wednesday the 17th, was day one of this weeklong plane-catching target, and it could have gone better. I had taken the decision at Lucknow to head slightly farther north than planned, to Varanasi, to get away from the terrible traffic. Often out of mobile contact and with texts coming through in piles, I was left to make this decision without a conversation with Base Camp. While succeeding in finding quieter roads, before long I found myself in an area hit recently by huge floods with makeshift shelters down each side of the road. After 140km there was no option but to stop at the town of Gorakhpur. Close to the border with Nepal, Gorakhpur is famous as a religious center, home to many well-known historic Buddhist sites. In more recent times it has become a business center.

It was only half past four, but it was now getting dark at six p.m. and I was told by a number of people through the afternoon that there was not another town and motel for another 120km. This was hard to believe, but enough people echoed the fact, and camping didn't seem wise. Once again I had been cycling below sea level all day. Even if there had been space I would have been nervous about camping in such potentially malaria-infested swampland.

Day 75 on the road went better, and I hit the magic 160km. It was a strange one, though: lunch was taken after 120km, and then I stopped for the day just a few hours on. It was therefore a long morning, but the saddle sores felt much more bearable after a superb rest. The people I'd spoken to the day before had been telling the truth: after the constant towns and villages since New Delhi, it was 120km until Gopalganj. The morning was very eerie, riding through thick fog in a swamped forest. The tall, branchless trunks rose out of the dark water and disappeared into the clouds, like hundreds of pillars supporting some dark world above me.

Breakfast had been rice ordered on room service the night before and was the best way to start the day—fuel for well-rested limbs before more tough but flat roads. A couple of times I stopped and asked people if there were towns ahead and where I could get food and water. Some didn't understand, a few said there were no towns at all to the east, and only one, a man pushing an overloaded Hero bicycle across a bridge, told me of Gopalganj. It was an incredibly poor area.

When the trees cleared, I passed mile upon mile of shanty-type housing down the sliver of dry land on the side of the road, surrounded by marshland. It was unclear if it had always been this way. I wondered if there had been some natural disaster, maybe a flood, which had pushed people out of their villages. But it seemed possible that this was actually the only long-term solution available to the chronic population problem, that people's only options were to build branch-and-sheet-plastic shelters that protruded onto the road. Their beds and cooking stoves sat on the edge of the tarmac and their children ran about barefoot and barely clad, oblivious to their situation. They seemed happy, but it is the side of India you will not see as a normal tourist. This was not some urban migration issue, large shanty towns of disenfranchised families looking for the better life; this was in the middle of the countryside, a population forced to live wherever there was dry land. A population at saturation point.

Near the end of the day I grew worried. I had not passed a single possible place to stay all day, not even in Gopalganj, and I was experiencing some of the most broken riding yet. The road was deeply rutted and the trucks lumbered along at walking pace as their suspension struggled to deal with the deep troughs and ridges. On a bike I could at least wiggle a smoother line, but it was slow going. The language issue meant that I was in the habit of asking the same question to a number of people, just to confirm facts. Again I stopped a number of times late on to ask if there was anywhere within cycling distance I could stay. The first few said no, or didn't understand, and then a few gave me a confident no.

I had almost resigned myself to a long evening's riding and a tough night sleeping out when I got a positive response. "No hotel here, but there is motel," said a young man on a bike, looking eager to help.

I could have hugged him. "How far?" I asked.

"Not far, maybe five hundred meters."

I had been expecting him to say 15 or 20km. I could see at least half a kilometer ahead, and it didn't look promising. However, sure enough, within a kilometer I almost passed a shabby building on the opposite side of the road at the start of a tiny hamlet called Sembhuapur. It was a motel, and an army of young boys, all less than ten, were sent out to help me lift my bags up some stairs to a very bare concrete room—a cell of a room, with a padlock on the door, but there was a bed and it was dry. I was hugely thankful that I wouldn't have to sleep at the roadside after all.

While writing my log by head torch, a boy came back, lit a mosquito coil, and placed it under the bed. There was no window and, like a few of the places I had stayed at, no mains electricity; the generator was only run for a few hours once it was dark outside, and until the guests were asleep. There had been a few times when I had gone to sleep cool with a huge fan swirling overhead and then woken up in the middle of the night in a pool of sweat. I had thought my last few nights at about 600 rupees a night were cheap, but tonight's was 200 rupees—a bank-breaking £2.68.

Rice and dhal were now my Indian staple diet, to be found in every kitchen. For the third time that day I tucked into some double portions and then had a dessert of three packets of dry biscuits and a few cans of Coke before bed. All for £1.30.

I woke suddenly. It was still pitch-black. I could hear that the hum of the generator had stopped. But there was a new noise. A scratching at the end of the bed, followed by a light patter. Wide awake now, fully alert, I lay there straining my ears and eyes to make it out, unsure if there was someone else in my room. I picked up my glasses from the floor as quickly and quietly as possible, switched on the head torch (I often slept with it wrapped round my left wrist), took my knife from my right pocket and flicked it open, and sat up.

Nothing. But then, as I looked right, toward my pannier bags next to the wall by the door, I saw something moving fast. A large rat jumped out of one of my bags then down the space between them and scurried along the wall. I jumped up, closed the bag, then sat back down, staring around for a moment, experiencing a mixture of relief and surprise. My door was closed and the only way into the room that I could think of was up the long-drop toilet in the corner. It was a disturbing thought, but there was nothing I could do about it, so I went back to sleep.

I felt really groggy in the morning, having slept badly, occasionally woken by the rustling of rats. I'd slept on the right bed of two singles pushed together, and as I sat there eating a packet of biscuits I noticed something on the left bed, near the foot. While I was asleep, rats had been pooing on the mattress right next to me. They had to be fresh as there had been a sheet there; during the night I'd pulled it off most of the bed, leaving the mattress showing. There was a scattering farther up the bed too, and then I spotted some at the top, right next to where my head had been.

Putting this awful night's sleep behind me, I wheeled out early. Before leaving, the young boys again helped me with my bags. Once laden up, I turned to them. They were standing in a group along with some older teenage boys, watching in awe as I clicked the ratchets on my cycling shoes and pulled on Lycra mitts. I wanted a photo with them and to give them each 10 rupees as a thank-you for their help, but when I beckoned them all over to set up a photo with the bike, the oldest boy called them back. I have no idea what he actually said but it seemed clear: "Do not go over to him, do not trust him, he is dangerous." I immediately became very self-conscious and embarrassed about the situation. I wanted to explain but had no way of communicating my intentions, so I put 40 rupees on a table at the side, pointed to the boys, waved, and left.

After 80km, the perfect morning on less than perfect roads, I stopped at an A2 service station. I had seen a number of these and was intrigued. They are India's answer to motorway service stations, with loud yellow billboards and all the normal chain identities that we are so used to in the West. However, apart from McDonald's, this was the first I had seen since leaving Europe. Despite the shiny outside, I was almost relieved to find another standard roadside food stop inside, with park-style benches and the same options of rice, dhal, and whatever else they had cooked that day. There was no generic menu or tacky packaging, and I was relieved at how average it was.

By the time I reached the larger town of Muzaffarpur my saddle sores seemed to be worsening. At 3:30 p.m. I realized that I had a big push to make the only town shown on the road signs. Digging deep, I did more than 25km/h for the next two hours, which was only possible because the roads improved. I felt incredibly burned out wheeling the last bit in the dark to Dalsing Sarevi, but I'd managed to cover 171km in ten hours.

It then took a while to find somewhere to stay. I was eventually directed to an unmarked resthouse that from the outside looked as bad as the rat hole. But I was shown to a great room at the end of a long corridor, simple but clean; it even had paint on the walls. The landlord was very excited to have me stay and bounded happily ahead of me, then showed me around the room, pointing out and naming items of interest for my benefit: "Chair, TV, toilet . . ." I suppressed my love for nouns and managed to keep a straight face until I'd subtly shown him out.

Over the next hour he returned a couple of times, first to ask if I needed any laundry done and then to offer food. When I did leave a while later to explore and find my own dinner, I turned around after five minutes to find him right behind me. He didn't speak enough English to make a joke out of it, so I tried to act as if this was normal and walked on. He actually came in useful when it came to choosing dinner, from very dark pots at a street stall. The food was served on a plate made of dry leaves, which my guide insisted on both buying and then carrying. My room was £3 and dinner was £1, but his hospitality was priceless, and I left him the money I owed in the morning on his desk with a thank-you note. I don't think he would have asked for payment.

That night I transferred all the data from my cycle computer onto the laptop—something I had to do every ten days to free up memory space—and realized that I had crossed another milestone: 7,000 miles. It felt like much more than that since Paris, seventy-six days ago.

By day four of seven to Calcutta, I was still on target for Tuesday evening's flight but not making it easy for myself. A few 180km days would make it much easier. At this rate I would be left with 100 miles on the Tuesday, then have to find the airport, box up the bike, and get my flight. This was my first transfer. I didn't want to be riding into Calcutta in the dark and I wanted as much time as possible to take the bike to bits—assuming the box was waiting for me.

On that subject Mum had had to deal with many issues. I had made contact with a Glasgow University alumnus who lived in the city and assured me that a ready-made bike box would be almost impossible to come by and that large bits of cardboard were in short supply. Many other options had been discussed, from getting a bike box flown out to getting a wooden one made, which included getting a quote from a joiner. This seemed over-complicated, and there were concerns about taking a pile of untreated wood into Thailand, so I reverted to plan A and insisted that there must be some way of finding a pile of cardboard I could use in Calcutta. The friend of a friend who had put us in touch with Ali in Yazd (Iran) came to the rescue again with a contact for a haulage company based at the airport. After weeks of frustrating dead ends on what seemed such a simple task, this was now sorted, and they promised Mum I would be met at the airport with anything I needed.

Under different circumstances it would have been the perfect day, again, bang on 160km in seven hours and fifty-three minutes. But it added pressure for my push to the end of leg 2.

For most of the day I was plugged into some audio books which I had not got around to listening to since Heather, my sister, had sent them out to Lahore on a memory stick. This was a miracle since I only had a 2GB iPod and had listened to music on loop every day. Lost in Bill Bryson's *A Short History of Nearly Everything*, I headed for a resthouse near the town of Naugachhia. I had set this as a target all afternoon. With so many people around all the time, the whole day was peppered with snatched conversations which added up to a pretty good overview of the areas I was passing through and a good sense of what lay ahead.

Only a few kilometers out, two men on a motorbike started up the same conversation for the umpteenth time. "What is your name? Where are you from? Where are you going? Do you like India? Why are you here? Are you married? How old are you?" And so on. No question seemed off-limits and I was getting used to their familiar way. Brits normally get awkward and bashful after a couple of questions, but in India there is no such problem and I would often have long conversations which felt more like interviews, despite every effort to ask questions back. However, once we had got over the initial standard set of questions I did manage to ask about the rest-house ahead and was told in no uncertain terms that it was not good and I mustn't stay there. "You must stay in Naugachhia," they told me. "It is the same distance, with good place to stay. Follow us." So I did.

By the time we entered town it was getting dark and I had followed the motorbike onto a side road, over a railway line, and back in the opposite direction. We had also picked up quite a following while moving at walking pace through a packed main street. By the time we pulled up in front of a big white building with a metal fence in front of an empty courtyard, there was a huge crowd around me and it was an effort to stay calm. It was utterly claustrophobic and I was surprised at my instant need to get out.

It turned out that the resthouse, if that is what it was, was shut. At this point a young man pushed through the crowds. He wore a smart shirt and dark-rimmed glasses, and looked educated. "Hello, can I help you?" he asked in perfect English. I explained that I needed to find somewhere to stay, and he smiled broadly. "I will show you, follow me." The men on the motorbike looked put out. A few words were said, and then they pushed through the crowds and disappeared. My new guide turned back to me and introduced himself as Dhraj.

We walked back to a small square I had just ridden past. Sitting in a wide circle outside a small shop were about fifteen men. Dhraj introduced them, and each shook my hand. "These are my uncle's and father's friends," he told me. "Please stay here with them and I will find you a room." The crowds that had been following me kept back: it was obvious that the men in this group were respected as elders in the town. None of them spoke English though, so I sat in silence for fifteen minutes, taking in the scene and drinking tea. Apparently there were rooms here, just above the shop, but the owner was away.

After another fifteen minutes he still hadn't returned, though Dhraj had. I protested that I must go on, it was getting late. It was now Dhraj's turn to look put out and he immediately came up with another option. I followed him through a number of tiny side streets to a 100-rupee guesthouse—half the price of the rat hole. The room was dark, dirty, unbearably humid, and smelled dank. The bedsheets were damp to the touch.

Dhraj seemed a nice enough guy, if slightly overexcited, and I accepted his offer of helping me to find food. His enthusiasm was very well meant, but I couldn't help the gut reaction of wishing I could hide away, far from this constant attention and human contact. It is hard to describe, but it gave me an insight into what it would be like to be a top celebrity. No one really seemed to stop and think about the net effect of their behavior. It was charming and friendly, but its constancy was a lot to take in.

I was touched by Dhraj's friendliness to a complete stranger, but I

felt resentful of being paraded through the streets like he had discovered me. He waved cheerily at everyone he knew, calling
comments in Hindi loudly about me, beaming like a kid with a new
dog. First of all we went to his father's cloth shop and then on to his
house, where I sat in his room and drank tea. He slept in a big double
bed with his older brother and was studying English at the local
town. His dream was to study for an MBA and go to work in a hotel
in Calcutta. "There is nothing I can do here. My friends will all have
to move away." In the kitchen-cum-living area, his mother, younger
sisters, and young cousins were all singing together before having food. It was lovely, a sweet home environment, and a privileged
thing to be let into. Back in his room, the walls were stacked with
drums of oil and bags of grain, enough food for the family to live
on for months. Apart from that there was a simple bookshelf and
desk.

Dhraj seemed intrigued by all things Western and asked question
after question about culture, fashion, and education. I told him
about Scotland, the farm where I had grown up, and then about my
university years.

"Do you have a girlfriend?" he asked.

"No, I don't. I did when I was at university but she left me when I
decided to cycle around the world. Do you?"

"No." He looked embarrassed. "My father will arrange my wife
when I have a good job."

"Are you happy with that? Do you want to find your own wife?" I
was unsure if this was appropriate, but felt bold considering the
degree of questions I'd been asked.

"Love marriages don't work," Dhraj replied, looking at me
confidently, as if he was trying to explain something important. "A
man must provide the money and the wife must provide the family.
It is up to my father to decide my best wife. In America everyone
divorces, in India nobody divorces."

From the way he said it, it had obviously been thought through
and said before; it seemed too conclusive a statement to have just
occurred to him.

I sat back, unsure what to say next. "Not everyone divorces in
America, but I agree that people are less close to their wider families,
for example their parents. In Scotland we mainly do love marriages."
I used his phrase, but it sounded strange.

The conversation moved on, and after a while he walked me back into town and left me at a restaurant.

"What time will you leave in the morning?"

"Very early, seven a.m., but don't worry, I will find my way out."

"No, I will come and see you in the morning." He waved cheerily and left.

After his initial over-excitement, I had really enjoyed talking to Dhraj about life here, and his life to come.

Over dinner, a man in his midtwenties introduced himself to me. I was on my third bottle of Coke as the food was fiery hot. He told me he was doing an MBA and lived in the town. As the conversation developed his story started not to add up. Eventually his eyes dropped and he looked ashamed. He had been studying an MBA and had planned to go and work in Calcutta in a major hotel but his mother had become very ill and he'd had to come home and work to support his younger family. He was now taking over a shop along the street. He spoke perfect English, was well dressed, and had spoken initially with enthusiasm and charm, though his tone turned to resignation and regret.

After a few questions I decided it was too sensitive a subject to dwell on. I could see the pain he was in, how his dream was his pride and without it the fire for life in his belly was out. The parallels between this man and Dhraj were not lost on me. How different the generations were, how fragile their opportunities.

Just after seven I lifted the bike down the narrow outside stairs. I thought I would escape alone, but by the time I returned with my pannier bags Dhraj was there, flanked by three of his friends. It had been a bad night. There was no mosquito cover on the bed and I had been bitten badly down both legs and on the neck. I was on anti-malarials but the thought of these mozzies feeding on me at their leisure in the night was horrid. I had woken a few times to their shrill buzzing and in the torchlight managed to swat a few. They were both fat and slow, and the largest I had seen.

I probably looked very rough, but Dhraj and his friends certainly did not: dressed in their smartest clothes, hair combed, they looked like they had been up for hours. One friend was the designated photographer, and for ten minutes, until I insisted that I had to go, he arranged us in various combinations and snapped happy. Then each of them produced a piece of paper and asked for a message and autograph. It was all very sweet but, groggy after such a bad night, I just wanted to get going.

It was early Sunday morning, and I felt like the pied piper walking through Naugachhia. On the 500 meters through the main street to where Dhraj was going to show me the correct road out of town, it seemed everyone dropped whatever they were doing. Dogs joined us too, attracted, I could only assume, by my moldy musk. I felt like a very sweaty tramp after my night of discomfort.

Dhraj waved and shouted something to a guy standing at the road-side, then turned to me. "He is my friend. I told him about you but he didn't believe me. Now he has seen you." Dhraj beamed happily; it seemed he would now be a celebrity for the day.

At the junction, he pointed and explained that I should go straight, over the railway, and then turn left when I hit the main road, that there was no need to go back the way I'd come.

"Thank you for your hospitality, Dhraj, you have been very kind." I threw my leg over the saddle and then leaned forward to shake each of the guys' hands.

"We will miss you, Mark," Dhraj replied loudly. "Will you miss us?"

"Yes, of course." I smiled, then clicked a shoe in and went to push off. "Good-bye." I waved before clipping in completely.

"I love you!" Dhraj called loudly.

My head shot around in surprise and I stared at the group, waving happily at me. I cracked another smile and kept pedaling.

On the railway crossing the barrier was down, and it took five minutes for the train to pass. A number of locals had cycled out with me. One of the young boys, in his early teens, wheeled forward and asked me to sign a newspaper page he had. I took a fresh page out of my logbook instead and after a number of attempts trying to spell his name as he said it I gave up and wrote a short note instead, and signed. The barrier lifted and I turned onto the highway and put in a fast couple of kilometers. Gradually the followers fell off my tail. I was very touched, but I craved space.

There continued to be very bad sections of roads all day. At the start I was still pushing hard for Tuesday's flight; by the end, a smidge short of the perfect 160km, this dream was over. As bad as these main roads were, I was still just about managing the 100-miles-a-day average, but before Calcutta the highway I was on cut northeast slightly then turned due south, forming a loop of extra miles. The most direct route was due southeast, and I planned to cut across a 100km section on a small road from the town of Kora to Ingraj Bazar ("English Market"). After the bad roads around New Delhi I had asked Mum to research how good this "shortcut" would really be. The British embassy did everything they could but information was hard to come by and their report was that the road was there and passable but in an unknown condition.

I got to Kora midafternoon, still undecided on what I was doing, and then stopped on the far side of the town at the turnoff. The first section, as far as I could see, was a dirt road. Within minutes I had a large group of locals around me and I called out for someone who spoke English. Almost everyone said yes, but only a few men came forward to talk. The first one said the road was bad all the way to Katihar, a town halfway across the shortcut, and from there it disappeared.

I pulled out my map and showed him the road, clearly marked, all the way to Ingraj Bazar. But there is a massive difference between knowing the roads from personally traveling along them and being able to recognize features on a map—something you take for granted when you are used to map reading—so my map caused confusion and a lot of shouting and pointing. A second man said that there was a route through but it was very bad indeed, not possible with a truck but possible by bike.

I thanked the men, put the map back, and closed my pannier. As I wheeled the bike backward out of the group, they continued to argue. It was a tough decision because I had been so focused on making that flight, but in factual terms it was already made. There is no way I could risk that unknown bad road, and by continuing on the highway it was too far to go in two days. I called home and asked to change flights to the Wednesday.

By the end of that Sunday I was still 404km from Calcutta, in a strange government hotel on the outskirts of Rai Ganj. It looked like a tourism initiative, surrounded as it was by a nature reserve with many rare birds (according to the signs), but seemed completely empty. I got myself the best room in a week for 300 rupees. It was blissful because it was so quiet, and I felt strangely joyful as I washed for the first time in days, cleaned all my clothes in the sink, and then dined in a deserted restaurant on two huge piles of Chinese egg chow mein.

The pressure was off: I now had a three day target of just 84 miles a day. But Monday morning was so fast, on the best roads for over a week, that I started to beat myself up for changing the flights. At this speed there was a slim chance I could do 126 miles a day. Then, in the afternoon, the roads became ridiculously rutted and slow again, so bad that I had to push the bike over a few sections, and I finished the day on 159km. Switching flights had been the right call, but when left in your own company 24/7 the slower option is never an easy thing to live with.

The town I ended up in was one of the poorest I had seen, and its lifeline was obvious: everything on the right-hand side of the road, for over a kilometer, was a power station. Huge transistors and capacitors were lined up and power cables left the compound in various directions. It was therefore utterly bizarre that the town itself had no power. The guesthouse and every place I passed on the walk into the center in search of dinner ran on personal generators.

It is a very eerie experience walking through a place of such poverty at night, with people working away in the dark or huddled around sources of light and power in food stalls. One place I passed was a wooden shanty-style shed filled with people crammed around a small TV, watching a film. I stood by the back window and watched for a few moments before going on to find dinner. I have never shared my food with so many flies—the main downside of generating light in muggy outdoor places—and was glad to walk back, climb the stairs, and crawl under a mosquito net for a massive night's sleep.

For over a week I had been cycling until or into the dark to hit the magic 160km target. The roads were so bad that it had been taking all day. It was no fun constantly trying to find a place to stay in the dark, not to mention how bad the insects were in the late evening. The day before reaching Calcutta I decided to break this pattern, and it made for a much easier day. Leaving an hour earlier let me pace the day so much better, and I arrived in the town of Shantipur well before nightfall.

I was now so close to the end of leg 2 that every bit of focus was on getting to Calcutta and making my first flight. It would be a massive milestone. It was getting harder to care about the world I was passing through.

Unfortunately, after a brief stop I discovered I had a broken spoke (though, due to terrible roads, it could have been broken for days without me knowing). Needless to say, fixing a broken spoke the day before the end of leg 2 was the last thing I felt like doing. Amazingly, these wheels, built in a tiny shed in Poland, had lasted over 6,000 miles on the toughest roads without problems. It took as long to clean down the bike and de-gunk the chain as it did to replace and true the spoke.

Actually, a fire in my room was the last thing I needed. As soon as I put the lighter to the stove, a flame shot out and instantly the whole stove, the top end of the fuel bottle, and the table were on fire. I jumped back as the flames licked up and panicked for a second, thinking the bottle would explode any minute. Without really thinking I hit the stove with a pillow. It flew off the table onto the floor, where I hit it again, which put the fire out. I then had to put out the flames on the table. I sat back for a minute after that, heart going like a sprinter, thinking about the disaster that had just been narrowly avoided, then I started scrubbing away at the soot stains on the table with a wet sock. Luckily, the varnish had prevented the table from burning badly and the stove itself had weathered the beating it took well. I vowed to be more careful in future.

I couldn't even tell you what those last miles looked like, I was so transfixed on getting there. I had expected getting to the airport to be a challenge, but I had a clear run in and I arrived at lunchtime, and from there everything was arranged for me. I was to go to a hotel by the airport to shower and repack, then the freight company that had organized the cardboard for the bike box would come around and I would simply have to package the bike for the flight.

Unfortunately, it happened the other way around. I found that the hotel was closed for refurbishments and I spent ages asking taxi drivers and a few pedestrians for an alternative, eventually backtracking 3km to another hotel. There was no option but to spend 500 rupees on a room for the night, even though I would only be there for a few hours, until nine p.m. This was annoying but understandable.

I called the freight company. Despite saying that they had a box, it was very clear that they did not, and that it would be a real problem to get one that afternoon. Since the arrangement had been made over a week earlier, Mum had been in touch on two occasions to double-check that it was there and ready for me. The messages she'd received had always been positive—it was all taken care of. What I later learned was something which I had observed on a number of occasions throughout India but had never understood: that it is rude to say no.

I immediately got back on the phone to Scotland to try to sort out the mix-up, and after four hours two men did turn up, after having been sent into Calcutta to find cardboard, which I then had to cut up and tape into a box. I had taken the bike apart once before and it is surprisingly fiddly because of the mud guards and pannier cages. It is also huge, the sixty-three-inch frame and many bits, even in Tetris-style formation, making a large package. The hoteliers wouldn't let me do it in their courtyard or hallway, so it took over an hour to take apart and box the bike under a streetlight on the pavement in a busy street in north Calcutta. This caused quite a crowd to form, and it was quite an effort to ignore them and focus instead on keeping track of all the bolts and washers and in which order they'd have to go back on. Once it was boxed, taped, and then cable-tied by one of the men who had brought the cardboard, I felt pleased with my handi-work.

Two hours later, after a quick meal, repack, and twenty-minute nap, I called a taxi. Calcutta taxis are all yellow and 1950s vintage, with huge rounded wings and a small hatchback. The only option, after much head-scratching, was to wedge the bike box into the back and tie the boot down, with the box protruding by almost half its length. This hazard did not make my driver drive carefully. The only blessing of that taxi ride, during which my heart rate peaked for the day, was that it was over much faster than it should have been. We were at the airport in minutes. After all the mayhem of the after-noon, I was actually early.

Calcutta airport was nothing like any other international airport I had been to. It had a very local feel, more like a European domestic airport from a few decades ago. This surprised me for a major commercial center like Calcutta.

The flight to Bangkok was called on time and I made my way through from the waiting hall, expecting to find check-in desks. Instead I came to a security check first and duly put the pannier bags through the X-ray. I was checking only two bags on, taking another as hand luggage; the others I'd used to pad out the box, worried about how the bike would fly encased only in flimsy cardboard. The box just fitted on the conveyor belt, and I went through to pick it up when the man waved me on. Then another man standing by the X-ray screens called me back.

"You have an electric device and some fuel with your bike, sir?" he asked.

Shit, that sounded like an accusation. I tried to look relaxed and think quickly what he could be talking about. "I am cycling around the world," I explained. "My camp stove is in there, but it is empty and not screwed up for the pressure. But I don't think there is anything with an electrical current. What did you see?"

"There is a box in there with lots of wires and switches and an electrical current."

I realized then that he must be talking about the GPS tracker. It only had one switch on it and I had no idea what was inside it, as it was sealed, but I could understand how it might look suspicious. "Oh yes, that is a GPS tracking unit so that people following my cycle on my website can see where I am, but it is switched off. There is no current in it at the moment."

The man looked blank, and I was not sure he'd understood. "I will have to look inside," he said.

My heart sank as he took a knife from his belt, cut the cable ties, and sliced the tape along the top. The box was absolutely crammed, the tracker unit was at the bottom, and the ties were needed to hold the cardboard sides together.

I was now drawing quite a bit of attention. I tried to unpack as subtly as possible to retrieve the unit while standing in the middle of a busy concourse. The tracker unit is bright yellow, and under a lid is a small input port, a switch, a red LED light, and a small magnet. Every morning I would remove the magnet, which would turn the unit on, and the red light would come on. It is not a high-street commodity with clear branding and to a suspicious mind could easily look like a more sinister device, especially when packed in a box with a petrol canister. But there was nothing more I could show him; it was a sealed unit and it was definitely off. A tiny magnet being placed on top was not the most convincing on/off switch though, I had to agree. Thankfully, he finally believed me and I repacked everything. However, I now had an open box to check in.

"Do you have some tape I can close this with, please?" It was fair to assume this sort of thing happened sporadically.

"No, we have nothing here."

I protested, as politely as possible, that I could not check in an open bike box crammed with all my kit, and I couldn't go back to buy some tape as I was past security. The man had now been with me for over ten minutes, slowing the progress of the queue behind. His colleagues were getting tetchy and started to call him back over to help. I repeated my problem with more force, as he looked like he was about to walk off. Saying something into his radio, he simply said, "Wait here," and returned to his duties. Another guard appeared a few moments later with some tape which read "Security Checked." It was thin and flimsy and only enough to put two straps around the box and one lengthways down the seam of the lids, but it would have to do.

The check-in desk was across the hallway and I went straight to the front, relieved finally to be over the afternoon's many hurdles. I handed over my passport and tickets.

The man checked a list, looked at my tickets, then looked up at me. "You were on yesterday's flight, sir."

"Yes, I was booked on that flight originally, but this was changed earlier this week. I now have confirmation that I am on tonight's flight."

"Can I please see your confirmation, sir?"

I paused, unsure what to say. "I don't have it on me. I have been cycling and the change was made from the UK, but the confirmation is on my email account."

"I am sorry, sir, but you are not booked on this flight." He paused, then said something to his colleague, who nodded in agreement. "All I can do is put you on the waiting list. Can you please wait over there until everyone has checked in and I will see if we can find room for you."

I didn't know what to say. After everything I had been through to save time over two and a half months on the road I was about to lose a day because of some administrative mess-up. I sat where I was told for over an hour, feeling absolutely drained. It had been one battle after another since getting here and I now faced a night and a day of waiting in Calcutta.

The first and only thing I could really do was call home and figure out what had happened. Mum was as confused as I was, but immediately jumped into action.

An hour later the check-in hall was almost empty, apart from me with my trolley filled with bike box and pannier bags. I felt utterly dejected. Mum had called back a couple of times to see if anything had happened and I had been up to the desk to speak to the same guy to explain what I was doing and how important it was that I got on that flight. He had agreed amicably but explained that there was nothing he could do to help. Mum had just called back for the third time. It looked like I would have to get a taxi back into Calcutta to a hotel.

"Mr Beaumont."

I looked up. It was the check-in guy.

"We have a seat for you."

I could have hugged him.

Good-bye, India. I have loved your unique charm but I am not sad to go. You have certainly been a challenge.

Leg 3: Bangkok to Singapore

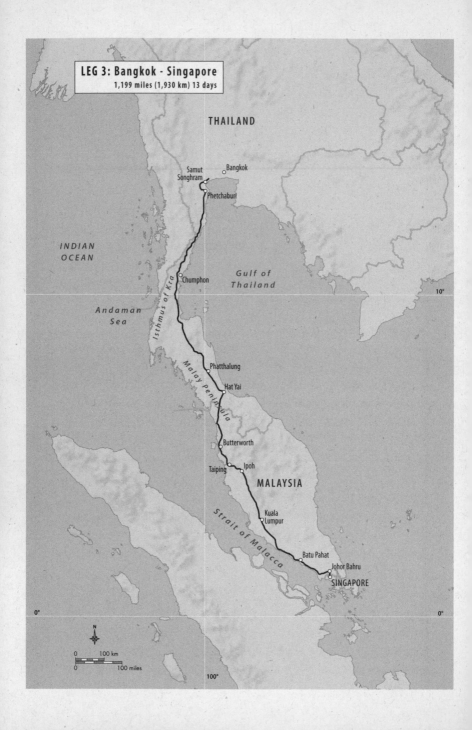

LEG 3: Bangkok - Singapore
1,199 miles (1,930 km) 13 days

THAILAND

Bangkok
Samut Songhram
Phetchaburi

INDIAN OCEAN

Isthmus of Kra

Chumphon

Gulf of Thailand

10°

Andaman Sea

Malay Peninsula

Phatthalung

Hat Yai

Butterworth

Taiping   Ipoh

MALAYSIA

Kuala Lumpur

Strait of Malacca

Batu Pahat

Johor Bahru

SINGAPORE

0°   0°

N

0   100 km
0   100 miles

100°

13

It was a restless flight. Trying to put the pent-up stresses of Calcutta behind me, I dozed briefly. Another distraction was my neighbor. He was an older Indian gent, with excessive gold jewelery and a linen suit. Soon after takeoff, and without introductions, he launched into a monologue about how much he hated India, its crowds and its poverty. This seemed highly contentious and I couldn't help but think him arrogant, with his Rolex flashing and his obvious Indian heritage. It turned out that he had been born in Delhi but now lived in Hong Kong, and that he was stinking rich, which was evident but he pointed it out a couple of times anyway. He had returned for the first time in years for a family occasion, which only reaffirmed his sentiments about the place. His off-by-heart speech did reflect some sad truths about India's poverty levels and demographics, but considering he was part of the top percentile in terms of wealth yet found it easier not just to escape but to talk with contempt of his roots, I found it a gloomy affair. I couldn't get much of a normal conversation going so gave up and tried to sleep.

I was the only non-Indian or non-Thai person I could see on the flight. After thousands of miles of self-propelled travel, the confines and speed of air travel seemed bizarre. The hostesses obliged me with a second meal but then apologized and declined when I asked for a third.

The plane landed as the first light crept over the horizon. Landing at this time is very special because you can see dawn from the air, and then you sink back into the night as the plane lands, only for the sun to catch up half an hour later. When I picked the bike off the carousel, it looked battered. Not having been able to reseal the box properly in Calcutta had left it with no structure, and bits of bike poked through on both sides. Hoping for the best, I pushed out of arrivals to be met by a friend of a friend's wife, a Thai lady called Toi, and her driver.

I had been so stuck in the moment getting through India as fast as possible that I hadn't really visualized Thailand, other than maybe landing at the airport. The changes were massive. Over the years I had always thought of my friends who backpacked in Southeast Asia as quite adventurous. It always sounded so exotic. However, while there are undoubtedly wild parts, this is defiantly still the developed world. The roads were superb and full of pickups, there was a 7-Eleven on every corner, and you could buy most of the familiar brands you would at your local shops. Thailand is incredibly Americanized, and coming out of the wilds of Iran, Pakistan, and India made this even more evident. I was constantly surprised by the feeling of being back in the Western world for the first time in months.

Bangkok is massive and would have taken half a day to navigate across by bike, so it had been decided to restart the race to the west of the city. Starting in the west also meant I didn't have to cycle westerly at all, and cycling in an easterly direction at all times was one of the most important Guinness World Record criteria. The airport access road was a busy expressway which bypassed Bangkok to the south. At dawn it looked an impressive cityscape, begging for further exploration.

It was already very humid. Even while standing my T-shirt clung to me. By the time I had pulled all the bits out of the battered cardboard box and put the bike together I was very sweaty and dirty. I was almost certain the bike would be damaged; it looked like it had been thrown about a lot. Another of the Guinness criteria was that the whole cycle needed to be done on the same bike. Inevitably many parts would be changed, but if the frame and whole bike needed replacing it wouldn't just delay me greatly, it would jeopardize the chance of qualifying for the world record. To my relief, the bike seemed to have survived. I already knew it was tough, and it had come out of that flight with evidence of bashes that would have crippled many frames. The only real damage was the front pannier rack, which had been twisted and needed to be bent back before its bolt holes would line up with those on the front forks of the bike.

I immediately realized that dehydration would be a real problem here. It had been humid in parts of northern India, but nothing compared to this. The temperature was in the midtwenties at most, which was much cooler than the hottest parts I'd cycled in Turkey and Baluchistan, but was much harder to bear, with humidity as high as 90 percent. The Southeast Asia I would be cycling through has a tropical climate. It is always hot and humid, and when it rains, it pours.

The western peninsula of Thailand, which I would be cycling straight into, stretches along the warm waters of the Andaman Sea. For the days leading up to November I'd be passing close to many of the famous tourist spots. The areas around resorts like Krabi and Phuket as well as the island of Koh Phi-Phi, where *The Beach* was filmed, receive over 350mm of rainfall in October, which drops on average to a still soggy 200mm in November. Bangkok and the north, which I wouldn't see much of, have a slightly dryer 250mm of rain in October dropping to a much drier 50mm average in November. Therefore heading south meant it would get hotter and wetter.

I was conscious of not holding up Toi longer than was needed. She had had an early start and I was, as always, grateful for the help. It took over an hour to build the bike, repack the bags, and quickly change. I felt wrecked and in no state to start racing for Singapore. Flying had messed up any balance left in my daily routine. As hard as it had been for the past few months, I could deal with the rigors of life on the road, but flying through the night and being dropped into this very different world to build the bike then go, go, go changed a lot of variables, and I felt completely thrown.

There was nowhere particularly iconic that I could find to start from and I ended up at a petrol station and coffee house to begin the 1,100 miles to Singapore. I waved good-bye to Toi and her driver in their luxurious white four-wheel-drive. If I was amazed to see this new world, what must I look like to them, I wondered, appearing out of the wilderness like some brainwashed Duracell bunny, obviously exhausted but manically keen to race on.

The roads were perfect, wide and smooth, the wind was behind me, and I spun the pedals lightly; but within minutes my head was dropping, eyelids doing that slow blink. It was like leaving Paris all over again, only much worse. After just a few kilometers I pulled in for a couple of energy drinks and some more food. It was such a novelty to walk into a service station and find shelves stacked high with a wide variety of products. No more small packets of dry biscuits and bottled water; I could start putting something back in the body's storeroom. It was a poor mileage day, but I was rolling. The bike was in good shape, and if the incredible tailwind kept up I had nothing to worry about.

In the town of Phetchaburi I was greeted by lots of monkeys running about the parks. Because it was the end of the rainy season in Thailand and Malaysia I had been advised not to camp, so was on the lookout for cheap motels. For the price of 300 baht (£5.50) I found the best room I had had since Iran, save that one night of ridiculous luxury in India.

My next challenge was food, and I walked into the center to explore. I passed a big group of students chatting around the gates of their college, and a couple of them spotted me. Two of the girls called across some pretty cringe-worthy chat-up lines in English followed by wolf-whistles from some of their other friends. I waved back, slightly embarrassed. It was all very lighthearted, but it was a shock after the lack of female conversation and interaction over the past months in countries where women just didn't have those sorts of freedoms. The girls could only have been late teens and wore short skirts and white shirts almost like a uniform. I was amazed by how shocked I felt at their public flirting. I actually felt intimidated, and rushed on.

Dinner was harder to come by than I had expected. Phetchaburi was a small town off the tourist trail, so the food was as authentic as it comes. I have always enjoyed Thai food, but like so many international cuisines it has been somewhat dulled down for the British palate. I like a good green curry and other subtle delicacies, but rustic food in Thailand tends to be less refined. I had found Indian food to be spiced with rich flavors; Thai food seemed to be spiced with fire. But at the time, I didn't know this. At an outside stall on a corner with a number of plastic tables and chairs I chose a mixed plate of rice and other undefined ingredients. I managed only a few mouthfuls of the very innocent-looking white rice before my eyes tried to escape my skull and I was sweating awkwardly. Plate one abandoned, plate two I managed to finish, but without a jot of enjoyment. The best part of dinner was the multipack of yogurt I bought from the 7-Eleven on the way back to the hotel. I was in bed by eight.

At seven a.m. I wheeled out again. It was now overcast and much cooler, and less humid, which was welcome. I felt fantastic, like my mind was starting to catch up with where my body was.

It was a phenomenal day. In just over seven hours on the bike I covered 201km at a stupendous 27.7km/h average. Any roadies reading this might be thinking this isn't that fantastic, but I would encourage them to try it with a bike weighing over 30kg. But I can't take all the credit: I was accompanied by a huge tailwind, and the morning was as flat as you could dream for. The afternoon threw up some gentle undulations, but they were a joy to cruise up at 25km/h and descend quickly. All day felt like cycling with a finger on fast forward.

Mum arranged with Toi for my cycle computer unit to be fixed, after it had died in the last few days in India. Her driver had been sent to meet me but ended up calling a number of times because he couldn't find me. He was miles past where he had expected to find me. Late in the afternoon he caught me with a look of disbelief on his face. I only had a 1,000 baht (£20) note to pay for the 400 baht repair, so he was delighted with the tip and happily waved me off on my way.

I ended the day well down the Malay Peninsula in the province of Prachuap Khiri Khan. En route I passed a road sign which denoted the narrowest part of Thailand, a mere 10.9km from the Gulf of Thailand on my left to the Myanmar land border on my right. I was amazed at how little English language there was in Thailand. Almost no signs were translated, and when I stopped to get food I found that people just couldn't understand me. I have never been anywhere that seemed so familiar in terms of brands and standards of living yet so foreign. Thailand is the only country in Southeast Asia that has never been occupied and administered by a European power.

Cycling into the tiny village where I stopped, I eventually spotted a building with an air-conditioning unit sticking out of every window and a small Thai script sign above the door. I thought it must be a hotel. It was.

I was on a complete high after such a big, fast day. The tall palm trees around the hotel seemed permanently bent with the prevailing wind. It was the direction I would be heading until reaching Singapore. The prospect of a thousand more miles of wind-assisted travel was hugely exciting and made all the other niggles seem very manageable.

One of these niggles was my left hand. Out of habit, I was aware of moving around my right hand on the handlebars far more than the left. Every time I used the video camera, my phone, adjusted my sunglasses, had a scratch, or anything else, it was with my right hand, and this habit was now showing. The weeks of bad roads had been punishing to each point of contact, my saddle sores being the obvious example, but my left hand was also now suffering from the constant trauma of judders to the palm area, and it now seemed that the nerve damage was getting serious. What had been occasional pins and needles was now prolonged periods of numbness, which meant that I had a very weak grip and pinch. This was fine when riding the bike, just a bit annoying; off the bike it was a real nuisance. It is amazing how limiting it is to lose the dexterity in even one of your hands. For example, it had taken twice the time it should have building my bike in Bangkok because I couldn't hold parts in place properly as I screwed them together. I called Fi, my physio, to figure out a cure.

Finding food was the next adventure. There didn't seem to be a lot of options as the whole village seemed to be along the sides of the highway over a couple of hundred meters. On the hotel side of the road I walked until I found an open roadside food place. In the central serving area there were a number of pots on a stove, and a small Thai lady serving into plastic plates; some people sat around on plastic Coca-Cola tables and chairs on the muddy ground. Most Thai women I had come across were small, but this lady was exceptionally tiny: I must have been nearly 2 feet taller than her.

Responding to my signals, she lifted the lid of the first pan to let me have a look. To begin with it just looked like a very thin gray soup, until she stirred it with a big metal ladle. In the swirling vortex some shapes floated to the surface which I immediately identified as some kind of poultry feet. They were bloated and podgy in the stew. There was no meat on them, just gristle. I smiled at the teeny lady and asked to look in the next pot. This one held what looked like chunks of pig. I say pig and not pork because most of it was either joints or sections of white fat and skin.

I gestured for a plate of rice with pig bits and a small bowl of chicken feet (because I couldn't not try them) and sat down to dine. The feet were not great, very tough with not much to them, and you had to nibble the gristly skin off the bone. It was how I would imagine boiled toenails might taste. It was the hottest thing I have ever faced. It must take years of conditioning actually to be able to taste such food, let alone stand the torture on the taste buds. Having numbed my mouth for the next 3,000kcal I still needed to eat, the pig bits were relatively palatable. I had by this point lost the luxury of taste, but its texture was how you would imagine medium-rare pig's fat to be, wobbly and smooth. I think the rice was also very spicy but I can't be sure as I was still in a pool of sweat and numb to the feet.

I couldn't finish either dish so went across the road to find another stall. The first waitress ran away after a minute of trying to communicate over her giggles. She joined a gaggle of giggling waitresses who spent the next half an hour standing at the back of the kitchen, pointing and gesturing. The man in charge didn't seem as excited to see me, and we eventually agreed that he should bring whatever he liked because we couldn't understand each other. Two small whole fish arrived, which I ate with difficulty off a skeleton of tiny bones. It had been a fun hour but I was glad to escape back to my hotel room, still hungry but having lost my sense of adventure for the evening.

When I woke I immediately went to the window and was overjoyed to see the trees still bending to the southerly wind. It wasn't quite such a fast day but I stayed on the bike longer to try to capitalize on the great conditions. After 210km I reached the town of Lang Suan, tired but euphoric.

But the last few days, while fast, had been frustrating. I was constantly passing brown signs denoting beaches, waterfalls, caves, and other stunning tourist sights within a few kilometers of the road. The sea was just through the trees to my left and had been for two days, but I hadn't seen it once. It was a place that promoted a lazier pace and every instinct wanted to turn left and spend a day recovering on the sand.

The thicker forests after the open ground or palm trees farther north helped to make it increasingly muggy. It was dry until late morning and I assumed it was just getting more humid until it suddenly started pouring, and then didn't stop for four hours. There was no point in putting on my rain jacket, firstly because it was so warm but also because the rain was so heavy that it would have been through in minutes. I was absolutely drenched, but it wasn't too unpleasant as I covered fast, hilly miles. The climbs were fine, but the descents were wild with so much water on the road.

I was now passing through thick mangrove forests into the Chumphon province. The town of Lang Suan got its name from the river I had crossed just before turning off the highway. The last few hours dried up and I assumed this would allow my clothes to dry as I cycled along. But the humidity didn't allow this.

I turned into a very simple-looking hotel. The sparse reception simply comprised a chair behind a wall of keys on hooks. The woman sitting there looked very bored when I peered through the window, but as soon as I entered she stood up and was delighted to give me a room. I cycled onto the courtyard of rooms set back off the road. The key wouldn't open the door, so I walked back over. Without a word she called out and a young man came through, took another key, and signaled for me to jump on the back of his motorbike. It was less than 50 meters but I got on and he sped down the path and stopped outside a different room. After unlocking it he stepped inside and walked around, as if checking everything was in place. I fetched the bike, wheeled it in, and took the key from him.

"Room OK?" he asked.

"Yes, thank you," I replied, expecting him to leave.

"You want me to organize message?"

I looked at him. "Sorry, what do you mean?" I wondered if he meant the internet.

"You want me to organize girl for message?" He looked straight at me, as innocently as if he was offering clean towels.

"Ah, a massage. No thanks."

I had heard about Thailand's liberal sex industry but assumed it was confined to red-light districts in major cities. This level of promiscuous opportunity in rural towns was a surprise, and I reacted strangely. I was fourteen when I first saw a lady sunbathing topless, on a Mediterranean holiday. I can remember blushing furiously and not knowing where to look. Here I was, ten years on, having made it through amazingly tough times in recent months and feeling like a man about it all, breaking into a crimson blush and quickly closing the door when a bellboy offered to organize a prostitute for me. "Pull yourself together, Mark." I laughed at myself and went for a cold shower—only because there was no hot water.

When I woke up on day four in Thailand I knew I had overcooked it on the previous two. My legs ached, and a niggling tightness down my left calf was now a completely locked muscle, which hurt when cycling and made me limp when walking.

The middle of the day was once again filled with torrential rain. At eleven a.m., like the day before, the heavens opened. It was pretty dramatic riding, cycling through some flooded dips in the road and bracing myself against the waves of water thrown up by passing trucks. The wet riding also didn't help the saddle sores. Apart from that it was beautiful, and I was constantly impressed with the passing landscapes. Thailand is stunning to cycle through, ranging from jungle landscapes to wide-open paddyfields. Pictures of the king and queen were everywhere on billboards at the side of the road, in shops, and in the media.

Every day I was also passing the most amazing statues at the roadside. At one point I saw a huge golden sitting Buddha on the hillside and a procession of costumed people came down the road banging drums and singing. They were carrying a big platform that looked more like part of a Chinese dragon festival or Brazilian carnival scene than anything I knew from the Buddhist faith. Regardless, it was an amazing sight in the rain. They seemed so happy and waved as they danced and marched by.

Compared to the last few days it was a fairly disappointing 160km, but considering how I felt it was a success. I felt much better the next day after nearly ten hours of sleep. It was increasingly muggy all morning, then it poured from lunchtime onward. After lunch I reached a junction to the town of Phatthalung to be told that the road ahead was blocked because of the rain. On the map I could see that it would be a long way around, so I stopped the next car that was driving back and asked why the road was shut. The problem seemed to be a big tree that had come down in the rains. I decided that I should be able to lift my bike over a fallen tree and carried on. As I got there it was being cleared but not before I had driven past 3km of queued traffic.

Phatthalung was both the province I was in and the major town I passed through 26km before the end of the day, just 120km from the Malaysian border. To the west was the Nakhon Si Thammarat mountain chain, which I could see in the distance off to my right. After 140km I had a quick ten-minute biscuit stop before heading through Phatthalung to finish on 188km. Somewhere in the middle of the downpour I crossed the invisible 8,000-mile mark.

I was glad to find shelter at the end of the day. The constantly wet shorts meant my saddle sores had now developed into open wounds, especially on the left-hand side. I was also worried about my left knee, which was twinging, and the muscle down the left calf was still locked. A very excited motel owner's son decided to show me across the road to somewhere I could eat and then called his sister, as she spoke better English. This was very sweet, but it was an awkward conversation, as neither of us knew why we were speaking to each other. But I was glad for the help with food: it was the best meal I had eaten since arriving in Thailand.

During the evening I got news from Scotland that the British embassy didn't want me to carry on through the border region of Thailand. I'd had no idea there were possible dangers there. This late revelation was a real spanner in the works and I spent the rest of the night making a chain of phone calls so we could decide what to do. The plan had been to carry on through southeast Thailand and then down the east coast of Malaysia. The east coast made sense to avoid the most mountainous roads of Malaysia as well as its capital, Kuala Lumpur, which had the potential to be very slow and dangerous riding. This route was now out of the question.

It appeared that the three southeast provinces of Thailand had renewed Islamic separatist terrorism in recent months. This was a little-reported issue which I had not factored into my risk analysis before leaving. In fact there had been four years of insurgency problems in the region, resulting in the deaths of more than 2,600 people. In the last three weeks a spate of small bombs had been set off in bars. The attacks targeting security forces and Buddhist civil servants had increased in October after a quieter period during the month of Ramadan in September. With over four hundred killings in the last six months the British embassy were now advising I use public transport.

By the following morning Mum had done a lot of research and we decided together that I could in fact carry on. However, I would have to change my route completely, cutting down the west coast of Malaysia.

14

By nightfall on day 87 I was safely in Malaysia.

Throughout Thailand I'd had constant problems with my cycle computers due to the rain. I rode with my Polar unit, which was a cycle computer as well as heart-rate monitor, on the handlebars and then I had a Cateye cycle computer positioned on the front forks of the bike. Since the first of the monsoon rains this had been misreading slightly, and the Polar wasn't fixed properly since its service in Bangkok. So far they had not misread at the same time, so the logbook had been kept straight, but on day 87 they both failed me: the Polar unit slowly faded as the day went on until I simply couldn't read the screen, and Cateye stopped after 123km. I was faced with the real problem of not being able to prove the mileage I had cycled for the Guinness World Record. Luckily, my GPS tracker showed exactly where I had gone with updates every two hours, and a border crossing that day was the best witness signature I could hope for, so I took the mileage from the map.

It was a bit of a late start the next morning as I fixed on the new cycle computer and tried to mend the old one. Three cycle computers would surely suffice. My remedy for the misreading cycle computer was silicon gel, which was a saddle sore ointment I used on the contact points. The Cateye manual warned of possible misreading in heavy rain and suggested using silicon grease on the contacts; I didn't have the grease, but the gel substitute seemed to work. At least it did during the morning's normal showers. After 78km it misread again for 12km through the heaviest storm, when the rain, doing its best impression of a waterfall, washed all the gel away. However, the new one kept working well.

It was nearly ten a.m. by the time I was off. I was about to turn on to the highway again, cycling out of Jitra, when a scooter pulled alongside with a big basket on the back. We stopped at the traffic lights and the man looked across at me. He had an open-faced helmet and was smiling broadly. "Where are you from?" he called out.

"Scotland."

"Come for breakfast."

It was more of a friendly order than a question and I didn't know how to explain that I was in a rush. "Where?"

"Very close."

The lights changed and I followed him. I hadn't eaten properly, so this was not a bad thing, despite the delay.

We stopped at a small food stall and he told me his name was Mat. He was a fishmonger, and his big basket was for carrying his trade. I thought that Mat was a strange name for a Malaysian but have since learned that it is an abbreviation for the Arabic name Muhammad. This little shack turned out to be his daily breakfast stop, and a familiar host fed us fish, eggs, and rice as we chatted about his work and my travels. He was charming, a worldly and knowledgeable man who had never traveled.

Until 1957 Malaysia was a British colony, and didn't exist as it does today until 1965. The British influence is everywhere. The two immediately noticeable changes when I crossed the border were that I was back in a Muslim state and that everyone spoke some English. Mat spoke excellent English, partly because he read newspapers and followed Newcastle United (the Malaysians have an obsession with the English Premier League).

After half an hour I had to leave, and he insisted on getting breakfast. He was off to the markets like he had done for thirty years and I was heading south toward Kuala Lumpur.

I didn't get far. After 20km a police car pulled alongside with its sirens and lights going. It appears you're not allowed on the expressway in Malaysia. I'd had an inkling of that, but I hadn't seen any signs. I came off at the next junction, which was a bit annoying, onto the old roads—a good thing as they were sitting there waiting for me. The policeman stopped me again and asked me where I was from. I said I'd come from Bangkok and he said, "Oh, very good." He obviously thought I was from Thailand, so I explained that I was from

Scotland. "Oh, a long way. Your English is very good." I didn't have the courage to put him right—it was well meant.

I hadn't researched any of the west coast of Malaysia, having planned on being in the east, so I quickly had to reroute without adding on too many miles. It didn't make sense to do any more miles than I needed to in the heavy rains. I was reluctant to get off this road as it was such fast going, but after a while I didn't mind the diversion: the smaller roads seemed fast as well and were proving much more interesting. This way I might get to see some of Malaysia. During the day I passed mile upon mile of paddyfields, the farmers knee deep, bent double, tending their crops of rice.

Early afternoon another man pulled alongside on his moped and beckoned me to stop. I was lost in my own world and reluctant to brake, but it would have been rude not to. The man pulled off his helmet with a huge grin under a fat mustache and introduced himself as David. "I was driving the other way and saw you and came back to find you," he explained happily. "Where are you going?" I told him about the world record. "Yes, I met another man doing that a few years ago near here." I didn't believe him, it was too unlikely, only a few people had ever gone for this world record. "Yes, I think his name was James or Phil, he was also from England."

"Did he have blond hair?" I asked, surprised. I didn't correct him about not being English.

"Yes, he did, he was in a real rush and didn't want to talk much."

I couldn't believe it. He had met Phil White, a young guy who had attempted the record in 2004 and with whom I had been in touch when researching my attempt. "Phil White!" I confirmed. "That must have been in 2004. Unfortunately he didn't get the record. Another Englishman called Steve Strange broke it at the same time."

"Oh well, when I saw him he was certainly going fast. He would hardly stop to speak to me."

This seemed a sore point, so I moved the conversation on. It turned out that David was a member of warmshowers.org, the cycle organization I had been helped by already in Istanbul, and was an avid cyclist. A few days later I managed to check his website to confirm his self-proclaimed status as host extraordinaire in this part of Malaysia. He had done some impressive tours of his own and he seemed very disappointed that I had already passed his front door and could not stop over. What a gentleman. He spoke about cycling as an international friendship, and after my friendly fishmonger he was the second kind Malaysian ambassador I had met that day.

The third came by a few hours later. The rain had started on time as I made my way toward the wonderfully named town of Butterworth. On the outskirts it suddenly doubled in ferocity and started pelting down with such force that it stung the skin. The road was instantly inches thick in water as it couldn't drain fast enough. This force of rain has to be experienced to be believed and I looked around desperately for anywhere to hide. Ahead I saw a boulevard of large hardwoods, and I dashed to the first one. Leaving the bike under the outer branches I stood upright as close to the trunk as possible to get shelter from the barrage of water. I didn't need to worry about the bike being slightly in the road: most cars had also pulled off the road in this deluge.

After five minutes I was still there when one car did approach. As it pulled up, it slowed, I assumed so as not to splash me, so I waved and smiled, realizing how absurd I must look. The car came to a stop and a man leaned across to hand me something. I had to step out from under my tree to take it. He shouted, "It's OK, I am a vet, get yourself a meal," then drove off. I looked down as I jumped back under the tree to see that he had handed me a 10-ringgit note and a business card—Dr. Sandhu. It was the equivalent of only about £2 but would have bought me a good meal at any roadside stop. You had to smile at such random acts of kindness, even when it was raining this hard.

I was worried about whether I would find anywhere to stay. There did not seem to be many options ahead and it looked like I might have to turn off. I pulled up at some traffic lights by the junction and got the attention of a man driving a Volvo to ask. Just before the lights changed he managed to give directions to a hotel in a town 5km away called Bukit Mertajam. I thanked him as he pulled off.

After a few kilometers, having followed his instructions, I was starting to wonder if I was actually on track when a Volvo pulled alongside and the same man rolled down the window and called out, "Follow me." It took another fifteen minutes to get to the hotel, and then he walked to the front door to make sure they had a room for me. I thanked him profusely and asked where he lived in the town. "I live in Sungai Jawi, another town further on," he said, which explained why he had carried straight on at the lights. "I thought my directions might be too complicated, so I came back to find you." I was lost for words. What a wonderful man. I offered him dinner but he insisted that he had to get home.

The hotelier was the first grumpy man of the day and was not at all happy with the bike going to my room, but I insisted that I could not leave it in the car park, and eventually he agreed.

It had been an interesting day, full of characters, but no great distance at 140km. Looking ahead, I targeted Singapore in five more days. Despite better energy levels, my left calf was giving me real issues, having been locked for nearly a week now. I took a long walk into town for dinner and then did a long massage, hoping the combination would ease it off.

The next day I left just after eight a.m., and battled humidity and saddle sores to cover 166km by a little after six that night, when I stopped at a hotel with a spa. I was now crossing the foothills of the Cameron Highlands. They were about 50km to my left as I cycled south, and all I could see toward the 5,000-foot plateau was magnificent jungle hillsides rising into cloud. I certainly noticed the change in terrain near Ipoh, the largest town I had passed in Malaysia.

My left calf was becoming a real concern. I needed to get the locked muscle treated. There was an option to wait until Kuala Lumpur, where a masseuse was standing by, but it was such a huge city and would undoubtedly take a lot of time to find the place, get treated, and then get going again. Moreover, if I kept going at this speed then it looked like KL would not arrive neatly at the end of a day, even if the masseuse could come to me. When I passed a hotel with a big SPA sign at the 166km mark I therefore jumped at the chance.

It was a smart-looking hotel, so I was prepared to pay a bit more than average, reassuring myself that it was worth it to get this leg fixed without taking too much time out of the day. After a quick shower I went down to the spa. It all looked very nice: a gym, a swimming pool, then treatment rooms. The lady on the front desk offered a back and leg massage for forty-five minutes for the very reasonable sum of 60 ringgit, or £11, and showed me through to a treatment room. It was like any other I had been to: a massage table with face hole, and a chair in the corner. The mood was set with low lights and quiet music. The only clothes I had for when I was off the bike were a pair of shorts and a T-shirt. I didn't carry any underwear. For times like this, and if I ever swam, I had a pair of Speedos.

After a minute a Malay lady came in. She was absolutely tiny and spoke no English. She gestured for me to get on the table facedown, which I did, then she covered my legs with a towel. All fairly normal practice. It started well, and I relaxed into a surprisingly good back massage. My shoulders and neck were amazingly tight after hundreds of hours on the bike. Just as I felt myself almost dropping off to sleep, she knelt on the table so she could get her whole body weight behind the moves, then started using her knees on the base of my back. I was glad she was so tiny: my muscles were so tight the massage was painful enough. I lay there wondering what might be coming next, trying to relax and accept it as the local way. I flipped over when instructed and she massaged my thighs and calves, ignoring me the whole time but inflicting considerable pain for someone of her size.

Eventually it was over. She stood back, at the foot of the bed, and waved to get my attention. I propped myself up on one elbow. She said something in Malay and made a movement. I apologized in English, said I didn't understand, and she repeated the action. I was completely confused, so I pointed at my calf like I had at the start and gave her the thumbs-up to indicate that I was sure it was better.

Without another word she walked out. I was about to jump off and get dressed when the door opened and she walked back in with another lady. I lay there in the dimly lit room on my back in a pair of Speedos, with two tiny Malay women looking down at me. The new lady looked me straight in the eye and said, "She wants to know if you want a massage without your underwear."

My heart-rate hit 180bpm in one fell swoop, and I stammered awkwardly, "No, thank you."

"Just forty ringgit to her for private massage."

They both looked at me expectantly.

"Thank you, but no, thank you. It was a very good massage."

I sat up and threw a towel over my lap until they both left. I then dressed and left a 40-ringgit tip on the chair for the masseuse. I didn't see either of them as I left the room and went upstairs for a huge all-you-can-eat buffet, laughing at myself again for acting like a teenager every time I ended up in these situations.

Singapore looked like a fraction under 100 miles a day away, so I asked Mum to confirm my flight for four days' time. Learning from my Calcutta experience, the plan was now to put in three big days and then do a half day into Singapore to allow time to take the bike to bits and prepare for the flight to Perth. In Singapore the director of the British Council was hosting me, so I hoped the logistics would be better organized.

Day 90 was fairly uneventful, save for some torrential rain that started later on during an impressive thunderstorm. The left knee was increasingly painful and I was now in a habit of massaging it every time I got off the bike. My only personal revelation of the day was a newfound dislike of fast food. I turned up at a small town called Bidor and could find nothing except KFC. I have never had KFC, but bit the bullet, assuring myself that it couldn't be that bad. It was, and I thought seriously about making myself sick as it made me feel so ill all afternoon. My logbook simply read, "I will never do that again. First and last. Terrible." I'd eat spicy chicken feet over KFC chicken any day. Farther down the road I found a huge plate of rice which put things right.

It had been a long, slow climb to the hilltop town of Kuala Kubu Bharu and I felt weak after the bad food. That evening I made it to Rawang and had a feast. I have never been happier to see a Pizza Hut than I was when I was in Southeast Asia: they meant regular non-spicy big-calorie meals. I started with a huge pizza, then a big bowl of pasta and garlic bread before finishing with a couple of chocolate brownies.

Kuala Lumpur was the next big challenge. KL is not a massive city on the world scale, but the wider KL area, known as Klang Valley, is home to over seven million people and is a busy place to navigate by bike. It is also quite a compact area, hemmed in by the Titiwangsa Mountains to the north and east and the Straits of Malacca to the west. This was the main reason I had opted to cycle down the east coast, until the terrorist attacks in the southeast put an end to that plan.

Kuala Lumpur is not the most exotic of names for quite a stunning city, as it translates as "muddy confluence." Crossing the city was a bit like running the gauntlet in a flow of traffic which barely let me take my eyes off the road, let alone stop. However, I was aware of the most stunning cityscape whenever I did glance up. At one point the road was elevated for a long section and passed close by the Golden Triangle, the commercial center of KL. The tallest twin buildings in the world, the Petronus Twin Towers, were close by and I had stunning views of a unique city which merges old colonial design with the postmodern fashion for mammoth glass structures. It was definitely a place to make a mental note to revisit in a more sociable way. I was fascinated to ride under *Blade Runner*–style elevated tram systems before passing a Hindu temple. The multiculturalism of the place was everywhere and reflected a capital with strong Malay, Chinese, Indian, Middle Eastern, and British influences.

My target was Kajang, a suburb to the southeast, and I would encourage you to zoom in on Google Earth to appreciate how easy it is to lose Route 1 while trying to navigate this labyrinth. I was relying on a country-scale map to get me through, so I eventually gave up on mapping altogether and just trusted my sense of direction.

Despite my grumbles about injuries I found a new focus from a break in Semanang and raced a fast 40km to the coast turnoff on Route 19, which then provided a cruisy 20km descent to meet Route 5 south.

The next day was memorable as it didn't rain for the first time since Bangkok, or at least not until I was off the bike in the evening. I made it to the coastal town of Pontian Kechil. After checking into a cheap hotel I walked out onto the rocks, looked over the Straits of Malacca, and watched a lightning storm roll in from Sumatra, Indonesia, which was on the horizon. The straits are one of the world's most important shipping channels as they link the Pacific and Indian Oceans, and today was the first time I had actually reached the ocean in 8,600 miles on the road. I was nearly halfway around and this was the first time I had seen the sea. It was a memorable moment. I was talking to home about the plan for arriving in Singapore and getting to Australia, watching this lightning storm roll in.

Down the coast, across the causeway, and across Singapore was all that was left to pedal of leg 3. I would be in Australia the next day, and I would soon be exactly halfway around the world. A thought that had been keeping me going for months was that in theory things should get a lot easier from Perth onward. I had done the logistical planning in seven legs but also thought about it as a race of two halves. The first 9,000 miles were through the unknown cultures, languages, and foods with difficult border crossings and bad roads. Part one was about getting through in good time and safely. The second half I saw as more of a straightforward race as it was mostly back in the English-speaking world, with foods I should recognize, through more familiar cultures and over good roads.

I was set to make it halfway around the world in about 96 or 97 days, which was hugely exciting. If all went to plan then there was no reason why I couldn't go even faster for the second half and take the new world record in well under 200 days, in doing so taking nearly three months off the old record. I was looking forward to Australia as somewhere I could escape from people for a while after the mania of Asia. I'd be back in my tent, racing across the Outback with the famous easterly winds behind me. The trip was almost bound to get easier, so this last 90km pedal into Singapore felt like a bit of a victory lap.

It was a scenic cycle inland for the last miles of Malaysia and I stopped only once, to buy a new pedal wrench so I could take my bike apart when I got to Singapore. The Johor–Singapore Causeway is the main link for road, rail, and water piping to the island and on an average day carries over 60,000 vehicles. The immigration system was very confusing and not built for cyclists. To start with I queued with tens of motorbikes and mopeds that would have taken ages, before giving up and pushing my bike past them into a car line where I was ushered to the front by guards and was through in no time.

I have never been anywhere like Singapore. It is the fifth-richest country in the world according to gross GDP and this standard of living is very evident. The causeway led onto Woodlands Road, which wound around the big central park of Bukit Panjang to the city center, on the south side of the island. Needless to say it was spotless, and made the very developed Malaysia I had just left behind look like a shambles. The last city in Malaysia, Johor Bahru, had been one of the most dilapidated I had seen in the country, which made the contrast even greater.

Partly because I spent my whole ride staring around me in awe rather than looking for signs, and partly because I didn't have a map, I got entirely lost. I hadn't figured Singapore would be that complicated as the main island is less than 20km across, but city riding is always disorientating. Mostly by luck, I ended up by a large London Eye–like structure where I asked a workman for directions to the center. I then worked my way toward my destination, the famous Merlion, opposite the Opera House. The Merlion is just what it sounds like, the head of a lion with the body of a fish. It represents the origins of Singapore as a fishing port and its original name of Singapura, meaning "lion city."

Phil, the husband of the British Council director, picked me up from there and I went back to their house to spend the afternoon preparing for a late flight to Australia. Halfway through cutting up bits of cardboard to make a bike box the physio arrived, and I received a professional sports treatment for the first time since Istanbul. The locked muscles, knee niggles, neck pains, and nerve damage in the hands were all causes for concern with 9,400 miles still to go. The physio was to feed back to Scotland with a full report which would be sent on to Perth so I could get further treatment upon arrival. The good news was that he thought I was in good shape, just very burned out.

I had forgotten that it was November 5. After the physio and packing, I found myself in the middle of a Guy Fawkes Night party for an hour before my taxi arrived. All the office staff from the British Council came around and we shared a buffet fit for a king. Apparently bonfires are banned in Singapore, but the novelty of sparklers was not lost on me.

I wish I could have stayed at Eunice and Phil's and flown the next morning. It was a beautiful house and the celebratory mood was a perfect unwind after a successful 1,253 miles from Bangkok, but I had a flight to catch. Waving good-bye to the guests, I squeezed the bike into the trunk of the taxi and left.

I was still 65 miles north of the equator. It was time to head south for the first time.

Leg 4: Perth to Brisbane

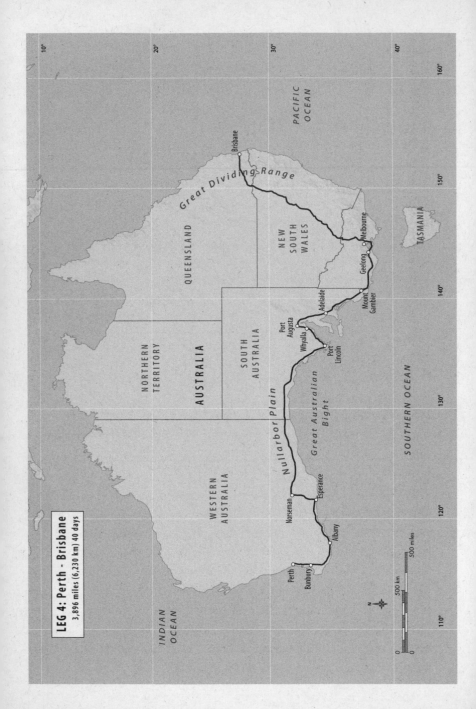

LEG 4: Perth – Brisbane
3,896 miles (6,230 km) 40 days

15

The best thing about Singapore Airlines was the stewardesses. Not only were they good at their jobs, they happened to be the most stunning women I had seen since the hotel in Ukraine. I couldn't sleep, so my mind wandered, thinking about my self-inflicted half-year sabbatical from any meetings with the female half of the race. I laughed. I never normally got hung up or bothered by these thoughts. Maybe women were on my mind as I had just cycled 1,100 miles in a world where I had been offered them on demand at most of the places I had stopped.

As the plane came in to land I stared at the expanse below me, mesmerized. Australia at dawn was everything I had hoped for. Space at last.

It took me a long time to get through Australian customs, but they did a fantastic job of cleaning up my muddy shoes. I'd arrived in Perth on the first Tuesday in November, Melbourne Cup day. The annual thoroughbred horse race is an event that stops the nation. Ian Pugsly, an old work colleague of DP's from Scotland, who now lived in Perth, was there to meet me with Margaret, a friend of a friend.

The day was a blur, and like all previous days off was more tiring than a normal day of riding. After dropping the bike off to be serviced, we all headed for a huge breakfast. A group of young road cyclists sat outside the café, their racers propped on the grass. The food tasted strange but familiar. Everyone looked like me. Everything was so familiar yet foreign: I hadn't seen "familiar" for so long and I was on the wrong side of the world. I marveled at every little detail, absorbing Western ways for the first time in two months. I found myself staring at people. This world felt millions of miles from where I had come, yet because I had traveled mostly by bike since

Europe, these once isolated cultures for me now felt so much closer. Iran, Thailand, and the like were no longer distinct, very distant wonderlands; they were real and accessible variants of the same small world I had lived my whole life on. People are naturally very here-centric, but many of my preconceptions that had painted the world in black and white before were now confused. I could no longer see the world in such isolated sections.

The deserts and rains of Asia had been a catalyst for wear and tear for all my kit, on top of nearly 9,000 miles of cycling. I needed to go shopping. With a new Polar watch, sunglasses, gloves, and many other bits from the only proper bike shop I had seen in 5,000 miles, I managed to spend what would've lasted me a couple of months of cycling in the Middle East. The sunglasses story was annoying. I had only realized mine were missing when leaving the airport and emerging into the intense Australian morning sun. I immediately knew where they must be. I took out my camera, flicked back a few photos, and sure enough there they were, sitting on a table just behind me as I held the camera at arm's length in southern Malaysia at the start of that last day. It was hard to believe it was just yesterday. It hadn't been sunny enough to warrant wearing them, so I must've forgotten to throw them on my head.

Bike and body needed to be ready for the 3,800 miles that lay ahead across leg 4, but then a call came in that jeopardized this. Aldo and Sats from the bike shop told me there were real problems with the bike and there was every chance they would not finish it today. The gearing cog had seized on (I hadn't been able to shift it without wearing mitts), the wheels were terrible and looked as though they'd had a very hard life, a couple of bolts were completely seized, and almost every moving part needed to be changed and tuned. The frame was fine, but everything else needed a lot of TLC. I am a lousy mechanic, so I'd completely underestimated this mammoth task. It was a far greater job than they had anticipated, too. As tired as I was, the thought of losing another day produced a knot of fear in the stomach and I urged them to do everything they could to get it done. Forcing this worry aside, I then joined Margaret's family, Ian, and the crew for a coffee back at her house and enjoyed talking about other things than the cycle for a while.

It wasn't long before Fiona, a masseuse, arrived. It hurt, but the diagnosis was good. Everything was tight but working well. By the end I was almost asleep on the table and it was hard to get going again.

Aldo and Sats worked hard all day to get the bike overhauled for the next leg. There's no way I would've got even halfway across Australia with the bike in the shape it was when it arrived in Perth. It was so strange testing it in the car park of the bike shop without 30kg of lateral weight on it. It felt unstable. Very helpfully, and for the first time since leaving Paris, both my banks then decided to freeze my credit cards due to fraud concerns. Half an hour later one was unlocked, the bike was in the van, and we shot off back to the airport, this time to meet a friend who had brought new kit supplies from Scotland. Unfortunately, due to the impossible levels of customs control, half of it had been confiscated, so I wouldn't have the ration packs I had hoped for when heading into the Outback.

Over dinner at a local pizzeria the idea of starting in Fremantle, a port city in Western Australia, instead of Perth was raised again. I had assumed I would start somewhere iconic in Perth, but the cons were that Perth is big, the roads out of it are big, and to then get to the coast I would have to go west before I went east. If I started slightly down the coast, near the mouth of the Swan River at Fremantle, I'd be on the Indian Ocean, with much smaller roads along the coast. It made no difference to the rules, so we decided to do it that way. The thought of starting at Freo, as the Aussies call it, also appealed greatly because of its iconic image in the circum-navigation yacht races.

I love Australia. I would like to state that clearly before writing about what a tough time I had there.

The late start at 9:30 a.m. was inevitable considering the final preparations that needed to be made. Fremantle was the perfect starting point. Its old market center had a sleepy charm. My ceremonial dipping of the toe in the Indian Ocean coincided with a freak wave and I stomped grumpily back up the beach with two wet feet. I then stopped at the end of the street and spent the next half an hour buying and sorting out an Australian mobile number. Little did I know that most of the Australia I was going to see had no mobile coverage.

The bike felt so smooth. Because of the gradual wear it had not been obvious just how much damage had been done. The gears shifted effortlessly and the chain set ran many times smoother. I had spent the last three months on that bike, but it was suddenly a novelty again, like a new toy.

Then there was everything else that was different. It is an endless list; suffice to say that there was almost nothing here on the road or around to remind me of where I had just come from. The most significant change was the weather. It was hot and dry, the coastal morning sun a modest warning of what I knew lay ahead. The roads seemed empty, which again was a sign of extremes ahead, but those vehicles I shared it with were all huge. Almost every car was a 4x4 and the trucks were all massive articulated rigs. There had been many warnings from trans-Australia cyclists about the infamous road trains. If these were their normal trucks, I could not imagine what else was in store.

Ian tracked and filmed me for the first 10 miles out of Freo, with incredible views over the ocean to the right. I got the impression that Margaret, who was driving, was a reluctant accomplice in this last errand. Mum had set up my visit to be as stress-free as possible. I believe she said something along the lines of "Mark will do his own thing and will just want to recover for the day." We hadn't realized how spread out Perth was, and Margaret had been chauffeuring me, feeding me, and helping in an array of ways since the moment I'd stepped off the plane twenty-four hours earlier. I could not have done it without her. It was hard to show my genuine gratitude while constantly rushing around.

As soon as I saw their vehicle do a U-turn and disappear, my momentum slowed. I had been honest about how tired I was but had tried to sound as upbeat as possible. However, the cheery demeanor and banter were not an exact reflection of how I felt, and I stopped less than a mile farther on at the first crossroads, parked the bike in a car park, and spent the next hour in a diner. I absently watched some rugby on TV and hungrily ate a bowl of pasta, drowning it with a couple of pints of Coke. It is a hard one to describe, but sleep deprivation and long-term exhaustion give you a weird feeling. My stomach and chest felt as if they were collapsing, utterly hollow, and my head felt incredibly heavy. You feel utterly removed from the world around you, as if it is a program you are watching.

Eventually I got out a pen and started doodling on a paper

napkin. I wrote absentmindedly—"3,800 miles. AUSTRALIA. 38 days. Good food. Good roads. Halfway there. On target. Small targets. You have cycled to Australia! Race on . . ."—and moved on to a second napkin, trying to use word association to get myself in the right frame of mind to start leg 4. I ended up laughing at the absurdity of this little world I was living in and got going, having found conviction again.

Writing my logbook at the end of the day, I could not figure out the discrepancy between the map distance and what was shown on the cycle computers. It appeared that I had reset the odometer on my cycle computer that morning by mistake, so had lost my total miles. It also appeared that I had reset the wheel size somehow, so the main cycle computer had under-read by about 5km. My annoyance at this might seem like an overreaction, but I had to verify every detail for Guinness World Records and it was a pain to work out and document exactly. But I was rolling again, the bike was superb, the body would improve, and the race was very much on.

I always got my deepest sleeps in a tent, and I woke with refreshed spirits, eager to get into a flow and lose myself in Oz. From all the route setting I knew every twist and turn that lay ahead, but what I had overlooked was every rise and fall. After the flatlands since Pakistan a 1,200-meter ascent that day came as a shock to the legs. The road had left the ocean on the first day and I would be riding through deep forests for much of the next few days, on constantly rolling roads. Part 1 of leg 4 took me southeast to the town of Denmark, on the Southern Ocean, along to Esperance, where I would cut due north for the start of the Outback. Part 2 was across this vast expanse along the Great Bight, then part 3 was looping south through Adelaide and Melbourne before cutting northeast to Brisbane on the Pacific Ocean.

Midafternoon I was glancing around, noting how little there was to note, when I spotted my first kangaroo. It was very dark, surprisingly small, munching away in the forest 10 meters back from the road. The experience was like my first elephant: exciting even though expected. The surprise in terms of wildlife was the number of parrots. Big gray ones, shimmery dark green ones, and white cockatoos were a very exotic discovery.

I didn't pass many towns, but those I did were quaint and sleepy. Ian Pugsly had told me he was going on holiday to the coastal town of Denmark, so we'd planned to catch up that afternoon and the following day. Ian and his wife found me just before lunch and we stopped at a granny's café for some of the best scran I could remember, which made me extremely lethargic in the early afternoon heat. On these vast empty roads I felt very pedestrian spinning up the long, steep hills. But with every climb I was eventually rewarded: the biggest hills since Turkey meant some great sweeping descents. The sense of space and freedom was overwhelming after the muggy confines of Southeast Asia.

At 150km it was very tempting to pedal on until dark, but a few people had warned me that the section to Denmark was 120km, without any supplies. I knew that there were greater gaps ahead so opted for stocking up on supplies and a big night's sleep before tackling this.

At dusk on Friday November 9, day 97 on the road, I reached 9,000 miles. Halfway around the world. I got there on a long straight in the middle of absolutely nowhere, with a stunning orange sunset behind me. I took out the camera to capture the moment but was lost for anything even vaguely profound to say.

At nearly 193km, and after sitting on the bike for just shy of ten hours, it was a big day. The nearly 2km of ascent made sure I burned over 6,900 kcal before getting to Denmark, with the promise of a bed at the holiday home of Ian and his family.

It is always slower and harder to leave a proper bed, so the second half of the race started by chasing the miles late into the day after starting at 8:30. After 10km of open rolling farmland with Ian, who again tracked me in his car, we stopped in a field gateway and said our good-byes. I was off on my own again. For all that the company was nice, it inevitably slowed me down.

After only six hours' sleep, I was soon feeling the effects. When pushing it physically every day I was finding that it took weeks to get over a full night's sleep deprivation, as opposed to just a day or two like it normally would. After nearly 200km of hilly terrain the legs were also pretty sore. The tendons behind both knees on the inside were really tight. I had to put this aside. It was so important that I got into a good rhythm in the first week in Oz.

I was actually more excited about getting to day 100 than the halfway point, and I was only two days away now. By the afternoon

I had bypassed the town of Albany and was in open scrubby countryside that thankfully was starting to flatten out. The beginning of November means early summer for Australia and I was burning easily, despite the sun not yet being as hot as I had been warned, with an average that day of 21 degrees.

For the last 60km I passed through featureless land, without houses, people, or vehicles for long stretches. I felt relieved when I got to the village of Wellstead—a strange new emotion after my craving for space. The village shop was empty except for a middle-aged, very bored-looking man who sold me a fruitcake, two mushroom pies, and an electrolyte drink.

"Where ya from?" he asked.

"Scotland."

"I'm from Wales."

This surprised me, mainly because of his strong Aussie twang, so I questioned him.

"I left when I was ten, me parents came over to work. You see, in those days it was all the pommy bashin', they would thump ya for being British, so I lost the accent pretty darn fast. It's different now, of course. A few jokes and the likes but no one gets a beating anymore."

He seemed like a man who bore the scars of early bullying, so I changed the subject. "Anywhere to camp near here?"

"Nah, you can't camp anywhere near the town, but there's heaps of space up the road. Where ya headin'?"

For the first time on the cycle, people were reading and understanding the cycle strip "Artemis World Cycle Challenge" on my Lycras, and asking questions.

Just 500 meters later I spotted a deserted playing field with perfect flat grass and some buildings as windbreaks and decided to hide myself away there. After a huge and superb dinner of couscous with soya mince followed by masses of fruitcake, washed down with a bottle of fine vintage Gatorade, I was in heaven, alone and in my tent again. For the first time in Australia there wasn't even phone coverage. There was nothing to distract me from my world.

Days 99 and 100 were spent riding due east to Esperance, where the road cut due north. And there is not much else to be said, for there was not much to see, hear, or do except ride. They were perfect days in terms of the 100-mile-a-day target, but that was as exciting as it got.

I had some new concerns though. Firstly, I realized I had lost my chamois cream. This was a small white tub of cream which I rubbed into the seat of my shorts every morning to reduce friction; it also acted as an antiseptic. The monsoon rains of leg 3 had aggravated already tender skin and I knew there would be little chance to clean the shorts in the middle of the Outback. The manufacturer recommended washing them after every ride, but out here I was lucky to wash them every 400 miles. The hotter it got, the more salt got deposited in the material from my sweat, which in turn rubbed into the skin sores, making for incredibly painful riding. The next chance to pick up chamois cream was Adelaide, a thousand miles ahead. So I knew what was going to happen to my saddle sores, and it wasn't pretty.

The second concern was the wind. At this time of year there was meant to be a westerly prevailing wind, and a good one at that. However, since turning east, and especially out of the rolling woodlands, I had been straight into it. For half the world I had been telling myself that things were going to get easier in Oz; days of unexpected climbing and riding into a headwind was not the plan, and I found myself cursing, agitated, and distracted on the bike.

False expectations are a dangerous thing. I had always told myself that if I got halfway around in less than a hundred days then it was race on for an even faster second half. This terrain and headwind did not fit into this thought, and I found myself pushing the same hourly average speeds as if I was back on the bad roads of India. Each day was getting gradually warmer, but I didn't notice because of the front right wind, so I ended each day feeling utterly weathered and a bit burned. As usual my nose took the brunt and began to bleed where the skin had burst off entirely.

Conditions did not improve over the next couple of days—on day 100, I ran out of water and became almost delirious before managing to refill. When I finally camped in a grassy field set behind some trees near the road, I was absolutely exhausted.

The following morning, number 101 on the road, started with a close encounter. As I zipped back the flysheet on the tent I was confronted by a big black spider with some red on its back. I still can't be sure what it was; what I do know is that it helped me go from groggy to fight-or-flight mode in less than a second. I had already opened the outside zip before I saw it crawling up from behind the pannier, which made me jump back inside. It was shiny, quite flat, and seemed to walk more like a crab than a spider, and it was now on the move up my pannier bag, which was in the tent porch. Sensing an opportunity as it paused right on top, I grabbed my logbook and flicked it for six, into the field beyond. That done, I packed away quickly and went to the roadside before having breakfast. More couscous. I was getting sick of that stuff.

I was now a one-hour flight from Perth, or nearly a week's pedaling. It would have been cool to pop in on the town of Esperance, a place founded by Scottish pioneers and an absolute haven by everyone's account. However, the wonderfully named Shark Lake Road offered me an earlier opportunity to cut north, away from the relentless headwind. To go into town would have been a bit of a there-and-back anyway, so I popped back out on the main road going due north to Norseman—the start of the great Outback.

At this junction it was the perfect 80km half day and I stopped for a pub lunch of lasagne and chips. I knew that such luxuries would be short-lived in the weeks ahead, so I ate up and treated myself while I could. I then stopped at Grass Patch for a late-afternoon revive of coffee, Coke, and an ice cream. Grass Patch is an ironic name, in a similar vein to Greenland: it seemed too dry to support much actual grass. Having said that, there was a huge amount of road trail haulage that had me riding half the day looking nervously behind me. These vehicles supported the arable harvest as well as the mining industry, so there were either huge irrigation systems in use or more rainfall than the parched verges suggested.

In seven hours and fifty-five minutes I covered 162km—a perfect day by all accounts, but in fact it was horrid. I still felt very demotivated on the bike and increasingly saddle sore. Finally, I stopped at the Salmon Gums Motel.

I walked into the motel and found myself in the local bar. It was full of hairy overall-wearing farmers fresh in from the harvest and haulage. The couple who ran it were a funny wee guy and his wife, who looked like a tough lady. When I walked in she exclaimed loudly, "Looks like a cyclist," then shouted, "What do you want?" I got a Coke and sat at the bar and chatted. She had a young kangaroo in her arms that she was petting and feeding milk. I asked if they had any rooms. She looked at her husband and he thought for a second and said yes. She said, "Where?" and he said, "Number two." She walked off behind the bar and came back a few minutes later. "You're a lucky bastard," she said to me. "We're fully booked but a room just came free and it's twenty-five dollars."

I took my drink and room key and found a barstool. As I did, one of the farmers asked for a pint, and the wife went to oblige. "No you don't," her man shouted, half serious, half theatrically, "not after touching that animal." They were lovely. Hard as nails but with that country charm which is the same the world over. Within this small village world this bar was the epicenter, and as such they were the heart of the community, rulers of the manor.

The wallaby (as they corrected me when I called it a kangaroo) was the newest addition to the family. It wandered about the bar being petted like a dog.

During a huge meal I had while sitting at the bar I watched the major dramas of the night unfold. I have worked in catering in small country hotels and can relate to how out of proportion these become. There were less than a dozen people eating, but their only waitress, a girl in her early twenties, ended up breaking down in tears because of the stress. This made the man shout at his wife, who in return gave him the silent treatment and caused the wallaby to hop off. So for half an hour, until she spoke to him again, the man chatted to me about his shoulder injury and the goings-on in Salmon Gums. Later on, a group of four farm-worker girls came in. They had been swimming in a reservoir, which they weren't allowed in as it was drinking water, and were proud of their escapade. This angered the bar lady but got a vote of support from the barman, which was enough to start them talking to each other again.

The motel was out the back of the bar and I was glad for a hot shower and bed.

Norseman to Ceduna is about 1,200km—roughly the same distance as John O'Groats to Land's End. It is often called the Nullarbor, but in fact the road only cuts through a small part of the actual Nullarbor Plain, in the eastern section. The Nullarbor Plain is about 200,000km square. Unlike the railway, the Eyre Highway, as this stretch of road is called, cuts through the southernmost part of the Nullarbor, along the Great Australian Bight. The word comes from the Latin for "no trees" and is fitting. This arid expanse of scrub is actually the world's largest single piece of limestone, and is about as interesting as this sounds. It is populated by absolutely no one save those who work in the sporadic roadhouses along the roadside.

It was still 100km to Norseman from where I started out. From there the Eyre Highway stretched 1,687km to Port Augusta. However, from Ceduna, 1,200km ahead, I planned to continue following the coast around the edge of the Eyre Peninsula rather than carry straight on inland, because I needed to be back on better roads to do extra miles while always heading eastward to make up my 18,000-mile target. My route had taken me as directly as possible through the Middle East and Asia, where I had assumed the going would be slower, but in Australia and the US my routes would not be anywhere close to direct, ensuring the most miles would be done where the going should be faster. "Should" is the optimal word here. As I said, the headwind had already given me a real reason for concern.

My saddle sores were feeling better after a shower and a big night's sleep in a bed, though, and overall day 102 was a much better day. The eccentric owners of Salmon Gums left me a packed lunch in the fridge, and I was almost sad to go. It would have been a cool spot to explore more. Before leaving Norseman I stopped at a garage to load up on food, and then stopped at another store for sandwiches, a map, and 10.5 liters of water.

Ten and a half liters was probably too much, but I had to cook that night and if something went wrong I needed to have enough water to last. I also left with a Powerade, three bananas, two buttered rock buns, a packet of Heinz baked beans, four sandwiches for the morning and lunch, and two packets of shortbread-type biscuits, and I had three army ration packs left. That should be enough food to get through the next twenty four hours.

The winds seemed to pick up massively in the afternoon, so despite the long daylight hours I decided to focus on early starts. It was also getting seriously hot in the afternoon. The next day was number 103 on the road, and the first full day of the Eyre Highway. I had a simple and very important target: 160km to Balladonia Motel, where I could get more water.

After everything I had been told about the Nullarbor, I was surprised to find myself in thick trees almost all day, following the wonderfully named Heartbreak Ridge. The first 45km was getting re-tarred and I had to run the gauntlet on a couple of very long single-lane stretches. Stopping at one of these traffic sections, I chatted to a large Kiwi lady who was in charge of the signals. She was out here for two-week periods, working in full trousers, jacket, gloves, and a mosquito net over her head in the 40-degree heat. She was in great spirits—must have been made of tough stuff—but obviously welcomed someone to talk to. "It's not that bad, you know," she told me. "Some of the guys working on the road have been out here for a couple of months." This is a job, I thought, which would actually drive you nuts.

Apart from the heat—it was the hottest day since Pakistan—the new menace out here was the flies. These were not your normal houseflies but big horseflies, or clegs, as they are called in Scotland. These wee buggers bite you and suck your blood, and they followed me in a swarm. They buzzed behind me and seemed to be attracted to the black material the most as they landed on my gloves and shorts, nipping painfully. I tried to out-cycle them, but whenever I glanced back I had a strange panicky feeling. They were slow and swattable but too many to take on.

Late in the afternoon the trees thinned and I was pedaling hard to make Balladonia by six p.m., with half a mind to keep going beyond, when a car pulled alongside. It was a bashed-up old blue hatch-back—not something I would trust to make it across the Outback. A Danish man shouted across at me, tracking me at cycling pace for a while. He seemed to be a perpetual traveler, midthirties, and off to find himself. He was incredibly excited to find me cycling alone out here, and I was cheered by his excitement.

But the last hours on the bike that day were hell. The wind was ferocious, whipping across the now open plains, and my shorts felt like they were made of very fine sandpaper. Over time this turned into a dull ache with the odd shooting pain as if I had hit a nerve. Real saddle sores put you in a strange state: your stomach tightens and you find yourself staring at the road through a complete daze, your head like lead on a tensed neck. Such acute pain affects your whole body and there is no escaping it without getting off the bike.

During this section a caravan with a tandem bike on the back passed and then pulled over. Carlos, an Italian, and his Australian wife got out and, without asking if I actually needed anything, plied me with glass upon glass of lemon juice, some cake, and an apple. He was originally from Turin and had lost none of the accent. It was another of those wonderful random acts of kindness, at the perfect time.

My average speed dropped gradually all afternoon because of the wind and I felt a broken man when the resthouse appeared. But it is amazing how brief this feeling is: as soon as I was off the bike I started a debate with myself about staying or stocking up and carrying on.

This was the first of the infamous roadhouses with a petrol station, restaurant, bar with motel, and campsite off to the side. I certainly didn't expect them all to be this well equipped. I was impressed as I walked into the big bar, with pool tables and about a dozen or so people eating and drinking. The Danish man was sharing a beer with two motorbikers who turned out to be from Holland. One of them was a student and had just been part of a team competing in the world's largest solar car race in northern Australia. His friend had then flown out and they had hired big BMWs to ride across Australia. They reacted to my bike and me with amusement.

I was still of two minds about whether or not to carry on but needed lots of food so agreed to join them for dinner. The Danish man made a comment about how extortionate the beer was and went off to cook his own meal, offering his camp spot for me to share. The place was expensive but I felt like a king tucking into a trucker's size bowl of spaghetti. It turned out that the bikers had a motel room with three beds and they offered me the third for nothing. By the time we finished it was past seven p.m. and I accepted. There was no point in fighting another 10 or 20km into that wind just to spend the night in the tent when I could get a shower and bed.

When I returned from dropping off my bags and showering, the bikers were being asked to play pool. The contenders turned out to be a group of volunteer firefighters who had been working on the same bush fire for two weeks. Every night it died down and they retired to the motel, and every morning it flared up, so they drove out and, using vehicles, tried to clear its boundary of further fuel, beat it back where possible, and contain it. They told amazing stories of how the fire behaved when it got windy. It could jump roads and clearings they had made. Each of them seemed to have stories of near misses. Their strongest views were reserved for the fires' source.

"Bloody Abos," one of the young men spat. "We found where the fire started, a campfire with empty cans of beer. Only Abos drink that stuff. They move about, get drunk around fires, then move on. When the wind picks up, the embers rekindle and you got a bush fire. It is so dry out there they will rage for weeks until the winds drop."

I somehow won a couple of games of pool. On top of the cycle, this won me high regard, and the firemen told me more of their stories of the bush. They had a great sense of pride about their work, and it sounded dangerous and impressive, but their stories also educated me in a level of racism I had rarely come across in open conversation. I wasn't offended by their views on the Aboriginal people: it wasn't my place to judge, and the firemen clearly weren't bad people. It seemed from the level of openness that such opinions had been with them for a long time, perhaps handed down by older generations.

I went to bed that night full of anticipation. Ever since I'd first learned about the 90-mile straight road in Australia I had been looking forward to riding it. The next day, number 104, I would be on it.

16

An hour after starting I got the 90-mile straight and was left wondering why I had been looking forward to it. A brown sign that would have looked gigantic anywhere else but out here looked insignificant stated 90 MILE STRAIGHT, AUSTRALIA'S LONGEST STRAIGHT ROAD, 146.6KM. After setting the camera up on self-timer for the tourist snaps, I set out for a whole day riding in a straight line; but, to be honest, you wouldn't have known it was straight, because it was not completely flat and therefore didn't feel completely straight.

One exciting feature about the road (though I admit only in theory, or if you have an active imagination) was the RFDS. The yellow signs read RFDS EMERGENCY AIRSTRIP and for the next few kilometers or so the road widened slightly, with different paint markings. Conjuring up memories of one of my favorite children's programs, *Flying Doctors*, I was impressed to find out that the only way to hospital out here was by air, and the only way for the air ambulance to pick you up was to land on the road. It took over an hour to fly from Perth, during which time some vehicles would drive out from the nearest roadhouse and stop the traffic. I couldn't imagine this would have been a taxing job. If you were to stop the traffic for an hour you'd be lucky to have a traffic jam of more than a couple of cars and a road train. Still, every time I passed one of these signs and landing strips I inadvertently looked up, as if a plane might be on approach to liven up my day.

Caiguna was at the other end of the 90-mile straight, and the only bit of civilization all day. I had to get there for the sake of water, so it had to be a 180km day. It is hard to imagine, though very easy to describe, but there really was absolutely nothing at the roadside, only scrubby bushes and open ground. There were no fence posts, no turnoffs, nothing at all human, except the mile markers. It is a purely psychological thing, but I dislike counting down miles. Kilometer markers, somehow, I can deal with. They are more numerous, and in some countries, like Iran, I enjoyed them punctuating my days. These markers, in this barren expanse, as the day got windier, became increasingly discouraging.

All afternoon the wind got stronger and stronger, blowing in from the front right. It was absolutely energy-sapping. I felt like I was struggling into a hot fan all day as warm gusts battered the front end of the bike around. The Danish guy passed me midmorning and seemed slightly put out that I had not joined him at the campfire last night. It amused me that he kept commenting how tough it was driving this vast distance: "So trying, I get so dehydrated and bored, you know?" I wasn't sure if he really expected me to agree and sympathize while I rode along beside him on a pushbike.

As the wind swung from the side to head-on, my pace slowed, and battling harder simply aggravated the pain from my saddle. The skin had split at a number of rub points and was deeply bruised. It was also starting to callus around these cuts, on small areas that had broken and healed repeatedly. All day I could not stay on the bike for more than twenty minutes at a time because of the pain. I couldn't take painkillers or I would lose all awareness of how bad things were. The loss of the cream was proving even more serious than I had feared, and using antiseptic and arnica wasn't making up for it, although they would hopefully help prevent infection. The worst moments were when I stopped for around five minutes, too sore to carry on. On days like this, the most important thing is momentum. When the hurt is greatest it is essential to carry on because at least then you are progressing. If you stop and sit alone at the roadside you are both in pain and achieving nothing.

While off the saddle, there was nothing interesting about the world I was passing through to distract from the pain and I felt like my resolve was slowly getting worn down. By midafternoon I was almost out of water. On the map of the Nullarbor I could see a couple of water stations. I had no idea what form these would take, but the first was luckily not far ahead. Pulling off the road into a large dusty car park, I saw a big water tank raised high off the ground with a tap at the end of a thin pipe. The car park was empty except for a small camper van.

After lining up my water bottles and looking forward to quenching my thirst after a day of rationing, I turned the tap, only for nothing to happen. It was dry. I had less than a liter left. Thankfully, the camper van was owned by a young English couple who had spare stores and kindly gave me a couple of liters to see me to the next rest-house. I don't know what would've happened had they not been there. I would've been in trouble.

By six o'clock I was still out there battling, and having been stubbornly focused on getting to Caiguna all day I suddenly realized there was no way I would get there by nightfall. I had less than half a liter of water left and very little food. I could have ridden into the night but I was spent. I just couldn't face another hour of that pain, into that wind. It was relentless. I had cracked. I just stopped pedaling, stepped off, and pushed the bike off the road without a second thought. It hadn't even been a conscious decision. My body had decided for me.

The power of recovery is amazing, though, and within half an hour the life was returning to me. With no food to cook I had little to do after pitching the tent. At this point, in the growing dusk, I spotted a short way off a family of grazing Big Reds, the biggest kangaroos and one of the largest species of marsupial. They are magnificent animals, with an incredible bound, and I set off stealthily to try to track them. They kept jumping a short distance ahead, so I had to follow, until they finally sensed me and fled, bounding gracefully toward the horizon.

I had been tracking for less than fifteen minutes, but when I looked up, for the first time, I saw that I was hundreds of meters from the road. The sense of space was awesome. A plateau as far as the eye could see in every direction, as the sun sank in the west. It had clouded over at sixish after another hot clear day, and the spectrum of oranges that were now seeping into the sky was mesmerizing. I couldn't even see the road from where I stood; I only knew it was there because my bike stood silhouetted and alone on the verge. It was a real moment. I just stood there for five minutes until hunger distracted me. My last ration pack, a banana and an energy bar, was almost all I had left.

I had covered 166km, probably the most painful 100 miles of my life, but was still 15 miles from the end of this incredible straight. It had taken over nine hours' cycling in eleven hours on the go at a painful 17km/h to get that far. It was unsustainable to keep battling like this. As the winds picked up massively in the afternoon, the only solution, despite being exhausted, was to get less sleep tonight, start very early tomorrow, and try to finish earlier.

It wasn't the best night's sleep. I was kept awake by strange noises. In the middle of the night a truck pulled in at the roadside nearby. The engine ran for a while before cutting out. There was no reason for anything to stop on the 90-mile straight. I lay there tense, straining to hear. Someone got out and there was scuffling and a cough. I had no idea if the moon was high enough to enable the driver to see the tent, and I didn't want to get out and draw attention to myself. I am sure it was all very normal and nothing to do with me being there, but I felt very vulnerable. Eventually I fell asleep again, though I kept waking till dawn.

At 5:30 I rolled the tent. The truck had gone and there was nothing on the horizon. I left without breakfast as I had nothing except my emergency pack left, and this was not an emergency yet. I had about 250ml of water remaining. Thirst increases through the day, so even though I would get dehydrated later, it was easier to ration water in the mornings.

After an hour, without a breath of wind, I reached Caiguna. There I met an older couple I had seen the day before at the last roadhouse. They were flabbergasted that I had got this far so quickly in the wind, and sat me down to have breakfast with them. They explained that once every couple of months their job was to drive across the Nullarbor filling up the small music racks and collecting the money from sales. The gentleman proudly showed me the rack with its range of CDs and tapes. I didn't know cassette tapes were still made. They were a lovely couple, but I couldn't help wondering at their choice of job and how profitable it could be. If I had to drop a box of CDs at every roadhouse every couple of months I would be tempted to buy a Harley and make it fun, or better still just get a trucker, who was going anyway, to do it.

A small spanner in my early start plan was that I lost forty-five minutes crossing from Western Australia into the Central Western time zone. Another was that because I had been in a "go, go, go" state of mind for so long it wasn't at all easy to get to midafternoon with plenty of daylight left and just stop. So I ended up sitting on the bike for over ten hours, pushing an average as slow as the previous day, over a total of 181km. For all that it hurt, it was a great day.

It took five hours to get from Caiguna to the next roadhouse at Cocklebiddy, and then I carried on until it was dark, making it over Madura Pass. As its name suggests, I spent all afternoon on a very gradual climb into the same afternoon winds. The final descent was, however, glorious, and I happily turned into a resthouse and motel feeling great for battling through another toughie. Then, to shatter this moment, the motel owner, during some typical chitchat over the settling of the bill, told me the story of how an incredible wind just the previous week had helped an amateur cyclist go 300km in a day—"and he wasn't even trying to go fast like you," he added helpfully.

The fact that there is so little in the Outback means that the smallest things are noticeable. Unfortunately, the three most memorable roadside occurrences will never make it onto the "I crossed the Nullarbor" postcards that every roadhouse sold: roadkill kangaroos, piss bottles, and porn.

I very rarely saw any kangaroos in broad daylight, but I passed hundreds of dead ones at the roadside. Apparently at night they are a real hazard for cars. If a Big Red weighing an average of about 70kg hits your car going at 80mph then you are both in serious trouble. However, if you are driving a road train, a huge truck with two or three trailers, you are hardly going to notice it. Most vehicles out here have huge bull bars, and the kangaroos are the reason why. In the afternoons I could always smell roadkill long before I saw it. The smell of rotting flesh in 40-degree sun was sickening. The Dutch bikers had been complaining about the odor getting into their helmets. And they were past each kill in a matter of seconds. On a bicycle at 12mph it took a couple of minutes to reach and pass each carcass, and on some stretches I passed many.

I assumed that the less organic litter was also thanks mainly to truckers. That Saturday a road train passed me heading in the other direction, and I saw that the driver was reading something. I could see the top of a book or magazine over the steering wheel so he could half look forward at the same time. This scared me. You could hear these monsters coming and I almost always took myself right off to the side as they were not very good at pulling out. People at a couple of roadhouses had told stories of how these men would do almost nonstop transcontinental drives. Driving from Perth to Sydney in one hit, I can understand how you might end up zoning out slightly and squashing the odd kangaroo or cyclist en route.

A side effect of these incredible commutes is that it seemed the norm to urinate in plastic bottles and chuck them out of the window. I might only have passed one or two an hour, but as there was almost nothing else out there it seemed like a lot. The pornographic litter I found harder to rationalize. If you have to urinate while driving I suppose it makes sense to get rid of it. No one likes a bottle of piss in the glovebox. But if you are a guy who likes porn, you wouldn't think you'd suddenly have a change of opinion on the matter while alone in the Outback.

I had to stop. Fatigue and saddle pains were developing into leg strains which could easily become injuries. I hadn't had any mobile phone coverage for four days now so called home reverse charge from Mundrabilla and asked Mum to call Dr. Niall MacFarlane at Glasgow University and get some advice. All day I could not raise my heart rate above 110 beats per minute. Normally if you spin your legs a bit faster the blood will pump around a bit faster and your heart rate will rise. For all the will in the world I could not make my muscles do anything that raised my heart rate. I could not spin them faster, and could barely raise my head from the front wheel.

Monday was only 5km better than the day before at just 124km. In two days I had dropped half a day on target, but there was nothing I could do about it into that headwind. At 16.9km/h average this was the slowest day of the whole cycle so far. There were, however, a couple of milestones to help me claw through the day: first, I crossed from Western Australia into South Australia; second, I'd reached 100 hours' ride time in Australia.

Just 16km short of the state border I met the Southern Ocean for the first time in over a week, at Eucla resthouse. This was the start of the Great Australian Bight, or at least where I joined it, an enormous 700-mile open bay. Unlike most shallow bays, the bight is not very fertile because the Nullarbor area gets so little rainfall that there is not enough outwash of nourishment to support much life. Therefore it is an area renowned for big sharks, tuna, and whales but not the more complex marine diversity of the Gold Coast and the barrier reefs to the east. It is spectacular, though, and I was excited to see the road running close to the ocean all day, near famous cliffs that rise to 60 meters. Apparently I was a few weeks late for the whale-watching season but that didn't stop me peering out hopefully.

The Eucla resthouse was quite posh and the first that looked to cater for anything more than simple stopovers. I was going to say budget, but while being simple, nothing in the Nullarbor is budget. Each establishment has a monopoly on trade for at least 100km so with a bit of collusion can charge whatever they want. Eucla was different: it had a nicer restaurant, an outdoor swimming pool, and touristy signs with distances to towns in each direction across Australia. I was heartened to find Norseman 712km behind me and Ceduna 495km ahead, as it was starting to feel like I had been out here for a long time. YOU ARE NOW LEAVING WESTERN AUSTRALIA. THANK YOU FOR CALLING. NEXT QUARANTINE STOP CEDUNA said the sign. It seemed that going the other way you got stopped here for quarantine, but I still had the best part of 500km to my quarantine check. In my mind this left a very large no-man's-land where whatever they were quarantining against could enter in either direction. This suggested that there was not much to protect over the next 500km.

My key purchase at the resthouse was a notepad as I had run out of logbook for all the Guinness facts and figures, as well as my own shorthand notes. They had nothing but a stack of postcards, but I got into conversation with an elderly couple. They were very excited to find me cycling out here, and the lady produced a small flowery notepad, wrote me a good luck message, and waved me off. It made me smile for miles.

Since Norseman I had passed signs every so often warning about wild animals. Keeping in mind the aforementioned roadkill these were understandable, but their style amused me—though maybe this says more about my frame of mind at the time. An average sign would be yellow with three diamonds showing a picture in each, normally a camel, a wombat, and a kangaroo. Then underneath, in a large rectangular sign, it would say something like NEXT 88KM. After 88km exactly I would pass another similar sign with another arbitrary number. I assumed that this would happen until I reached the first dividing fence line after 1,200km of open plains. Maybe the authorities thought they would be more memorable if they were at surprise intervals.

I lost another forty-five minutes on the border with another time change. The road didn't turn out to be the clifftop ocean route I had expected, but the map did show a couple of points where you could turn off to viewing points. By midafternoon it was painful progress, both literally and in terms of speed. Day after day this was indescribably demoralizing. The wind simulated a constant hill climb, which hour after hour became pretty mind-numbing. My saddle sores were bleeding and a constant pain.

That afternoon a camper van pulled alongside, and I chatted with its occupants. A dreamcatcher was hanging from the rearview mirror. "Are you Canadian?" I asked. The lady seemed delighted that I had guessed. Her Aussie boyfriend was behind the wheel, and we had a shouted conversation for a few minutes before he raced on. I envied their spirit. They had each other, were young, happy, and on an adventure together. Their laughter put into context how rubbish I was feeling, how alone I was.

I only rode for seven and a half hours that day, then couldn't face it anymore. At the closest cliff point I turned off and cycled the few hundred meters of dirt path to a wide parking area, busy with a surprising number of camper vans and caravans. I kicked the bike on to its stand and walked over to the cliff edge. Moments like that are good for the spirit. For that day's tough climb, this was my summit moment. It was breathtaking, falling 50 meters below me into raging seas. The wind was ferocious, but I didn't care now—it added to the wild charm of the place. As the sun sank over the sea to my right, I turned to find the Canadian lady standing there. I hadn't noticed their camper van parked up. Her boyfriend soon joined us, but in the wind we still had to shout to be heard.

There was no sense in trying to camp near the campers, it was far too windy with no soft ground, so I said good-bye and pushed the bike back down the track. I'd hoped for more shelter away from the cliffs, but there weren't even any dips or ditches I could drop the tent into. The only cover I could see was a couple of low bushes no more than waist height about halfway back to the road. Pitching on the northwest side to use the bush as a windbreak was not ideal, but there was no alternative. The couple had offered me a space in their camper, and while it had been a very genuine offer, I felt uncomfortable about accepting. It looked cramped enough for two, and they were a couple. It was pretty disheartening to have had two really poor days, but I tried to reassure myself that there would be others at the other end of the trip that would easily average these out.

I woke just as the tent collapsed on top of me. It took a second to orientate myself and remember where I was, then stretch out through the canvas to find my glasses. There was a reasonable moon, so I didn't need my head torch. The wind had changed direction, picked up, and was now coming from the west, so the canvas was blowing across me instead of lengthways.

There was no way I could get back to sleep in a collapsed tent, so I fumbled for the porch zip and crawled out, assuming my kit inside would be enough to pin it down. This assumption proved wrong. I was sitting on the ground putting on my trainers when a gust whipped in and picked up the whole tent and everything in it, including shoes, helmet, and cycle clothes. It traveled quite a distance. I threw myself on it as soon as it landed, quickly tucking it under me so it could no longer catch in the ferocious wind. The noise of loose pertex canvas flapping, cracking, and whipping in the wind was amazingly loud.

After bundling the canvas up I got to my feet and went back over to where it had been pitched. There was kit strewn everywhere, and everything that had been in the porch was in danger of blowing away now, so I quickly threw the bike on its side and on top of the tent while I chased after my cooking pan and food as they too flew off into the night. It took a few minutes to find and weigh everything down. The wind was utterly relentless.

There was absolutely no point in even trying to repitch in these gales; my only choice was to sleep on top. However, with the direction change had come a marked drop in temperature. It wasn't anything dangerous, but the windchill from this cooler air in the middle of the night was surprising. I threw on all my cycle clothes, trousers, fleece, shoes, and hat and crawled into my sleeping bag, but still felt cold. For the next four hours, until first light, this is how I tried to sleep, on top of my tent with any loose kit thrown inside until it was light enough to see properly.

The upside to this terrible night was that the wind I had been expecting and hoping for since Fremantle had arrived. It was now right behind me. I had lost a bag of food in the night, which left me without much to start the day, but I was itching to get rolling. Nine hours later I had ridden a stunning 206km. I had the same saddle sores and was on the same terrain with the same food and hydration levels, so the wind had added over 80km to previous days. That tail-wind literally and psychologically pushed me along. By the end of play I had passed another major milestone—10,000 miles.

In the middle of the afternoon a camper van drew level as I pedaled along, and I looked over to see three beaming faces and a video camera looking at me. Down the side of their vehicle were cycle brand sponsors and a website address, raceacrossaustralia.com. I laughed as they filmed the shouted introductions.

"What are you doing?"

"Going for the world record for cycling around the world. What are you doing?"

"My husband is going for the world record for cycling across Australia," the lady shouted back. "What is your job to allow you to do this?"

"For now I am a cyclist." I laughed.

"Are you married?" she asked.

"No, I'm only twenty-four."

We chatted for a while. A guy called Damian was somewhere behind me, racing about sixteen hours a day across the continent. It was not going well. He had been banking on the same tailwind as I had. This had been bad news for me and I was having a miserable time, but it had been disastrous for Damian. He didn't have thousands more miles ahead of him to average out any slow miles. They all had to be fast, and after a good first day he had fallen behind target, unable to battle into the headwind faster than the previous record holder had gone without the wind as a hindrance. I agreed that I would stop and see them all at the next roadhouse, and they drove on.

Damian was supported by a number of friends, but all of them seemed to be struggling to keep up with the hard man. Over a quick lunch I properly met his wife, young son, a young friend who was the driver, and a couple of these support riders. The second support camper van was driving behind the riders. It was an incredible record to chase. Damian aimed to ride at an average of 30km/h for four sets of four hours every day. He had a bike for the flats, a bike for the hills, and plenty of spares. The flats bike was a single-piece time-trial bike built for speed and pain over a short distance. The idea of riding in that compact position for tens of hours was excruciating.

On top of the tailwind, I was motivated all afternoon by being chased by Damian. It seemed likely that I would be caught and passed late in the day. There was no way I could compete, but I was up for giving it a go.

Much of the day was spent in the real Nullarbor Plain, a treeless expanse of gently rolling scrub. I was excited to get there, but unsure why. However, at the end of the day I was in woodland for the first time since the day after Norseman, spindly hardwoods in sandy soil over increasingly rolling terrain. By nightfall I was climbing impressive dippers, and there was still no sign of Damian. The camper van caught me again to give an update and I agreed to meet them at the next available camp spot. It's strange losing control of where you stop, distances seem much farther, and I was soon looking around muttering to myself, "Where are they? That would have been a perfect camp spot." I found them in the first proper lay-by, a track looping off the road. It just showed that my idea of a good camp spot differed somewhat from the norm.

After putting the tent up I joined them in the back of their camper. I was being fed sandwiches when Damian arrived. He was in incredible shape considering what he had just come through. A man in his forties, Damian had an efficient, compact frame and a tough mental resolve which was apparent from his handshake to his style of conversation. He was all about pushing boundaries, and we spent a very enjoyable twenty minutes loading carbs and chatting before I crawled into my tent, and he turned on his lights for another four hours into the dark.

Damian's motivation was to raise money for orphans in Africa; a documentary on the subject had moved him and his wife. He was behind target, but you wouldn't have known from his banter. Like all true competitors he was focusing on his own inputs and performance and not getting distracted by what he couldn't affect. You can't focus on winning—there are too many variables out of your control—but you can focus on your best performance; and your best performance, in the right circumstances, will be a winning performance. Damian exemplified this approach, and through meeting him I gained strength.

It had been a fantastic day—206km—but I had overcooked it. The next morning the wind had turned back and was up from early morning. The only cover was the trees for the first few miles. Once again I simply could not raise my heart rate. I had spoken to Damian about this and he had experienced the same. When the body is truly exhausted and has depleted reserves there is no way to raise the HR, so I sat at an average of 102 beats per minute pushing a painfully slow 17km/h.

I lasted five hours and nine minutes on the bike and covered just 89.8km. I had blown up, the value of a 200km day lost. I simply couldn't keep going. Just before stopping I passed a sign that read DROWSY DRIVERS DIE. NUNDROO 5KM. Drowsy didn't even come close to how I felt. I was miles away, completely spaced out. I was almost numb to the pain of my saddle sores and couldn't find anything in my mind to focus on. I needed something to clutch at that would enable me to refocus. It didn't matter what—a single memory, idea, or wish that would allow a spark of interest or passion, and let me build momentum. But I was numb, removed from the world.

At Nundroo I saw another bike parked outside. Marcus was from Germany, had been living in Sydney, and was now cycling home. I joined him for some food, which turned into a lot of food, and was glad for the company. The plan was to carry on as it was only three p.m. when I arrived. To be honest it was not a plan as my mind couldn't focus, but I had assumed I would carry on, as I always did. An hour and a half later I was still there. It would be one of the worst days of the race yet if I stopped, but I couldn't go on. What was the point of fighting that wind for another few hours, getting another 30km down the road, sleeping in the tent, and then doing the same tomorrow?

"Come stay with me, I have a spare bed in my room," Marcus said. He had heard me arguing with myself about the pros and cons for ten minutes now. "You will make up the miles. You need to eat, sleep, and recover or you won't make it."

I had only just met the guy but his perspective and honesty were most welcome. If I had been alone I am sure I would have carried on, out of a sense of obligation if nothing else. It was a hard decision to make, but once made it felt right. I had two more courses of food, showered, then turned in for an incredibly early night.

Meeting Marcus renewed my confidence about what lay ahead. He was not very experienced but from what he said it sounded like the worst was definitely behind me. "Get up really early with me and we will miss the afternoon's wind," he advised. I agreed for a moment, then I remembered he was going the other way. "I have had a headwind as well, the first week from Sydney," he explained, "and yesterday it was a headwind again. It was only today that was better." This was also encouraging: I might be in for a tailwind in the east.

At seven a.m. the following morning we shook hands on the roadside and headed in opposite directions. His ambition and very open naivety about what lay ahead were charming. He planned to cycle to Perth, get a boat to Singapore, hopscotch up Asia, and then pedal home to Germany, and vowed never to take a plane again in his life.

The early start worked: it was completely calm. After a couple of hours I passed a couple of tall, old-fashioned wind generators, for lifting water out of underground wells. This meant that there was livestock nearby, I reasoned. Half an hour later I passed a dilapidated stone farm shed. It was the first sign of civilization. At lunch I reached Penong, the first houses in nearly a thousand miles, and at 4:30 I finally made it to Ceduna. I was through the Outback; the sense of relief was absolute.

17

I'd had enough of the beard. I hadn't had a shave since Pakistan, and it was getting a bit ridiculous. I was back in the civilized world, so it was time to look civilized again. There was no cutthroat barber in Ceduna, so, armed with a pair of scissors and a pack of single-blade disposable razors, I began hacking off the rat's nest. Under my burned nose and dark cheeks my white chin looked unusual.

Civilization also meant the first phone coverage for over a week. To amuse myself I tried to guess the number of messages I'd received, with the reward of an ice cream if I got more than fifteen. My trip was filled with little games like this; they were so important. It seemed the web blog had continued well despite my lack of communication, and people had rallied to get me through this tough bit. I had some amazing messages of support which, despite having not reached me until now, meant a lot.

The GPS tracker had failed. It seemed that the batteries had died in the middle of the Outback. They had not been tested before in this way, sending a location every two hours up to seven times a day for half a year, but it was hoped they could last for the whole world. Those following the cycle online had grown concerned that I had somehow broken down and was stuck in the middle of nowhere. Base Camp was immediately working on the logistics for getting a charger or replacement unit to me. I had to be very careful about my verification for Guinness World Records.

That evening, taking stock of what I had come through so far in Australia, I was stunned to find that I had spent over £1,000, not including my purchases in Perth. For somewhere with so few places to spend money I was doing a pretty good job of getting rid of it.

The next day, Friday November 23, felt like a fresh start, despite being less than fresh in body. The plan was to cut off the Eyre High-way and continue to follow the coast around the Eyre Peninsula. It was two sides of a triangle, and while necessary for the miles, I did stop for a long moment when I got to the sign that read PORT AUGUSTA ROUTE 1 462 (STRAIGHT ON), ROUTE 1 (ALT) 739 (TURN RIGHT).

This was still one of the most rural areas I had ever been in—only the odd house here and there—but it teemed with life compared to where I had just been, and it was a stunningly scenic route. I set out without many supplies as I could see a small town called Smoky Bay en route. I got to the dot and found that it was actually a coastal town on a 6km there-and-back detour. The fact that I was chasing a big daily target made this frustrating, but I needed water. Smoky Bay was a beautiful, quaint fishing town with no through traffic. It reminded me of the world I was missing just off the highway. This little town was named by Captain Matthew Flinders in the early 1800s after seeing the smoke from fires lit by the Aboriginal people.

I sound like a stuck record, but it was a grim afternoon. The trees swayed and grasses were flattened by the gusts. The only time I have ever experienced anything in the northern hemisphere that can com-pete with this is in the high mountains, and they are not conditions you would normally try to go for a cycle in. However, lunch was the most fun I'd had for weeks, in another place with a cool name, Streaky Bay, where I picked up the GPS battery charger Mum had arranged to be sent to me.

It felt like a perfect sleepy holiday. I sat on the pier, swinging my legs like a little schoolboy in the sun, eating watermelon, and tucking into a superb pick and mix of bakeries. I'd run around the super-market with such glee after living off roadhouse food for so long. Truckie food is great, but it doesn't seem to have the nutritional value to aid cycling 100 miles a day into an unrelenting headwind, plus it was insanely expensive. Here I had a full choice, and for my first few shops I bought far more than I could eat and carry. That day I spent an incredible £25 on food and didn't have much left over.

Friday's 180km was a massive success, taking me as far as Port Kenny. For such a small town, the hotel was buzzing. I only popped in for water, but the need for a cheap room was assumed by the land-lady when I walked in, and I wasn't going to refuse.

It was the night before the Australian general election. John Howard, from the Liberal Party, had been in power for nine years, the second-longest tenure in the country's history, and was going strong for another session. But he faced his strongest competition yet from a young contender, Kevin Rudd from the Labor Party. The pre-election debates and scandal had kept me amused since arriving in Australia, and tomorrow was the big day.

The most amazing scandal had hit the headlines the day before, just two days before the polls opened. I had thought that UK politics was sometimes dirty and a little underhand, but the Aussies seemed to have taken this to another level. The husband of a Liberal MP had been captured in the early hours of the morning distributing fake election flyers from the fabricated "Islamic Australian Federation," claiming that the Labor Party sympathized with Islamic terrorists. They were being left in letterboxes in a marginal area. The damage to John Howard's campaign was immense. It was a malicious act, and some of their comments linking in the Bali bombing and the obvious anti-Muslim sentiment were entirely inexcusable and very serious, but I couldn't help laughing. It was a wonderful mess and seemed rather ridiculous. You had to wonder at the conversations which led to that seeming like a good idea. It was so amateur that the leaflets had misspelled Allah Akbar—"God is great"—as Ala Akba.

The next day was one of the hardest afternoon slogs yet. What had been the devil coming front right all the way across the Nullarbor was now right on the nose. In eight hours I managed 142km—not a disaster, but bit by bit I was dropping serious miles. I passed Elliston fast, then the headwind picked up and I slowed through Sheringa. Eventually I pitched the tent in a lay-by at the roadside by Mount Hope, a tiny hamlet. I felt like I had battled again and not been beaten.

The day threw up two wild and surprise attractions. The first was a huge lizard tucking into a roadkill kangaroo. It lazily eyed me as it chomped down on the rotting carcass. The second was a South African cyclist coming in the other direction who was trying to circumnavigate Australia. He must have been at least fifty but could have been much more, and he looked as if he had spent every moment in the baking sun. With long gray hair, a completely open cycle shirt, and what appeared to be darkened, oversize swimming goggles hanging around his neck along with a shark-tooth necklace, he looked like a character out of the film *Waterworld*. He also resembled the fatherly figure in Wesley Snipe's *Blade* trilogy: haggard, worldly, tough as old boots.

If there was a reward from taking on this wind, then I reasoned it would be heading back up the east side of the Eyre Peninsula. This stayed in my head throughout Sunday morning, which started and remained windy all the way to the headland at Port Lincoln. Having turned the corner, the afternoon was then wind-assisted, and I cruised to the cutely named Tumby Bay. This really was Toytown country, and both Port Lincoln and Tumby Bay begged for further exploration.

Port Lincoln, THE SEAFOOD CAPITAL OF AUSTRALIA as the signs proudly claimed, was simply showing off as an idyllic beach town when I wheeled in. A harbor wall, along the top of which ran a grassy area with footpaths, closed in a wide sandy beach. Behind this the road ran along a front with cafés and shops, where I pedaled along, considering which beautiful spot to dine at. I wanted to celebrate the end of the winds for at least a couple of days. A pizzeria café looked perfect, and I kicked the bike onto its stand.

I turned to see a guy with two girls about my age walking over. He was interested to know about the bike. They were going for lunch as well, so I joined them. For half an hour we sat in the sun, eating pizza and chatting. It was fantastic, one of the first normal conversations I had had in days. He was here working with his girlfriend. The other girl was a friend, a marine biologist called Sarah; she was diving daily for a study on the marine biology systems in the area. He was an avid cyclist and wanted me to stay and talk more about our adventures, and Sarah was stunning with great chat, so it was hard to drag myself away. That night, as I walked down the beachfront at Tumby Bay to find some food, she texted, simply to say keep in touch.

I have never been so excited to find a laundry. My clothes had not been properly washed since Perth and the side effects in terms of the salt wounds don't need any more explaining. Suffice it to say they were now pretty chronic. I still had no new saddle cream, so a proper wash would go a long way toward easing the situation.

Before going to bed I spoke to Dad for the first time since leaving Paris. It sounded like a lot of people were starting to follow my progress back in the UK.

The following day, with clean clothes, a girl on my mind, and a huge tailwind, I flew. It was in fact the greatest daily distance of the whole cycle at 226km. And when your arse feels like it's falling off, 141 miles is a long way.

For the first part I followed the coast along to Cowell, and then the Lincoln Highway swung inland and over wooded climbs to the town of Whyalla. I completely zoned out for most of the day, loving the sense of flow from spinning away at 23km/h for hour after hour. It hurt, and I didn't want to repeat my 200km experience in the Nullarbor when I blew up the next day, but there was nowhere sensible to stop, so I just kept going. At one point I slowed for fifteen minutes to scan the roadside for a good spot to camp. Finding nothing, I stopped and was amazed to read 190km on the cycle computer. I then looked at the map and realized that Whyalla wasn't impossible. It would be tough and I would have to speed up, but it wasn't impossible. The road cut back toward the coast and was mainly a very gradual descent, and I covered the last 36km in an hour and twenty minutes. My heart rate was high because I was really pushing, and it felt incredible to break out of that seemingly never-ending slow march across Australia and really go for broke for a few hours.

My logbook that day contains the simple note "Saw Emu—dumb birds." I was cycling through the woods at one point with a high fence between it and the road when I startled an emu. It was the first time I had seen one and it ran away and hit the fence every few meters for about 500 meters, grunting away, sounding more like a pig than a bird. They are big, clumsy-looking birds with "form without function" wings when they are standing still. When they are striding along, smacking their disproportionately small heads on a fence, they are hilarious. My laughter made my front tire wiggle down the road.

It was almost dark when I raced into Whyalla. The road was completely deserted. A mile later I saw the Sundowner Hotel Motel and pulled in. It turned out to be an edge-of-town gaming venue. The reception hall had rows of slot machines and a bar in one corner. The receptionist gave me a very strange look when she handed me my room key, which I understood when I looked in the mirror. I was a sweaty, muddy mess, and pretty stinky.

Still, I returned for food without having a wash first as I was too hungry to care. They had closed the kitchen, but seeing my face fall the bar lady asked me to wait and she ran off to get the manageress. She seemed pretty abrupt to start with, until I said, "I have just cycled from Tumby Bay and really need to eat—I'll have anything."

She looked at me for a long moment. "You cycled from Tumby Bay today? That's nearly two hundred kilometers."

"Two hundred and twenty-six," I corrected.

"Anything?"

"Pardon?"

"You want anything?"

"Oh, yes, and I'll take a couple of whatever 'anything' is."

She laughed and walked off to make the arrangements. A few minutes later she was back and I chatted to her until two huge chicken schnitzels with gravy and all the trimmings arrived. I scribbled down my website at her request and thanked her for her help.

Food had rarely tasted better. I didn't care that it wasn't vegetarian, I was so hungry. There had been little choice at any of the roadhouses and I'd eaten quite a few meat meals.

Just as I got up to leave the lady came back through having visited the website. "There's fifty dollars for your charities," she said. "Please let us know how you get on."

It was a lovely gesture, a fitting end to a great day.

After that wee epic I allowed myself a short lie-in and a huge buffet breakfast, and didn't leave till nine a.m. Until the top of the peninsula the winds were still with me, and despite pretty tight legs, I managed some fast early miles.

Port Augusta is where my coastal road, the Lincoln Highway, rejoined the main trans-Australian, the Eyre Highway. After the wild beauty of the last few days, Port Augusta was a bit of a shock. Signs called it THE CROSSROADS OF AUSTRALIA with slogans like BRIDGING THE OUTBACK AND THE SEA, but this overlooked the fact that it was a rather dull industrial area. From there the road cut south again, following the coast toward Adelaide.

It had been decided that I should take a recovery day in Adelaide, with Shonnie Pascoe, a Glasgow alumni contact, and her family. The plan of a day off every fortnight had worked out perfectly so far, keeping me on target. At Adelaide there was no reason to stop, but after such a fight to get across the Outback the team back in Scotland advised me to take the day of recovery to keep on track in the long run. I was back into the wind but didn't care now. I was close to a break and my spirits soared.

Before I even started the race, and through leg 1 with Piotr, I was taught how to strip the lactic out of my legs and work out any niggles and frozen muscles. My IT bands, which run on the outside of your upper leg from hip to knee, always got particularly tight. Throughout Southeast Asia some of the muscular niggles had become more serious, and in Australia the endless fighting into a headwind had left the legs with constant pains. Every night I would sit in my tent or motel and strip them out; if I didn't I could barely get back on the bike the next day. When I forgot or was too tired I always paid for it. However, the process was very painful, and I had long known that a part of this pain at least was avoidable.

I have never been a roadie, an indoctrinated road cyclist, who has found it socially acceptable to shave my legs. But now was the time. I had months of leg massages to go and if I could avoid pulling the hairs and making myself squeak every evening then it had to be done. I'd bought myself a packet of disposable razors and some shaving gel in Ceduna and had been psyching myself to take on the legs ever since. The pain from the massage after the 226km ride was what finally made me do it.

Respect to ladies, it is not easy, especially with a very hairy start. Propped on a chair, with one leg lifted onto the toilet seat, the process took nearly an hour, and by the end I had two razor cuts behind my right knee and a big one where I had taken the skin off straight down my left shin. At this depth, the cuts would not stop bleeding.

After a shower I threw on my shorts and went over to the diner to eat. I felt so self-conscious and embarrassed when I looked down. They looked weird, like chicken legs. I found myself walking back to my room with my knees together because it felt funny.

Apart from my new sleekness, the next day was fairly uneventful through a mixture of farmland and over 164km to the small town of Dublin, where Shonnie met me. I was just so excited about my day off that I hardly noticed what I was passing.

Adelaide was by far the most restful day off yet. Shonnie and family were the perfect hosts. Every few days on the road I would meet people or be in a place where I wanted to stop and explore, but few could compare to the desire to stay at this home from home. After a visit to a clinic for a professional massage and picking up a few new supplies, we managed to find time to relax and chat.

Base Camp and the BBC had managed to send out a good amount of replacement kit, most importantly some new chamois cream: at last I could start fighting these saddle sores. Shonnie also raised motherly concerns about my pretty bad sunburn and we ended up hunting around town for some zinc cream.

The next day, number 118 on the road, I was given a lift back to Dublin to start afresh. Shonnie waved me off and I set out, with a few hours' riding ahead of me before I reached Adelaide. Just 20km out from the city I was spinning along a flat road, feeling great on the bike, when I heard a loud twang from the back wheel. I didn't need to look, I knew it was a broken spoke. If this had happened anywhere between Perth and Adelaide it would have been serious, so I was grateful for this small blessing at least. But I kicked myself for not having got the bike serviced on my day off—not that a weak spoke would necessarily have been spotted. I phoned Shonnie, who'd only just got home, and explained that I needed a bike shop; could she kindly call around?

Twisting the broken spoke around its neighbors and not worrying about fixing it, I undid the back brake so the wheel wobble would not hit it and pedaled slowly on. Shonnie and her husband met me on the outskirts of the city and took me to the first shop, where two slightly dour men took a while to get on board in terms of the urgency of my request. Once the bike was on the wheel rig I left them to it and walked around the shop for a while until I was called back.

"Your whole wheel is bust, mate." He pointed at a hairline crack coming out from one of the spoke holes and along the rim.

There was no way the spokes would stay tight with that. It would last a while, but one big bump would split the wheel completely. And they couldn't fix it: they had no parts and were too busy. Trying not to stress about lost time, I reminded myself that I was in the best place in the last 1,500 miles to break down, so any lost time would be minimal in comparison. I immediately wrote off the rest of the day, and accepted that I now had another full rest day. It was out of my hands, so why stress? The mechanic phoned another shop in town, which agreed to see me immediately.

This new shop was evidently where the pros went. In the dimly lit room, filled with expensive kit and posters of the pros, the owner-cum-mechanic greeted me warmly and I explained the problem: "I need a double-rimmed very strong rim put onto a thirty-two-spoke

Rohloff hub." Each part of this request was unusual, as double-rimmed is not the norm in road wheels, a standard rim has thirty-six or more spokes, and these spokes would have to be shorter because they were for an unusual hub.

"Sure, no problem, come back at two o'clock."

I looked at my watch. It was just coming up to midday. I looked back in disbelief. I checked, and he was sure; it would only take him two hours and I could get back racing that afternoon. I didn't know what to say. Strangely, I didn't know whether I was grateful or disappointed I wasn't getting the afternoon off.

After a quick lunch back at Shonnie's, we picked up the bike and went back to shop number one so that I could start where I had finished. And then I was off, having lost less than four hours in total. By the end of play I had covered 141km—only an hour's riding down on target.

I had not expected the Adelaide Hills. There was nothing before them to suggest they were coming. Straight out of the city to the south I started climbing, and by nightfall I had climbed 1,300 meters—more than I would have done in a week of Nullarbor riding. The ascent out of town began on the main highway, then cyclists were taken off onto the old road, which went much higher than the main road, winding through thick woods. I was accompanied by a number of road racers who shot past me. There was no way to compete with the amount of weight I had on my bike, regardless of how fresh I felt. One man paused for a few words and I told him I had ridden from Fremantle before he went on.

A few kilometers later I was pausing at the top, a place called Eagle on the Hill with a stunning view back down over Adelaide, when I heard rustling nearby. I looked up and saw a koala bear looking down at me from halfway up a tree. It was tiny and moving so slowly, hand over hand, up the branch. I have rarely seen anything so cute. My first koala.

Getting back on my bike, I pushed on, quickly realizing that I wasn't actually at the top. Ten minutes later I did summit and also finished the cycle path, coming onto a minor road. It wasn't at all clear which way to go. The cycle path I had been on wasn't on my map, so I wasn't sure exactly which little road I was now on. I made a good guess at the correct direction and pushed on. Just around the corner, a few hundred meters later, I came across the cyclist who had spoken to me before; he'd decided to wait for me at the top in case I didn't know the way. He must have been there for ages.

We headed off and for half an hour raced on some tiny roads, making a number of turns I would never have found as he explained the history and beauty of the Adelaide hills. It was like being in parts of Europe with small scattered villages made up of stone cottages, craft shops, and cafés. Some had very German names, others very English names, and my new guide explained how their founders had established traditional towns from wherever they were from.

At the end of the day I came off this high ground and spent the last few hours sweeping down the most spectacular country roads lined sometimes with open hardwoods, at other times with small fields, and then, as it started to flatten out, with wider arable land. It had been a more scenic day than the rest of Australia put together.

The next day was the first of December. It was 40 degrees in the middle of the day and didn't feel the least bit like December to me, but the date did make me appreciate how long I had been going for. I had left in the middle of the UK summer and it was now the UK winter.

Another milestone, 11,000 miles, passed a few hours after setting out.

After the Murray Bridge I stopped at a garage to get a new map of South Australia. My last detailed one had run out at Adelaide and I was hoping a national-scale map would tide me over for my last few days of SA, but it was hopeless: none of the roads I was on were shown.

Another 25km farther on I stopped at Tailem Bend for a second breakfast. My eating routine now reflected that of a hobbit: first and second breakfasts, elevenses, lunch, tea, dinner, then a bedtime snack. It was still 50km until lunch, I was already chasing the miles after stopping for longer than I should have, and then I got a puncture after 35km. It was baking hot and the flies were insanely bad. I was forced to wear my mosquito head-net to keep them off. They were like a plague, clambering all over my bags.

A morning's headwind became an afternoon's sidewind and it was genuinely good fun being back on the bike. The café owner at lunch loved hearing about the world cycle and promptly plied me with two huge veggie burgers, two slices of homemade carrot cake, two mega chocolate cookies, and a homemade ice coffee with an ice cream and cream float. That was 3,000 kcal right there, and I felt the food coma all afternoon.

The terrain flattened out and I hardly passed a thing as I followed the coast south toward Melbourne. After 50km I passed the well-named Policeman's Post, although I'm not sure why it had been deemed necessary to post any law out here, and then on to Salt Creek. The map suggested there was a motel in Salt Creek, and I craved a shower and bed. My plan was to shower for a week and keep the saddle sores clean so they'd hopefully heal. However, when I arrived I only found a roadhouse, which was closed. I had little food and only 200ml of water left, so this was a nuisance. The only people in sight were three men by a pickup, so I wheeled over to ask them if there was anywhere else.

They were dressed like laborers, in jeans. Two had T-shirts on and the other a checked shirt. The shirted one had a handlebar mustache and impressive tattoos down both arms to his wrists, and a swallow on the back of both hands. One of the others was smaller, less well built, with a shaved head. The last of them was fairly nondescript: white, short hair, average build. He was maybe ten years younger, in his midtwenties. They were all leaning on the back of the pickup when I arrived.

"Hi, is the roadhouse shut for the day?"

"Yeah," the big guy answered, and they all stood up and looked at me. "What are you looking for?"

After I'd explained, I was told there was nowhere in the area, but the younger guy suggested I knock on the door of the roadhouse as the guy would be in. "He has a couple of cabins in a swell that you can rent but they are full with fishermen," he added.

"So what do you do here?" I asked.

"Construction. We're working on a house down the road." It was said hesitantly by the big guy, at which the baldy burst out laughing, along with the younger guy. They looked at each other, sharing the joke for a long minute. "We're convicts, mate," the big guy owned up eventually. "We've been moved to a minimum security prison and we're working for National Parks renovating a building near here. We're all getting out next year, so we're on minimum security." It turned out that each of them, especially the shaven-headed guy, had been at this stage for a while, and kept getting his sentence extended for drugs and fighting. They laughed about this with laddish comradeship.

"So you're a professional cyclist?" Baldy piped up. I had already told them I was cycling around the world.

"Yes, it's an eighteen-thousand-mile race, just over eleven thousand to here."

"Shit, you're a strong man then?" He lifted his arm and flexed the biceps, laughing. I couldn't tell if this was friendly or mocking so didn't react. "You must have some stuff with you to keep going?"

"Stuff?" I guessed what he meant.

"You must use some pretty good performance enhancers?"

I laughed. "No, I don't use any."

The big guy muttered something to the others which I could only assume was a "yeah, right." I don't think they intended to be threatening, but I was completely alone and they were big guys whom I had no reason to trust.

"Come on," the big guy continued, "you must have some spare performance drugs, you guys always use the good stuff."

"I have nothing, seriously. If I did you could have some." I was a bit out of my depth and didn't want to sound completely negative. "I need to head on for the night, but I will try the roadhouse," I said, changing the subject. I felt that locking the bike might cause offense since they were the only people around, so I left it with them.

A light was on and a man answered after a long wait. He wasn't very pleased to see me but did agree to sell me a few supplies and pointed at an outside tap I could fill from.

Back outside, the men called me over. "You want to stay with us tonight?" the big guy asked. "We have a cabin up there." He pointed back down the road.

"Thanks, but I have to head on."

"Yeah, our parole officer probably wouldn't let you anyway."

It was a strange but kind offer and I left them where I had found them, chatting away by the pickup, waiting for their parole officer to come back.

I kept going until exactly 160km, now in a pine forest, by which time it was nearly nine p.m. and dark. There was no chance of finding a room, so I threw the tent up in an unused field gateway behind some trees. I had to have a ration pack for dinner and went to bed hungry.

18

I woke, bleary-eyed, unzipped the tent, and stepped over my pannier bag in the porch to go for a pee. I was outside before I put on my glasses and then wandered over to the trees. Back at my tent a few minutes later I stooped to crawl back inside and saw a massive hairy spider on the side of the pannier bag I had brushed on the way out. The spider was dark brown, furry, and about the size of the palm of my hand. You always think you are going to be cool and calm in such situations, but I jumped back with a rush of adrenaline, wide awake in an instant, my senses heightened.

With outstretched fingers I leaned forward slowly, naked except for a pair of trainers. Pinching the edges of the porch, I pulled it back and leaned farther inside, now within a foot of the spider. I reached for the smaller pannier and the spider moved and ran across the bag toward me and down the side. I froze. It stopped. I then jumped back into the open. The wee monster stayed put.

I don't know much about spiders, but this one was pretty unique-looking. It could have been a tarantula, except I didn't think you got tarantulas in Australia, so I guessed it was a huntsman. With a name like that, and from the look of the bugger, I assumed it was another killer. Most were out here.

I picked up a long stick with my right hand. The plan was to flick it away from the camp, but every time I touched it, it stuck to the bag and scurried around a bit. "Scurrying" sounds small and cute; better to say this beast trotted. For five minutes we played cat and mouse, or scared man and pissed-off spider. Eventually I caught it off guard and it fell off the bag onto the ground, still right next to the camp. I beat it repeatedly. In retrospect it was a bit of a cowardly killing, which I regretted, especially once I learned that huntsmans are kept as pets and are rarely deadly (I think "rarely deadly" is a wonderful criterion for a house pet). I could have moved it farther away; I'd only killed it because I was scared of it.

The wind had changed again in the night and was in my favor. On average the wind seemed to make at least a 5km/h difference if it was ahead or behind, adding up to a difference of at least 40km a day for the same effort and time on the bike. And after a day into the wind managing just 120km I would feel twice as knackered and battered than after a tailwind-assisted 200km. That day—December 2, day 120 on the road—I managed 183km. As well as the wind change it was also overcast for the first time in Australia, and it rained in the afternoon.

Since Paris I had changed the back tire in Istanbul, Lahore, and Perth. After just over 2,000 miles since the last change I hadn't even been checking wear, assuming there would be plenty of tread left. But the Aussie roads were more abrasive, and midafternoon I noticed a blue bit on the tire. Looking closer, I found this was the inner mesh, under the worn-through rubber. The only other time I'd worn a tire this thin was as a student riding from the south of France to Belfast; I couldn't afford a new one and for the last few days of the ride had to put inner tube patches on the outside as a makeshift tread. I had already swapped my front and back tires so that they would wear evenly, so there was no point in swapping back. That night I decided I should be able to make it the 50km to Mount Gambier the following morning where I would have to pick up whatever I could find.

One welcome distraction was Sarah, the marine biologist I'd met in Port Lincoln. She had continued texting every day after our half-hour lunch meeting. I was surprised, but it was in no way unwelcome: she was beautiful, had an amazing job, and was great fun. She had hoped to be back in Adelaide where she lived before I passed, but missed me by a day. Her text that afternoon caught me off guard: "Hi Mark, crazy thought but I have decided to take a week off work and road trip with you into Brisbane. Wot do u think?" This was out of the blue, and surely every traveling single guy's dream. The pros and cons raced around my mind all afternoon.

That evening we spoke for the first time. I was a month up on the old world record, she had said in subsequent messages that she would not distract me and just catch up every evening, and that it would be a cool road trip anyway so not to worry about her. It seemed perfect. I was close to agreeing.

I called her again that night, having decided against it. It was hard to explain, and it sounded ridiculous even as I tried to, but I needed to be left in my own world. In previous experiences on the road, whenever I spent a night unwinding with someone I struggled to get motivated the next morning. We spoke for a while and kept in touch over the weeks that followed, but I felt like I had missed an amazing opportunity. I beat myself up for days about it and was close on a number of occasions to calling her back. But I knew in the long run I would regret anything that might slow me down. I was here to race.

As well as phone calls, the evening was spent handwashing clothes and treating wounds. The saddle sores were still bad but no longer worsening. Some of the skin was now forming calluses where it had been repeatedly opened, which I guessed was a good sign. However, I now had a painful rash down the inside of both legs which was like having itching powder in my shorts.

Apart from my brief logbook entries, my memories of the next three days into Melbourne are sparse. I wasn't in the happiest place mentally. Australia seemed to be going on forever. On day 121 I managed to pick up a cheap replacement back tire and I made arrangements to pick up the correct quality replacement in Melbourne (I had ridden the German-made Swalbe tires throughout). From Mount Gambier I crossed the state line into Victoria, adjusted my watch by another half an hour, and stopped for a new map.

Day 121 started with a front puncture in the rain but got much better, along an awesome coastal road. The puncture took ages to fix because of another conditioning injury: just like my backside, my hands were now also grumbling about the long hours on the bike. Since Perth I had been getting pins and needles in both hands when I forgot to change my hand position regularly. In the last week my left hand had got worse, and down the thumb side was becoming numb for increasingly long periods.

I had spoken to the team about this. My sports doctor had fed back that this nerve damage was not unexpected and I must try to use a different position to let the hands recover. This wasn't easy:

there were a limited number of comfortable options and the nerve damage was also affecting my pinch badly. I had struggled to open some tins and do simple camp tasks. Changing a puncture was the hardest test yet. I had almost no pinch so could not hold the levers, and it took over half an hour to change the inner tube. I couldn't believe how weak my hand was.

In the afternoon I had a choice to make: stay on the coastal road, which became the famous Great Ocean Road, or go inland through more dull farmland. Cycling to the opposite side of the world and not seeing the Twelve Apostles rock formations by a few miles seemed like craziness, but it would undoubtedly be slower, along a windy, hilly coastal road. I stood at the junction for five minutes, torn between my wish to cycle the Great Ocean Road and to make faster miles. I decided that I would have to go back for the tourist sites.

That evening was another busy one of phone calls and forward planning. I had managed without phone reception for over a week, but now that I had it the phone never seemed to stop and everything seemed important. A big idea, and potentially a very good one, came from Guy, who had sent the tire to Perth. He suggested I make a major route change from Melbourne, going inland due north and missing the coastal road through Sydney, which would be busier and slower. It would be 200km shorter but a lot faster. I left this with Mum to check. It was almost a no-brainer, a great idea, but was a big change and needed to be researched and decided on quickly.

I opted for plan B, the inland option: south of Melbourne, across the bay using the Queenscliff Ferry to the town of Sorrento, and then due northeast. The Queenscliff Ferry was a perfect 100 miles away and I was confident of reaching it when I started out. However, the insane winds changed again and I had to fight hard all day, making the last crossing with just ten minutes to spare. The last two hours I had to crank hard, pushing it far more than I wanted to, knowing I would pay for it.

Early in the day I passed a message on the tarmac on my side of the road: JESUS LIVES. This graffiti was repeated every kilometer for the next 50km. I was left wondering how and why.

The roads that day were by far the busiest I had been on in Australia so far, and I was glad to cut off toward the ferry. If I had been worried before about cash then I certainly winced to find myself in a $120 hotel in Sorrento. It seemed to be the place for rich

Melbourne residents to escape. My only choice was to sit in the posh restaurant for a plate of risotto and chips. Surrounded by dining couples and families, in absolute luxury, I found myself feeling pretty lonely for the first time. It was idyllic, but I craved to be back in my tent, somewhere I didn't feel so out of place and alone.

I was kindly asked for drinks by a group who had seen me arriving, which broke this unhelpful mood. I joined them for half an hour, and went to bed much happier.

That unrelenting headwind had eventually beaten Damian on his trans-Australia record attempt. He had battled on for a few days after passing me, but it was futile and he had been forced to abandon, too far down on target. Grant, our Melbourne contact, had mentioned how dangerous and busy the city roads were, so Mum had decided to email Damian to ask if he could join me for the day.

He turned up very early on a superb full-carbon race bike. "You should have come on a mountain bike," I jested. "This thing is built for big miles, not big speeds." I was thrilled to have him there—my first proper cycling company since Paris, after four months on the road. Before setting out he inevitably asked how I was doing. I didn't need to tell him how tough the wind had been, but I did tell him about camping less in an effort to fight the saddle sores. "You should use pawpaw cream, it's amazing stuff," he said. I had never heard of it.

We were cycling through a town at the time and Damian shouted a stop, pointing at a pharmacy. Five minutes later he came back with a small red tub of what turned out to be fermented papaya fruit. Over the next week I used this every night and morning as well as rubbing the chamois cream into the shorts. I had almost resigned myself to the fact that the only real cure was to rest up, which obviously wasn't an option. I was therefore astonished to find that the sores healed over within days. There was no way the sores were going to disappear, of course, but the improvement was incredible.

I was doubly glad of Damian's company when I saw how confusing and busy the eastern suburbs of Melbourne were. An unexpected delay came midmorning when Damian's back tire exploded. It went with a loud bang, leaving a long rip down the sidewall. I had been planning to pick up my new tires a bit farther on, so I called ahead to Guy at the Bike Box, who kindly jumped in his van and came out to meet us. While I changed mine, Damian got a lift back to the shop, and we joined up a bit farther down the road.

After all the stop-starting and slow city cycling, it was frustrating to only make 125km that day. It was scary riding in Melbourne. Many drivers tooted us, gesturing rudely as they passed, cutting in aggressively or giving us no room. As I understood it, it was the law to allow two cyclists to ride abreast; cars had to slow and overtake properly. It blatantly infuriated them. Damian was obviously a veteran at this fight and defended my wide bike heroically, but I was left with an unfortunate bad taste about Melbourne, a city which people seem to love.

This feeling was reinforced the following morning. I needed new maps now that I planned to cut inside the coastal mountains, missing Sydney. After breakfast I went over to the garage and started looking through the selection. It wasn't at all clear which ones covered the areas I was heading into, so I opened three or four to check what they covered.

Without warning, the guy in the store shouted, "This isn't a library. Are you buying it or not? Buy it or f*** off!"

I said to him, "Look, there's absolutely no reason to be rude. I'm not from here and I'm trying to figure out which map to take. Can you help me?"

I had the New South Wales one in my hand, and he said, "Well, it's not that one, is it?"

I would have thought it was just one grumpy man being exceptionally rude, but the day before I'd never seen so much road rage toward cyclists. There seemed to be a real them and us between cyclists and other road users in this area of the country.

Though it started strangely, day 125 was ultimately a success at 176km. Working on a best-case scenario, I was now a week from the end of Australia. The road out of town was a very long, gradual hill through a forest and it rained heavily the whole way. It was perfect to dispel my rage and I reached the top puffing and soaked to the skin but with a clear head.

This deluge caused my main cycle computer to misread and blank out for 13km for the first time since the monsoons of Malaysia. But the storm cleared to leave a fast, flat afternoon. The dream was that the tailwind would stay with me until Brisbane, now that I was heading northeast. It was a very different area I had cycled into, more like Italy than what I had got used to Australia looking like, with huge vineyards for most of the day.

The dream looked like it might come true as on day 126 I woke to a roaring tailwind. I was becoming wind obsessed; I'd rush to check the wind direction as soon as I woke. It took nine hours to cover an almost unprecedented 217km at 24km/h. It wasn't a lot easier to force myself into staying on the bike, though, especially for the last few hours, as I promised myself a bed if I made the next town. There was nothing of interest in the world I was passing either—I was now into wide-open farmland—so I spent the day racing the clouds.

Set a few hundred meters off the road was a small pub. Outside were about a dozen locals, who greeted me warmly. After going in and establishing that there were no available rooms, the barmaid suggested I pitch my tent across the road in a small park and then come back for dinner. I took her at her word, placed my order, and said I would be back in half an hour.

I would never normally have camped somewhere as open as a small public park in the middle of a row of houses, but it was a stone's throw across the street from the pub and I couldn't help but trust the people there. Also, part of the park, which was about 10 meters square, was a large and immaculate public loo, which acted as a private en suite to the tent.

After pitching the tent I walked back across the road and was introduced to Pommy Dave and a number of other characters. Moira, a tough-looking woman, introduced her son and a few other people, then offered me an apple from a huge bag she had just picked. We sat in a big semicircle and I listened for a while to the local gossip until the food was ready. It seemed that Pommy Dave, an interesting guy who had drifted here after leaving the merchant navy, was, as the nickname suggested, originally English, and had some sheep. These were his pets, though the country folk, led by Moira, saw them as prime candidates for the table. A long conversation (which I sensed was a rerun) ensued during which offers were made to kill and butcher them and split the meat between the villagers.

After eating, Moira turned to me and asked, "Have you seen our Opera House?"

"No." I laughed, assuming this was some sort of joke. She looked offended, so I backtracked. "You're serious, I didn't know." They seemed the least likely bunch of opera-goers you could imagine.

"Come and see."

She got up, and I followed.

Next to the inn was a huge structure which I had assumed was a dark poly-tunnel. Moira pulled back the tarpaulin to reveal a huge stage and wooden floor. The innkeeper was apparently a famous chef—people came from miles away to eat here, and I had to admit the food was superb and really cheap—and his idea was to bring a touring opera to the country after building this amazing structure. The locals, for all their farming chat and simple lives, had bought into this and were now all avid fans. Every year operas by major companies from Sydney, Brisbane, and other places visited, and seats would sell for up to $500 each. It was amazing to watch Moira standing there in her Wellington boots and farmers' clothes talking about *Carmen* and *The Marriage of Figaro*.

Back at the inn I said my good-byes and left for the tent. One of the men, Dave, shouted after me, "Watch out for the sprinklers, they sometimes come on early." As I was about to crawl into my tent, Moira came across to offer a shower back at hers. It hadn't even crossed my mind to ask, but I was quick to accept. It was a wonderful community of friends.

By day 128 I passed 12,000 miles. When I arrived in Australia I hadn't quite reached 9,000 miles yet, and here I still was 3,000 miles later. I craved the excitement of crossing a border and immersing myself in a new culture every couple of days like Europe. This inland expanse from Melbourne to Brisbane was turning out to be exceptionally dull. At least in the Outback I'd felt I was truly in the wild; here I was in the developed world. These were days of scorching heat and wide-open and fairly featureless farmland. It's simply not true to say that the world tour was packed with nonstop action.

The only exciting prospect out here was that if this wind kept up I could save a day by pushing 700 miles in six days. This was very much on my mind as there were now daily discussions about my flight to New Zealand, which needed to be confirmed soon.

I realized that if I could keep up these distances I could cross Australia in thirty-eight days, and 3,800 miles in thirty-eight days meant a daily average of 100 miles, which would completely cancel out the day off in Adelaide. This prospect was insanely exciting and I set my absolute everything on making that happen. I couldn't wait to get out. It had been the hardest month of all, but the thought of being able to leave Australia on target was incredibly uplifting.

The flies were incessant and gave me another incentive not to stop, though now, with the tailwind, they could keep up far better than they had been able to. I rode past lots of dry farmland before stopping in a small town called Tomingley.

The pub in Tomingley, next to the motel, was mainly filled with long-haul truckers. For such a small place it had a huge truck park across the road. I walked up with a couple of drivers to order my food at a kitchen window at the back of the bar. The first asked for a "trucker's plate" and I saw him handing over some coins—far less than anything on the menu I was holding. The guy in front of me did the same, so I quickly put the menu behind my back and said, "Same for me, please."

"Three dollars, please."

What a bargain!

I went to the bar for a Coke and joined my fellow long-haulers outside. The man I sat next to had one front tooth at the top and a wide gap on either side; his cheeks were sunken and he had short, wiry, unkempt hair; his arms and legs were underdeveloped, and he had a stoop. To me, the stereotypical trucker is large and strapping, but this man looked like a human version of Gollum. He looked like he had spent his whole life driving.

He told me he drove all over Australia and had done so for twenty-seven years. I told him that I had cycled from Perth, and there were some comments from others sitting near us.

"Have you driven the Nullarbor?" I asked, to make conversation.

"Yeah, hundreds of times. I've had to drive Perth to Sydney non-stop a couple of times," he boasted.

I looked at him incredulously. This was surely not possible.

He obviously enjoyed this reaction. "If it is an emergency," he continued, "we can get across in two and a half days."

"Are you not worried about falling asleep after missing two nights' sleep?"

"No," he replied, "you've already taken care of that . . . that's the last thing you're worried about."

I was called for my dinner, enough to feed a trucker or three average men, but I couldn't get this comment out of my head.

Back in my room, the pawpaw cream continued to work miracles on the wounds on my backside, but it still hurt a lot sitting on the saddle all day. I had given myself a hard time about staying in motels (in a bid to stay clean and prevent any infection) rather than camping, but with good miles each day I no longer cared. I reminded myself I was out here to get the world record, not to make it as tough as possible.

In fact I was on a high after the big miles, and I was optimistic that Monday night when I called home. I asked Mum to book a Sunday morning flight. I wanted to try to save that day. I was convinced I could push 182km a day for five days.

The next morning I was cycling into the town of Dubbo—known as the crossroads of New South Wales, as you can head north to Brisbane, east to Sydney, west to Adelaide, and south to Melbourne—when I came across a cyclist heading the other way. He slowed, swung across the road, and stopped in front of me. John had found my site on the internet and, following the GPS tracker, had decided to ride out and meet me. A geography teacher and family man, he was great company for the miles into town, over a second breakfast, and for a couple of hours farther on. It was very welcome as I had started out feeling utterly terrible, the effects of a 200km day, as always, hitting me hard. By the time he left I had found a fresh mood, was in the flow, and pushed a much faster afternoon, finishing at 7:40 p.m. on 176km, just shy of the day's target.

For a day with over a kilometer ascent, I was more than happy with this progress. The last section was through Warrumbungle National Park. What a fantastic name. Warrumbungle National Park is of course in Warrumbungle Shire, where little teddies live. It even looks like a fairy-tale land after the parched farmlands I was used to, and I made up a song about the wild Warrumbungletons as I climbed their hilly roads. Sadly I can't remember it to recount fully, but I do recall that the chorus repeated my favorite new word—a lot.

I knew I would be camping by lunchtime, so I'd stocked up. It was a very cool camp spot, in a wooded glade with picnic tables, near a huge tumbling waterfall. A few caravans were in the car park but I was able to wheel right into the woods and hide away. After cooking up some pasta with baked beans I had a bag of dried fruit and nuts as dessert while sitting on the rocks by the waterfall. It was the most spectacular spot I had visited in Oz, save for the cliffs on the Great Bight, and I sat there for half an hour having a nice wee think. I ended up laughing aloud. It was as much a release of tension as anything else. I realized that I had been blindly focused for so long and was ultimately not having a great time. It took a place like this for me to let go for a moment and appreciate the unique journey I was on.

But my optimism had all but gone when I called it a day after just 100 miles. I can't describe the pain of sitting on those saddle sores for nearly eight hours. They are worse for the first few hours and then the nerves in the backside stop reporting the pain to the brain as much and if you have the right focus you can almost blank it out. However, even once you get to this state of mind, it is no fun. Your world is one of dulled senses and suppressed pain.

Those first few hours had been particularly bad in some tough hills and it was slow going to the town of Coonabarabran, the gateway to Warrumbungle National Park and supposedly the astronomy capital of the nation, being the closest town to the largest optical telescope in Australia. Some friendly banter with a retired copper and a farmer who were sitting outside a café, shooting the breeze, cheered me up hugely. It was good to be distracted from my own wee world when it was this tough.

At the end of the day I felt like I was giving up on the dream of making Sunday's flight by stopping when I did, but I simply couldn't face going on. I would have ground to a stop the day after without treatment on those sores.

I woke the next day with a renewed fire in the belly. It was make or break on that flight, so I went for broke. I sat on the bike for just shy of ten hours in eleven hours and forty-five minutes on the go and covered 217km. My backside wasn't any less sore, but it proves that mind-set is everything. I found the zone and managed to push it that much further.

However, perhaps inevitably, I paid for this effort. For all that it had put me back on target, on Friday morning I struggled to get out of bed. I looked at myself in the bathroom mirror and saw a ghost staring back. My eyes were heavy, I was pale, and I was shocked at how old I looked. Both my legs were cramped up for much of the day and I barely noticed the world I passed, just focusing on staying on the bike. At one point I found tears silently rolling down my cheeks as I cycled along. It wasn't really crying, it was just that the pain from the saddle sores, my tight neck, a headache, and my cramped legs was almost unbearable. I think it was just my body's way of getting some sort of release.

My energy levels felt at stalling point all day and after seven hours I had to stop, after 151km. It was all I could manage; it would have to be enough. After the 217km the day before I had confirmed that I would definitely make Sunday's flight. This left me over 200km for Saturday, the final run to Brisbane. That evening I spent a full hour massaging my legs, ate like there was no tomorrow, and was in bed by nine p.m. If I repeated my Friday performance I would be left 40 miles short, and missing the flight would mean losing at least a day. It didn't matter that I still had New Zealand, America, and the rest left, I had to approach that last day as if it was all that was left.

I was rolling at 5:44 a.m. The first few miles were insane. I have rarely felt worse, yet I knew I had no choice but to carry on for the next 130 miles. The roads were empty, it was Saturday morning so everyone else was in bed, and my only option was to smile wryly at the absurdity of my situation. Seeing the humor seemed a far healthier option than simply stopping.

The road had been on a northeast tack since Melbourne, west of the mountains. Now, on this last day, I would cut almost due east and have to cross the top end of the chain. Therefore, the 210km to Brisbane also involved nearly 1,500 meters of climbing. I hadn't remembered that the clocks would confusingly go back not forward as I traveled northeast, so it was fortunate that I'd left so absurdly early.

For the final few miles a local cyclist had agreed to come and show me the way in. Adam had represented Australia, and he turned up in a similar style to Damian, ready for a ride. I had to quickly point out that I had already done over 100 miles that day, 3,800 miles in the last thirty-eight, and was not going anywhere fast. Slow and steady; this was a tortoise's race. He was fantastic company and we cruised those final miles sharing stories.

My contact in Brisbane was Jo, my Scottish physio's best friend. She met us at the Brisbane River for the final mile to the finish of

Australia. It was 12,632 miles to this point and I had just spent 303 hours on the bike to ride across the biggest country I have ever cycled. That last day had taken nearly eleven hours of pedaling, so it was Jo who made up for the excitement I didn't have the energy to feel or show. It was a fitting finale to Australia, looking across the river to downtown Brisbane.

It had long been a dream of mine to cycle across Australia, and it was strange to feel a bit numb to the joy of accomplishing it. The reality was that I would now have to box up the bike, fly to New Zealand, and the next day I would be setting a new target: Dunedin to Auckland—the best part of 900 miles. But for now I needed a few hours off, a massage, a shower, and some clean clothes.

Australia had been the greatest test yet, maybe even more so because I had expected it to be so much easier. Europeans naturally find it hard to imagine the amount of space and emptiness in this magnificent country, the largest island on earth. I loved the Australians, when I could find them, for their no-frills friendliness, but I was glad to be moving on. It is, I think, a place to revisit with company and an engine.

Leg 5: Dunedin to Auckland

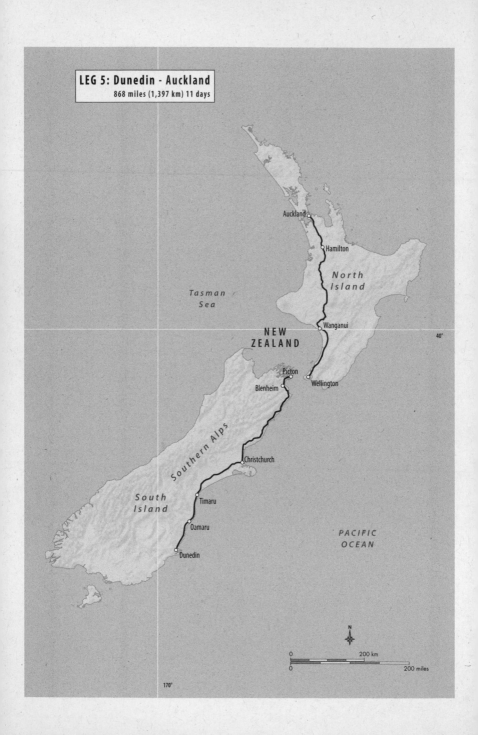

LEG 5: Dunedin - Auckland
868 miles (1,397 km) 11 days

Auckland

Hamilton

*North
Island*

*Tasman
Sea*

**NEW
ZEALAND**

Wanganui

40°

Picton

Blenheim

Wellington

Southern Alps

Christchurch

*South
Island*

Timaru

Oamaru

*PACIFIC
OCEAN*

Dunedin

170°

N

0   200 km

0   200 miles

19

My last night in Oz was spent getting a massage and resting. Switching off, even for a few hours, was important before setting a new target and going again. There were no night flights and it would take two flights to get to Dunedin, which would take up the day. Effectively I flew from Brisbane to Auckland, then to Dunedin, to cycle back to Auckland. I didn't care about the time lost as I needed the transfer day for recovery.

Sunday December 16 started early, though, as I still had to take the bike to bits and box it up for the flight. But it was such a thrill not having to get into the Lycras when I woke, which made up for not being able to lie in.

Auckland airport is in two parts, the international terminal half a kilometer from the domestic one. There should have been plenty of time to transfer and it was arranged that contacts from Glasgow University alumni would meet me in Dunedin. I'd stay the night with them, build the bike, and leave first thing Monday morning. However, the flight to Auckland was delayed and I landed within an hour of my connection.

I could still just make it, at a sprint, but then the immigration officers insisted on taking my tent away and giving it a clean. It was eventually handed back smelling of chemicals and in a big pile. "Sorry, we aren't allowed to fold them up so you can see all the parts are there," the young man muttered. Rubbish, you just can't be bothered, I felt like calling back as I grabbed it and stuffed it unfolded into the pannier bag. Why would an immigration guy steal a tent pole? It wasn't a big deal, but missing my flight was, and despite having explained my situation the immigration men were on autopilot and moved with the same lethargy, just working their shift.

My contacts in Auckland were from a Christian Fellowship where a university friend had lived during his gap year. Two slightly startled men welcomed me as I stormed out of arrivals.

"Where are departures?" I called before even getting their names.

"Follow that dotted line," one of them answered, pointing at a painted line on the floor.

"Can you please bring my bags?" I didn't wait for an answer as I set off at a sprint, clutching my tickets and passport.

I hadn't run for over four months, and in that time had cycled over 12,500 miles. This does strange things to your legs. I made it halfway to departures at full tilt when a sharp pain shot down my right calf and I pulled up, limping to a halt. Something wasn't right. I made it to the terminal at a fast walk, still limping. Sweating and panting, I reached the check-in desk.

"Sorry, sir, that flight is fully boarded."

The check-in lady listened to my story and to my surprise immediately sympathized. I had got into the habit of expecting to be fobbed off by authorities. However, a friendly face was not enough to get me to the South Island of New Zealand today. She booked me on the early flight, and I left her desk in time to meet the men from the fellowship arriving with my bags. I was in Auckland for the night, and they kindly offered a bed, so we wandered back to their car. There was no point in stressing, it was an unavoidable delay, but after everything I had done to make that flight it was frustrating to lose half a day because of a flight delay. In the process I also seemed to have given myself a calf injury.

Dunedin is the most Scottish place I have ever visited outside Scotland. I was told a joke about how when the Scots came to New Zealand they landed in the sunny North Island, looked around, then moved gradually south, exploring. Eventually they came to the southeast corner, where New Zealand is at its wettest and most barren, and felt at home. There might be some truth in this. On my arrival it was pouring and alarmingly cold. After following the summer sun for four months I was not feeling at home.

After warring with local Maoris in the early nineteenth century, Europeans first set up permanent occupation in Otago, near Dunedin, in the form of a whaling station. Fighting subsided as epidemics wiped out huge numbers of the native peoples and in the mid-nineteenth century the town of Dunedin was commissioned. Charles Kettle, the city surveyor, wanted it to emulate the spirit of Edinburgh: Dùn Èideann is the Gaelic name for the Scottish capital, and Dunedin's main street is Princes Street, just like in Edinburgh. I found the town both quaint and quite grand. After the wide-open and fairly bland towns of rural Australia it was bizarre to find this very cozy and elaborate European-style town where all the names I saw reminded me of home. Interestingly, the Reverend Thomas Burns, a nephew of Scots poet Rabbie Burns, was the minister of the Church of Scotland in Dunedin at the time.

Dunedin's airport lies 35km south of the city and was tiny compared to the last few I had seen. A local taxi driver kept me company with his life story as I built my bike on the tarmac under the canopy at the front entrance, and then ripped the big box into pieces to stuff into bins. Building, repacking, and getting some food took a few hours, and all the while I wished for the rain to ease.

After parched Australia, New Zealand in the rain seemed artificially green. It was so busy, so stuffed with plants of all shapes and sizes. I was used to weeks of landscapes with one type of shrub or just burned grass. This was a much smaller world, from the roads to the houses and cars. Australia has immense horizons, the sense of space is absolute; now I seemed to have been dropped into a strange toy world.

I felt pretty rubbish by the time I actually reached Dunedin. My little run in Auckland airport seemed to have resulted in a pulled muscle in my right calf, and this was now aggravated by the cold. I could cycle, but with a constant twinge. It was only ever going to be a half day, so I was pleased to make 90km to the small town of Palmerston. It poured most of the day, only clearing at the end, but once on the road I actually loved the ride. It was many times more interesting than the land I had just left. Out of Dunedin I faced a long, steady climb through lush rolling farmland; I could easily have been back in Perthshire, where I was brought up. The descent I earned was twisty and technical, especially in the wet, but the roads were all mine with the rest of the traffic on the newer highway. This was the stunning terrain of north Otago.

The heavy rain caused both main cycle computers to misread, but the Polar unit agreed exactly with the miles on the map, so I wrote the log from that instead.

The plan was to get through New Zealand's 870 miles in nine days. Eight would have been the best-case scenario, but the missed flight and half-day delay had put an end to that plan. If I had been fresher and New Zealand wasn't so mountainous it might have been realistic to make up this lost time, but not with another 3,800-mile race across America to come. It was decided, with the team back in Scotland, to try to get a good recovery ride through New Zealand.

The following day was not fantastic, even though I felt so much better on the bike in terms of aches: the day and a half off had done miracles to ease the saddle sores. The problem was I just couldn't refocus. I felt my mind was tweaking out slightly and I was constantly restless on the bike, unable to zone out and find a flow. New Zealand was also proving to be much cooler than Australia, which was taking some reacclimatization. The average in Oz had been over 30 degrees, but in the South Island it was midteens. I knew it wasn't actually that cold, just relatively, and appreciated that it would be a good prelude to winter in America.

Day two ended in the holiday town of Timaru, which was over-priced and home to the now extinct but wonderfully named volcano Mount Horrible. On day three I hit the flatlands for the first time, which helped me hit the magic number. Mentally it was a much better day as well, but it was hard to know if this was the cause or effect of the better progress, though it's all connected. The Canterbury Plains between Timaru and Christchurch are used mainly for mixed farming. The towns are concentrated on the edges of the plain as it is prone to drought when the wind comes from the north, so I passed little all day. The only memorable punctuation was crossing the country's longest road bridge at Rakaia, just before lunch at Ashburton.

By day four in New Zealand I was starting to enjoy it again, back in the flow. By the end of play I was just 4km short of 13,000 miles around the world. My mood was reflected in the fact that I could start the day doing four hours without getting off the bike.

Through the entire length of New Zealand, except short sections when leaving places like Dunedin and Christchurch, I was following Route 1, the main linking road of both islands. For most of the way it seemed to be a normal single-lane road but was considerably narrower than similar roads back in Australia. Like in the UK, there was simply less room to build such wide roads. Without a hard shoulder I was more nervous, but I soon found the Kiwis to be very careful drivers. I shared the space with HGVs but I didn't have the same fear as I'd had in Australia with the road trains on much bigger roads. Every second vehicle on the road in New Zealand seemed to be a camper van, giving the wonderful impression that everyone was on an adventure.

Heading north out of Christchurch, I soon reached the edge of the Canterbury Plains and started climbing again into the Hundalee Ranges. Most of the day was spent inland on this roller coaster of a road before dropping back to the coast at Kaikoura. It was spectacular, especially the last descent and section along the coast. The right calf had eased well over the last four days, helped by daily massages, but I still tried not to push it on the long climbs.

Kaikoura is a cool town, a backpackers' haven. The name translates as "meal of crayfish," and it came into existence because of the abundance of marine life. The Kaikoura Peninsula, which kicks out just south of the town, produces currents that sustain this ecosystem and caused the town to be originally established as a whaling port. Whales, in particular the sperm whale, are still the major draw, which makes the place quite touristy.

In the Hundalee Ranges I met two other cyclists within a few hours of each other. I had met so few touring cyclists on the road in 13,000 miles and these two could not have been more different. Nigel was English, looked to be in his late forties, and was hugely friendly. He explained that he had spent the last five years, alone, cycling around the world and had covered 70,000km. As soon as he saw me coming the other way he crossed over the street and started talking excitedly, delighted to meet another world cyclist. He was extroverted and eccentric, that was for sure, and I admired his nomadic adventure. However, I wasn't the least bit jealous. A five-year solo trek like that is no longer an expedition, it becomes your lifestyle. It is not a break from your normal world, it is your world. He had no intention to write a book, kept no journal, and had no website for friends to follow him. It was an incredible achievement. He seemed a nice guy but I couldn't help feeling that he was a lost soul.

Energized by this friendly encounter, I was excited to see another cyclist a couple of hours later, and this time I crossed the road to say hi. He was another middle-aged man, this time from America, and after an introduction and a few questions it was clear that he just wanted to be left alone. He was completely introverted and mumbled incoherently into his beard, looking around like he wanted to escape. I bid him good travels and carried on, wondering what motivates people to take to the road alone.

For me, I needed a target and focus; I found the prospect of being a solo nomadic traveler intimidating. However, a couple of friends of mine, Alistair Humphreys and Rob Lilwall, represent this type. Both have completed three- to four-year solo epics, covering vast distances. In response they say that they would hate to do what I do, racing through and never stopping to engage with the places I visit. Meeting these guys today made me realize again that I was, of course, in the minority. I had the mind of a racer but the ambition of a tourer. Maybe I was in the wrong sport, I reflected with amusement.

Day five in New Zealand was a simple race for the Picton ferry. My ride into Kaikoura had been a good 112 miles, which left a perfect 100 to finish the South Island. From there it was a three-hour ferry across Cook Strait to Wellington in the North Island. I had to make it in good time to sail at six p.m., so I set off with a renewed urgency. However, after a few hours' cruising at 23km/h I relaxed, realizing I was making great time, and enjoyed one of the most spectacular day's riding of my life.

For the first five hours the road hugged the coast on a strip of flat land that it shared with the railway. The Pacific Ocean crashed in on my right, relentlessly angry, and on my left the Kaikoura Ranges reared straight up to 2,500-meter peaks. Some sections of road ran out of room entirely and cut through short tunnels in the sea cliffs. Narrow strips of grassy field bordered other parts with thick woodlands to my left that covered the lower mountains. The whole section was postcard perfect.

From the town of Blenheim, where I stopped for lunch, the road turned inland again and across the flat Wairau Plain before a last 30km hill section over to Picton. For some unexplained reason these hills were more arid, unlike the rest of the lush South Island, and I climbed slowly, following the Tuamarina River. The final descent was fast and short, and I wheeled into the ferry port with over an hour to spare.

Jonathan, our contact at the British High Commission in New Zealand, had very kindly organized and paid for my ferry ticket, so I didn't need to do anything. With an hour to pass I went in search of food, and once aboard I sat on the top deck to enjoy a feast fit for a king.

The Interislander boasts that it is one of the most beautiful ferry rides in the world, and I could see why. It is 92km between ports and the first hour is spent cruising up Queen Charlotte Sound and Tory Channel, where the land on either side reaches out in long fingers, revealing coastal villages in the bays between. Marlborough Sound continues through sheltered waters with small islands and the rugged mainland on both sides, before the open waters of Cook Strait. It was freezing on deck but I stayed there for the whole journey; it was spectacular, and passed in a flash.

Pushing off the car deck, I was met by friends of the family, Mary and Sandy MacFarlane, who were taking me in for the night.

In Wellington, a bike shop had agreed to open at half past eight to do a quick half-hour service to check that everything was aligned for the rest of NZ and the first section of America. The bike had done a lot of miles since Perth. The guy at the shop couldn't fit a new chain as the sprocket was so worn, and neither he nor any other shop in town had the part, so after wasting a few hours I left late, having achieved nothing. The Australian roads seemed to have punished it quicker than the Asian roads, which was unbelievable. I wouldn't have time to get it fixed in Auckland and I wouldn't be able to get it fixed in San Francisco until Boxing Day.

Flying into America on Christmas Day was asking a lot of my hosts. I was thinking it might be wiser to arrive on Boxing Day, use the afternoon to rest, get a massage, give the bike a full service, then get back on the road the next day. So it was decided that I should not push it and arrive in America ready for the last big leg. This decision caused some frustration considering the relatively easy target of just over 400 miles in five days, after busting a gut in Oz. However, as it turned out I needed all this time and was glad for it. The North Island might not have the Southern Alps and wild reputation of the South Island, but it turned out to be tougher riding.

After a late start and a long climb out of Wellington, the road summited and rolled back down to the ocean, this time following the west coast. The next section flattened out but was very narrow, considering the amount of traffic, and a couple of cars tooted as they passed. My pannier bags did make my bike wider than a normal bike, but I tried to hold my line and not be pushed onto the edge. At the first opportunity I jumped onto a cycle path that started along-side. The road and path now followed the Tasman Sea, with steep hills and rock faces on the right.

After a few miles the path pulled slightly away from the road and I paused, wondering if I should get back on the road. They must go to the same place, I concluded, as they shared a narrow strip of flat land on the seafront. My path diverged even more until I found myself among houses. Ten minutes later it ran out entirely, ending up at the beach. I saw a number of teenage girls wearing lifeguard T-shirts, so I asked how to get back to the road. Their directions saw me pushing my bike through a very soft beach, onto a wooden bridge, through a car park, and then up "Queen Elizabeth Park" and through a small town. It had been a big loop and I was not much farther north. The strange looks I got from swimmers as I tried to push my sinking bike across the sand made the detour well worth the half an hour it took. I decided to stick to the road regardless of how ratty the drivers got.

Despite this and a gusty headwind I almost hit 100 miles and finished in a town called Bulls. It was a town with a sense of humor, with puns on its name almost everywhere you looked. A big sign in the town center announced BULLS, A TOWN LIKE NO UDDER, and the small police station read CONSTA-BULL above the door. I got a good feeling from the people in Bulls, as though they were happy with life. I certainly benefited from their thriving food culture. Every small town and places in between were producing proper home cooking, which was ideal for my fuel. That evening I dined on some amazing and utterly gigantic falafel kebabs in a small Turkish café.

Day seven was a huge shock to the system. In the South Island you have big mountains but also big valleys and the road normally finds a gentle route though the high ground. In the North Island you have huge old volcanoes in the middle and there is no easy way around them. I had two options: first, I could do some extra miles, with the possibility of flatter ground, around the whole coast by New Plymouth; second, I could cut straight over the top as I had always planned to. From Bulls the hills started straight away but were only gentle undulations for 40km until Wanganui.

The pros and cons were debated at length with Mum until I opted for the direct route, as I didn't know enough about the coast and didn't want the pressure of the extra miles, which would have put me back up to over 100 miles a day to Auckland. The deciding factor on top of this was that following the coast would mean going slightly west and then east, which would need explaining to Guinness World Records. The direct route over the volcanoes avoided this and seemed to make most sense.

Just before Wanganui I met Tim Cooke and his wife. Tim was another Glasgow University alumnus, a dentist and keen cyclist, and had agreed to join me for a section. He was invaluable company, not just up some seemingly never-ending climbs toward Raetihi, but because he had ridden the exact route I planned to do across America. I spent the afternoon quizzing him about what lay ahead between California and Florida. He had loved the ride but he hadn't done it in the middle of winter and shared some understandable concerns about this.

Tim's wife was a doctor, so before leaving Wanganui it was a good opportunity to get some of the slightly personal ailments I had picked up checked out. On top of the skin rash and saddle sores, one of my more interesting beds, most likely in India, had given me bad ringworm on the right leg. This was constantly itchy and had been a growing and unidentified concern, so we wheeled down to the pharmacy to pick up some potions after lunch.

It was overcast all day and the skies grew increasingly threatening with the occasional shower as Tim and I climbed. It was slow going, but a beautiful road, coming out of lowland forests into barren open ground higher up. All along the route was evidence of the harsh weather with huge erosion and subsidence along the roadside. A few corners were completely caved in and the road narrowed to one lane. We loosely followed a river upstream which on a couple of occasions fell through rapids or over waterfalls. One of these was particularly spectacular, wide and fast-flowing with white water crashing into a huge black plunge pool. It was one of those sights you immediately stop for, without thinking, regardless of how focused you were a second earlier.

After about 60km, Tim turned back. It was a valiant effort as he had the same distance back, albeit mainly downhill. Later on, the heavens suddenly opened and I was caught. The thunder crashed instantly after the lightning, and the rain drove in sheets across the road. I might as well not have been wearing Gore-Tex, because I was soaked to the skin within minutes.

The next day was Christmas Eve. I had an easy three-day target into Auckland so just wanted to focus on getting there feeling as good as possible. The first few hours promised some of the best views in New Zealand as I pedaled through the National Park and under the shadows of three volcanoes, Taupo, Tongariro, and Ruapehu. Fortunately the rain had cleared by morning but a thick fog had settled and I saw little more than my handlebars for the first three hours. The first two of these were a gradual climb into a headwind at a slightly disheartening 15km/h. But I didn't care. If I only got 100km today then I could still make my flight and there was no point in getting there early as everything was booked now.

The afternoon brightened up and it was a great day on the bike, though fairly uneventful, passing mile upon mile of sheep farming and forestry. A few bits of my shoes and bike were coming loose, so I had a very enjoyable "stick everything down" session at lunch in the town of Taumarunui. Maybe it's a guy thing, but I find it hugely therapeutic to glue stuff together and neaten up edges with strips of electrical tape.

The afternoon was full of long descents with a few climbs and a couple of steep ascents to finish the day in Te Kuiti, known as the "shearing capital of the world" and home to the world's largest shears, which sit at 7 meters high. After 164km I now had an easy two-day ride into Auckland. Considering the weather and hills I had just come through I was grateful I had not attempted it all in three days.

I didn't feel bad when I woke up on Christmas Day, just not particularly festive. There were no presents to open, no tinsel in sight; there was, however, another day on the bike. The prospect of cycling on Christmas Day hadn't worried me, though, as I have never been a big Christmas person.

I cycled out of Te Kuiti to the town of Te Awamutu in a couple of hours. The roads were almost deserted, it was cold and raining, and it wasn't that much fun. I passed a number of houses where I could see families together in living rooms. I didn't miss Christmas, but seeing these scenes I missed home, for one of the first times.

The worn sprocket and chain were a concern; it needed changing as soon as possible. Te Awamutu was home to one of the only shops in New Zealand which had the parts. I will never know how, but

Mum had persuaded the owner to open on Christmas Day for me. Brett had arranged to come and meet me on the road as it was apparently only a two-minute job. I made good time first thing and was in town before he left home, so he told me just to wait at the shop. When he eventually turned up, he did so with his wife and young daughter, ready to go for lunch at his in-laws.

It was a good thing that I did meet him in the shop as the sprocket was completely locked on and a workbench and torque tool were needed to release it. Once a new chain and sprocket had been fitted I popped outside for a test cycle. After a few seconds the chain slipped, five seconds later it did the same, and sporadically thereafter. Brett wasn't worried to start with and set about the necessary adjustments.

Over an hour later we were almost out of options, having changed the front chainset, changed it back, and fiddled seemingly everything. We were out of ideas. It just didn't make sense that a new chain and sprocket would not fit together. Brett finally decided simply to turn the sprocket over, so it was back to front. The sprocket was symmetrical, so switching it around should have made absolutely no difference, but to our surprise it somehow ran perfectly. By this time an apology seemed pretty weak, but I offered my heartiest thanks and apologies to Brett and his family, who had now missed their lunch. His wife was, understandably, not outrageously friendly, but I truly was grateful. It was my only chance to get this fixed in New Zealand.

I had my Christmas lunch in a petrol station, eating cookies and a sandwich. Graeme, a good friend from university, called from Canada. It was great to hear from him. Lots of people had texted, which was lovely, but that made me feel farther from home; actually chatting and laughing with a friend was what I needed. Another mate, Dave, had called earlier but only for long enough to tell me that I was costing him a fortune and hanging up. This had amused me greatly, but it wasn't the friendly banter I wanted for Christmas on the other side of the world, on my bike, in the rain.

All afternoon, to the big town of Hamilton, was over rolling roads into a stiff headwind in the pouring rain. It was so miserable that I found myself laughing aloud at the absurdity of it. Almost every car that passed flashed its lights, or I got a wave or thumbs-up. Mid-afternoon there was a rush on the otherwise empty roads as everyone left their designated lunch destinations. I could imagine how many dinner chats I would feature in that night. "You should have seen the guy I saw today"; "On his bike, at Christmas"; "Yeah, I know, it was pouring, he looked miserable, must have no home, poor sod."

At Hamilton I hid out in McDonald's for half an hour as it was the only place open and warm that I could find. In the car park as I left a middle-aged lady approached me and started to spin a long yarn about needing money to get her car which was somewhere and her keys were somewhere else and she was alone and . . . Her story made no sense and she probably just wanted money. Without thinking, I interrupted, gave her $20, and pedaled off. It felt good to give something for no reason, especially when you are soaked to the skin and having a rubbish Christmas yourself, and when you have been on the end of generosity from strangers. I looked back to see a very surprised lady. "Wait, I will post it back to you!" she called after me.

"No need, Merry Christmas!" I shouted, and pedaled into the rain again.

I planned to stop in the town of Huntly after just 110km as this was the last town for a while and would leave a reasonable 90km ride into the airport. However, I rode through the town center and out the other side before realizing that was all there was. There had been nowhere to stay and I was slightly concerned at the thought of camping in this weather.

Five kilometers later, in the middle of the countryside, I spotted a motel. Wheeling up to the office, I saw a note pinned to the door, and my heart sank: "Office closed." But below it continued, "All inquiries please come to the big house."

I stood on the porch of the big house, which was down the next driveway, and rang the doorbell. A lady came to the door, saw a drowned man in tight Lycra, and let out a small squeal. Without a word she disappeared and I could hear the sound of laughter inside. I was definitely imposing but had no option but to remain there, feeling awkward. The motherly figure who came to the door was immediately friendly. "Of course, let's get you inside and dry. Come over to the office and I will get you a room." She put on some big boots and a rain jacket and walked me back across.

After signing in, she asked, "And where are you going to eat tonight?"

I had been so busy trying to find somewhere to spend the night that dinner hadn't even crossed my mind. "Well, I have a bit of food in my bag, but is there anywhere near here?"

"Yes, there should be a few places in Huntly, it's just 4km that way." She pointed.

I didn't immediately reply, but she must have seen my face fall. There was no way I was going back. There is nothing more demoralizing than that, especially in the pouring rain. An 8km round trip was too much to face.

"Don't worry, you get a shower and I'll bring you some leftover Christmas lunch. We have loads."

I could have hugged her.

It was one of the best Christmas dinners I have ever had. It wasn't a particularly fantastic meal, but in context, sitting cross-legged on my bed, dry and warm, tucking into three courses after the day I'd just got through, it was one of those moments I knew would stick with me.

The last 88km into Auckland was very cold but it had stopped raining. Paul, our contact in Auckland from the Christian Fellowship, came out to meet me as a surprise and saved time by showing me the fastest route in.

New Zealand had been a strange leg. I had felt better on average than most of Australia, but it had thrown up some surprise challenges. For some reason I had almost overlooked it, tagging it on to the end of Australia as "a bit more of the same." It could not have been more different, like going from the south of Spain to the Scottish Highlands.

I was now 13,504 miles around the world and 144 days in. New Zealand had been within miles of the expected 872, but many of them had been at a tougher gradient than the distance alone had suggested. For all that it had thrown at me, it had been many times more interesting and varied than Australia and I'd loved it. I also felt much fresher than when I reached Brisbane. I was ready for my biggest flight yet, into my first winter riding across America.

Leg 6: San Francisco to St. Augustine

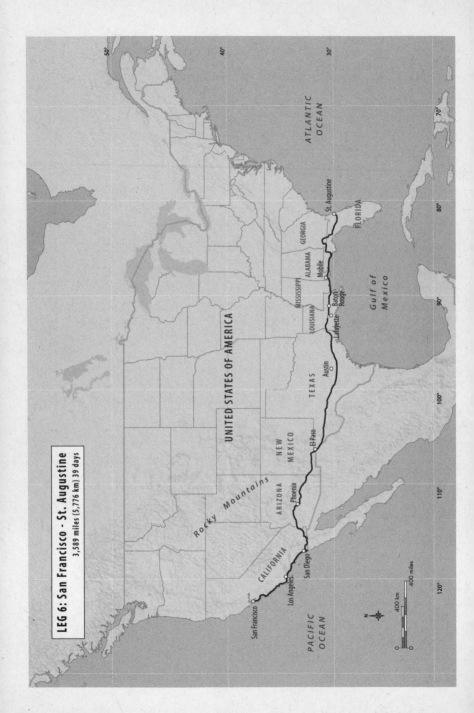

LEG 6: San Francisco - St. Augustine
3,589 miles (5,776 km) 39 days

20

It was the strangest Boxing Day in a quarter of a century. I flew out of Auckland on a seven p.m. flight, was in the air for eleven hours, and landed at eleven a.m. on the same day, having crossed the International Date Line. I couldn't sleep, but I got into America without issues.

San Francisco at the end of December meant winter for the first time, and from early December most of America had been hit by a series of storms. Ice in many areas from Nebraska to Illinois had caused tens of thousands of power outages and sixteen deaths in less than a month.

My second Boxing Day was spent taking the bike in for a service, eating lunch, shopping for a few bits of warm kit, having a massage, and then making my way back to the house of Joe, a friend of the family, who had met me off the plane. The bike shop rebuilt the bike from the box and serviced the bike, hopefully for the last time. A long time was spent discussing possible handlebar alterations to try to ease the numbness in my hands and wrists, but it was eventually left alone. Bullbars and tribars seemed too much of a risk as they were unfamiliar. Better the devil you know.

Set a target, go, focus, dig deep, keep going, finish, box the bike, fly, build the bike: it was a tough routine to repeat back to back. I had found it hard enough to find the mental zone in New Zealand without any break to recover from Oz. The planned route for America took me from San Francisco through LA to San Diego, across the mountains and into Arizona, New Mexico, and Texas, then the smaller southern states of Louisiana, Mississippi, and Alabama, before finishing in just over a month's time in St. Augustine, Florida. It was another massive leg and it was hard to find the reserves to start setting another gigantic mile target.

The first day started on the southern city boundary of San Francisco. I had no idea what to wear as it was so cold. I ended up in my new swanky spaceman foil bib shorts with three layers on top, including a down-filled body warmer. In real terms, even by Scottish terms, it was not cold, but after nearly five months of sun it was unbearable. There is no flat land out of San Francisco—in fact there is almost no flat land down the entire Californian coastline—and the climbs meant I was soon overheating under my layers while my face froze. I needed to reacclimatize.

The US was the only country where I had not done my own route setting. It is a country built for the car, with a labyrinth of interstate routes and other major roads, many that you cannot cycle on. In addition, most US cities are too spread out for public transport, let alone an easy traverse by bike. The western coastal route south to San Diego and the trans-America southern route came in small, very useful cycle maps.

Straight out of San Francisco I missed the first turnoff that would take me through small coastal towns rather than on the major route, and had to cut back. As I wound my way through these towns I immediately had doubts: surely there was no way this was faster than the main road? But I persevered, unsure of my options, and regretting having not researched a plan B. Within hours I could see that this route was designed for the tourist cyclist, there to amble through the countryside, and would not be the fastest route.

I woke at six a.m. the following day very groggy. After fighting through the first night, the jet lag hit me hard now. Sunrise came at 7:15 and I wheeled out for what would be a very long day on the bike. On the toughest days it is even more important to hit your targets to feel that the struggle has been rewarded with a successful outcome. I stopped after a perfect 161km.

The morning from the town of Aptos until the aptly named Seaside was inland for the first time, and pretty dull, pushing into a tough headwind. This was the Santa Ana wind, a seasonal phenomenon I had been warned about. The Santa Anas are strong, extremely dry offshore winds that sweep through California every winter and are a result of the buildup of air pressure in the high-altitude Great Basin between the Sierra Nevada and the Rocky Mountains, the motel owner informed me. For just a couple of kilometers I turned inland and faced the strongest section of wind yet. I genuinely struggled to keep the bike on the road. Not even the worst of Australia competed with this, but it was over quickly, as soon as I was back on the coast, sheltered by hills.

After the flat farmland early on in the day, the hills grew bigger and in total I climbed nearly 2km—the biggest single day's climbing yet, bigger even than Turkey. I hadn't expected this. Mum had let me know but I had argued that I was not allowed on the inland interstate and that it wouldn't be that bad. It was beautiful riding but I should have taken the warnings more seriously.

At Big Sur after 115km it was too early to stop, but going on to the next town would take me into the dark so I pedaled slowly through the deep forest looking at each log cabin, stopping at every possible accommodation. Americans seemed to be on holiday between Christmas and New Year, because every window showed NO VACANCY. No room at the inn this Christmas, I mused. The next 100km looked to be along a steep coastal road with cliffs, but I had no choice but to carry on.

Before leaving town I stopped at the last hotel and asked them for the phone number of the hotel at the next town, 30km ahead.

"No, sir, we are full tonight," I was told when I rang them.

"I am on a bicycle, are you sure there is no space at all?"

"No, sir. Big Sur is just up the road from here, please go on to there."

I hung up, feeling dejected. I had told him that I was calling from Big Sur, and anyway, 30km is not "just up the road" on a bicycle on roads like these.

Apart from the jet lag there was another reason I was trying to find shelter for those first few nights. For all the care I'd taken to get the right winter kit sent out to San Francisco, I had made one big mistake: I had turned down Mum's repeated offer to send out my warmer sleeping bag, as I thought it would be unnecessarily bulky and heavy. I had made this decision when sweltering in the middle of Australia. Now all I had was my one-season bag, for temperatures of 8 degrees and above, and tonight would be below freezing again. I knew I'd be used to the cold soon and able to brave this, but that night I fancied a big recovery sleep indoors.

Heading south, I found myself with steep craggy hills on my left and rocks which fell away on my right almost vertically to the Pacific. The drop varied but was often 50 meters as the road weaved and dipped, hugging the cliffs to cut a path through this most dramatic scenery. It was breathtaking, truly one of the most scenic rides of my life. Once on the move, having accepted I was in for a tough night, I loved it, and a new idea occurred to me. If I switched on my lights and rode into the night it meant that I would hit my 160km target and I would spend less time in a freezing tent. And also, if this kept up there would be no flat land off the road to camp for tens of miles.

As the sun went down and the waves crashed onto the rocks far below, the colors over the ocean were mesmerizing. The road was narrow, and the markings and crash barrier often disappeared, making it incredibly dangerous as the light dimmed. Many passing cars tooted their horns. You think I'm crazy, I chuckled to myself.

Such periods focus the mind absolutely on the moment; nothing else matters but the stretch of road in front. In the pitch dark, my dynamo-powered headlight was tested for the first time and was superb. But it was freezing. I pulled my hat down and my neck warmer up so that just my eyes peered out, trying to pick up the road paint.

Cycling at night is like cycling in a bubble: you have no idea where you are and are almost surprised when other things like signs or cars enter your small world. Many of the cars going the other way left their lights on full beam and I would get a rush of adrenaline from riding blindly for a short way. By the same token it was great when cars coming in the same direction cast light farther down the road, giving me some greater vision.

It was dark when I stopped at Lucia, outside the hotel I had called, and I was amazed at how quickly I got cold off the bike at night. I had no target, having not even looked at the map since Big Sur. I did, however, start riding with my head torch as well so that I could scan the roadside for possible places to pitch the tent. The bike light had kept me in a blinkered tunnel that would have led to dawn if I hadn't started looking around.

An hour later I was starting to fade when I suddenly picked up a CAMPSITE 1 MILE sign on the right. It seemed unlikely, as there had been no space to put up a single tent, let alone erect a campsite, for 50km. However, sure enough a gate soon appeared and I wheeled in, staring at the big information board and AFTER HOURS HONESTY BOX. I took a form from the box and scanned the sketch to figure out the layout. The good thing about my dynamo light was its immense strength; the bad thing was the fact that it stopped working as soon as the bike stopped. I slowly pushed the bike down a hill, trying to make sense of the site. It was all quiet as I nipped into the toilet block. As I left, someone was waiting.

"Hi, I'm Amy, I saw you arrive. If you are looking for somewhere to camp we have space next to our camper down here."

So I joined Ted and Amy Knudsen for a cup of brew and a chin wag, in the freezing cold, before crawling into my sleeping bag, wearing everything I had, tired but content. The ball was rolling for America.

I woke at 6:30 to a heavy fog. It had been a restless night due to the cold and I quickly packed away the soaking tent. This was the coldest I'd been on the road so far and it was hard to get going, especially leaving the offer of a friendly chat and breakfast.

The road continued like the night before and within miles I felt incredibly saddle sore, having slept in the Lycras to keep warm. I had to stop and take them off; it was simply too painful to keep going. It took two hours to do the first 24km. I set myself up for a tough day's riding where I might not make the 100 miles again. I was sure I was missing some spectacular scenery but couldn't see anything due to the heavy rain and sea fog. Again, some of the cycle computers began to misread.

Just as the coast opened up and I came off the hilly ocean road, the sun burned through the fog and I started flying. It felt wonderful to have come through that night and miserable morning ride into this clear, warm Californian winter's day.

The day before, while at a shop getting supplies, a shopkeeper told me to stop and see the elephant seals, something that sounded at the time like an unnecessary distraction. The road continued to veer inland across rolling plains, then at one point I came back to the ocean and saw ahead a huge car park and hundreds of people lining a half-kilometer section of beach. Curiosity got the better of me, and I've never seen anything like them. Each elephant seal was over a meter long and looked like it weighed as much as a small car. Most were lying motionless on the beach but some were lazily playing together. The sound they let out was similar to that of a seal only lower, a bit like a "moo." I'd never seen such weird-looking animals and stood there for a full twenty minutes filming and photographing them.

A man approached and asked what I was doing. I obviously stood out from the crowd in my Lycras, but I soon realized that his real interest was in the camera I was holding. He introduced himself as the "guru guy," a TV presenter on some gadget sales program, and was interested to know if I would be in LA and wanted to come and be a studio guest. I declined. (I was going to describe guru guy as a short man with a mustache, but on reflection, half the people I'd met in the last 140 or so days on the road seemed to match this description.)

When I got back to my bike I found another guy peering at it closely, with his notebook and camera out. He introduced himself as Richard and as we chatted his wife and kids came up. Turning to them, he said, "This is the guy we passed on the bike near Big Sur last night." A spark of recognition lit up their faces. "We thought you were crazy!" Richard continued. "We were going to stop and see if you wanted a lift but decided you must've known what you were doing." Richard and his family were from Florida and were in California on holiday. I didn't think much of it at the time, but as I left he gave me his contact details and told me please to get in touch when I made it across in a month's time.

Everything had been packed up wet from my cliffside camp, so I was determined to find a bed and somewhere to dry things out. Despite the frustrating start, I very nearly hit the magic 100 miles to the town of Oceano. Before that I passed through my first major town since San Francisco, Morro Bay. For the first time that day I managed to pick up phone coverage and call Scotland, mainly to try to sort out how to get a warmer sleeping bag sent out. Once again the cycle route I was following sent me on a crazy loop to miss the busy roads, giving me an incredible but frustratingly slow tour of this stunning town. In the dark, cycling into Oceano, I then misread the map and overshot the town center by a couple of kilometers and had to backtrack to the motels I'd just passed. Only one out of the dozen or so along the sea front didn't have NO VACANCIES on the door, and luckily, I got the last room at the inn.

The following day was much easier, and despite continuing over some big coastal hills it was a perfect day, hitting the 100-mile target in eight hours. It was also getting noticeably warmer as I headed south, though I knew this would be short-lived after leaving the Pacific and heading over the coastal mountains at San Diego. It was also amazing to see the contrasting standards of living as I traveled through California. That day I pedaled past some of the most lavish properties imaginable in the Santa Barbara suburbs, which the rich and famous call home.

In the town itself you could also see this influence, and I ended up paying nearly twice as much as normal for somewhere to stay. (I knew that there would be plenty of time to camp in America, and while there were so many coastal towns and I was getting used to this new world I found myself justifying somewhere to stay every night.) Santa Barbara had a fun feel about it, a bizarre mix of surfer cool and urban chic. Like so many of these places it was somewhere I wished I could stop and explore more. All I got was an hour to wander through the main streets and pick up another family-size burrito, which easily provided half the calories I'd burned that day.

As I set out on New Year's Eve, it was bizarre to think that I'd been on the road since August 5, trying to push 100 miles a day. I followed the harbor front down a boulevard of palm trees which felt like something straight out of *The OC*—a stereotypical Californian scene. Once again the road cut inland and I found myself passing through large stretches of arable farmland, battling into the Santa Anas.

One local explained that this wind was sometimes referred to as the devil's breath because, aside from its discomforting heat and dryness, it is associated with wildfires. In Raymond Chandler's novel *Red Wind* the Santa Anas are introduced as "those hot dry winds that come down through the mountain passes and curl your hair and make your nerves jump and your skin itch. On nights like that every booze party ends in a fight. Meek little wives feel the edge of the carving knife and study their husband's neck. Anything can happen." Having cycled into it, I know what he meant.

I was glad to get back to the relative shelter of the coastal road, though the Adventure Cycling Association's map routes were a continuing frustration and I again misread and underestimated the afternoon ride. I'd already spoken to Mum about looking into other options as there was no way I could do another 3,000 miles on these routes.

The target for that night was Los Angeles, where Simon Levay from our global contact list was offering to host me. At lunchtime it looked like I'd get well past LA, but in the end I was lucky to get that far. I met Simon on the very outskirts of the city at a place called Canyon Road after 145km. As it was the end of the year and I was entering such a major milestone, it felt important to hit my daily target, so I asked if I could go on.

LA is a ridiculous city to try to cycle through but, luckily, down the oceanfront I found a cycle path that meandered through the beaches. I cycled in at dusk to a beautiful sunset over the sea and had to weave my way slowly through the many runners and dog walkers. It was everything I'd ever imagined LA to be, with *Baywatch*-style lifeguard towers and yummy mummies rollerblading and pushing their strollers. Every social stereotype of modern America seemed to be there, making the most of the last of 2007. Down past Muscle Beach and across the end of Venice Boulevard, I felt like I was riding through a film set.

By my calculations it was already New Year's Day in Scotland, which meant it was my birthday. Twenty-five. If you have to be alone on your birthday, cycling into LA at sunset is a pretty good way to do it.

As arranged, Simon was waiting by the lighthouse near Venice Beach and we drove back to his house in West Hollywood. I guessed he was in his midfifties, and he introduced himself as an avid cyclist. He certainly had the build of a hill climber. We chatted in the car about some of the incredible coastal climbs he'd trained on in the area, some of the best in the country; he mentioned that Lance Armstrong also came to train there. "I hope you don't mind that my partner and I are vegetarians," he added. I was, of course, delighted. What I wasn't expecting, as we arrived at his small white house, was to be met at the door by a very excited, flamboyant Indian in his twenties.

Simon was an Oxford graduate who had been professor of sexuality at Harvard. For the past decade he'd been living in LA and had written a number of books on the subject. I hadn't even known sexuality was available as a university course, but his heavy workbooks, which I leafed through, were an in-depth guide to everything you could imagine relating to the world of sex, from prostitution and diseases to sexual positions. After an awesome homemade dinner, Mike, Simon's partner, headed out to a party to see in the New Year.

I'd become so used to being stuck in my own world, meeting people for short periods and building momentary friendship, I already knew that my greatest memories from the road would be the people I met, but because of a lack of time I almost never got beyond first impressions. That evening, thrown into a situation that was so different from my first impressions of Simon, was a notable exception. I was warmly welcomed into his domestic world, where he lived with his young lover. I was fascinated to learn about his life's work, which stemmed from a personal desire to discover and explain sexuality.

LA, the end of 2007, and a relaxing evening off the bike in fascinating company. It was a perfect time to reflect on what I'd been through so far.

21

I should have learned by now the effects of relaxing too much when off the bike. As I cycled out of LA on New Year's Day I'd rarely felt more burned out. I found it impossible to focus on the miles I had to do that day, let alone the big picture. This had happened before a couple of times after I'd stopped, wound down, and shared stories with people on the road. As much as it was great in the moment, it was detrimental to the momentum on the bike.

So I made the decision right there and then to change my plans in the US.

I had many contacts in America and many of them were offering to meet and look after me at different points. As antisocial as it might be, there was no way I could maintain my mental focus if I kept distracting myself with company. The first of these contacts was due that day, and I called Mum to say that even if I made it as far as Don Macleod's, 150km down the road, I didn't want to stay there. I realized this would be a tricky one for Base Camp to explain, that I would stay in a motel within a mile or so of a friend's house, but I felt it had to be done. I was too tired and easily sidetracked to meet people every evening.

Despite leaving before seven a.m. I only managed six hours on the bike. Heading south out of LA was an awesome feeling as surfers, a karate school, and early-morning dog walkers made the most of the New Year. To start with the path continued to weave through the beaches, which was slow going where the sand had drifted. Then I was into grid-section suburbs with tens of stoplights, which did nothing to help progress. In 120km I hardly saw any countryside, riding from suburbs into areas of industrial oil refineries and then back into coastal towns.

By lunchtime my spirits had picked up. It was a remarkably warm day considering it was the start of January, and I kept stopping for birthday phone calls coming through from friends and family. Laguna Beach, where I stopped for lunch, was lined with expensive townhouses and chic cafés. As it was my birthday I treated myself at a hippy falafel bar that overlooked the surf. Another cause for celebration was that today was the 14,000-mile mark; only 4,000 to go. It was almost tempting to start counting down. By midafternoon I'd managed to get back into the flow and was excited to ride into the dark to get my 100 miles.

The next day was the final part of the southern stretch and the end of what was probably the most scenic week's riding I'd ever done. I woke with a new plan to be on the go between seven a.m. and seven p.m. every day from now on, which meant riding predawn and post-dusk but would give me loads of time during the day to space out the miles. That last stretch of California was the most industrial yet, and I could see San Diego approaching from miles off. I didn't get to see the city, however, except for its impressive skyline, as I turned left, away from the Pacific for the last time.

The only way was up and I knew the rest of the day would be a slow climb over California's coastal mountains. They trace an 800-mile course from the Mexican border to the northwest corner of Del Norte County in northern California and form a continuous series of ranges and valleys which separate the coast from the Great Central Valley and the deserts of the interior. Though the coastal ranges didn't look too severe, I knew it was about to get a lot colder. After the regular towns and coastal commerce of the past week I also knew the next section, along the Mexican border, was going to be a lot emptier.

By nightfall I'd made it to the aptly named town of Alpine, at 3,000 feet. After throwing a couple of foil-wrapped burritos in my panniers I layered up, switched on the lights, and headed into the night.

The I-10 is the major coast-to-coast southern highway in America, and it was pretty hairy riding in the dark as huge trucks labored past me as I clung to the hard shoulder. There was no flat land to be found up here, but as I passed the 4,000-feet elevation sign I spotted another sign for a vista point a mile ahead and hoped to find some-where to camp there. The small lay-by was completely open with a view back down the valley I'd just climbed up. Far from ideal, but there was one small tree and I locked my bike to it, put my tent up, and climbed in. It felt great to have finished the day with that massive climb, but looking ahead, I could see some more for tomorrow.

As I cleared up camp the next morning a couple of cars and trucks pulled up at the vista. One man and his wife gave me a particularly strange look; it was obviously an ill-advised campsite. The first couple of hours I had three big passes to cross. Each time I climbed I was boiling, layered up against the cold, but as soon as I started descending, it was freezing. The cold air actually hurt my face on those fast downhill sweeps, but apart from that it was spectacular riding. After one particularly long descent I came across a diner and decided I had to stop to warm up. Over a mountain of a second breakfast, I realized that I'd definitely left coastal California. Already the people, houses, accents, and lifestyle seemed so different—all lumberjack shirts and lazy drawls.

Warmed up, I pushed over the last mountain pass. The one great thing about the route maps I'd been following is that each section showed a relief map. Up ahead, I could see that the road literally dropped off back to almost sea level in an unbelievably short distance. Sure enough I was in for one of the best descents of the trip. I froze my arse off for half an hour from the craggy mountaintops down into a sandy desert.

And that was it. For the week since San Francisco I'd built up this crossing of the mountains to be a major event. As it turned out, I'd done the worst of it during a three-hour night ride and was now through.

Just 15km into the desert I stopped at the roadside and checked the map. The spaces between towns were about to get vast and I realized I'd already been caught out without enough supplies. I'd never imagined the mountains and desert could meet each other in such a short distance. To start with it had been gravel and scrub, but I was now on a long straight road with sand as far as the eye could see. At the start of the desert there'd been an option to cut onto the old interstate, which I thought would be safer and just as quick, so I found myself alone, on a very poor road. I didn't have nearly enough food for the next stretch but dug out a packet of fig rolls to keep me going.

There was a roar of an engine a good way off. It looked like one of the desert race cars I'd seen in the Paris-to-Dakar rally on TV. The vehicle stopped 100 meters off to the left and the driver pulled himself out of the window, took his helmet off, and started talking to two men standing next to a pickup. One of the men spotted me and quickly walked over. He was a gaunt, Mexican-looking man with an accent I could barely make out. I'm not sure I would've normally trusted him, but he seemed friendly enough.

"What ya doin'?" he asked.

I explained that I was cycling from San Francisco. He cut in enthusiastically before I could go on, and I couldn't get a word in for the next couple of minutes through his excited chatter. I decided that adding that I was actually cycling around the world would perhaps be too overwhelming for him.

"D'ya wanna ride?" he asked, gesturing to the dune buggy behind him.

I was about to say no—my automatic reaction to any distraction—when it occurred to me that I was stopped anyway for a break and that this was a unique offer.

Five minutes later I was clambering into a bucket seat and securing a full face helmet to an air vent so I could breathe. I questioned this, and my driver explained that without any windscreen or windows you couldn't breathe when the sand filled the car. There was also a five-point safety belt and a neck brace, so by the time we were ready to go I felt like I was strapped in for a roller-coaster ride. The car itself sat on massive tractorlike low-pressure tires under huge flared wheel arches. Compared to the size of the ground clearance, the huge suspension, and the tires, the cabin looked tiny sitting on top. The entire back of the car was the engine, which sounded like a jet starting up.

It felt like we were out for half an hour but afterward he told me that we'd actually been driving for less then ten minutes. I also thought we were going the fastest I'd ever been in a car, but he assured me we hadn't even hit 70mph. The massive coil suspension made the vehicle float and wallow as the unsilenced engine barked an incredible din behind us. We basically did a huge figure eight. Going down the straights I could see we were passing over deep sand dunes, often over a couple of meters from peak to trough, but it was hard to tell, partly because we were covering the ground so speedily that all the motions of impact and flying happened so fast. We got thrown around a huge amount, but because of the suspension these bumps didn't seem to relate to the ones we were passing over. Every time we went into a corner the vehicle wallowed dramatically to one side and I was sure we were going to go over. The only way I could speak was through an intercom in my mask, but I hardly got a word in and found myself laughing uncontrollably for most of the ride.

When we stopped I clambered out, took some photos, thanked the driver, and returned to my bike, which I'd left by the road. As I pedaled off down a completely flat road, my heart rate was sitting at over 100 beats per minute—twice what it should've been. I could think of nothing else for a couple of hours. Nor could I wipe the smile off my face.

Into Arizona, after a couple of days pushing over 100 miles, things continued to go well. It was another mental boost crossing the state line, an old, narrow footbridge over the Colorado River. The riding had been easier because there was nothing to distract me from the miles to be ridden.

The entire right-hand side of the road that day was given up to a motorsport playground. There were signs everywhere explaining where the motorbikes, quads, and dune buggies could go. I guessed there wasn't much else you could do with land like that. I certainly had never expected to see such landscapes in America. It looked like something out of Saharan Africa, with massive dunes stretching out across my view.

It was a wild landscape to cycle through and I rationed my supplies, assuming I could get things at the next town, Glamis. When I eventually arrived, hungry and thirsty, I found a couple of houses but nothing else, so I ended up doing 70 miles with two liters of water and a couple of energy bars. Luckily, it barely got above 10 degrees all day, so I wasn't sweating too much. It was still a massive relief to get to Palo Verde, where I found a small, dark country inn full of poker machines and pool tables where I could get a pizza and water.

The old man at the bar next to me spent the whole hour I was there telling me how he'd spent the last eight years of his life doing up a house he didn't own. Ever since he'd moved in, the ownership of his whole neighborhood had become a matter of dispute with a local mining company, but despite this he'd invested his entire savings and all his time renovating the house. From what I could see, he now spent his time telling his tales of woe to anyone who cared to listen. After the modern bustle and buzz of the California coastline it was certainly a big change to find myself in small-town America.

After 120km, in the small town of Blythe, a kind Latino shop owner gave me my bag of shopping for free, without a word of explanation. Just before the town I had passed through the first of what would be many border security posts. These seemed strange, as they were located in the middle of nowhere. The young guard explained that they were vehicle checkpoints close to the Mexican border, looking for smuggled people and narcotics. He quickly checked my passport and waved me on.

The clocks had changed by an hour into Arizona, which meant that when I left the town of Quartzsite at 5:30 p.m. it was dark. There's something hugely satisfying about climbing in the dark, but this day ended crossing a massive flood plain where the road zigzagged at 90-degree angles around mile-wide fields. This meant that despite being perfectly flat fast riding, the road was annoyingly farther than it needed to be.

I had never realized that modern man migrated within a country. In America it seemed to be a big thing. This year the storms in the northern states were particularly bad, which meant that every town I was passing boasted a full RV park. Recreational vehicles are the Americans' bigger and brasher way of doing caravanning. Snowbirds, as these migratory Americans are called, were apparently flocking south in even greater numbers this year. As a result I was finding that many campsites catered to every form of accom-modation except for camping itself. This caused a particular issue that day in the small town of Brenda, where I spent nearly an hour traipsing around three campsites and a motel in the dark until I gave up and camped a kilometer outside the town by the side of the road next to a hedge. It wasn't a very good hedge and I ran about for a few minutes testing different places as cars drove past, trying to figure out the best spot to pitch my tent and hide from the road.

It was still very dark when I woke the next morning at 5:30 and I felt surprisingly tired. I guessed I was still on California time (4:30) where it would get light between 6:30 and 6:45. It was still fairly dark at 7:15 when I finally left. For the most part it was an incredibly dull day on the bike with long straight roads through tumbleweed towns of half boarded-up houses with patched roofs, and front yards strewn with old wrecked cars and other waste. Loads of people seemed to live in caravans permanently within the town's boundaries. Most of the houses had a DIY look about them and the only obvious commerce in the area seemed to be the RV parks. Half the land and houses seemed to be for sale, and I spent hours sitting on the bike wondering who would buy and what you could do with an area like this.

I was, however, starting to enjoy small-town American country dining. I stopped after an hour in Hope for scrambled eggs, toast, and hash browns. After hours on the bike I was starting to look forward to the next conversations I would have in such places with the locals.

There was only one obvious target that day, and after 120km I hit the sprawling suburbs of Phoenix. Like a number of US cities, Phoenix has no natural geography to hem it in, so it's not dense at any one point: it simply spreads for miles and miles in every direction. After a pretty mind-numbing ride on a slow climb up to the Black Mountains, it rained heavily for a couple of hours through Wickenburg to Morristown. From there I hit a two-lane highway, flew the last two hours in the dry, and stopped at the first motel I could find.

Phoenix is where I started to give up on the Adventure Cycling Association route maps. I did use them for sections over the following week, but for the most part I made it up as I went along. Don't get me wrong, they're fantastic if you want to tour and see America properly and possibly take the safest routes, but they are almost never the fastest way. This made little difference when I was between towns, but traversing Phoenix was hugely frustrating and took most of the day. The previous three days had been over 180km each but it was going to be hard to keep that up.

To make things worse, the breakfast news on Sunday warned about snow and storms in the area I was about to enter. The headlines were also about the huge storms that were now hitting California; by the look of it there was no way I could've got through in the same time if I'd been a week later.

Later on in the afternoon I stopped at the town of Superior for supplies, and from there I could see a long climb ahead. It was nearly dark and the weather was bad. As I was getting ready to leave a man walked over from his family car, handed me a big paper bag of sweets, and said, "You'll need these more than us, man."

After the boring scrub of the day before, that afternoon ride out of Phoenix had actually been pretty spectacular, through craggy hills scattered with large cacti. Before reaching Superior, I stopped at the wonderfully named Apache Junction, where an awesome mountain backdrop was bathed in the late-afternoon light.

As I set out from Superior, it stopped raining. It'd been raining for most of the afternoon. The road quickly climbed and I stopped after 5km to reassess the situation; this was my last chance to go back and get a motel room for the night. Ahead I could see that the valley narrowed and the road got steeper. I rode on and soon found myself in a gorge, with river rapids off to the right of the road. Like the Californian coast road, I was about to miss some of the most interesting parts of the ride by cycling on into the night. About 10km later it was completely dark and the road took me through a couple of tunnels. I got a real buzz cycling into the steepest part of the gorge as it got dark and I didn't care about the numerous passing cars tooting at me. I was sure they were trying to tell me I shouldn't be on the road at that time of night and that there were no towns up ahead, but my lights were on and I had everything I needed.

Halfway up I decided that I would try to push on for at least another hour and a half, especially now that it had stopped raining. Suddenly I felt bumps in the road behind me and realized the back tire had blown out. You couldn't have picked a worse place to puncture. I pulled into a small gravel lay-by. Assuming it was a slow puncture, I decided simply to pump it up and ride to the top of the hill; it looked like it would rain again and I had no desire to sit at the side of the road in the night fixing punctures. Within 50 meters it was flat again, and this time I had no option but to fix it. By the time I'd finished I was freezing and wet, and I decided my best option was to cycle to the top and find the first bit of flat land to get the tent up and warm up.

Five miles later I reached a turnoff in the road with a wide gravel turning area. It was in full view of the road, with no shelter from the wind and rain, but it would have to do as a campsite. It was nearly eight o'clock, it had been dark for three hours, and the rain had started again.

I woke at about one a.m. with the tent sheets lying on top of me, the soaking material on my face. In a moment of confusion I forgot where I was. I crawled outside and tried to put the tent back up, but it was raining so hard, the ground was now so soft, and the wind was so strong that the pegs pulled straight out. It took me twenty minutes to move the tent to a drier bit of ground and then set the bike up so I could tie the tent ropes around its frame to hold it up. Everything I'd been sleeping in, which was almost everything I had, was drenched. Even the one-season down sleeping bag, which had been bad enough in the cold Californian nights, was absolutely worthless now that it was wet through.

By five a.m. I'd hardly slept, having found it impossible to get warm, just hoping it wouldn't snow as forecast. There was no point in wishing I'd stopped earlier now, but the couple of moments of hesitation I'd had when starting the climb into the dark kept entering my mind. As soon as it was light I packed the camp and set off, but I simply couldn't keep warm and the twinges I'd felt in my left Achilles and behind my left knee the day before felt far more acute. It continued to pour freezing rain all morning and I can't remember ever feeling colder. At least it wasn't snowing.

After just 28km I came to the town of Globe. By that stage I needed to do anything to get warm and raced into the first diner I saw, simply with the idea of resting for a while, warming up, and carrying on. After half an hour, a few cups of coffee, and a big breakfast I was still wet and cold, and the downpour looked like it was going to continue.

An hour later I was still there. The locals told me that the road ahead had been closed the day before due to mudslides in the heavy rain. This rain was forecast to continue for at least the rest of the day and there was no way I could risk being caught out for another night in that weather with everything already wet. It seemed an obvious decision: I had to stop. However, it took calls to Mum and David Peat before I convinced myself that I really had no choice but to stay where I was after just 28km. It was less than a kilometer to the first hotel I found, but even after that short distance any doubt left in my mind disappeared. It would've been an unbelievably tough day's ride in those conditions.

After sleeping that afternoon I couldn't sleep at night. I lay there for hours feeling guilty about having stopped early, absentmindedly watching films until a power cut ended that. This actually helped me sleep: it showed how bad the weather was out there. It was reasonable to assume that further mudslides had brought down power cables.

My alarm woke me at 5:30 a.m. with all the lights on, and I could see that the storm had passed, leaving a crisp, clear morning with blue skies and a heavy ground frost which made it look like it had snowed.

It was the coldest yet, truly bitter for the first hours. After 40km I made it to a Native American reservation and got distracted for a while speaking to a full-blooded Apache over a warming mug of coffee and a pastry. He told me the history of the area and his family with the charm of a natural born storyteller. "Wee fat man in a baseball cap" is how I kindly described him in the logbook.

As I went to leave, another guy walked over from the petrol pumps where he had been filling his car. "Hey, are you the guy we saw on Sunday way back?"

"Maybe, yes," I replied with a smile. "Did you pass me near Superior?"

"Hey, Tanny," he called back to his truck, "it's him. You are one crazy guy." He beamed at me and shook my hand vigorously. "We passed you in the rain, in the dark going strong. Where ya headin'?"

That day was all about getting back in the zone, picking myself up after the lost miles. A couple of reassuring texts from Scotland helped me feel less alone. It was a long rolling day through wide plains with the odd cactus, the stereotypical three-pronged ones. It was exactly what was needed. I had momentum again, and I sat on the bike for over nine hours, covering over 180km.

There was no sense in heading for more high passes as my set route suggested: there was a lot of snow on the hills, especially past Mount Turnbull, which looked spectacular. So I bought some new maps of Arizona and New Mexico and set a new route, mainly back on the interstate.

The problem with heading back onto the interstate became evident the next day. There was almost always a wide, hard shoulder to cycle on, but by lunchtime I had had three punctures. Apparently, in the summer, when it is incredibly hot, the tires on the big semis melt. To strengthen them, the tires have tiny wire meshing in the rubber, which gets thrown over the road in tiny shards when they melt. Not even my

Kevlar-lined tires, which had made it happily over some of the roughest roads in Asia, were strong enough for this almost invisible menace.

After the first puncture on the front wheel I regretted throwing away my last damaged innertube after the puncture in the gorge. There were no spares left and I was almost out of patches. By the third puncture, on the back, the same as number two, both inner tubes had multiple patches and there was only one left. A number had been wasted trying and failing to patch my only spare inner tube. A quick call to Scotland confirmed that there were no bike shops in the next towns, and by one p.m. I had covered only 80km despite a howling tailwind. It could easily have been a 200km day, but each tire had so many gashes and puncture marks; I had to stop every 5km to pick out bits of glass and wire before they went all the way through. It was slow going, but I had no choice: one more puncture and I would really be stuck. On the bright side, the long breaks gave me a chance to dry out the tent after the frost and condensation had soaked it. I also used the time to clean out the chain and sprockets, which were all gunked up. I was fast learning that winter riding was much tougher on the bike.

My habit was now to stop just before dark, eat, pick up more food (normally burritos), and then do two or three hours of night riding. I was once again in a ghost-town area, with half the buildings boarded up and no supermarkets to be found, and I eventually camped at a rest stop off I-10. A huge sign just before my very open camp spot told me I was on the Great Divide. I had no idea what this was, but I'd been aware of very gradually climbing all afternoon. I texted Val Vannet, my old geography teacher, who was following the cycle for a school blog, to find the answer. The Great Divide, also known as the Continental Divide, marks the watershed between the rivers flowing west and the rivers flowing east and south downhill to the Mississippi.

It was a freezing camp, in contrast to the sunburn I had got during the day. There was a large parking area with a number of covered picnic tables, and I pitched my tent in the shadow of the one farthest from a floodlit truck area, sheltering the tent from the chill wind. It was one of the first nights when I woke just because of the cold, and I struggled to warm up and go back to sleep. In a few days I would get a warmer sleeping bag; for now, this one was hopeless.

The following morning was more fast interstate cruising with the same tailwind, but the start was painfully cold. I tried to think warm thoughts as I snuggled into my neck warmer and shivered under the down body warmer, a fleece, and two base layers. After 7km, just about warm, the back punctured again. I used my last patch, and it was an arduous task due to the cold. After that I only made it 15km before having to stop to thaw out over an omelette and coffee. While there I spoke to DP, who was planning to fly out and join me in west Texas. I was looking forward to seeing him. It had been over two months since I'd seen anyone I knew.

However, Clay and Shannon, a couple I'd met in eastern Turkey four months earlier, had been in touch by email a few times and were now living in Las Cruces, the second-biggest town in New Mexico, and the place I was heading to. Over lunch I decided that my puncture situation pretty much dictated when I stopped, and I texted to confirm that I would welcome the offered place to stay.

I spent the rest of the day in a strange state of mind, thinking up a life business plan, amused by where my ideas took me. They went from more expeditions to huge corporate enterprises, but all hinged on my main goal in business, which I had decided on while at university: to get paid for who I was and not just for what I did. In my mind this was the only way I could earn true value for time and effort invested in whatever I was doing.

These thoughts were punctuated by a strange meeting later on. I was cycling through a wide plain with mountains on the far left and right when I saw a bike ahead. I was gaining on it fast and could soon see that it had some sort of trailer attached to it. Closer still, I saw something written on the back. I had to halve my speed to take a proper look before catching up. The trailer was one of those contraptions parents tow toddlers in, but the cyclist was no parent. The sign on the trailer read "WWJD."

"What does WWJD mean?" I asked him.

"What would Jesus do?" He said he was cycling from Florida.

"You know that you are cycling toward Florida, not away?"

"Cycling from Florida," he repeated.

"Why are you doing this?"

"Society is lost."

I had only met two such characters on the road so far—the other was walking aimlessly in Turkey—and they had both claimed to be living as devout Christians. I would say they were actually living against most Christian principles by turning their backs on society. They were examples of religion not as a catalyst for greater good and community but as something divisive and mindwashing. I thought about this for days.

Clay found me in Las Cruces, in a bike shop. The young guys who worked there told me about the legendary tire-breaker that was the I-10, so I armed myself with a pile of patches and a number of thicker inner tubes, each with slime in them. Slime in your tire means that if you get a simple puncture as opposed to a rip you can just take out the shard or nail, pump the tire up and fill the hole without having to patch the inner tube. The downside is that it can be messy and is slightly heavier.

I was sleeping on the floor, but after the storm and cold nights I was glad of the home comforts. During an all-you-can-eat buffet Clay and I looked ahead and set a new route for heading into Texas. The local advice was invaluable. I still needed to ask Base Camp though, to make sure I'd still be doing the correct number of miles. Mum, with some help from Bobby, agreed to get on the case in the next couple of days and reroute through Texas, Louisiana, Mississippi, Alabama, Georgia, and Florida.

22

WELCOME TO TEXAS. THE PROUD HOME OF GEORGE W. BUSH read the state boundary sign.

Most of day 160, Friday January 11, was gradually downhill, and for the first few hours, into the city of El Paso, the road followed the train tracks. It looked like a nightmare of highways on the way in, so I picked up the old cycle maps and turned onto Route 20 when it crossed and wiggled through miles of suburbs.

El Paso is not as big as Phoenix but is very industrial. It looked more Mexican than American, with many shop signs in Spanish only. My road took me west of the city center and then east along the south side by the Mexican border, a high wire-mesh fence at the roadside that followed the Rio Grande. The Rio Grande is a name that conjures up images of an expansive delta in the same league as the Ganges or Mississippi, but at that point it was no more than a muddy stream, maybe five meters across, with lots of junk and old tires in it.

The contrasts around this border area were incredible. The road had just come past a huge, dirty factory on the left which looked like some sort of raw material refinery, but behind that you could see the main city with its modern housing and offices, SUVs, Starbucks, and 7/11s. I stopped and looked through the small diamond-shaped wires at a shanty town in Mexico, on the other side of the road. A number of children were kicking a football on the dirt road that ran down the far bank of the Rio Grande and some stray-looking dogs ran around. All the buildings looked like home-builds, patched and unpainted. The fence I was peering through was about ten feet high and I ran my fingers over it while taking Mexico in. Along the bottom were a number of sections that had been cut and then patched up where people had jumped the border.

After being stopped and questioned by patrol guards for filming at the border—having visas in my passport for Iran and Pakistan did not help me—El Paso took ages to cycle through. All big towns do, but I enjoyed being able to take it all in. There were endless rows of garages and tire shops, and the majority of people looked Mexican. It had a unique feel, a million miles from the Californian towns I had passed through.

On the far side of town there wasn't much at all, and as the afternoon became evening I got worried about food and somewhere to sleep. The days were getting colder, but thankfully staying clear. It was as flat as you could wish for but not fantastically exciting. Eventually I stopped at the only village shop I had passed since the city and bought some minging-looking sandwiches and a tin of beans in case I had no options.

Fort Hancock, the next village, looked a similar size. I was not hopeful, but I set my sights on getting there and rode into the dark. It was such a flat, open valley I could see the lights from a long way off, which was deceptive at night, so I ended up riding late, in a strange trance in the cold, staring at a dot of light on the horizon.

Fort Hancock, Texas. I love the name. It was where Andy and Red crossed into Mexico after escaping prison in one of my favorite films, *The Shawshank Redemption*. The interstate and the minor road I was on converged slightly and touched either edge of the village, which was just a single street maybe a kilometer long. An old man walking his dog in the dark told me that there was a motel next to the interstate. Like most American motels, a young Indian couple ran it. I was so relieved not to be camping out.

Across the street I discovered Diane's, evidently an institution in the area. It was a tiny, greasy, cheap road stop, but the food was fantastic. About five older ladies seemed to share the cooking, waitressing, and evening's entertainment—a running barrage of jokes and banter with all the tables. My waitress announced me to the room. "This one's from Scotland," she said, beaming. Dinner took ages, but I left with more than enough sustenance. Laughter is the best medicine, but I was tired after a ridiculously early start and was so glad not to be in the tent. It was the coldest night yet easily.

While scribbling in my logbook before bed I found another reason to celebrate: 15,000 miles done, only 3,000 to go. I had cycled nearly that far before this trip, so it was a distance I was happy to compute in one part. I could now start counting down.

Breakfast at Diane's. It had to be done. The ladies were different but the banter was the same. The customers were mainly truckers and farmers drinking coffee from vast mugs, laughing themselves into gear for the day ahead over a plate of heart attack.

West Texas, before hitting the hills, was big valley riding on a slow climb, back on I-10. There were often long sections of "frontier road," parallel access roads set off the interstate that gave me a road to myself. I hardly stopped in the first 110km to Van Horn, then pushed on toward Kent at 170km. The plan was to meet DP at the end of the day for three days' filming; he had traveled for twenty-two hours from Scotland to get to Texas and was now driving eight hours to meet me. Tomorrow I would be back into the mountains and the plan was to film the big climb over to the town of Alpine at dawn. It was noticeably colder, but a crisp, dry chill which you could layer up against. DP and I were both out of mobile reception, so there was nothing to be done but carry on until our paths crossed.

I had gained another hour having come into the Central time zone, so had a longer day. As the afternoon went on, I scanned every passing car in the other direction. I was looking forward to seeing my friend again; Lahore seemed a long time ago indeed. I noticed more and more passing trucks blowing their horns at me. This had happened frequently throughout the US, and the farther out from town you were the more acknowledgment you seemed to get. Little did I know that DP's driver, Kaye, was a storm tracker for the news networks, had a radio in his car, and had a call out for me. Any truckers tuned in were picking this up and reporting back where I was.

Finally they found me, and the last 20 miles to Kent, gradually steeper along the busy I-10, were spectacular in the evening light. The trucks lumbered past as I sat on the hard shoulder, a dot moving slowly eastward. I felt proud to share even a small part of this experience with DP.

I was camping—again, there was no choice—but DP had brought supplies from Mum, the most important of which was a warmer sleeping bag. I set up the tent behind some shrubs, off the small road

I was turning onto from there, leaving the I-10 behind. DP and Kaye drove off to find a motel.

The evening logbook was an absolute habit: 870 meters ascent, 172km, 21.4km/h, minimum temperature freezing, rode for eight hours and one minute in ten hours fifty-four minutes. Dinner was two tins of soup, a yogurt, some bread, and a "Bear Claw" pastry. Bear Claw is made from almonds and tastes like marzipan. I found them very addictive. If I hadn't been riding 100 miles a day, I'm sure they would have helped toward an exponential waistline. After that, I zipped myself in. I was utterly content to be warm at night and excited about the next few days with company.

For the next three days I came out of my own wee world and road-tripped with David and Kaye. Kaye's job was to drive fast toward tornados when everyone else was driving away. He was of Native American descent and looked it, with long hair and dark skin. His jeans and leather jacket usually hid a beaded leather medicine pouch, traditionally used to collect plants and herbs to be used as omens and cures, which was tied around his waist.

It was a beautiful, crisp, and clear morning as I climbed the pass by the McDonald Astronomical Observatory. The road was deserted, only a handful of cars passing all day, and it wound gradually steeper until it switchbacked up through woodlands. When the trees cleared, the view was stunning. I was in a very different place mentally from normal, constantly aware of DP driving past and back.

By evening it had flattened out again but I was heading into a fierce headwind. I desperately hoped it would ease overnight as I was on this tack for the next few days. My campsite was hopeless, down a shallow bank at the roadside. In eight and a half hours I had only covered 154km at a sluggish 18km/h.

The following morning the wind was as keen as ever, cutting bitterly into my face as I set out. I could feel the big day in the hills in my legs and struggled to wake up. After just a few kilometers DP passed, having found me quicker than expected. "I'll see you for breakfast in the next town," I shouted. "It's too cold to stop."

It was hopeless. I was going to be fighting into this wind for days at this rate. It seemed ridiculous to do two sides of a triangle, but it made sense to cut back onto I-10 or risk losing days to slow, energy-sapping riding. It would be like the middle of Australia again, only much colder. By the time I reached the town of Marathon it was still minus 2 degrees with the headwind and I was struggling to warm up properly, giving me fears about injuring cold legs.

At the next junction I turned left, back toward the I-10. I needed time alone; our food stop had taken twice as long as it would have if I had been alone. That knot of frustration I was feeling needed time to pass. It seemed unreasonable—DP was only with me for three days—but the slight delays and distractions were not as welcome as I had imagined they would be. It annoyed me that these things got to me. I just needed to do some fast miles and feel the freedom of momentum. I think DP sensed this, and by the time he did eventually find me the mood had passed and I was thinking clearly again.

We got back onto the interstate at the town of Mobil. The last miles had been quick and I couldn't keep the smile off my face as I cruised fast, now with a tailwind. Inevitably, because of the slow start and long climb from the junction it had been a slow day to Mobil at 117km. But with hours of daylight left, 100 miles was easily possible.

The plan was just to stop for food, but on the outskirts I looked at the map again. There was no town we could aim for that night. I found David in a car park after a few kilometers and quickly made the decision to stop there. We had so much to do before DP left that it would be a late night. I could make up the miles back on the interstate, so this should be the last delay in America. It wouldn't hurt getting a short recoup and recovery, even though I hated stopping short.

I woke feeling fresh to spend the day tracking down distant interstate horizons. My resolve was doubled both by the missed miles to be covered and the stolen recovery time.

This was Middle America at its best. Huge horizons in wide-open valleys on transcontinental interstates. When your landscape is closer, the illusion of speed is greater. Here, landscapes seemed to last half the day.

Later on, DP stopped for the last time and bid me a fond farewell. In Istanbul and Pakistan he had been there with and for me on my days off, and in Perth it had been his old friend Ian. It was only now, five months in, that David had experienced the realities of my daily routine. Being left alone again left me in a strange mood, almost canned anger, which made me feel like I could do anything. This was just as well as I had a mammoth finish to the day.

I cycled well into the night having ridden ten hours and stopped at a cheap motel, where I was given a vast room. Without food or means to cook, I then cycled back into town, stopped at a gas station and diner called Town and Country, and scanned the boards for the healthiest thing on offer. I sat there, alone again, in the red plastic diner in my Lycras, munching on chicken and gravy, slurping a Coke and ignoring the strange looks from the customers. They were as much a stereotype as I was, except mine wasn't the norm here. They were mainly potbellied, hairy men with baseball caps and workman's shirts and jeans. It was a bit lonely, and I actually enjoyed the cold night cycle back to the motel. It seemed appropriate.

Big days are often followed by a false start, and the late push hit me the next morning. It was 8:30, after a breakfast of egg burrito and muffin, when I dragged myself away from the warmth of Town and Country. For the very first time since leaving Paris I had reset the alarm for 6:40 when it woke me at six. However, once going it was a faster day by a matter of 3km/h. This might not seem much but the difference in perceived momentum and morale is huge.

By the 120km mark I was almost out of water and had not eaten for hours, so I peeled off to do a small detour to the village of Roosevelt, as there were no towns on the interstate. I cycled completely out the other side of the small row of wooden houses before realizing that was all there was. Turning around, I found a small petrol station and village shop. There were a couple of steps onto a wooden walkway with a row of bench seats outside. It looked like something out of a Wild West film. All it lacked was the swing doors.

Inside, it was so dark it took a minute for my eyes to adjust. I nearly walked straight back out. The walls were covered in stuffed heads—boar, deer, and a moose—hunting awards and photographs, including kids as young as twelve killing wild boar with crossbows and other teenagers killing guinea fowl with huge pistols. Next to the cakes and chocolates you could buy shotguns and knives big enough to skin a dinosaur. I felt utterly naked wandering around in my Lycras with the eyes of the shopkeeper and a few "hunters" following me. These men were sitting at a table near the door drinking coffee. The lady behind the counter was also middle-aged and wore a thin pull-over and no bra—that was very clear, even in the low light. She looked tough, the sort who would start a bar fight with you for not drinking as much as her. She seemed to be saying, "I am a tough country girl, look twice at my breasts and I will stuff your foot in your mouth," so I tried not to. I also tried not to linger or look too impressed.

I discovered a pastry being sold that claimed to be 500kcal—equivalent to a quarter of your daily recommended calorie intake. That is incredible. It was a pecan cake about twice the size of a Mars bar, and I bought four of them. I was relieved to get back into the daylight, but I felt terrible after eating a few of these bricks of food, so I decided to ration the other two. I turned on my phone to find I had reception for the first time in four days and read the ten or so texts from friends and family before leaving the strangest country town yet. It was a small time warp, a forgotten world, less than a mile from the interstate.

Despite big rolling roads, a tailwind allowed me to fly to the town of Junction by late afternoon. Junction, like so many of the towns I was passing, and like the name would suggest, existed, it seemed, simply to service the transcontinental diesel flow. All I could see on approach was gas stations, fast food joints, and a few retail outlets.

At this point it seemed sensible to leave I-10 again, although my exact route ahead was unclear. I cut onto a small, bumpier route with winding roads, coppices, and scrub that looked like Scottish heather. But it was soon dark, so there wasn't long to enjoy this. The wind changed late in the day and it was slow going, not helped by the saddle sores, which kept reminding me they were there as I headed for the town of London.

With such a name I was expecting it to be at least big enough for a small motel. I scanned the roadside with my head torch and was through London, a tiny hamlet without even a shop, almost before I realized it. My passion for pushing on and camping wild was waning. I felt I could keep doing the daily miles but craved a bed and shower. Energy for anything above the 160km target and the novelty of a cold tent was leaving me.

The forecast that morning had warned of storms coming in, so I pedaled on into the dark reluctantly, hoping for some kind of cover to materialize out of the darkness. Finding a safe place to camp at the roadside in America at night was proving hard enough without having to stormproof everything. It was miles later that an idea hit me. Remembering Iran, I realized that I had passed a couple of large viaducts, and pushed on to find another. Of course, the next one was much farther along. It was half an hour before a low wall appeared at both sides of the road. I stopped and waited for a couple of cars to pass before throwing the bike over the barriers and scrambling down the steep bank.

It was more of a bridge than a viaduct, with three underpasses, each a couple of meters across and easily high enough to stand in. The two on either side were filled with branches and junk like discarded fuel drums, but the middle was clear. On its concrete floor was evidence of flooding: a bank of sand and grit a couple of feet deep on one wall that stretched most of the way across. I could hear a couple of cars passing overhead but they sounded distant. My only concern was that this was obviously a storm drain; I could see the watermarks in the sand. As I left my bike and wandered off to the woods for a pee, the thunder started, far off but threatening. If there was torrential rain I didn't want to be in that waterway; but if there was moderate rain and high winds I did want to be under-cover. Taking a gamble, I decided to pitch the tent at the highest point of the bank of sand, under the road, and went to sleep to the sound of rain starting to fall.

That night in my tent on the sand under the road, I dug out the photos of family and friends I had been carrying all along. In five months it was the first time I had looked at them, undoubtedly because spending time with DP had reminded me of home. At 190km it had been a great day, but I felt sad for the first time, dreading how far I still had to go. The reality was that I felt strained. I could keep doing what I was doing, but any events above the 100-miles-a-day targets were getting harder to deal with, like this imminent storm. The fire in my belly was not the same; I felt I would be glad for the cycle to be over any time. Trying to put these thoughts aside, I switched off the head torch and fell asleep, listening to the rain.

It was minus 3 when I woke, but thankfully it had stopped raining in the night. The road was deserted for the first hours and I pedaled unclipped as there was so much black ice on the roads. After an hour I stopped at the first town, where most shops seemed to be butchers, gun sellers, or taxidermists, went into the gas station and bought a woolly hat. It was the best $6 I spent in the US. I stayed cold all day but at least my ears thawed, albeit slowly and painfully. In the cold and with so little traffic I completely zoned out, and the next few hours passed without leaving any memories.

I came to after noticing a gold Jaguar heading the other way. It wasn't just that it was an odd color; being a Jaguar, it stuck out from the average SUV or white pickup. As we converged it pulled up and someone jumped out of the driving seat and started waving a St. Andrews flag wildly at me. Bemused, I pulled to a stop. The man ran across, promptly dropped his camera on the road, and greeted me. "I'm David Grossett, a relative of the Muirheads."

My uncle on my mum's side is a Muirhead, and I'd known he had lots of family in the US, but had completely forgotten that I might meet some en route.

"We've been following your tracker so have driven out from San Antonio to find you."

It was a lovely gesture, and I could not help but appreciate his enthusiasm, despite the impromptu break.

"Shall we stop for food?" he suggested.

"It's very cold for me here, can we stop in Fredericksburg?" I suggested. It was only 9 miles ahead.

"Yes, of course," David replied, beaming. "My son-in-law owns a diner there."

I had just been getting back into the solo zone after DP's company, so I slightly resented being stopped and taken for lunch. I tried to shake off this negativity, but my efforts were not helped by the fact that I overshot the diner and had to backtrack a couple of kilometers. David and his wife were charming and very excited to meet up and I did enjoy a huge lunch with them. He gave me his clan crest off his beret—a very kind good-luck gesture that I hid safely in a pannier.

This meeting left me in a poignant mood all afternoon, musing on how the cycle was affecting others. It had touched me to see David's enthusiasm in sharing a small part of my journey; the hundreds of messages on the website and texts from friends reflected this feeling. To be honest, this was a personal ambition which had grown to have schools and charity aspects. I had underestimated the less structured externalities of such a venture, the number of people associating with my journey and being affected positively by it. I felt so far removed from normality it was hard to grasp, but I tried to imagine going to an office every day and logging on to follow an expedition for half a year, and working out what that relationship would be like.

After the 64 miles to Fredericksburg, it was a fast 32 miles to

Johnson City, the birthplace of Lyndon Johnson, where I would have stopped except that there looked to be an easy 13 miles on to Blanco. I was now skirting Houston and big oil country.

From the Turkey/Iran border through to the Pakistan/India border I had spent $500, but I was now spending nearly $100 a day on food and accommodation. I could have camped more and each day I fought my conscience about this, but it did not feel as safe and easy as Europe, Australia, or New Zealand had been and it was so cold at night. I craved any possible comfort to keep going. Tucked up in bed in Blanco, I ate heartily and watched the news on the primary elections. Barack Obama was the underdog who seemed to be threatening Hillary Clinton, but it appeared to be a one-horse race for the Republicans with John McCain. It was like being back in Australia when their general election was going on: the Democrats and Republicans tore shreds off each other, the gloves off. After the news, the weather warned of more storms for the Deep South and Texas, as far south as Houston. Hopefully they would stay north of me.

"The Devil's Backbone" is the apt nickname for the road east of Blanco. I only know this because I met Kaye again, 5 miles out of San Marcos.

It was 1 degree and raining hard when I set out. Thankfully the downpour eased over the narrow, rolling and pretty dangerous first 20 miles, and I thought only of getting to San Marcos, scrunching my toes to warm up. I was in my own world again when I spotted a man in a long coat and a Stetson standing at the roadside. I recognized the jeep before I realized it was Kaye, taking photos. He had also been following the tracker and had come out to see how I was getting on, concerned about the storm.

The last few miles into town had been a steep descent and the rain had started again, this time for good. I jumped into the jeep's front seat, turned the heating up, and hungrily ate a pile of homemade nachos and a couple of yogurts that Kaye had brought. They were what I needed, and I didn't resent for a minute being stopped.

After lunch I had passed two other cyclists—only the second time this had happened, if you count the guy with the kiddie trailer. They were just as intriguing, if slightly more normal. They were both in their early twenties, from California, and were following the same

Cycling Association route, having taken thirty days from San Diego. They had a vast amount of kit so were struggling with constantly breaking wheels which they had no idea how to fix.

After passing them, and congratulating myself slightly for getting to this point twice as fast as them, I embarrassingly had to stop within 5km with my own wheel problems. I had hoped I was imagining the back wheel wobble, blaming an uneven road, but it soon became unmistakable and I feared the worst: my first broken wheel since Adelaide. Fortunately there were no broken spokes, but two were massively loose, which was odd. They should break or stay taut, not self-loosen. Unless . . . I examined the rim. There was a crack along the metal, allowing the spoke to pull through slightly. I took all the bags off, turned the bike upside down, and sat at the side of the road trying to tighten them all evenly, making it run straight again. It was the Californians' turn to pass now, with a cheery wave. I would have offered to help. I cursed after them, even though I knew I didn't really need help; it was just my annoyance with the wheel showing.

Eastern Texas was far more inhabited, though in the open countryside there were far fewer places to hide and camp. I had been barked at by dogs behind high-security gates a number of times. Even miles from towns people seemed paranoid and every farm track or field gate was bolted. The high-security gates, which would have looked at home only in the most expensive parts of a big city, looked bizarre here, but the signs were clear: NO TRESPASSING. I reflected on how nervous Kaye had been about camping wild or even stepping across fences—"if you cross, they can shoot you." It seemed ridiculous. I was doing no harm, and was so used to the Scottish right-to-roam attitude. There was, however, something about the area that made me nervous every time I stopped, more so than at any other time on the cycle. I had been worried many times in countries like Pakistan and India, but I had never been afraid of being robbed like everyone seemed to be here.

All land I passed in the growing darkness was very open, without the cover of hedges, walls, or trees. Eventually, my only option was to pitch the tent behind some road-building machinery parked in a gravel car park by the roadside. There was one of those massive scraping machines with a big blade underneath, a road roller, and a Bobcat-style digger. They formed a wagon camp shield in all directions from sight and wind.

*

Two days later I finally made it to Louisiana. Texas seemed to have gone on for a long time. The last full day in Texas was uneventful, and short: I managed only 150km, and it started well below freezing. This caused a new problem: the oil inside the hub gears, or part of the mechanism, froze solid, and it stayed that way until midmorning. As a consequence, hills were a real struggle. With all the weight on the bike it was not possible to get out of the saddle and climb the way you would on a mountain bike, so stuck in a high gear my legs burned as I tried to power up the long climbs.

The ride into Louisiana was pretty memorable, into the dark with lightning on the horizon to the north. The state boundary is a small bridge and the sign is pretty understated compared to the likes of Arizona and Texas. I aimed for the town of DeRidder before finding somewhere to camp. The border itself had been in trees—the first time I had ridden any distance through forests in hundreds of miles. And it continued that way.

When the trees cleared, the road slowly climbed. Off in the distance were huge chimneys billowing smoke upward, sitting in a sea of white floodlights. There was none of that orange glow you get from far-off streetlights; this was brilliant white. You could smell the massive pollution this plant was causing. The air seemed thick and slightly sweet. In the dark it was eerie, especially with the lightning storm flashing in the background. I assumed it was some oil refinery or grizzly metal plant, but when I passed its huge gates I was amazed to find that it was a paper mill.

It was nearly midnight by the time I finished making calls and eating, so I set the alarm for 6:30. The main delay that evening had been trying to fix my back wheel again—the spokes kept loosening. I resolved to find a shop as soon as possible, probably in the state capital Baton Rouge, two days away if all went well. Despite the deep tiredness I was feeling and the wheel problem, there was reason to celebrate: I had now covered 16,043 miles. Only 2,000 miles to go.

23

Tuesday January 22 went very well, until 3:30 p.m.

Louisiana was a nice change, fairly flat with quieter roads. Crossing out of Texas had seemed like a massive milestone; it was now only a short hop across Louisiana, Mississippi, and Alabama, just a couple of days across Florida, and I'd be back in Europe for a 1,100-mile sprint to the finish. Less than 2,000 miles! I smiled all morning, the fire well and truly alive in the belly, regardless of how low the batteries felt. The saddle sores and leg pains would fade; it was nothing I hadn't dealt with a hundred times over in the last half year. The finish in Paris played time and time again in my mind. It had done so many times before, but it was different now. It seemed so close.

I was suddenly into an area of flooded fields, with small paddle boats in them—for what I had no idea. The town of Mamou is surrounded by them. I had missed the turnoff for the route I was supposed to be on; I was still heading in the right direction, but now on very minor roads. The final miles before the town were being dug up, so after a fast first 100km it was like mountain biking and very slow going, bumping across corrugated roads. This quickly shook the back wheel out of shape again and I tensed with every bump, fearing the wheel would break entirely. The dirt went on and on, around every corner, when I kept expecting to find fresh tarmac. It wasn't long before the back wheel was all over the place and starting to rub the brake pads, so I stopped and disconnected them. There was no point in fixing it there, with more bad roads ahead, and at this speed there was no need for both brakes anyway. The front ones were working fine.

Just before Mamou the tarmac started again. I pedaled thankfully

into town to find some lunch. I could see from the map that the road
I was on cut sharp left, down the main street for maybe half a kilo-
meter, then cut sharp right at the other end of town. That was it, so
I knew I would be lucky to find a good place for food.

It was like many tumbleweed towns I had passed through. The
streets were amazingly wide despite the town's size and the main
street was very spaced out, with big sidewalks and wooden houses
giving way to shops in the center of the street. I was cycling fairly
slowly, looking around as I approached a crossroads. The traffic
lights hanging high above were green, so I didn't pause.

A white car was slowing into the lights from the right. I looked at
it, then glanced away left. A second later I looked forward to see that
the car hadn't stopped and was still rolling, and an old lady in the
driver's seat was looking right. I screamed—a gut reaction, without
thinking; no words, just a bellow of fright. I threw on the brakes but
my left hand pulled limply on the disconnected wires and the front
wheel skidded. The bike skewed sideways and the front wheel hit
hard behind the front wheel arch of the car. Immediately unclipped
from the pedals by the force of the impact, I flew over the bars and
onto the hood and bottom of the windscreen before sliding forward
as the car skidded to a halt. I landed on the tarmac and instinctively
curled up, believing the car was about to hit me.

I had been thrown forward a good meter, but the car never got that
far. I lay on the ground, completely still.

From the moment I realized she hadn't seen me, it had all
happened so slowly. I was aware of everything. In all, it took probably five seconds.

"Why did you jump the lights?" I heard the lady saying in a
panicky voice, but I couldn't look. I just lay still, closed my eyes, and
swore silently, over and over again. All I could think was that it was
over. The race was over. Just as I'd started to believe I was there.

I felt someone touching me but still couldn't look up or move. I
sensed nothing was broken, but I felt paralyzed. There were more
voices now, and someone screamed, "For God's sake, call 911!" The
first voice was close over me now. "He jumped the lights, I didn't see
him, he just cycled into me."

It took a few minutes of telling myself to get up for my body to
react. I eventually rolled onto my back and stretched my fingers out,
checking my arms. The right elbow was dead and the forearm

scratched. I looked down at my legs. The right one was pretty cut up but it didn't look deep. A man offered a hand and pulled me to my feet.

The car was dented badly at the side, its side window broken. Other cars were stopped at each junction of the crossroads. The bike was lying on its side, the front left pannier broken off and in front of the car, having followed my path. The front wheel was completely buckled in, sitting about 30 degrees from straight.

The old lady looked petrified and I tried to reassure her. "I'm OK, it was an accident."

"Why did you miss the lights?" she repeated.

"I saw it all." I turned to see a lady in her midthirties. Looking around properly for the first time, I realized quite a few people had gathered. The young lady pointed back in the direction I had been traveling. "The cyclist was in the right, he had the green, you ran the lights."

The old lady stood silent, stunned.

At that moment the police arrived. Their station can't have been far in a town this size. I started walking over to the pavement slowly, checking my legs more closely. The greatest pain was in my lower back; I must have landed on my tailbone. At least it wasn't a striking pain, it wasn't broken, only the dull pain of bruising.

The police picked up the bike and I watched them trying to wheel it off the road. Of course it wouldn't, which seemed to baffle them. I walked back over, lifted the bent front wheel, and pushed the bike to the side, then went back to pick up the bag and sunglasses, which were still in front of the car. The police were very friendly, almost jokey, but seemed utterly clueless about what to do. The old lady looked as terrible as before. They took her to the station to give statements, along with the lady who had witnessed the accident.

An ambulance then arrived and they checked me over as best they could at the roadside. "You need to go to the hospital," one of the policemen said. The paramedic agreed.

"I don't think I need to go to hospital."

"Yes, sir, you do. This is a serious road accident."

"I really don't think I need to go to hospital. I am just bruised and cut."

The paramedic checked my right elbow, which flinched, but there was nothing broken, of that I was sure. "OK, please sign here, then."

The medic produced a clipboard with a legal disclaimer saying that I had been checked at the scene and had refused hospital treatment at my own risk. They left quickly.

"Is there a bike shop in town?" I asked one of the policemen.

"No, there's nothing near here."

"Is there a motel in town?"

"No."

"OK. I'm cycling across America," I tried to explain. "It's part of an eighteen-thousand-mile race around the world to break the Guinness World Record. I need to get my bike fixed as fast as possible."

Neither of them replied immediately, just looked at me as if I had taken a hit to the head. It took a couple of minutes to convince them I was for real, but I was still no closer to getting any help.

"I'm not sure what you can do. There is no bicycle shop near Mamou."

We went in circles for a few more minutes before another man came up. He introduced himself as Tim, the old lady's son. He was a big chap, probably in his midforties, in working jeans and a grubby T-shirt. He had a kind face for a bear of a man and was hugely apologetic. "I came as fast as I could, as soon as my mom called." I reassured him that I was not badly hurt and repeated my situation to him. "Geez, of all people to run over she runs over a world-record holder." He ran a hand through his hair, obviously relieved I was at least fine.

"I'm not a world-record holder yet," I observed dryly, laughing for the first time and pointing at the bike.

My helmet was lying on top of the back pannier, completely smashed in, flattened down one side. I decided this was not the time to point out that my back brake had been disconnected and that the helmet had not been on my head, that it had been the weight of the back of the bike which had crushed it. I needed all the sympathy and support I could muster to get out of there quickly.

"I need to find a bike shop today to get that wheel fixed," I repeated to Tim.

"Of course. I can take you in the pickup, whatever it takes." He looked very concerned. "She's getting old. I should have known this would happen soon."

I called home and explained what had happened. Mum's reaction, as always, was very reassuring: she was concerned but didn't sound panicky. She immediately turned her attention to helping me get the bike fixed, and we agreed to speak later once she had found the nearest repair shop.

A policewoman then took charge of the situation, arranged for the bike to be put in the police truck, and took me back to the station to use the internet to find the nearest bike shop. The closest turned out to be 50 miles away in the city of Lafayette, and the shop she got through to said it would be no problem if I brought the bike in first thing the next morning.

Half an hour later the bike had been transferred onto Tim's huge truck and we were on the road to Lafayette. Tim was a crawfish farmer and explained the flooded fields I had been confused by that morning. When he got the call about his mother's crash he had been out in his little boat. He was born-and-bred country Deep South and I fought laughter as he started to tell me about the joys of crawfish and all the many ways you can cook them, as it reminded me of another of my favorite films, *Forrest Gump*. I enjoyed his company. His dark humor cheered me as the shock of the last hour's events wore off.

It was after six o'clock when we arrived in the city and Tim's GPS took us directly to the bike shop. Inevitably it was shut.

"The nearest motel?" Tim asked.

"Yeah, perfect, thanks. If it's close I can just walk down in the morning."

We had just come off a main road, so I was hopeful. Tim hit a button on his GPS and it gave him a list of accommodations close by. "You're in luck, less than a mile."

The motel was a big purpose-built building like so many others I had seen in the States. The reception was to the left of an arched driveway, which led through to a large car park. The rooms were on two floors with walkways along each and metal stairs between levels. At a guess, there were fifty rooms. Tim admitted not knowing this part of Lafayette, but he was sure it was all right. It looked clean enough; in fact, there was hardly anyone around.

"If you need to get back to Mamou in the morning please just call, it's no problem," Tim said.

Mum had not been able to contact Guinness World Records out of office hours, so I still didn't know if I had to go back once the bike was fixed. Lafayette was just over 50 miles from where the crash had happened but only about 20 miles east, as we'd traveled in a mainly southerly direction. Ideally, to save time, after an "out of my control" event I would be allowed to restart from the city.

My room was very basic but fine. Bottled emotions were bubbling inside me and I just wanted time alone. That morning I had been cruising into the Deep South thinking of Florida and the finish; now I was in an unknown city with a damaged bike and feeling pretty bruised after a car crash.

A young black man was walking past the door just as I called back to Tim that I couldn't find the light switch. "Here it is, behind the curtain," the young man said, popping his head in and switching them on.

"Thank you."

"No problem, man." He gave a cheery wave and walked on.

All things considered, I was in good shape, so I accepted Tim's offer of dinner and we drove across town to a diner. His son was studying in Lafayette and he claimed this was the best food joint in town. It certainly did "big," and we ate like kings. It was amusing to sit there for an hour swapping stories. We had nothing in common, except maybe that we were from farming backgrounds. He had only once been out of Louisiana, and that was to go skiing in New Mexico. OK, that was another thing in common—a love of skiing—but in terms of outlook we were a million miles apart. However, I really liked the guy. He was genuine.

Back in the motel, I peeled my Lycras off and had a shower, which stung massively. I felt strangely at ease. I had got away almost unscathed and if all went well I would easily be able to make up the miles. I had only been two hours down on target that day despite the crash. If I could get fixed in a similar time and start from Lafayette then I would lose less than half a day's riding in total.

I dozed off at about ten p.m. but woke suddenly less than an hour later to screaming at the door. I sat up; I hadn't even got under the covers. The TV was still on. A girl's voice was shouting; a man answered. There was a moment of silence and I felt every sense heightened, craning to hear what was happening behind the curtain. My room was dark except for some streetlight that was creeping in through the curtains.

I pulled them back very slightly but stayed back with the lights still off. Outside two girls and three men, all young and black, were arguing. I only caught the odd word. It was all slang and heavily accented. It was clear that the girl I had heard initially was going berserk at a man in a dark puffy jacket. In response he was getting more and more angry. After a few rounds he walked over to her, arms outstretched, screaming in her face. They were about five meters from my door, in the parking lot.

One of the other men who had been standing at the side now came forward and pushed the first man off the girl. The shouting was now going three ways. Were they drunk or on drugs? I guessed the latter. The girl seemed to be getting the upper hand again—certainly she was shouting more, and louder—and then the man suddenly turned and walked off, shouting that he would kill her. She screamed after him again, calling him a coward.

I had no idea what to do. I had never seen anything like it. I didn't know how serious it was. Certainly the adrenaline was pumping. I was thinking fast again, like in the crash, focused and trying to react sensibly.

I couldn't see any weapons and hadn't been unable to decipher enough words to know what was actually going on. It seemed irresponsible to go to bed, so after another minute I'd decided to call 911 when there was a quick knock at the door. I fell back into the dark in fright. I had been staring so intensely through the curtains, trying to make out what was being said, that this noise a couple of centimeters from my left ear made me react like a kid caught spying on his parents arguing. I jumped out of my skin.

I threw on my shorts and a T-shirt. Maybe it was the police, maybe it was the motel owner; the argument was sure to have woken everyone. In any case, I wasn't thinking clearly when I opened the door a crack without putting the chain on.

"Hey, you OK?"

I looked out and recognized the man.

"You remember I helped you with your lights this afternoon?"

I breathed easier. "Yes, thanks, what's going on?" I spoke quietly, opening the door to shoulder width now and jamming it with my foot so I could speak to him.

"Yeah, don't worry, they're all drugged up. They'll be gone in a minute. I saw the curtains moving so guessed you were still up. Everyone is out watching." He smiled as if it was a spectator sport. "Sorry to bother you."

"Should we not call the police?" I asked. "They seem pretty serious."

"No," he said, less laid-back now.

Behind him were two other young guys. He saw me scanning them and smiled again. "Hey, this will be over in a minute, can we chill with you for a minute? You seem cool. I can bring some ladies—you want ladies?—and we can forget all about this. Where are you from?"

"Scotland."

"Hey, he's from Scotland," he shouted to a skinny guy standing behind him. "Come on, let's chill for a bit and I'll call the ladies."

"No, thanks, I'm going—"

He put his hand on the door. "We won't stay long. Come on, man, I want to talk to you more."

I had no idea what to do, but I let my foot slip from behind the door. I stepped back as he walked over the doorstep, still trying to think of how to get him to leave. He walked straight past me and sat on the farthest away of the two beds. It was still not a threatening situation, but I was now wishing I had just closed the door.

"I'm sorry, but you have to go," I said. "I'm going to sleep. I'm not being rude but I just don't know what is going on around here."

I sensed movement behind me and turned to see the other two men in the room, one by the television and the other by the round table next to the door.

"Come on, let's go," the first guy said, and ran past me.

"Hey, stop, what are you doing?" I called stupidly after them as they disappeared out of the door.

I stood completely still for what felt like minutes, but was probably all of twenty seconds, before noticing that my wallet, which had been on the table by the television, was gone.

I picked up the key and bolted for the door, turned left like they had, and sprinted to the end of the building. The parking lot was a dead end with a turning area and high fence around it. There was a group of three or four guys and two girls hanging around the steps at the end of the building.

"Did you see where they went?"

"Yeah," one of the guys replied, pointing unhelpfully toward the fence.

I couldn't see how they could have got over it but walked around the back and up and down for a few minutes, trying to think what to do.

The group by the stairs stared at me. They were all rough-looking characters. I suddenly realized how out of control this situation had become, how vulnerable I still was. It was very early in Scotland but I had to get help, plus I figured it would be good to be on the phone to deter further attack.

Mum answered after a couple of rings. "Mum, I've been mugged. I'm OK, but they've taken my wallet." This was a tough call to take as a mother, after dealing so well with the crash that afternoon.

I walked back parallel to the rooms, in the middle of the car park. The guy and girl who had been fighting had gone, but there was the other group now. Because they were near my room, I decided it would be sensible to walk past them and go straight to reception. Maybe they could call the police.

As I drew level with my room, a black sedan pulled in under the reception arch going fast and swerved left to a stop by the stairwell. With the engine still running, a tall black youth wearing a black vest top and jeans, despite the cold, got out of the passenger seat. Almost running, but with a slight limp, the youth moved forward to the group and without a word threw his right fist at one of the men, catching him on the jaw with a dull thud. It was a huge punch, and the man fell backward. Not a word was said by either as he picked himself up and ran off.

The attacker turned and stared at me. I was still on the phone. "Hang on, Mum, something's going on." Without thinking I had stopped when the car had pulled up, rooted to the spot. I could have been at reception by now; instead I was still the wrong side of the gang. I cursed to myself and walked forward, avoiding glancing at them again. The youth paused for a second as I set off, but I could sense him still staring at me; then he burst forward, half running, half limping, like before. He grabbed me by the chest and pushed me back, letting go but blocking me. His face was scarred across one cheek and he looked haggard, though he couldn't have been more than thirty. He was a lot shorter than me, maybe five nine, but strong.

It was his eyes that scared me: they were wild, bloodshot, with huge dilated pupils. He was not in control, acting paranoid and anxious, almost certainly on crack.

"I will call you back in a minute." I hung up.

"You scared?" He lifted his right fist and held it back.

I didn't answer. What could I reasonably say in the situation? I tried to ready myself for the attack.

"Give me some money and you'll be safe."

I patted my pockets. "I don't have any money. I have just been mugged. That's why I'm here." I was surprised at the venom in my voice—probably not the best way to pacify this guy.

Before he could reply, the car horn sounded and he turned. I could see the driver signaling frantically, and the attacker turned away. I took a few steps back as he shouted at the driver. The room was closer than reception and I was now in the background, so I quickly walked back, putting some parked cars between the gang and me, onto the walkway. I unlocked the door to my room, went inside, and quickly locked it again behind me.

I sat on the bed, shaking, then called home. "I'm fine, I'm back in my room . . ." I didn't know what to do, but Mum said she was off to do what she could; I had no idea what that might be. I sat around for ages, then Mum called back. I explained that I was going to try to speak to reception and get the police.

It was now half past midnight, over an hour since the incident, and looking out of the curtain I saw that the car park was empty. I decided to make a dash for reception as the room phone wasn't working.

The man behind the desk was quiet and timid, not the hard man you might expect in a place like this. I explained what had happened, the whole chain of events, as simply as I could. He came out into the car park and I showed him where my room was, and where the events had taken place. "There's no point in calling the police," he told me. "The best thing to do is just stay in your room, you're safe there, and don't come out until it's light."

When I got back there, I found that, luckily, I had one other card in my spare wallet. Unluckily, I realized the video camera had been stolen too.

I woke at 5:30 after just a few hours' sleep and called Mum again. She told me that she had spoken to David Peat, and the BBC had called the Lafayette police, who were coming to take a statement. She had also spoken to Guinness World Records. While they were really sorry to hear about the crash, the rules were clear and I had to restart where the accident happened.

While on the phone to Mum I marched past reception and walked the 400 meters to the gas station. The spare credit card worked— a massive relief—and I tucked hungrily into a big breakfast. On the way back I phoned David Peat, just so I would look less alone.

It was completely light by the time I got back to the motel and the short walk and food had done me good. As I walked up to my door some people appeared, descending the spiral stairs from the first-floor walkway. The man in front was the one who'd come at me earlier. My heart sank. He approached me, like before, but with none of the aggression. "Hey, are you cool? Sorry about earlier, man, I was just playing. Can we come and chill in your room for a bit, smoke some?"

"No, no way." I didn't pretend to be nice and made to go into my room.

"Come on, we just want to get high and need a room. Here." He produced a $20 bill from his pocket and held it out. "All we want to do is smoke and chill, man, no trouble."

"No, not my room." I walked past him, unlocked my door, and locked them out. He had looked a shadow of the pumped fighter I'd seen a few hours before, and I sensed he couldn't be as dangerous now.

At about eight a.m. a couple of police cars arrived and took me to the bike shop. They took notes and looked around, but did nothing with conviction. "You're just in the wrong part of town," a police-woman explained. "These gangs just rent rooms for dealing and taking drugs."

I don't think the shop owners knew what to make of me turning up in a police car, my bike protruding from the trunk of another.

The shop was disappointingly basic. It was run (down) by a couple of brothers, one of whom proudly showed me the back room and attic, a vast place twice the size of the shop floor crammed with a jumble of hundreds of bikes he claimed dated back to when his father owned the place. It was a tip. The only 700cc wheel (a road-bike as opposed to mountain-bike wheel) they had was a cheap factory-made single rim. Good wheels are handmade (trued) to get the tensions even, and mine had a double rim for extra strength. Another important element of my front wheel was the hub dynamo, which generated electricity for my lights so I could night-ride. They had no spokes the right length and lacked the ability to cut them, so I had to put their factory wheel on as it came and buy cheap battery lights. At least I'd be able to keep going until the next major town with a proper bike shop.

While they stripped the old wheel so I could take the dynamo hub with me and straightened out the front rack, I called Tim. He didn't sound surprised to hear from me. "How are ya, all sorted?"

"Nearly, but I have to get back to where the crash happened and you are my only option. Can I please take you up on your offer of a lift?"

"Of course, no problem, when will you be ready?"

What a relief. It was a 100-mile round trip for him and he had been telling me how much work he had on the farm today.

"Well, I can be ready any time. I'll explain when you get here, but I had a bad night."

He asked there and then, so I explained the adventures I'd endured. There was a silence at the other end of the line for a few moments. "Man, I shouldn't have left you there. I thought it looked fine." He sounded genuinely upset.

The ride in the pickup was painful as my tailbone was badly bruised. On the way out of town we did a slow drive by the motel so I could take a last look and a photo out of the window. The wrong part of town is what the policewoman had said, but you would not have known it by day.

Tim insisted on dropping in on his insurance company. From my experience of insurance companies, I couldn't believe what happened next. We walked into a small office and were shown through to meet a man whom Tim greeted personally. There was a form on the table already filled out which included a short description of the accident, which the man asked me to sign.

"What is this?" I asked.

"Your settlement for the crash," Tim replied, as if it was obvious.

The other man was looking at me expectantly, so I didn't want to complain or question. I picked up the form and read it carefully. A quick signature later, I was handed $500 cash and we walked out. I don't think I have ever received a claim return in under a month; this had taken less than ten minutes.

"I didn't ask for compensation, it was an accident," I explained to Tim as we got back into the pickup.

"After what has happened to you in the last twenty-four hours this is the least we can do for you. It will at least cover the bike fixing and new camera."

I thanked him, and gave him $50 for the fuel for driving me around all morning.

By this time it was early afternoon and we were en route back to Mamou talking about crawfish again. Tim certainly liked his craw-fish. Best food in the world, he believed. "You have time for a late lunch at Mom's before you go?" He glanced across at me, suddenly realizing that this was a slightly strange question. His mom had run me over less than twenty-four hours ago. Still, I was hungry.

She lived 100 meters past the police station, so about 400 meters from where we had crashed. Lunch was a meaty stew, leftovers, but delicious. For all the debt they owed me, I decided they would probably still throw me out if I mentioned I was normally vegetarian, so I tucked in gratefully. She was a lovely old lady and apologized for hitting me for the entire hour I was there.

The meal was a nice way to dissipate any bad feelings but I craved space and just wanted to leave this town behind me. I put on my new cheap replacement helmet and cycled away.

The pain was worse than expected, each pedal stroke aggravating my bruised seat. I felt strange, kind of wretched, and void of any emotion. My jaw was locked all afternoon and I felt numb to the world, not really thinking anything. After only 42km I could not muster the will to keep going. As I pushed the bike into the room of a cheap motel, I burst out laughing. The relief caught up with me as my mind raced through the events of the last twenty-four hours.

After a quick shower I walked back to a Chinese restaurant I had seen on the way in. Halfway there, lost in thought, tears rolled down my cheek. They caught me completely by surprise. I didn't feel upset. I wasn't crying, at least not in a normal way, I just couldn't stop the tears flowing as I walked along in the dark.

My mobile suddenly rang, and without looking I answered, assuming it was home. It wasn't, and I tried to pull myself together.

Inside the restaurant was an all-you-can-eat buffet, brightly lit and very busy. I was shown to a table in the middle. As I looked over the drinks menu the silent tears started again and I pulled the menu higher so no one could see. A young Chinese waitress came over to get my drinks order, caught me off guard, and looked very uncomfortable as she watched me sitting there alone, silently crying into my menu. "Coke, please," I said, and she left quickly. The food was fine but I couldn't eat much.

On the way back to the motel I called Brendan, one of my best university friends, up in New York—the ultimate pragmatist, and son of shrinks, the perfect mate to call. He had been there to speak to before, when I was heading into Iran, camped under Mount Ararat, and after making it through Baluchistan to Quetta. I felt a bit shell-shocked, and very alone. It was not my style at all to have to talk issues through, but this time I needed to and by the end I was laughing again. I was overcome with exhaustion. Not the tired-legs, sleep-deprived kind of exhaustion I was now accustomed to, but an emotional void like I have rarely experienced, having spent the last day living on my nerves.

24

The following morning, Thursday January 24, I was in much better shape mentally but far worse physically. After only a few hours' sleep on Tuesday night and constantly being on the move the aches from the crash hadn't had time to seize up; now, after a big night's sleep, I struggled to stand up from the bed to begin with, my whole lower back in pain. The cuts and scrapes were not serious but the tailbone injury was. Niall, my sports doctor, and Fi, my physiotherapist, had been informed as soon as the crash happened and were helping with advice, but the only real cure was absolute rest, which obviously wasn't an option.

It rained for the first hour, which matched my mood. My right groin also ached until it was warm. I felt I really needed to rest up. Moreover, the bike had only done 40km on its new front wheel but I could tell it was not up to the job. Mum got in touch with a bike shop in Baton Rouge, the state capital and second-largest city in Louisiana. They were initially too busy, but after a long conversation in true Mum style they were now ready to drive out and meet me, build my wheel, service the bike, and get me back on the road as soon as possible.

From the outskirts, Baton Rouge looked very industrial. I was met with chimneys and factories on the waterfront as I crossed an old red metal bridge, which I later learned was the Mississippi Bridge. Not entirely sure of the arrangement, I was caught off guard when a car pulled alongside, a young guy shouted, "Follow me," and sped on.

Josh was the driver; he was also the main mechanic at The Bicycle Shop and an all-around good guy. I arrived agitated and keen for a quick fix. It soon became evident that was not going to happen. But it was the company and time I needed for recovery. Though I didn't leave until the following morning, I felt great for it.

It was hard to figure out who actually worked in the shop and who was part of a wider social group; there were always many young guys around. We were still there at 7:30 p.m., locked in for an hour past closing to finish a complete service. It was a problematic job from the start. The new front wheel had done only 111km but went straight in the bin. They then didn't have the right spokes to build onto the old dynamo, so they had to build a new wheel around a different dynamo. The disadvantage of this was not just the extra cost but also the much higher rolling resistance. A dynamo works by two rings of electromagnets spinning over each other, which causes electricity, but also causes drag. My old dynamo disengaged and so could freewheel when the light was not on; this new one was constantly dragging. We then ended up changing all the lights, mounting the front one on the handlebars instead of above the mudguard. On the back, there was still the problem of the self-loosening spokes. After cleaning, it turned out to be another hairline crack in the rim coming out from one of the spokes, like in Australia. But as I said, my impatience with the delays soon dissipated as I soaked up the friendly banter. It made me realize I had become quite icy in my solo world.

After Josh had rebuilt a new back wheel and serviced the entire bike it was dark and it made no sense to carry on through the city at night. Before heading off to find a motel I took the bike for a spin to check everything. Five of the guys grabbed bikes and came with me through a garden with winding paths, down a tree-lined boulevard, and around some old buildings on the university campus. For those short minutes I loved the comradeship of these new friends.

Josh only charged me for a new helmet and a few parts; he would not take anything for the wheels or the team's afternoon's work. "Come on, you can stay at my house," Gary, one of the guys, said. I followed his black Jeep Wrangler to the other side of town. Gary was my age and a real free spirit. He had spent the previous year traveling across northern Africa with one of his university professors. He lived at home with his doctor dad and mum, who were both wonderfully welcoming. I could have stayed up all night chatting with them. His mum was obviously the source of Gary's wild side, a redhead with a quick smile and mannerisms that reflected a hippy youth.

I woke a new man. The company and my time off the bike had

gone a long way to heal mind and body. It was hard to leave Gary's family, a home from home. I left Gary on his doorstep, dressed for court. Ironically he was off to testify against a woman who had run him over on his bike.

Around the corner I stopped for a second breakfast, unable to focus yet on a big day of riding. I called DP and home. The crash and mugging were apparently a front-page story in all the local papers and in a number of nationals. It had also made the ITV Scottish news and BBC news.

It was hard to get back in the flow and I managed only 145km as I had to keep hopping off the bike every half an hour with groin and tailbone pains. At half past three the heavens opened and it poured until six o'clock. Like any hardships, the rain actually helped focus my mind and the afternoon went a lot faster.

Eastern Louisiana was stereotypically Deep South—farmlands and swamps. The last miles were pretty hairy riding along a very busy, narrow, wet, and slippery road. The new lights didn't help. They weren't bad, but didn't have the same range. Traffic kept pushing me onto the painted line, which raised up from the road, so the front wheel skipped off it if it hit at too shallow an angle. After a number of wobbles I bit the bullet and decided to ride wide, forcing the cars to slow and overtake; I just ignored the odd horn. Despite poor miles and aches, it felt great to be moving again.

Time speeds up when there is more to punctuate it. The smaller states of the Deep South gave me regular milestones, adding to my growing sense of the end of America. And after that only 1,100 miles through Portugal and Spain back to Paris.

Crossing the Mississippi was not as clear-cut as it might sound, and the following morning I continued across the swamped delta, constantly on a raised road, surrounded by water, often through flooded forests. And it continued to rain, hard, until lunch, when it decided to drizzle on and off all afternoon just to make sure I couldn't dry out. But I didn't care. It was a big day with a fun target. If all went well I planned to cycle out of Louisiana, right across Mississippi, and into Alabama. Three states in a day was something better to focus on after the unchanging landscapes of Texas.

The swamps were continuously dull, not helped by the patchy fog, until I rounded one corner and suddenly found myself facing open water. It took a minute to figure it out. I had not really looked closely at the map as I knew I was staying on the same road all day. It was the Gulf of Mexico. I laughed out loud as I pulled on the brakes and stood there, mesmerized. The Gulf became the Atlantic when it got around the corner. It felt like I had made it across America. There were quite a few days to go until St. Augustine, but after my land-locked adventures it was an incredible lift to see the ocean.

I continued on the same road, but that was all that was the same from that point on. With the coast came the population. I was out of country America and back on what looked like the crowded coast of California, only tackier. Everyone was squeezed in on beachfront real estate but they were not the bling homes and resorts I had left on the West Coast. There were rows of hotel complexes and casinos. It was how I imagined Las Vegas looked, a world of flashing neon and building-sized billboards. There were also no more country diners. However average the food they produced was, it was at least real food. Along the Gulf front all I passed was miles of fast-food joints. I couldn't risk going on and finding nothing, so I stopped at a Wendy's burger restaurant. I was used to not finding veggie options in the States, except at a few places in California, but this meat feast of burgers and chips was terrible and made me lethargic.

The next day, Sunday January 27, I would be in the panhandle of Florida. Being midwinter, it was development season for this prime holiday strip, so I was in for a lot of patchwork roads.

In the afternoon I left the coast and started rolling into Alabama after a very flat Mississippi. By evening I was heading for the city of Mobile, which I was not looking forward to entering at night, though it probably wouldn't have bothered me before Lafayette. Just short of the city I crossed I-10 again, a much bigger road than I was on. Where the two intersected was, to my relief, a large enough area to warrant a rest stop, which I had not expected. After 180km, that was perfect. A great day, in spite of the weather and sores.

The motel was unexceptional but dinner was fun. I wandered out across the huge parking lot between the motels and diners and stood amid a number of generic fast-food factories trying to guess which was the best of a bad bunch. I spotted Hooters on the other side of the lot. I had never been to Hooters and had no idea what type of food they did but thought it was bound to be more interesting than the others. The table next to me was occupied by a family with young teenagers and there were at least as many women as men in the place. Coming out of a day in the rain, it was simply a very memorable hour watching big sport on big screens, being served big food by young ladies with big . . . smiles.

As soon as I crossed into Florida the following day the sun came out. Every American state has a slogan, and Florida's, aptly, is "The Sunshine State." That wasn't the only change. East of Mobile the houses suddenly got nicer. There were no more trailer parks— a regular feature since Arizona. It seemed California and Florida were not dissimilar worlds, sandwiching a very mixed filling.

After fighting the cold for weeks across middle America I got sun-burn for the first time in a while. But it was another great day, 180km, and the groin and tailbone were feeling much better.

Since Louisiana, the question of setting a finish date had been debated on and off. It was now time to commit—a slightly scary prospect. I had always simply made the most of each day as an isolated unit, trusting the big picture to take care of itself. Now, how-ever, the UK press, family, friends and sponsors needed to arrange their flights to Paris, so I had to tell the world when I thought I would get there, despite still being over 1,600 miles away. If all went smoothly I planned my finish for Friday, February 15, midafternoon, though Mum agreed to make it clear that at least until Portugal this was a target window and not an absolute date.

I knew (or thought I knew) that from Lisbon through Madrid to Paris was 1,100 miles. Working back, I therefore wanted to finish on the Atlantic Ocean in Florida having cycled 17,200 miles. For the world record I only needed to cycle 18,000 miles, but I'd had a nagging fear from the first weeks, and especially since the crazy roads of India and the cycle computer problems of Southeast Asia, that Guinness World Records might turn around and say that my mileages were short. The thought of this outcome was almost unbearable. I almost always cycled more than the map said. The deviations varied and were mostly very small, but add them up over half a year on the road and you have a major discrepancy. My fear was that Guinness would only accept the "miles on the map," so I decided to give myself a 300-mile margin of error so there was no comeback on my logbook. I was on target to break the existing Guinness World Record by over two months, so I was willing to sacrifice a possible three days to secure it.

While in Texas, these thoughts had rattled around my head so much and for so long that I'd ended up convincing myself something was wrong. The bedrock of my expedition was the fact that Steve Strange had set the Guinness World Record in 2004 at 276 days. Since I'd first learned this I hadn't been back to check it, and the margin between that number and my personal tally started to seem ridiculous. With too much time alone to think I ended up believing that I must have made a mistake. It seemed unlikely that it was possible to break a world record by over two months and far more likely that Steve had actually done it in 176 days. After a couple of days I was almost resigned to the fact, and called Mum to ask if she could check this, feeling very silly indeed. She came back later that day with confirmation that I was indeed two months up on the old record. It is amazing what thoughts the mind can entertain and justify when you're so alone.

The clocks went forward another hour into the Eastern time zone on the Florida state line, but from there my route would swing north into Georgia, where, despite going farther east, I would be back into Central time and would go back an hour again. This felt bizarre, and was something which even when explained to me still didn't make sense. The route was frustrating, as every instinct wanted to make a beeline for the end of America, but Mum and Bobby had invented this big S-shaped final week to give me the perfect miles. They were needed because the original American route plan had been dropped weeks ago and we had simply been planning my route stage by stage.

Lunch on Monday was had on white sands on a huge deserted beach at the town of Panama. I looked out across the Gulf and realized that the next bit of land to my south was probably Cuba. A lone police pickup drove down the beach at one point, sliding all over the sands, looking like it was joyriding rather than on patrol. Apart from that only a few dog walkers passed. Compared to the struggling single figures of a week ago, it was an unbelievable 25 degrees, but obviously still too cold for the fair-weather locals. I sat on the wooden steps of a closed-up beach house eating a big pasta salad, some yogurt, and a pastry. It was hard to get going again. I had reached the ocean. Having now crossed America, the anticipation of getting back to Europe made the last miles across Florida frustrating.

The afternoon was on much busier roads and I finished the day angry at all the road rage. More than any country I had ridden in, the car ruled the road here, but I had not yet received much aggravation from drivers except the odd toot when night-riding. That afternoon it all came at once, making me think that there must be a local story behind it. All afternoon cars revved and tooted, and drivers shouted at me as they drove past. It happened tens of times until I found myself in the habit of nervously checking behind.

In one town center a guy sat on my tail revving, despite loads of room to overtake, then shot up parallel and shouted out of the open window, "Get on the sidewalk!" He blared his horn and sped on. I was already wound up and I reacted without really thinking when he stopped at some traffic lights ahead. I cranked harder to catch up before they changed, cut into the center of the road, and stopped at his window. "Bikes are meant to be on the road, not the sidewalk, you idiot!" I shouted. He shouted something back that I missed, but as the lights changed I popped onto the pavement to stop him swerving into me. He drew level again, livid, and screamed, "You little punk, go home, you f***ing immigrant!" I thought he was about to get out, so I clipped out of my pedals, ready to defend myself, but instead he floored the accelerator and skidded into the street off to the right without indicating, so I had to slam on the brakes to stop in time. Luckily they were properly connected this time.

This annoyed me for hours, reflecting my state of mind at the time. In normal situations you would vent to someone, gain perspective on the incident, and simply dismiss such an ignorant comment. This time I couldn't get past it. It seemed that every time I stopped and met people properly in America they were as genuine and warm as anywhere else, but superficially many seemed to have a show on, an arrogance I couldn't get used to.

To distract me from this destructive mind-set, a roadie (road race cyclist) joined me—the first I had seen since California. It was great to chat and exactly what I needed for the next 10 miles. It wasn't healthy going along resenting the world I was passing through. Geoff had to slow down a lot for me, so he eventually sped on, but I valued his friendship, especially at that moment.

Just before he joined me, an old girlfriend had called. It had been over a month since we'd spoken. When Geoff pulled alongside me on the bike, I quickly told her I would call back. During our chat he turned and commented, "I knew you weren't American straight away as you hung up your phone call to speak to me."

That afternoon was punctuated by a number of calls home to sort out my targets for Florida. I was now booked on a Sunday flight to Lisbon, which left me 560 miles to cycle in five and a half days, which was perfect.

I had slept in for the first time in ages and didn't start until nearly nine a.m. This, compounded by the broken afternoon, meant a poor mileage day, but it didn't matter as much. I had a set target now for the end of Florida, based on averaging 100 miles a day, and there was no sense in burning out and getting there much before my flight.

As soon as I cut north off the Gulf I left behind the busy holiday world for dense forests along incredibly straight roads, all the way to the Georgia state boundary. The beach industry was less than a kilometer deep, and once clear of it I found myself in quiet country America again. There had been a keen headwind coming off the Gulf so I was glad to cut left, expecting it to blow me inland. The covering trees dashed that dream.

Day one of my new five-day target, 175km, passed without event. I couldn't wait to get to the Atlantic now. In the motel room there was no phone coverage but I could connect to the internet. There were tens of comments on the website and emails about Paris. There seemed so much excitement and a building sense of a finale. But it was still over 1,400 miles away. Sitting on my bed, tired, within my wee small-town motel room, in a forest in southern Georgia, I couldn't have felt more removed from this movement. Paris wasn't on my radar yet. I just hoped that from Lisbon I would at last feel able to start sharing this growing excitement.

The new challenge was how to get a new camera. Ideally I would get one while still on the road in the States, but apart from Amy, my final host in St. Augustine, a colleague of my sponsors at Liberty

Mutual Insurance Company, I didn't really know anyone in Florida. Then I remembered Richard and his family, the man I had met for all of fifteen minutes by the elephant seals in California. Mum took him up on his offer of help and phoned, explaining the whole situation. Without pause or query, Richard emailed back saying it would be no problem to drive out and meet me with a new BBC video camera. It was a twenty-hour round-trip to drive to me, but Richard didn't seem worried at all. While I spent the next day on my big loop north, ending up heading southeast, he and his wife, Chris, were road-tripping the length of Florida to help. It is genuinely one of the kindest acts by a near stranger I have ever benefited from, and once I got over feeling bad about it I started to look forward to meeting them again.

All night I kept waking to torrential rain. By the morning it had eased a bit but was still steady. The news carried stories of the huge storms not far north with massive damage and a number of deaths. That was day two of five, more deep forest riding, undoubtedly beautiful but ultimately lost on me. I was forever craving the next mile and the next day to finish America. I struggled to bring it back and live in the moment, daydreaming of what lay ahead.

It had been another late start. I felt exhausted, and no amount of sleep seemed to help. I had a cold, my throat glands were swollen, and my eyes streamed. To overcome this, as always, momentum was important, which forced me to stay on the bike, almost without break, until I reached 111km. I had to be mindful of the route to get my mileage right and I was map reading all day long.

My plan for that second day had been to keep going until the Florida border town of Monticello, but it was already late. The second suggestion was to stop up ahead in Thomasville, which would only be 150km for me. Only 10km short of target didn't seem like such a sacrifice and I wanted to thank Richard and Chris for all they'd done.

When I turned up in town, they had already paid for the nicest motel room I had stayed at in America, and then took me for a huge dinner at an upmarket buffet. They would accept nothing from me and we had a great evening. We chatted about the world I had seen, the travels Richard had been on, and our views; he acknowledged cultural challenges and gave balanced ideas. It was a refreshing conversation. His personal strength and guidance was religion, that much was clear, but it was not something he imposed on others, which meant I found it easy to chat for hours without barriers to viewpoints. It was great therapy talking away the evening with them both, and we were one of the last tables to leave the restaurant.

By day three of the five, and the end of the last full month on the road, I had every reason to be excited but felt as though I was on autopilot. My standards continued to slip: it was nearly nine a.m. when I finally left, which meant that I spent the afternoon chasing tough targets. The rolling hills of Georgia flattened out into Florida and I had the joy of cycling back into a place called La Fayette, this time a county in northern Florida.

Friday February 1, the last month, 17,000 miles. This penultimate day in the States was a big one at 190km: eight a.m. start, 22km/h average, 73km by noon, and 160km by five p.m. I was back in the zone, despite it having bucketed with rain all night, until the moment I sat on my bike. It was glorious after that with a fantastic tailwind. I finally found a great campsite after eight p.m. in a recreation area in a big forest. Only 70 miles to go!

I woke at six a.m. to my alarm, and again, with a start, at seven a.m., suddenly realizing it was now light. Thankfully it had not rained in the night as forecast, which meant I could pack my tent away dry for the flight.

My last day in America, and despite being tired to the bone I was on a new high. I couldn't wait to be back in Europe. The US and India were the only two countries I developed this love/hate feeling for, loving them for what they were but almost frantic to leave. Places like Pakistan and Australia were tougher in many ways, but neither had filled me with the same claustrophobia and desire for change. America was about the same distance as Australia had been, but that is where the similarities ended.

It was another relatively hot, sunny Florida day. After a frantic start and fast forest riding until Silver Springs the day became more leisurely. The victory lap of America was the chilled ride through Palatka and then on to Fort Augustine for midafternoon.

When I called home at lunch I sensed the growing hive of activity back at Base Camp. Heather, my big sister, and Inge, her best friend, had been drafted in to go through the mountain of data that needed organizing and summarizing before being presented to Guinness World Records when I finished. This included my daily statistics taken from three cycle computers, all the GPS tracking data, and thousands of receipts, itemized phone bills, and bank statements, all of which needed cross-referencing and signatories to prove beyond any doubt where I had been for over half a year.

I stopped for a photo at the WELCOME TO ST. AUGUSTINE sign but then took over half an hour to reach the Atlantic, where Amy was waiting for me. I stood for some time looking out over the ocean, not quite knowing what to think. It felt fantastic to arrive at this point, of course it did, but the cheers and raised hands I gave to the camera were a bit for show. I just felt exhausted and relieved. It felt a bit of a letdown not to share in Amy's family's excitement for me. Despite being happy, it wasn't a jumping-up-and-down sort of celebration for me. I still had over a thousand miles to go.

Leg 7: Lisbon to Paris

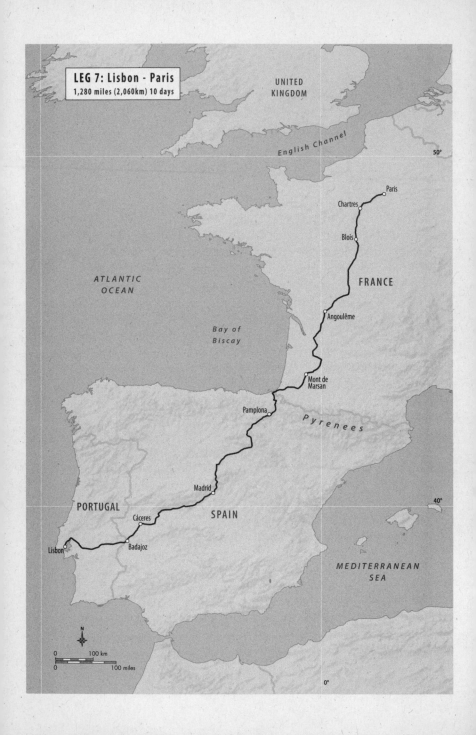

LEG 7: Lisbon - Paris
1,280 miles (2,060km) 10 days

UNITED
KINGDOM

English Channel

50°

Paris

Chartres

Blois

FRANCE

ATLANTIC
OCEAN

Angoulême

Bay of
Biscay

Mont de
Marsan

Pamplona

Pyrenees

Madrid

PORTUGAL

Cáceres

SPAIN

40°

Lisbon

Badajoz

MEDITERRANEAN
SEA

N

100 km

0

0

100 miles

0°

25

I had never been to Portugal but was looking forward to getting there as if it were home. America had been quite the adventure, and I left with mixed emotions. Before the trip I'd found it easier to feel closely related to America because I understood the language and, from what I saw on TV, their culture looked similar; Europe, on the other hand, always seemed far more foreign, in part because I heard far less about it in the media. Having now spent a good amount of time in both continents I see things very differently. The commonality between European countries, the UK included, and the way they make me feel at home, wherever I am, is something far more subtle than language. America, on the other hand, which is so familiar on the surface, is harder to understand.

Compared to the other long-haul flights I slept well, but still only for a few hours. Mentally I knew it was going to be tough to get going again—it always was at the start of a leg—but it was exciting. It was the last big challenge.

Leg 7, Day 1
Date: Monday February 4, 2008
Location: Lisbon, Portugal
Expected distance to Paris: 1,100 miles
Actual distance to Paris: 1,258 miles

I had twelve days to get to Paris. It was exactly 1,100 miles away, if my calculations were correct, so I could do it (as it turned out, for a number of reasons, I'd given myself a brutal race to the finish). If I managed it then I would have circumnavigated the world in 195 days.

This was exactly what I had targeted three years earlier when I first dreamed up the expedition.

However, as I stepped off the plane in Lisbon the world record was not what excited me most. I just wanted to finish now and see my family again. It seemed that a lot of people were coming to Paris for the finish. On top of the pressure I put on myself, the expectations of the press, friends, family, and sponsors motivated me as well.

Five months earlier, back on the Ukrainian border, Piotr, my masseur and physiotherapist, had waved me off after shadowing me for the first few weeks. It had been an emotional farewell. At the time he had promised to road-trip to Lisbon to join me for the end. I couldn't see the fun in spending every day alone, driving only to help me each evening, but I had thanked him and looked forward to meeting him again, not really expecting him actually to do it. David Peat and Piotr were the only people from home who had shared any part of my journey on the road. I was touched by how it obviously meant a lot to them. Having not known either of them before the cycle, they were now both great friends.

However, when Piotr stuck to his word and got in touch about coming to Portugal, I had doubts. Throughout the United States I had struggled to maintain the necessary level of focus and was now almost scared of any company that would distract me. By Lisbon I had been on the go for 183 days, and I felt like I was running on vapors; there wasn't much energy left and I just wanted to be left alone to get the job done. But the team back in Scotland had the wisdom of perspective, which I lacked, and persuaded me that it could only be of benefit to have Piotr on hand again.

When I walked out of departures with a big cardboard box and pannier bags piled on my trolley, Piotr was there, smiling. It was great to see him again and all fears were immediately dispelled. While I would still ride alone every day, unsupported, I realized that this was the end of the big solo. Being with Piotr was going to be a good way to re-engage slowly with society before the finish, and make sure my legs made it.

The madman had driven from Edinburgh to Lisbon almost without break and looked shattered, but he was still jumping around, excited to be back on the adventure. Somewhere in the middle of France he had smashed the back window of his station wagon by closing it onto the massage table. Apart from shards of broken glass everywhere, this had meant hours of very cold and noisy motorway driving, but he didn't seem to care. "It's nothing, I will get some plastic later," Piotr laughed as he picked more shards of glass out of the boot and handed me some new supplies.

With twelve days to the finish there was no margin for error; I needed to build the bike and get back on the road as fast as possible. There was no time for a lazy breakfast and catch-up. Just outside the entrance canopy of the airport we found some space off to the side and I set to work putting the bike back together. Unlike a normal bike, where you just throw the wheels on and put the chain back on, this custom-built bit of kit was a good bit trickier. The mudguards and pannier racks each had multiple bolts. After being taken off and put on a number of times, and after three crashes, not all of them lined up perfectly anymore. I also only had a tiny multitool. But I persevered; it was the last time it all needed to fit back together.

I'd planned to stay with Piotr's car until the outskirts of Lisbon, but within meters of leaving the airport I'd lost him. These city roads were not cycling-friendly and were certainly not built for the amount of traffic that now uses them. After half an hour, mostly spent standing at the roadside getting increasingly frustrated, he found me. Twenty minutes later I lost him again, and didn't find him until the end of the day.

Lisbon is built on the west bank of the Rio Tejo (the Tagus), which spills into the Atlantic as a wide estuary. It was unclear which roads I was allowed on as I cut northeast through the city. The main bridge across the estuary was nearly 10km wide and I was heading for it in heavy traffic when I realized beyond any doubt that bikes were not allowed. There was no way I was going to run this gauntlet against the law, so I quickly pulled to the side, already 50 meters onto the slipway. By this time Piotr was in the flow of traffic and gone. There was no point in asking him to come back as I was probably faster without him, so I texted him to carry on, that I would find him later, and to get some sleep.

Digging out the map, I could see that my only option was to cut north to a smaller bridge upstream, which was an annoying diversion. It wasn't clear how to do this, however, and I ended up weaving my way through Lisbon's suburban backstreets in a rough direction to avoid the IC2 and E80, two major roads I was sure I wasn't allowed on. The map suggested that these would merge and become the A1, which looked like I was allowed on. I had to ask a couple of locals for directions, and one guided me in his little Fiat 500 through a couple of kilometers of backstreets. My attempt to squash French and Italian into one language surprisingly did not result in Portuguese, so I gave up and spoke English, slowly, pointing enthusiastically at places on the map. It was early afternoon by the time I made it to Vila Franca de Xira and across a bridge to head in the correct direction, due east to Badajoz on the Spanish border.

The N4 was the old road going due east to Spain and ran roughly parallel to the newer E90 motorway, so promised to be fairly peaceful riding. To get to the N4, which I had been planning to take from its start by the bridge I hadn't been allowed on, I had to cut southeast on the N10. Leaving Lisbon had been more complex and slower than I had hoped, but the cycling now looked flat and cruisy. Long may it last, I thought. It was also warmer than I'd thought it would be, never dipping below the midteens. Things were looking up. I just had to find Piotr. This was made harder by his having run out of phone credit; the easily avoidable challenges of the first few weeks came flooding back. I couldn't quite remember if he could still receive texts, so I just let him know where I was heading and hoped for the best.

Portugal was a joy to ride through and I was so excited to be back in Europe. However, having expected something similar to France or Italy I was surprised to find it was far less developed. Most of what I was passing seemed like peasant-style smallholdings. At lunchtime I walked into a tiny café attached to a garage and immediately smiled from ear to ear: it was effortlessly charming, European culture in every detail, everything I had dreamed of getting back to after commercial America. Perching on a bar stool, I enjoyed a superb espresso and a panini as a couple of old farmers in flat caps sat next to me with their glasses of beer.

Later in the afternoon I entered a section of woodland and was surprised to pass prostitutes at every lay-by. It took a while to work out what was going on after passing a number of these scantily dressed girls, alone at the roadside. It was daytime and in the middle of the countryside, so prostitution didn't immediately spring to mind.

Turning onto the N4, I pushed into the evening to make up for the lost miles leaving Lisbon. Late on, Piotr passed me, having had an adventure of his own trying to patch up the back window and then track me down. The back of his car was now all black, covered in tarpaulin and tape. We set my target as Montemor-o-Novo and Piotr headed on to find somewhere to stay. It wasn't decided if we would camp or find accommodation from now on, but it seemed likely, with the early darkness and availability of massages, we would find cheap hotels if possible.

At 122km it wasn't a terrible first day but it did put me a quarter of a day down on target. Piotr had found a small hotel in the town center. It was simple, rustic, and wonderful. I smiled at every detail, thrilled by its style. The room had two very narrow wooden beds and badly painted off-white walls. The furniture didn't match and the doors didn't quite fit their frames. The dining room had a huge open fire and the barman was having a cigarette as we entered. It seemed a crime not to crack open a bottle of local red with the meal, but we refrained.

After eating we pushed the beds to the side of the room and set up the massage table. And then I promptly fell asleep. An hour later I woke to Piotr shaking me. He had also fallen asleep, on his feet while massaging me. Almost without a word we crashed out.

Day 2, 1,181 miles to Paris

I woke with a start, realizing it was fully light. Switching on my mobile, I found that it was still on US time. My body clock thought it was three o'clock in the morning; no wonder I felt rubbish. After throwing back a quick breakfast I was on the road as fast as possible, but two hours after I had planned.

It was a stunning day, racing due east to the Spanish border. Most of the day was through gently rolling hills covered with vineyards and I was fast making up lost ground, until the 105km mark. Cycling fast into the town of Elvas, I hit a join in the tarmac and heard the dreaded sound of a spoke breaking. Ever since the rebuild in Louisiana this had been my nightmare, because I had stupidly forgotten to ask for spares. I did have the spares for the original wheel but these would be slightly different—it was a different wheel rim. I kicked myself for simply hoping for the best and carrying on.

I might have been stressing, but Elvas was in party mode, a big carnival in full swing under the shadows of a stunning viaduct bridge. Mum swung into action to track down the nearest bike shop. It appeared that there wasn't one, so after a quick lunch I disconnected my wobbling back wheel and headed for the Spanish border, 15km away.

A few miles from the border I was about to swing onto the major road the N4 merged into when a police car screamed up behind me, siren blaring, lights flashing. Bikes weren't allowed on this road, I was told; I must take an unmarked side road that ran parallel. The two policemen were comically dramatic and walked around my bike as if they were checking it over, before giving me a lecture about the rules of the road. It might have been scary if they'd had the English, but as they had to keep asking each other for the right words, the effect was lost.

On the tiny farmer's track I was directed to there wasn't even a sign to let me know that I had crossed the border, and I was in the Spanish town of Badajoz before I realized. Meeting up with Piotr, I then followed him and his demented GPS system for a very confusing hour in search of a bike shop. It was a complete wild-goose chase, and by that time it was late.

At only 123km I had lost another quarter of a day on target. In two days I was now half a day down and had a broken wheel to deal with. I called a stop to the search and went into the first hotel I could find. Inside our room, I got to work. The old spare spoke I had wasn't exactly the same length or width but it did fit. It took half an hour to replace and tune the spokes so that they were all the same tension. I would have much preferred to get it properly fixed at a shop but could not afford any more delays. This was also a good chance to put the last set of tires on and clean all the gearing. Once finished, the bike looked spotless, but unfortunately the hotel room floor did not, so we did some quick furniture rearranging.

Speaking to home, I found I wasn't the only one with challenges. I felt bad about the amount of work Mum had, juggling the logistical planning and coping with media relations for the finish. It was hard for me to gauge exactly what was going on, but I could hear the strain in her voice and was aware that she was telling me only as much as I needed to know. Many journalists wanted to speak to me personally over the next week. There was also continued interest from Radio Scotland, including *The Fred MacAulay Show* and *Sports Weekly* with John Beattie. They had been on board since the start, so, though it was a distraction, I wanted to make time for them.

Day 3, 1,105 miles to Paris

I had cycled in almost every country in Europe, so I thought Spain would be similar. Ten years ago this might have been the case, but since then an influx of money from the EU has helped develop an almost impenetrable network of motorways. From the moment I left Badajoz I knew I was in trouble. The types of road I'd highlighted on the map had looked similar to those I'd cycled in places like France and Italy, but from the first road sign I realized this wasn't so. The Autovia de Extremadura was very much out of bounds for bicycles, which meant that my entire route to France was back on the drawing board. Considering that my distances and timings to Paris had been planned in detail and it was already a tough target, this discovery was a disaster. The roads I now had to use would be considerably longer.

My first target was Madrid. I had to get to Madrid. One of the main Guinness World Record criteria was to pass through two points on opposite sides of the world within 5 degrees. Wellington was my first antipodal, Madrid was my second, but I could now see that to get close and out the other side fast would not be easy. Unfortunately, this was another job for Mum, as there was little I could do from the bike. She got straight onto the Madrid police to see if they could escort me through by the fastest means possible. I had to admire her style. However, I was still at least two days' riding from Madrid and it wasn't even clear how I would get that far. All alternative routes to the main highway were much farther.

To save time that morning I decided to take the only other road that was heading northeast, leaving Piotr and Mum to try to figure out a way through. The detail of the smaller roads was not obvious on the map I had. By the end of the day Bobby was also on the case, trying to use aerial maps to see if there were ways through on the service roads, which often paralleled the motorway. If this wasn't possible then I would have to take a major detour on minor roads. This would end the dream of making Paris on time. Spain was turning into another America, my lack of research showing again. I had spent far too much time on the Middle East and Asia and overlooked the parts of the world I had assumed would be straightforward.

This lack of research soon showed up in another way. I had always assumed that the mountains in Spain were mainly in the north, along the Pyrenees. I now know that Spain is the second-most mountainous country in Europe, and the big hills started soon after the Portuguese border.

All day was slow going, over big rolling roads to the town of Trujillo. From there the E90 trunk road ran north for about 60km before cutting east in a beeline for Madrid. But there were no obvious small roads paralleling the E90 for 30km after this turn and the alternative was to cut over the huge bank of mountains to my east. One look at the tiny squiggles of roads in that area told me how slow this terrain would be.

As I got some food in, Piotr went ahead to scope out the situation. Bobby had spotted on Google Earth what looked like a small service road, and another source reassured us that this was the old road, which ran all the way alongside. However, even when Piotr came back with the green light I had my concerns. It was eight p.m., it was dark, and the prospect of doing another few hours on an unmarked road and then having to camp at the side of a busy highway seemed crazy. Therefore I called an end to the day at just 149km.

This decision, on top of the daily mileage since Lisbon, now seriously threatened the plan for Paris. My legs were already very tired but there was no time for a massage.

Day 4, 1,012 miles to Paris

Finally I had an incredible day—167km, which was about 25km more than the highway I was trying to shadow. I went north-ish down the service roads for the first section, which was mainly tar and light gravel through little dips and waterways but fairly good going. For the first hour and a half it was really dark, and Piotr followed me with the headlights of the car. Then it got light. It was quite cold to begin with, near freezing.

The service road then became a bigger road and after the next town I could see a large ridge ahead, which proved to be a massive climb and then a huge descent. I was boiling because I still had my leggings on but then the descent was freezing. It was a fantastic downhill section, though, one of the best I'd done in the last couple of months.

Early on Piotr had given a Peruvian guy who was working on the crash barriers a lift; he had described the road ahead and mentioned a good petrol station and café to stop at near Almaraz. After 55km I saw this but dismissed it as I hadn't yet reached Almaraz, then I wasted a lot of time trying to find Piotr. From there I turned directly east onto tiny roads on the south side of the Ibor River whereas the highway followed the north side. This section looked flat on the map.

As soon as I turned east I found a tiny gravel track for the first section which opened out into a better road, but there were a couple of other really dodgy sections farther up the road. After about 10km we stopped across a little bridge by a dam and I went into a little restaurant to ask for directions. There was a bit of confusion as there was no clear road onward, only one that looked like a driveway. This turned out to be the way, so I followed a really narrow single track up steep switchbacks for the next hour. It was beautiful cycling but, until it met up with a bigger two-lane road, really slow going. Every time it opened up, came out of the woodland, or came over the brow of a hill the headwind was a real problem; apart from that it was just hilly. It was a really long day, so I managed to get the miles in, but it was tough.

I was feeling the pressure now. Paris was everything I thought about and I focused every possible moment on riding. I had assumed that leg 7, with Piotr, would be similar to leg 1, when I saw him every evening only, but with the wheel breakages and new route setting I was seeing him far more regularly. He had managed to find more spare spokes in case the wheel went again and I was grateful for his company on some of the dark early-morning sections, but I insisted that he not assist in any other way. There was no way after carrying all my kit for over 17,000 miles I would let him carry anything for the last few miles.

Day 5, 939 miles to Paris

The plan was to be on the road at 6:30 a.m., with a 190km average to do to get to Paris in time for next Friday—a big target for eight days' riding. It was an epic day, and I finished on an absolute high. I rode for ten hours and managed 225km, including a 2,400-meter ascent, with an average heart rate of 130 beats per minute—insanely high for me—because I spent most of the day being chased by the Madrid police patrol, the Guardia Civil.

After about 60km on my own at the start of the day along some very dodgy service roads I met my first police car by a service station. From there I rode a very fast nonstop three and a half hours to Madrid, and then around one of its ring roads. Piotr followed me throughout, despite being worried he would get into trouble for his broken back window. He had nothing to worry about: we were being given VIP service through the capital by the country's best.

The roads were massively busy and I would not have been allowed on these motorways without an official escort. This escort was perfectly coordinated and changed patrols without stopping. Their main challenge was to stop the traffic flying in at speed on the slip roads to my right. For this the motorbikes would race ahead, stop in the middle of the roads with their sirens and flashers going, let me pass, then race on to the next one. I was on an absolute high all the way and had no problem pushing harder to get through as fast as possible—so fast that after a few hours I started to wonder how long this would take. The pace I had set out at seemed sustainable for an escort for a couple of hours, but it seemed Madrid was much bigger than I had anticipated. Every time I looked back to see the Audi on my tail, I caught a glimpse of Piotr with a grin from ear to ear, hazard lights going. The Guardia Civil seemed to be having a great time as well, causing a considerable traffic jam in the remaining three lanes.

I had been told the previous day that the old road north to Burgos still existed and went up the side of the major trunk road E5. When we finally stopped on the road north I was so hungry, in disbelief that we had already covered 165km, almost without stopping. I was now with two motorbike policemen, one tall and thin, the other shorter and slightly stout. They both wore immaculate uniforms with knee-high black boots. The taller one spoke a tiny bit of English but we struggled to communicate. I was trying to thank them, assuming they would be turning back now, but they were hanging around. I had to eat, and left Piotr talking to them.

Feeling slightly better after ten minutes sitting down and eating as much food as I could in that time, I went over again to the policemen. They were being emphatic about something to do with the road ahead but I couldn't understand what, so I decided, in order to speed things up, to call Alberto, the policeman who I knew spoke English. One of the motorbike policemen spoke first, then I took the phone. Alberto explained that there were no minor roads going north like I had been told and that I was still on a motorway. Because bicycles were not allowed on the motorway the police escort had to stay with me until the border of the Madrid city jurisdiction.

"And how far is that?" I asked.

"The Burgos border," he replied.

"OK, and how many kilometers is that?"

"It is near, maybe sixty kilometers."

I thanked Alberto and hung up. He obviously wasn't a cyclist.

My initial response was that there was no way I could do another 60km that day. I was shattered already. As I talked it over with Piotr the bikers stood waiting, expectantly. There was nowhere to stop near here, no way to carry on the next day without calling back the escort, and it was only midafternoon so hard to explain why I couldn't go on. "OK, let's go." I gave the thumbs-up to my police escort and got back on the bike. I was out of ideas.

Before pushing off I got the map out of my pannier bag to check where the Burgos district border was. The taller policeman came to my shoulder and pointed to the boundary. My heart sank again. It was on the top of a col marked at over 1,500 meters. "Shit, this could actually break me," I said to a worried-looking Piotr. My legs were already tired.

The Guardia were riding big BMW motorbikes and for the next three and a half hours they idled as I climbed and climbed. I was maxed out, pushing as fast as I could, my heart rate sitting at over 150 beats per minute the whole time. As fast as this was on a fully laden bike, 12mph is not fast enough for 1100cc engines to climb at and they had to keep falling back in turn to let their engines cool off. We only stopped once, at a petrol station for ten minutes for a couple of energy drinks. I also stuffed my pockets with food to be eaten on the go.

I knew what I was in for as the summit was in view for most of the climb. The road was down to a single lane in each direction now and not particularly steep, just a long grind at a leg-sapping gradient. However, once you are in that zone, sweat pouring, legs pumping, time blurs slightly; every time I started to fade I just had to look back to see the encouraging faces of my escort. There were almost no slip roads so very little for them to do except shadow me.

From the petrol station I'd sent Piotr on to find somewhere to spend the night, and he texted when I was about half an hour from the top saying that he had found a hotel just 5km down the other side. I shouted this back to the Guardia, who seemed to understand.

The sun was low over the mountains and I was still climbing. Pushing myself on for what looked like another fifteen minutes to the top, the road ahead suddenly flattened out and then disappeared into a tunnel. I sat up; I had done it. Just before the tunnel mouth I passed a sign for the top that read 1,444 meters. I turned and threw up a thumb at my escort. They both beamed back, returning the signal, one of them pointing at his legs and shaking his head.

The tunnel was short but I switched my lights on. As I came out the other side the valley opened up before me and I was faced with a long, sweeping descent as far as I could see. The sun was setting over the snow-lined ridge to my left and the road was completely empty. I was covered with sweat, roasting and exhausted, but on a complete high. What an incredible climb.

I was soon going faster than my pedaling could keep up with, so I just hunched down to get as aerodynamic as possible. My eyes were close to the handlebars as the ground flashed under the wheels. I watched the speedometer on the bars accelerate up to 60km/h, then slow toward 70km/h. At that point I looked back for a split second to check the bikes were with me. The taller Guardia was close but I couldn't hear the engine over the wind. He was beaming back at me, then, when I looked forward again, his siren started up, followed by that of the second bike, not far behind me. I glanced back in surprise to see their blue lights flashing and grins on both their faces.

Despite my sunglasses my eyes were now streaming with the wind speed. I hunched forward again. It was absolutely freezing, and I had to tense my arms to stop the shivers wobbling the bike, which would have been catastrophic at this speed.

Out of the growing dusk, streetlights appeared ahead of us and the road started to flatten out slightly, but we were still flying. I flicked the bike computer to check the top speed: 86km/h. The hotel was easy to find, and we pulled into the car park in time to meet Piotr coming out of the front door. Tears were streaming across my cheeks, I was frozen, but I have rarely felt more alive.

The two motorbikes had turned off their sirens before entering the town, but their lights were still flashing as they flanked me into the car park. They stepped gingerly off their bikes, laughing and gesturing about being saddle sore, and met me with warm handshakes. "You are Superman," the taller one said. I'd thought they would be bored spending the afternoon escorting some guy on his bicycle, but they'd bought into the adventure entirely. I had put a lot into the day, more than at any other time, and I knew I would pay for it. But at that moment I didn't care.

My new friends joined us for a coffee in the hotel café before heading back. The other men sitting around the bar parted with respect as they approached and the barmen served them for free. As we sat and chatted, as best we could, I kept catching the locals looking over.

These policemen certainly had the respect of their countrymen and I felt privileged to have shared this adventure with them. They waved a fond farewell before a much faster return trip to Madrid.

Even after that climb, my average speed for the day was nearly 23km/h. My computer also told me that I had burned just shy of 8,500 calories, and when the adrenaline left me I could immediately feel this. I needed to eat fast; I didn't care that my only option was a pile of steak, chips, and bread. In my haste to order I was lucky not to end up with carpaccio, which I didn't realize was raw beef.

I can't remember much after that, but I do know that I completely crashed during the meal, after buzzing with energy all day. Piotr says that he gave me a massage but I can't even recall walking back to the room. The next thing I remember was waking the following morning feeling like I had gone through twelve rounds. My legs were so sore that I limped to breakfast.

Day 6, 800 miles to Paris

Over breakfast, I felt utterly rubbish. I was fully awake but just didn't feel very connected to the world around me, and I replied to Piotr's questions absentmindedly. Then came a call from Alberto. He had put in a request that the Burgos police come and pick me up that morning; they had to as I was stuck on a highway bikes weren't allowed on. But they had said they were too busy to give me an escort. Alberto apologized, telling me there was nothing else he could do as it was out of his area and stressing that I would need to find another route off the highway. Easier said than done.

It made sense to get going as fast as possible, so we quickly packed and rolled out. I soon forgot how rubbish I felt in this rush. For the first 5km I had no option but to carry on using the highway, then take the first exit, regardless of where it headed, though Mum managed to research the route ahead and figure out a way to keep me on track. Piotr sat on my back wheel for those 5km with his hazard lights flashing, but the roads were almost empty in the predawn.

For the first time in Europe it was bitterly cold, and I wrapped up in many layers including a down body warmer, hat, and neck warmer over my face. The first three hours after the turnoff were utterly stunning, through the highlands with snow-topped mountains to my right and frosty ground all around. As the sun came up Piotr left me and I was completely alone in this frozen world. The sense of stillness was absolute. I had a week until Paris but for those hours I could have been anywhere. It was impossible to be anywhere else but stuck in the moment, freezing cold but loving it. I had borrowed Piotr's iPod at breakfast, bored with my own, so a bizarre mix of Polish hip-hop and eighties rock accompanied this winter wonderland.

It was a mixed blessing that the first three hours remained on average downhill: it helped my sore legs push a good average speed but meant that it remained bitterly cold. I almost craved a quick climb to warm up a bit.

A cracking headache developed during the morning caused by tightness in my neck and dehydration. Piotr therefore floated the idea of a massage at lunchtime. I wasn't mad keen on it, especially when we pulled up in the forecourt of an ELF petrol station in the industrial outskirts of Soria. In true Piotr style he simply didn't care, just threw the massage table up. I am sure we drew many strange looks from passing cars. However, apart from being a bit cold, it was a great idea and eased the headache noticeably.

The day finished with a superb descent into the dark to the industrial town of Agreda. If you had told me that morning I was going to cycle 187km in nine and a half hours and climb nearly 1,500 meters I would have simply said, "I can't." This success meant that I was back on track for Paris. The last big hurdle (I hoped) was continuing over the Pyrenees at a good speed.

After a hearty meal, I slept through a two-hour massage. It didn't matter how tight my legs were, I was utterly exhausted.

Day 7, 683 miles to Paris

The first 40km of my last day in Spain were a fast descent, which was again bitter predawn with the temperature well below freezing. After 30km I had to stop for twenty minutes as my feet were so cold it was painful. At 7:30, just before it got light, I passed through a single-street village called Valverde where everyone seemed to be having an all-night party. Still descending fast, I was through the other side within seconds, laughing aloud at the mutual looks of surprise. People were falling about the street, arm in arm in fancy dress made from hessian sacks with wigs on. The epicenter was a bar, which was still full with the music blaring. Their drunken looks of shock matched mine as I flew out of the still frozen countryside into this all-night bender.

Thick freezing fog surrounded me until late morning when a stiff tailwind, the first in Europe, blew it away. I was unsure which route I should take from the large town of Pamplona but I covered fast miles to that point. It then took over an hour to get across town, only to end up on the wrong road. Mum, who was doing the research into the options for crossing into France, had decided that while the inland border might be hillier, it would ultimately be shorter and therefore faster. These instructions came in by text message from Base Camp while I was cycling and I completely misread them. After 5km riding in the wrong direction I made a quick call home and then spent the next hour cutting back and skirting the city again to reach the N135 north.

The climb to the border was stunning. It was Sunday, and I was amazed at the number of road cyclists on the long ascent, which was reassuring. Unlike the mountains north of Madrid, which were bare and open, the Pyrenees were craggy where the road followed a deep river valley and then at its steepest point rose in sharp switchbacks. Over three false summits I kept climbing, each time assuming I could go no higher. It was getting late. The final crest was on the border and marked with a small chapel. I quickly layered up for what promised to be a hair-raising descent.

It did not disappoint. I was heading for the town of St. Jean Pied-de-Port, 15km ahead and a long way down. The entire section dropped in half the time I had spent climbing to this height. By the time I was halfway down it was completely dark and I was constantly hard on the brakes. The more tense you get, the worse you are at descending well on a bike, but that theory doesn't really make any difference when instincts take over. I couldn't help my whole body freezing as I flew into each switchback, lit by the ghostly beam from my front light, petrified that my front wheel was about to disappear under me on black ice. It was exhilarating, the coldest descent I have ever done, and certainly the hardest one I have ever taken on at night. Downhillers will know the feeling of getting to the bottom with forearms feeling completely burned out, arms weak. I had managed to get that feeling from a tarmac road having spent the whole time tensed and wishing I was going slower. I might have nearly cycled around the world but I was still rubbish at descending.

At 197km with a 1,900-meter ascent in nearly ten hours' riding it had been another tough but brilliant day—and I was now in France.

I checked into a tiny and almost deserted hotel on the main street of St. Jean Pied-de-Port. The town looked picture perfect with its small white chapel and busy rows of ancient-looking houses. The sense of excitement about being back in France overcame any tiredness as I pulled to a stop, buzzing after that descent. I had made it back to the country I had started from 190 days earlier.

Spain had been far tougher than I'd ever imagined. Then again, maybe the problem had been that I hadn't really imagined it, I'd just assumed it would be more average miles. In the grand scale of things I had overlooked leg 7 as a simple "sprint finish" to Paris.

The hotel owner and the only other guests, a couple who were eating, spoke French and I was delighted to wheel my bike into the bar and join them in conversation. I knew that French would not be the first language in this border region; locally they probably spoke either Basque or Occitan. That dimly lit wooden bar seemed a fitting scene for my first night back in France. I felt, aptly, like I had been around the world and was now back.

The old man brought me a huge pile of meat and chips and chatted happily. His wife, however, remained far less friendly and stood at the kitchen door, barking at him and scowling at me and the other guests. She was an integral part of the rugged charm of the place and there was something about her harsh tone and manners that made it strangely homely. In my dirty state of fatigue, a polished hotel would have been charmless compared to this. I fitted in here. It felt right.

Piotr had been away all day, backtracking to Madrid to pick up his girlfriend, Jagwega. It was nearly eleven when they made it back with stories of slipping on ice all the way down that amazing descent.

Day 8, 560 miles to Paris

France comprises twenty-six regions, and I had cycled into Aquitaine. I would spend the day riding through Gascony, coming out of the Pyrenees. It is a stunning area of medieval towns, or *bastides*, and the perfect welcome back into France.

The morning was freezing again as I wheeled out of St. Jean Pied-de-Port, nervous about the ice on the roads. The weight on the bike with the bags and the fact that I was clipped in made me feel very vulnerable indeed going into every corner. The road dropped away through lowland alpine scenery, with scattered smallholdings wherever the land was tame enough to farm. After a few hours I came out of the wilderness and onto the river valley at Orthez before setting my targets on Mont de Marsan.

I had quickly dropped out of the Pyrénées-Atlantiques and within half a day was in the plateau just south of Bordeaux known as "les Landes de Gascogne." Piotr and Jaga left me for most of the day because my route was much simpler now that I was back in France. They had not seen each other for ages and headed off into Bordeaux while I pedaled through tens of miles of vineyards not far to the east.

When Piotr left me in Poland all those months ago, he had been racing back to Paris to propose to Jaga. She had said no, not yet, but they seemed to be great together. Piotr is exactly a year older than I am, born on New Year's Day 1982; Jaga is four years younger. I'd had no idea how she would adapt to life on the road with Piotr and me, but I immediately realized I had nothing to worry about. She was constantly smiling and quick to laugh, using any spare moment to clown around and cheer me up. It was just nice to have someone else willing to share this tough routine with me. Like Piotr, she never complained, and in the most miserable moments would make us laugh. One such memorable moment was her crazy dancing in the freezing cold on an empty street to a song on the car radio.

I had five days to get to Paris and I thought about nothing else all day. Passing through some of the most scenic parts of France, where half of Europe seemed to have its holiday homes, I retained just about enough perspective to realize that I was almost entirely switched off from this world. I didn't care that I was cycling through the famous Bordeaux vineyards, or how cute each village *boulangerie* was, as long as the vineyards provided fast rolling roads and the bakeries had enough food to keep me going.

Eight hours and forty minutes of riding later I had covered 170km—still on target but not giving myself any margin for error. Ideally I would roll into Paris early on Friday afternoon, in four days' time; I would need to push out some bigger days to make that possible. All I was thinking about on the bike was the passing miles, the available daylight hours, and a constant supply of food and water. I was tired beyond what I had ever felt and pretty sore as well, so the end still seemed frustratingly far away.

What surprised me is that every time my mind flitted to the world record I wasn't the least bit excited; it didn't motivate me at all now that I was this fatigued. My motivation was to finish when I said I would, and to see my friends and family. The thought of waking up and not having to get on the bike was so thrilling that I tried to blank it out. It made me relax too much. "The big picture will take care of itself if I do the most I can now" was my mantra every time my mind wandered.

Another reason why the world record was not a sufficient driving force was that I was over two months ahead of the old world record. Despite that being exactly what I had set out to do, it was hard to believe how anyone could take two months off any world record. To get to that stage had meant focusing so hard on my own target for so long that the record no longer seemed to have the same draw. Success lay simply in hitting my own target.

Day 9, 455 miles to Paris

Alarm at 5:30, get up, and go. Day two in France, and hopefully the third last on the road, had a similar feel to the one before. I felt like I was going through the same long and challenging routine every day out of habit. I definitely felt that my senses were dulled to the realities of each day, as one blurred into the next. It had been this way since leaving Paris to some extent, but the days since Lisbon had been at a whole new level of intensity. I didn't feel like I had switched off at all. At night I would be asleep before I hit the pillow and then be racing from the moment the alarm sounded six or seven hours later.

I had started to take a number of calls from journalists, either while riding or when taking breaks. Mum was doing a great job of answering as many of their inquiries as possible, but they wanted to get quotes and have quick chats with me. I was very happy to do this but was finding it harder than I'd expected. Journalists' questions are normally fairly predictable: after contextualizing where I was in terms of the race for the finish, they would ask about the best and worst points and for some humorous, dangerous, or unusual anecdotes from the road. I wanted to answer them but really struggled. I felt so stuck in my blinkered now-centric bubble of a world that I lacked the perspective to talk about events that had happened months ago. Every story ended up sounding like simply a statement of facts, such as "and then I got run over and mugged" or "and then I passed through a two-day sandstorm while under armed police escort for 800 kilometers through Pakistan." "And how did you feel about that?" they would ask excitedly. "Um, fine, yes, I kept cycling." The stories lacked the human element and any insight into how I'd actually felt and reflected on my experiences, but they were all I could offer.

Three days from the finish, I was expecting to start feeling excited. I must have played the finish over in my mind thousands of times. Most of these daydreams had me cycling the last few days as a sort of victory lap. It certainly didn't feel like that. There was this building sense of a finale from the UK but I still felt completely removed from it. Friends, family, and sponsors kept texting me to say they were packing their bags and getting on flights, or to tell me how they were watching the tracker getting closer. I desperately wanted to feel a part of this climax, to see the big picture like people back home. They were seeing the 18,000 miles, the world, and how much I could break the record by. Theirs was a macro view; I, on the other hand, was seeing it from the bottom up in every micro detail, and simply pushing to get through each kilometer, hour, day. Anything bigger than that was out of my control, so I couldn't get my mind to focus on it long enough to get excited.

The midpoint of the day coincided with the greatest milestone to date—18,000 miles. Anything past this point was surplus to requirements. My plan since the 9,000-mile point had been to cycle 18,300 miles so that Guinness World Records would have absolutely no comeback. A 300-mile buffer had seemed reasonable all along, until this point; it now seemed like a lot of unnecessary miles. I tried to bury the thought that I could be finished now, but it kept resurfacing.

By nightfall I was cycling through some very empty countryside, facing my first night in the tent since Lisbon. The village of Chalais had been the last reasonable chance of accommodation, but I'd met Piotr driving back out toward me with the news that there was nowhere. "OK, let's find somewhere I can camp, maybe some woods so I can get out of the early-morning frost." Piotr and Jaga would have to sleep in their car, but they said they didn't mind.

Twenty minutes later, still cycling along in the dark, some head-lights appeared up ahead. They had found somewhere, but not to camp. They wouldn't tell me where we were going but Jaga kept giggling as Piotr simply said, "Keep going, another five kilometers, I will wait at the turnoff." He sped on, turned, and passed me again.

At the turnoff there was an old battered sign which I couldn't quite read as my lights didn't cast light that high. I then followed the Audi for a kilometer down a single track into some woods and into a big courtyard. It looked like the courtyard of a small castle. Piotr and Jaga were obviously very excited about their find.

"This is someone's house," I stated simply.

"No, it is a hotel, it is just there is no one here. We came and met the owner, we have room, no problem."

"No problem" was Piotr's favorite phrase.

I couldn't see much in the dark. Leaving the bike outside, we all moved into the hallway. It certainly didn't look like a hotel, more like an old stately home, and we stepped into a long, high hallway running left and right. It was dimly lit, with heavy wallpaper, a desk, and seats off to the right-hand side, and strange ornamentation everywhere. On some shelves off to the left were many bottles, including some malt whiskeys and some very strange and old-looking home brews. One of them had a whole pear in it.

I was peering at this when a man called in a strongly accented voice, "Good evening." I turned to see a small man in his sixties wearing a thick knitted jumper. He had a fantastic mustache. He looked very French but spoke very good English. It turned out that his wife was English but was very ill and in bed, so we had to keep quiet. This was the off-season for them but we were welcome to stay. He got a key and showed us up a spiral staircase and along a very long corridor past tens of rooms. Finally, he unlocked a heavy wooden door at the very end.

Once *le patron* had gone we all ran around excitedly, exploring our castle room. The main bed was a huge old four-poster but there were also two other single beds at one end and enough room in between for a couple of pool tables.

Back downstairs, we caught up with the owner, who was as eccentric as his home. This was not a commercial enterprise, just the French gentry having to open their doors to the riff-raff to pay for their opulence. His stories reflected a life of pursuing random hobbies and a mind allowed to wander without the constraints of the rat-race mentality. He was a fascinating man, a born entertainer and host, but after he'd explained how to grow a pear in a bottle and where he had visited in Scotland, and after he'd introduced most of the stuffed animals, I politely had to make our excuses and leave. We had to drive to the next town to find a small restaurant where we could eat as *le patron* had to look after his sick wife so couldn't cook.

After 183km and a 1km ascent it had been a great day on the normal scale of things. However, looking at the map spread out on my bed, I realized it wasn't enough. There was a real risk that reaching Paris on Friday was beyond what was possible. I had to find something more.

I went to bed after midnight, shattered and worried.

Day 10, 340 miles to Paris

When I woke it took me a second to remember where I was. Of course, a mad French castle, which didn't seem to have any heating. Breakfast was served in the huge kitchen and consisted of nearly raw eggs, toast, and coffee that could have woken the dead. Just before I left, my host insisted on showing me one more thing and ran back through carrying the largest gun I'd ever seen. He stood there in his hallway pointing the blunderbuss at bits of taxidermy and laughing heartily, which made his very shapely mustache quiver. It was a wonderful place, lost in time, just a mile from the real world. I would love to find it again, but then I happened upon it by night and left in the dark, so perhaps it would lose its magic if I revisited by day.

I had two and a half days to ride 340 miles—a hard target. The last two days had been disappointing at 106 and 114 miles respectively. Any other week this would have been above target. I realized I had been back in cruise control. I was hurting and tired so hadn't been pushing it as hard as I had in northern Spain. I needed to do a 200km day, and I set off with a renewed fire in the belly.

After 25km I broke a spoke. It was bad news at the worst possible time, and I pedaled slowly into the next town, Angoulême. Sitting in a bus shelter outside a church, I fixed a new spoke as fast as possible, trying to get the wheel to run straight. Piotr and Jaga got entirely lost trying to find me—a sign of things to come. With 320 miles to go, I could do without any more wheel breakages.

Like most towns that are over a thousand years old, Angoulême was a nightmare to navigate through and I lost over two hours fixing the spoke and trying to find the right road out of town. In doing so I found myself on a motorway and had to backtrack. While frustrating, these delays were all irrelevant really, excuses for nothing. I had to make 200km, however long it took.

Jaga had had the thought, over our mountain of pasta the night before, to get a carry-out tub of food to save time. The chef at the tiny restaurant had risen to the challenge of fueling a cyclist through 200km with great excitement, and my parallel challenge that day was to work through the vast basin of tagliatelle he had donated to the cause.

The afternoon had a better flow about it but there was a stinking headwind over rolling roads. This might not have been as spectacular as the mountains of Spain but the relentless undulations added up to a 2,210-meter ascent, which put that Wednesday in the top-three hilliest days of the entire cycle.

Just before it got dark I completely hit the wall for about an hour. I felt nauseous and struggled to concentrate on the road ahead of me. I worked through this, found some more reserves, and flew the last few hours. The wonderful thing about the dark is that you really are left in a bubble. There are no distractions beyond the pool of light cast by your headlight beam. It was cold, very cold, and I had stupidly left my hat behind the night before; I had to borrow a goofy striped one from Piotr. I realized how shattered I was when I found myself choking back tears for that lost $5 hat, which I had bought at a gas station in Texas and had never really liked.

At 10:30 p.m. I pulled into the village of Bellac, and almost fell off the bike. I had been on the go since 6:30 a.m. I could only see one hotel and it looked boarded up. I was about to give up and pitch the tent in the park, too tired to care, when I saw someone coming out of a side door. He was the caretaker and could give us a room, but could not take any money as it wasn't his job. "Just put sixty-five euros in an envelope and leave it on the bed in the morning," he explained in French before leaving, looking as tired and dejected as I felt. Slightly confused, I went along with this, only caring about the room.

Jaga went on the hunt for food and came back with a pile of pizzas, which was another surprise success in a town that looked completely shut up for the night.

At 12:15 I set my alarm for 5:30.

Day 11, 203 miles to Paris

It was the penultimate day. When I woke, Piotr was already up. He had somehow jumped behind the bar of the closed-up hotel and made me a double espresso. I propped myself up on one elbow and threw this back before munching some leftover pizza. My whole body hurt. Piotr kept stressing that my legs were fine, but I begged to differ.

Eight hours after getting off the bike having ridden 137 miles, I was rolling again for at least another twelve-hour day on the go. It would be light in an hour, and I pulled my neck warmer over my face, hat down, and just tried to zone out completely. My backside screamed, my head hurt, my legs felt like lead. There was nothing to do but stare blankly into the pool of light ahead of me and wait for dawn.

I had no idea what I was passing. I had to cycle 200km to leave myself a reasonable roll into Paris the next day. I still didn't feel the least bit excited about the finish; I was simply too tired to care. My every thought was focused on making the next mile, knowing that eventually I would get there. My phone beeped all day with text messages but I hardly read any of them.

During my last night ride I found myself quite nostalgic as I pedaled along in the peace and quiet, lost in my own world again. "This time tomorrow it should all be over," I thought to myself. "I have cycled around the world and I will break the world record." I found myself smiling at this thought. It was a nice feeling, but no more exciting than the quiet acknowledgment you might give when someone wishes you happy birthday or says well done for a good day's work.

The only thought that really moved me and filled me with excitement was seeing my family and friends at the finish line. I had no idea how many to expect but from what I had heard it sounded like thirty or forty at least. I'd left to a group of ten, so it should be fun. I couldn't believe that so many people had come all the way to Paris for the finish. I just hoped I would feel a little bit more inspired about it all tomorrow.

After 199km (124 miles) in nearly thirteen hours of cycling I was half a day's ride from Paris. I couldn't have cared less. After finishing the logbook I fell asleep without giving it a second thought.

Day 12, 79 miles to Paris

I woke at 5:30 and have never felt less enthused about riding a bike. I ached, and my head spun and was fuzzy. I was barely able to talk as I pulled my Lycras on for the last time and ate cold leftover pizza again. It was like I was on autopilot, a half-year routine enabling me to do what otherwise I would have found impossible.

The street outside the hotel was dark and cold, completely still. Not a single car passed. I tucked my chin deeper into my buff, under a woolly hat, fleece, and down body warmer. It was still well below freezing.

I was easily agitated. It was the last morning and I was fighting a personal and literal darkness. After about 10km I found that with my thick gloves on I had missed the button to turn on the cycle computer. Such things would normally have been trivial but I struggled to deal with such failures in my current state of mind.

At one point Piotr raced off without explanation for twenty minutes. When he returned I pulled up, got off the bike, and wandered around a frosty field sipping a mug of coffee and eating some fresh pastry they had brought, while Jaga snapped away happily. I took great strength from their warmth and enthusiasm.

As for the finish, it could have been another continent away for the way I still felt about it. After picking up the first few texts that day, I stopped reading them. I was not celebrating and could not relate to the words of congratulation.

The sun came out, the wind continued, and the first 80km passed in a blur. The BBC car tracked beside me at times and at others raced on to capture passing shots, but I was largely oblivious, increasingly concerned about my lack of emotion so close to the end.

In the small town of Rambouillet, just 40km from Paris, we stopped and met Pierre, a camera biker, used to driving motorbikes for cameramen in the Tour de France and other cycling events. The final hurdle was an inevitable one: how to safely and lawfully reach central Paris by bike. I was no help during this animated discussion in a café: I was under the impression that we should just follow Pierre, who should know best, and took the opportunity to get in an espresso and some more breakfast. The café was filled with elderly men in flat caps and thick jackets who watched our wee theater closely. Back outside, still waiting for the master plan to be confirmed, I stripped down to my Artemis World Cycle Challenge strip, and put on my helmet, glasses, and mitts. If I didn't feel the part, I would at least look it, I decided.

Irrational thoughts about last-minute breakages, one final incident that could trip me up, had been nagging me over the last few days. But as I set out again, for the final time, I realized that nothing could go wrong now. I could ride to the finish from here on a broken wheel; hell, I could run it, pushing the bike if it came to it.

I would like to think that it was more than the caffeine, but from nowhere the adrenaline of the finish hit me and I sped up, pushing the bike over the rolling hills southwest of Paris. Through Versailles, I cut through the traffic and up one incredible last hill, a kilometer-long steep road. At the top I stopped, my legs pumped, looking back in disbelief. "The last 18,300 miles has been good training for that at least," I said with a smile.

The *périphérique* is Paris's formidable ring road, and the city police's jurisdiction was anything inside this. The majority of Paris spills out in every direction far wider than this, so it was our hope that the police escort Mum had managed to arrange would pick us up in good time. Unfortunately they didn't, so the last miles from Versailles in through suburban traffic were slow. I had hoped to be at the finish at about two p.m.; it was already nearer three, and bitterly cold. But at last, our small convoy arrived at the Porte de Saint Cloud, the point I had pedaled out from on August 5, 2007, for my slow spin down to the start line. I was back. I just needed to retrace those last few miles.

When the police turned up, a man and a woman, they were on scooters. The man turned to me and spoke in French. What I thought he said was "Would you like to take the tourist route or go directly?" I was surprised by this; it clearly hadn't been explained to them what I was doing. "Directement, s'il vous plaît," I answered simply. The policeman nodded, turned to inform the policewoman, and immediately turned on his lights and sirens.

"Directement," unbeknownst to me, didn't just mean directly, it meant as fast as possible. Those last 3 miles were insane. The busy Friday-afternoon traffic was pushed aside as the red carpet was laid out for a straight run to the finish. After setting off at a crazy speed, the police seemed slightly disappointed that I could not keep up like a Tour de France rider on a 7kg bike. They soon adapted to my fastest speed as I cranked hard and puffed and panted my way to the center of Paris.

At one point the policewoman almost put her bike on its side, saving it only with a quick foot down, as she screeched to a stop in front of me to stop cars coming across me. Every traffic light one would jump ahead and stop the traffic from either direction and push us through, even if it was on red. The most memorable moment was pulling up behind a great fat gold Bentley Continental. The driver was obviously too lost in luxury to notice a hairy man on a bike, two police on scooters, a cameraman on a motorbike, and a car with its hazards going pulling up behind him. The policeman pulled level and rapped his knuckles on the car window furiously, pushing him through as if the queen was coming. I hadn't asked for this but didn't want to object; besides, they seemed to be having a lot of fun with their whistles constantly blaring from their lips as they darted back and forth, taking turns to clear the way and then shadow me. Some shouts went up from pedestrian bystanders, wondering at this bizarre spectacle.

As I turned onto Avenue Victor Hugo I looked up and there it was, the Arc de Triomphe. I was suddenly lost in my own world. My legs felt light and fresh, and I stared down at the wheel in front of me. I had absolute clarity. The fog of the days of blind focus lifted and I realized I had done it. It was all about to finish.

Six and a half months of pushing mind and body, and the race was almost run. I was about to achieve my three-year dream of 195 days. I was also about to see my family and friends. Mum had been on an amazing parallel journey. I hadn't seen her since Belgium but as mother and son we had become even better friends through the challenges we had faced together. I could not have got around the world without her.

In the last 500 meters I looked up and saw the Arc getting closer, the people walking by oblivious, and wondered what was around the corner. Within a minute of finishing I felt like I wanted to stop and have a moment to myself before seeing everyone. All of a sudden I felt quite choked up.

As we reached the most dangerous roundabout in Europe, the police thankfully paused for thought before pulling out. Within seconds they had me out and the three-lane traffic under control. I bumped over the cobbles circling two-thirds of the way around to reach the small pedestrian crossing at the top of the Avenue de Wagram. As the Arc cleared from view I looked ahead and saw a lot of people. I couldn't actually see which was the correct road or recognize anyone. These people could be anyone, perhaps not there for me.

As I pulled closer a few people ran out to spot me coming in and clapped from the pavement. Flanked by my escort and concentrating on the finish, I didn't see who. The street was filled, traffic stopped, with a wall of people from the central island across two lanes to the pavement.

I stopped pedaling and clipped one foot out as I approached this wall of people, then saw Mum running out from the middle. I threw my arms around her as the bike came to a halt. But all I could think about was that I wasn't actually finished yet; the line was still 5 meters ahead. I broke away from Mum and walked the bike forward, still straddling it. Cameras and microphones walled me in and a din of questions met me. I smiled and pushed on. They cleared enough for me to get through, and I saw Bobby pulling a finish cord across the road. I walked through it.

Standing with my sunglasses firmly in place to hide the tears in my eyes, I faced a media scrum like I'd never dreamed of. I had left with ten friends on the start line; I came back to many, many more. Before answering anything I just wanted to see my family. Mum appeared again and I gave her another warm hug; she had tears streaming down her face. Then Heather appeared. She looked fantastic and gave me the briefest of hugs because she couldn't keep back a secret any longer. Standing aside, she revealed Hannah, my little sister, whom I hadn't seen since long before the cycle; she'd flown back especially from Shanghai as a surprise. I then saw Dad, Grampa, and many more family and friends before I was swamped by the media.

I had no idea how to react. I'd never seen anything like it. I stood there on my bike, blocking the road, as they bombarded me with questions. Flashes went off and microphones were thrown forward. People shouted over one another and I felt it was getting quite aggressive. I felt like saying, "Guys, I'm not going anywhere." I saw the BBC camera lady get shoved aside by another, which prompted her soundman to shove back.

Sir Peter Westmacott, the British ambassador, had been waiting like everyone else at the finish, in the freezing cold for a couple of hours now. He was there to be the official last signatory, to witness the finish—not that it was entirely necessary with half the British press there!

It took over three hours to move away from the finish area after interviews and official photographs. By that time most of my friends and family, except Heather and Mum, had got too cold and had gone. I'd hardly seen any of them.

It wasn't until that evening that I caught up with everyone at a grand reception back at the Radisson at the Porte de Saint Cloud. I was on an absolute high as I got ready in my room, chatting to Mum, Heather, and Hannah. It didn't seem over at all, and I wasn't the least bit tired anymore. So many people had made the trip to Paris that I hadn't yet got to grips with the scale of the finish.

As well as the finish itself, I remember best the beginning of the reception. I went downstairs with Heather, Hannah, and Mum and walked around the corner to face a crowded bar full of friends and family. David Fox-Pitt, the man who had made my first major sponsor possible, had made it across in the middle of a skiing holiday with a bust ankle; my ex-girlfriend's parents were there, despite the fact that we'd broken up years earlier; and there were many more surprise faces. Most of all I remember my uncle's face. He rowed for Cambridge, and ever since I was a boy I'd wished for the oar he has on his wall. I hardly knew him, but the handshake and smile he gave me will always stay with me.

I was one of the last people to go to bed, and everyone kept mentioning that they felt bad calling it a night before me. I was exhausted, and halfway through the night I was struggling and went and sat by the bar with Heather for a bit and just chatted, but I was determined to see everyone and savor every moment. The fact that I had finished the cycle just didn't feel real at all.

The next morning I woke at 5:30 and jumped out of bed. I smiled the smile of a free man. I laughed out loud and punched the air.

After a while I went downstairs and for the next hour sat at the empty bar drinking a cappuccino and reading the papers. Front page on the English papers was the story of a Man Who Had Cycled the World. I couldn't stop smiling, but it still didn't feel real. For a long time I had been thinking daily about cycling 100 miles, but at no one point had I been focused on cycling around the world, so I couldn't grasp the big picture. Not yet.

It would be four days before verification came through, but I had set the Guinness World Record for the Fastest True Circumnavigation by Bicycle at 194 days 17 hours, in which time I'd cycled 18,296 miles.

Epilogue

Breaking the circumnavigation world record was the launchpad into the expedition world I had always hoped and worked for. A couple of years later and life has continued to accelerate. That boyhood excitement about world's first and fastest has never left me.

My next expedition, in 2009 and early 2010, took me from Alaska to Tierra del Fuego, in the far south of Argentina. However, this hadn't always been the plan.

For half a year after the world cycle, I had been training to row the North Atlantic as part of a twelve-man team. As ocean-rowing records go, this is as coveted as they get. I couldn't wait to be part of the world-record attempt to row the 3,500 miles from New York to Cornwall in less than 55 days.

In January 2009, Leven Brown, the team leader, took a different crew for a crossing of the mid-Atlantic, as a crack at that record but mainly to test some new onboard systems that we would undoubtedly need in the much colder and stormier North. A week into the crossing, the rudder broke while in high seas, and the boat, carrying no spares, was tossed around like a cork for three days until a passing cargo vessel rescued the team. While the crew survived, very shaken but unscathed, *La Mondiale,* our 55-foot rowing boat, was broken by the crashing hulls during the rescue and has never been recovered.

I had been writing this book and so was unable to go aboard this fated expedition, but I was following closely online from the comfort of my flat in Edinburgh. I watched, concerned as the boat's daily average went from over 100 nautical miles a day to nothing, before news reached me that *La Mondiale* would not be coming back from the Atlantic this time.

Considering that it took over a year to train and gain support for the world cycle, I had concerns that 2009 would now be a lost year. However, within a month the BBC offered to back another expedition I had been planning. Just a few months later I was en route to Anchorage, Alaska, for what would be a nine-month journey following the Rockies and the Andes south.

The mountainous spine of the Americas is one of the longest continuous geographic features on earth, and I had longed dreamed of a journey along it. To race from north to south could have felt like the circumnavigation all over again, and I craved a different challenge. My idea was to climb the highest peaks in both North and South America while cycling between them in a single climbing season.

After a three-week ascent of Denali (Mount McKinley) in Alaska in June 2009, I then had about half a year and 11,000 mountainous miles to pedal before attempting Aconcagua, the highest peak in the Western Hemisphere, in Argentina. The statistics suggested that the chances of summiting both at first attempt were about one in five.

Both of these mountains were a test of perseverance in the face of tragedy and incredibly harsh conditions. The cycle drew on all the experience from my circumnavigation and took me through some unforgettable landscapes. To mention just a few great memories, I experienced the wilds of the Yukon, the wildlife (and wild people) of places like Montana and Utah before the deserts and jungles of Mexico. Into Guatemala and Panama I met and filmed the most wonderful characters before exploring the high Andes in Ecuador, and then crossing the Atacama Desert, the driest place on earth.

After climbing Aconcagua, I was back on my bike for a final two thousand miles of headwind, alike to those I had battled in Australia, to reach Ushuaia, the most southerly city in the world. At the same time that this book is being published in the U.S., I am just finishing writing my second book about this nine-month journey down the Americas for publication in the UK.

I hope that it's obvious from this book that no major expedition can work without the goodwill, hard work, and support of many friends and my family. My career is quite a family affair, with Una, my Mum, still working with me full-time as the manager of "Base Camp," back in Scotland. When I am on the road this is a considerable logistical task, and when I am between expeditions she is my talk-tours and events manager, all-around agent, and, most important, still Mum!

I often get asked about the other characters who feature in this book. Top of the frequently asked questions would have to be Sarah in Australia. I have been in touch with her since we met, but we have never met again, so that fairy-tale ending never happened! Piotr and Jagwega remain good friends but have moved back to live in Poland to set up their own sports physiotherapy company. David Peat, the BBC director who first believed in my world cycle as a documentary, remains a great friend whom I speak to most weeks and who was with me in Alaska to film the start of the last expedition. Many people mentioned in the acknowledgments at the start of this book are still in some way involved with my expeditions.

Working in television and having a career that most people comment "sounds amazing . . . but not for me, thanks" is great for keeping in touch with people, and I have been very lucky with the support from everyone around me, all the way back to school days.

At this point most people in the UK know me as a cyclist. When I go shopping I rarely get recognized as Mark but regularly as "that cyclist guy!" However, those close to me know that it has never been about the cycling alone, and my idea was always to attempt original journeys that I can capture for TV and write about. You can't cycle everywhere on earth, and so my future plans for very different journeys may surprise people as I continue to explore this wild world we share.

About the Author

Mark Beaumont was born on New Year's Day 1983 and grew up in the foothills of the Scottish Highlands, where his parents ran an organic smallholding. When he was twelve, he cycled across Scotland from Dundee to Oban, then a few years later, while still at school, completed the 1,000-mile solo ride across the length of Britain from John O'Groats to Land's End. His next long-distance ride took him the length of Italy from Sicily to the Alps, a journey of 1,336 miles, helping to raise £50,000 for charity. After graduating from Glasgow University, and having also qualified as a professional ski instructor, he decided against a conventional career and devoted himself full-time to raising money for his endurance cycling adventures.